ROYAL HISTORICAL SOCIETY
STUDIES IN HISTORY

New Series

PROTECTION AND POLITICS

Studies in History New Series

Editorial Board

Professor Martin Daunton (*Convenor*)
Professor David Eastwood
Dr Steven Gunn
Professor Colin Jones
Professor Peter Mandler
Dr Simon Walker
Professor Kathleen Burk (*Honorary Treasurer*)

PROTECTION AND POLITICS

CONSERVATIVE ECONOMIC DISCOURSE,
1815–1852

Anna Gambles

THE ROYAL HISTORICAL SOCIETY
THE BOYDELL PRESS

© Anna Gambles 1999

All Rights Reserved. Except as permitted under current legislation no part of this work may be photocopied, stored in a retrieval system, published, performed in public, adapted, broadcast, transmitted, recorded or reproduced in any form or by any means, without the prior permission of the copyright owner

First published 1999

A Royal Historical Society publication
Published by The Boydell Press
an imprint of Boydell & Brewer Ltd
PO Box 9, Woodbridge, Suffolk IP12 3DF, UK
and of Boydell & Brewer Inc.
PO Box 41026, Rochester, NY 14604–4126, USA
website: http://www.boydell.co.uk

ISBN 0 86193 244 7

ISSN 0269-2244

A catalogue record for this book is available
from the British Library

Library of Congress Cataloging-in-Publication Data
Gambles, Anna, 1969–
    Protection and politics : conservative economic discourse, 1815–1852 / Anna Gambles.
      p. cm. – (Royal Historical Society studies in history. New series, ISSN 0269-2244)
    Includes bibliographical references and index.
    ISBN 0–86193–244–7 (hardback : alk. paper)
    1. Protectionism – Great Britain – History – 19th century.
2. Free trade – Great Britain – History – 19th century. 3. Free enterprise – Great Britain – History – 19th century. 4. Conservatism – Great Britain – History – 19th century. I. Title. II. Series.
HF2044.G35 1999
382'.73'0941–dc21   99-37129

This book is printed on acid-free paper

Printed in Great Britain by
St Edmundsbury Press, Bury St Edmunds, Suffolk

FOR M.

Contents

	Page
Acknowledgements	ix
Abbreviations	xi
1 Introduction	1

PART I: PROTECTION IN PRINT

2 Debating the corn laws, c. 1814–1830	25
3 Protectionism and Conservatism, 1830–1847	56

PART II: CURRENCY, BANKING AND CONSERVATIVE DISCOURSE

4 The politics of convertibility and deflation, 1809–c. 1830	89
5 The limits of economic sovereignty, 1830–1847	117

PART III: INCORPORATING EMPIRE

6 The imperial frontiers of Tory political economy, 1809–1830	147
7 'The patriotic principle': the empire in Conservative economic discourse, 1830–1847	176

PART IV: AFTER REPEAL

8 'Dead and buried?': the protectionist challenge, 1847–1852	203
9 Epilogue	230

Biographical appendix	243
Select bibliography	253
Index	279

Acknowledgements

This book grew out of my research as a graduate student at Nuffield College, Oxford. I would like to thank the Warden and Fellows of Nuffield for welcoming a historian of the early nineteenth century as a graduate student and for electing me to an Open Prize Research Fellowship in 1995. Without the unique intellectual resources and interdisciplinary climate of Nuffield this book would not have taken the shape it has. I will always remain indebted to the graduate students and research fellows who created the demanding and stimulating environment which moulded this book. I would also like to thank the British Academy for awarding me a Post-doctoral Research Fellowship in 1998 and the Master and Fellows of Clare College, Cambridge for the opportunity to pursue my interest in nineteenth-century economic discourse and in the British state beyond the boundaries of this book.

Like any other author I have accumulated debts – intellectual and personal – which are almost too numerous to mention. I would like to thank the librarians at Nuffield College, the Bodleian Library, the British Museum and the British Library for helping me to navigate the vast volume of printed primary sources upon which my research draws. Maureen Lynch at Denbigh High School first made nineteenth-century Britain exciting and inspired me to study modern history at university. While I was an undergraduate at The Queen's College, Oxford, John Davis guided me through the Peel Special Subject, introduced me to nineteenth-century economic discourse and became a valued friend. I owe my principal intellectual debt, however, to my tutor and doctoral supervisor, David Eastwood, who has offered intellectual generosity, constructive criticism, astute advice and friendship in Mahlerian proportions. My examiners, Peter Ghosh and Patrick O'Brien, tendered valuable criticisms which helped transform a doctoral dissertation into a piece of publishable research. Donald Winch, Peter Mandler and Martin Daunton read the entire manuscript at various stages and made focused criticisms and judicious suggestions which proved extremely helpful. The jacket illustration, from *Punch*, 19 April 1845, is reproduced by courtesy of the Syndics of Cambridge University Press.

I owe deeper debts to my friends and family whose support has sustained me through the long and often lonely process of research and writing. I would like to thank Victoria Campbell and Susannah Morris for combining true friendship with uncompromising intellectual honesty. My grandparents and my parents, John and Chris Gambles, have encouraged me constantly while Caroline and Helen have endured and even applauded the bookish eccentricities of their older sister. My book is dedicated to my husband, Malcolm, who married me three days after my doctorate was finished and has lived with this project ever since. As a musician and scholar he not only tolerated the unreasonable aspects of this author's behaviour but also understood them: without him this book could not have been written.

Anna Gambles
July 1999

Publication of this volume was aided by a grant from the Scouloudi Foundation in association with the Institute of Historical Research.

Abbreviations

AgHR	Agricultural History Review
BEM	Blackwood's Edinburgh Magazine
CHJ	Cambridge Historical Journal
EcHR	Economic History Review
EHR	English Historical Review
ER	Edinburgh Review
FM	Fraser's Magazine
Hansard	Hansard's parliamentary debates
HJ	Historical Journal
HPE	History of Political Economy
JBS	Journal of British Studies
JEcH	Journal of Economic History
JMH	Journal of Modern History
JPE	Journal of Political Economy
NAPIC	National Association for the Protection of Industry and Capital throughout the British Empire
ParlHist	Parliamentary History
P&P	Past and Present
QR	Quarterly Review
SH	Social History
SJPE	Scottish Journal of Political Economy
TRHS	Transactions of the Royal Historical Society
VS	Victorian Studies

1

Introduction

> 'The "sensible men" of their age were, at one time, for burning the Lollards and drowning old women with bleared eyes and hook noses; – nay, theorems in sciences more positive than political economy professes to be – in Astronomy, in Chemistry – which not twenty years ago "sensible men" were agreed on, are now maintained to be errors. The history of Truth is the history of her opposition to "sensible men".': E. Bulwer Lytton, *Letters to John Bull, Esq., on affairs connected with his landed property, and the persons who live thereon*, London 1851, 10–11.

This study is an intellectual history of opposition to those 'sensible men' who could see no alternative to the prescriptions of free-trade political economy for Britain in the first half of the nineteenth century. It shows how free-trade theory and policy were challenged and how an alternative political economy was moulded and sustained through half a century. Upon this broad canvas a distinctively 'Conservative' current of economic criticism consistently challenged the claim of free trade to intellectual hegemony over economic argument. In a wide range of policy arenas, from agricultural protection to monetary reform and the consolidation of the empire, many Conservatives rejected the assumptions of economic liberalism and replaced them with an alternative set of arguments about the foundations of stable economic advance and the role of government in securing it. This economic discourse was forged in specific political contexts and was articulated in Conservative constitutional languages. That is to say, Conservative writers tended to locate fiscal and economic questions within a political and constitutional idiom where fiscal policy was understood to contribute directly to the preservation of the propertied constitution; by representing the interests of property, by constantly renegotiating the relative positions of different forms of property, and by demarcating acceptable limits for the intrusions of the state into the realm of private property values, fiscal and economic legislation was perceived to be a set of political and constitutional mechanisms. This fiscal discourse embraced a problematic partnership between protectionism and Conservatism which persisted from the Napoleonic period until the dramatic schism of 1846. And, even though the party leadership surrendered protection as an electoral incubus at the general election of 1852, this partnership was revived when Conservatives returned to the panacea of protection after 1903. In order fully to understand this apparently doomed relationship it is essential to take protectionist ideas seriously and to trace their precise relevance for Conservatives during the first half of the nineteenth century.

In a historiographical sense this study challenges the pervasive assumption that British Conservatism can be wholly understood as a journey towards Gladstonian Liberalism. Of course, as Philip Harling and Tony Howe have recently shown, the history of nineteenth-century public policy can be persuasively told as one of progressive liberalisation.[1] Indeed, from the relaxation of mercantilist controls in the 1820s to Gladstone's retrenching budgets, it was the history of financial and commercial policy which largely forged the 'liberal' historiographical consensus. Yet the effect of imposing this policy-driven teleology on economic debates is to homogenise the more varied and complex intellectual reality of Britain in the first half of the nineteenth century.[2] For Conservative critics responded to free trade not merely as a set of theories about commercial policy but also as a more expansive philosophy of government.[3] They combatted the 'laissez-faire' trilogy of free trade, retrenchment and liberal political reform with an alternative discourse about the extent and character of government intervention. Here, the most pervasive critiques of the nascent 'laissez-faire' state were neither mounted by proto-Socialists nor by advocates of government growth but largely by those who conceptualised fiscal policy as an acceptable mode of social, economic and political intervention.[4] Fundamentally, these debates kept the boundaries of government firmly confined behind the limits established by the unreformed, propertied constitution.

Intellect, political economy and Conservatism: the historiographical setting

Many previous histories of nineteenth-century political economy have been 'doctrinal' accounts of the development of formal economic thought. That is to say, they have been concerned with the canon and the clerus – with analysing the theoretical foundations of the economics and the original contri-

---

[1] P. Harling, *The waning of 'Old Corruption': the politics of economical reform in Britain, 1779–1846*, Oxford 1996; A. C. Howe, *Free trade and liberal England, 1846–1946*, Oxford 1997.
[2] In this vein C. Schonhardt-Bailey includes only a limited number of protectionist texts in her recent anthology of nineteenth-century economic argument: *The rise of free trade*, London 1997, esp. i. 1–51, 119–338; ii. 159–262.
[3] Indeed free-trade liberalism often reached far beyond economic theory: M. Ceadel, *The origins of war prevention: the British peace movement and international relations, 1730–1854*, Oxford 1996, esp. pp. 121–30, 276–7, 346–55, 367–8, 426–31, 459–69.
[4] For a teleological perspective on the history of government growth see D. Roberts, *Victorian origins of the British welfare state*, New Haven 1960, 12–18. For correctives see W. Lubenow, *The politics of government growth: early Victorian attitudes to state intervention, 1833–1848*, Newton Abbott 1971, 12, 15–29, and O. Macdonagh, *Early Victorian government, 1830–1870*, London 1977, passim.

butions of key thinkers.⁵ Such approaches have, albeit unintentionally, tended to deepen the fissure between the historiography of political economy and that of ideas and political philosophies more generally. Numerous historians have, of course, attempted to knit this fracture in a variety of ways. For instance, historians of the Scottish Enlightenment read the history of political economy as one element in a broader set of debates on moral philosophy and on the purposes of civil government.⁶ Most recently, Donald Winch broke down artificial distinctions between histories of economic and political thought in a sweeping survey of the approaches of Adam Smith and Robert Malthus to the inequalities of economic change.⁷ Others have been concerned to explore different 'registers' of political economy. Indeed one purpose of Maxine Berg's history of Ricardian thought was to search for Ricardianism's variety of social bases and voices.⁸ From a different perspective Biancamaria Fontana attempted to escape the abstractions of 'pure' theory by connecting the economics of Ricardo, Mill and McCulloch with the less formalised political economy of the *Edinburgh Review*, and with the intrusions of political economy and Philosophic Radicalism into parliamentary debates and policy.⁹ With prominent exceptions, however, such welcome shifts away from conceptualising political economy purely as 'Economic Theory' have largely been restricted to exploring the development of, or contradictions within, an essentially 'liberal' orthodoxy.¹⁰ This monograph steps outside free trade to expose an alternative political economy which was critical of the social and economic capacities of the free market. It neither postulates rigid theoretical consistency nor searches out strict intellectual genealogies for economic argument. Critiques of free-trade theory are instead located in the historically specific contexts which were furnished by debates on public policy.

---

5   M. Blaug, *Economic theory in retrospect*, Cambridge 1962; W. J. Barber, *A history of economic thought*, London 1967; D. P. O'Brien, *The classical economists*, Oxford 1974; S. Hollander, *Classical economics*, Oxford 1987.
6   See 'Comments' by D. P. O'Brien and D. Winch in A. S. Skinner and T. Wilson (eds), *Essays on Adam Smith*, Oxford 1976, 63–72; I. Hont and M. Ignatieff (eds), *Wealth and virtue: the shaping of political economy in the Scottish enlightenment*, Cambridge 1983, esp. pp. 1–44, 137–78, 179–202, 253–69; J. G. A. Pocock, *Virtue, commerce and history: essays on political thought and history, chiefly in the eighteenth century*, Cambridge 1985, 193–212.
7   D. Winch, *Riches and poverty: an intellectual history of political economy in Britain, 1750–1834*, Cambridge 1996, esp. pp. 221–405 'Robert Malthus as political moralist'.
8   M. Berg, *The machinery question and the making of political economy, 1815–1848*, Cambridge 1980, 75–110. On popular criticism of Ricardo see N. Thompson, *The people's science: the popular political economy of exploitation and crisis, 1816–1834*, Cambridge 1984, 9–12, 17–25, 112–13, 153–5.
9   B. Fontana, *Rethinking the politics of commercial society: the Edinburgh Review, 1802–1832*, Cambridge 1985. See also M. Milgate and S. C. Stimson, *Ricardian politics*, Princeton 1991, pp. ix–x, 49–77, 144.
10 For example F. W. Fetter, *The development of British monetary orthodoxy, 1797–1875*, Cambridge, Mass. 1965; B. Semmel, *The rise of free-trade imperialism: classical political economy and the empire of free-trade imperialism, 1750–1850*, Cambridge 1970.

This study should, of course, be situated beside previous treatments of nineteenth-century critiques of economic 'orthodoxy'. Morton Paglin's analysis of the thinking of Malthus and Lauderdale was designed as an anatomy of the 'Anti-Ricardian tradition'. Yet he did not consider the contributions of less formal thinkers to contemporary economic criticism and presupposed the 'failure' of the 'Anti-Ricardian tradition' and the 'victory' of the ideas of David Ricardo.[11] Other historians have emphasised the pervasiveness and persistence of a 'tradition' which was critical of free-trade political economy. Indeed, Barry Gordon's account of the intrusions of political economy into parliamentary debates exposed a persistent critical counterpoint and raised doubts about the wider influence of Ricardianism.[12] Various shorter surveys of economic argument in early nineteenth-century periodicals, in particular those of F. W. Fetter, confirmed the wider diffusion of economic ideas which were critical of the so-called 'Ricardian orthodoxy'.[13] Some of these contributions have, however, introduced different teleologies into the history of nineteenth-century economic ideas. Harold Perkin, for instance, imposed a determinist model on intellectual debate perceiving an inevitable battle between an aristocratic agrarian ideal and a middle-class commercial one in the pages of nineteenth-century periodicals.[14] Naturally, this study would not have suggested itself in the absence of previous studies of the 'Anti-Ricardian tradition'. Indeed in some senses it confirms previous challenges to 'binary' approaches to the history of ideas which have tended to cast Ricardian theory as modern and progressive, and its critics as retrogressive and negative.[15] Where this book differs is in its insistence that economic debates should be rooted firmly in contemporary political contexts: in a nineteenth-century setting 'economics' cannot be separated off from political, partisan and constitutional discourses.[16]

---

[11] M. Paglin, *Malthus and Lauderdale: the anti-Ricardian tradition*, New York 1961, 157–68.
[12] B. Gordon, *Political economy in parliament, 1819–1823*, London 1976, and *Economic doctrine and Tory-Liberalism, 1824–1830*, London 1979.
[13] F. W. Fetter, 'The economic articles in *Blackwood's Edinburgh Magazine*, and their authors, 1817–1853, pts i, ii, *SJPE* vii (1960), 85–107, 213–31; 'Economic controversy in the British reviews, 1802–1850', *Economica* xxxii (1965), 424–37; 'The economic articles in the *Quarterly Review* and their authors, 1809–52', *JPE* lxvi (1958), 45–64; and 'The economic articles in the *Quarterly Review*: articles, authors and sources', ibid. 150–70; B. Gordon, 'Say's law, effective demand, and the contemporary British periodicals, 1820–1850', *Economica* xxxii (1965), 438–46; H. Perkin, *Origins of modern English society*, London 1969, 218–70; S. Rashid, 'David Robinson and the Tory macroeconomics of *Blackwood's Edinburgh Magazine*', *HPE* x (1978), 258–70.
[14] Perkin, *Origins*, 249–50.
[15] See Winch's objection to binary approaches to Ricardian and Malthusian political economy: *Riches and poverty*, 25–7.
[16] Others have recently explored the interface between 'politics' and 'economics' and have re-evaluated the role of the state in the economy during the long nineteenth century most notably M. J. Daunton, 'Payment and participation: welfare and state-formation in Britain, 1900–1951', *P&P* cl (Feb. 1996), 169–216; T. Alborn, *Conceiving companies: joint-stock politics in Victorian England*, London 1998, 1–19.

INTRODUCTION

Recent contributions to the history of ideas in nineteenth-century Britain have, from various perspectives, challenged the ideological hegemony of free-trade liberalism. Michael Turner has emphasised the catholicism of economic thinking in the Manchester Chamber of Commerce, erstwhile considered to have been a haven for economic liberalism.[17] Similarly, Tony Howe has questioned the dominance of free-trade thinkers such as David Ricardo and Richard Cobden over the minds of merchants, bankers and city financiers.[18] Historians of Whigs and Liberals have also challenged the ideological prominence previously afforded to free trade. Consistent with his expansive reading of the characteristics of the Scottish Enlightenment, John Burrow showed that 'laissez-faire individualism' played a relatively minor intellectual role in early nineteenth-century Liberalism.[19] Peter Mandler presented the revivification of an interventionist and populist Whig aristocratic style as an ideological response to the perceived political and moral weaknesses of both free-market economics and Philosophic Radicalism.[20] Richard Brent and Jonathan Parry identified religion, not political economy, as the centre of gravity of Liberalism and of intellectual life in the nineteenth century more generally.[21] Most recently Philip Harling has presented free-trade liberalism as one element in a broader movement for the reform of the late Hanoverian state and for the destruction of 'Old Corruption'.[22] Despite these major historiographical revisions, however, free trade seems to have retained its normative status in the history of nineteenth-century ideas. This phenomenon can only be explained by examining the impact of another major new departure in the intellectual history of the nineteenth century; the concept of Christian political economy.

Rejecting the tendency to impose a secular late twentieth-century idea of economics on the previous century, A. J. B. Hilton and A. M. C. Waterman transformed our intellectual map of the nineteenth century. They argued that the purchase of free trade over nineteenth-century minds can be explained in terms of contemporary theological languages and religious contexts.[23] They

---

[17] M. J. Turner, 'Before the Manchester School: economic theory in early nineteenth-century Manchester', *History* lxxix (1994), 216–41.
[18] A. C. Howe, 'Free trade and the City of London, c. 1820–1870', ibid. lxxvii (1992), 391–410, and *Free trade and Liberal England*, esp. pp. 17–18, 70–92.
[19] J. W. Burrow, *Whigs and Liberals: continuity and change in English political thought*, Oxford 1988, 1–49.
[20] P. Mandler, *Aristocratic government in the age of reform: Whigs and Liberals, 1830–1852*, Oxford 1990, esp. pp. 1–9, 33–43, 170–99, 218–35.
[21] R. Brent, *Liberal Anglican politics: Whiggery, religion, and reform, 1830–1841*, Oxford 1987; J. P. Parry, *Democracy and religion: Gladstone and the Liberal party, 1867–1875*, Cambridge 1986.
[22] P. Harling, 'Rethinking "Old Corruption"', *P&P* cxlvii (1995), 127–58, and *The waning of 'Old Corruption'*, 136–266.
[23] A. J. B. Hilton, *The age of atonement: the influence of evangelicalism on social and economic thought, 1785–1865*, Oxford 1988; A. M. C. Waterman, *Revolution, economics and religion: Christian political economy, 1798–1833*, Cambridge 1991.

emphasised the dominance of an idea of the free market as a divine mechanism in early nineteenth-century economic thought. Both Hilton and Waterman argued that contemporaries conceived of free trade as an arena for the moral trial of individuals and governments where God's providential market could operate without human interference.[24] Of course this study neither disputes the existence of Christian political economy nor underestimates the seminal contributions of its historians. It does, however, suggest that the historiographical 'Christianisation' of free trade during this period has, perhaps unintentionally, tended to reconfirm the hegemony of free-trade liberalism over the history of nineteenth-century ideas.[25] By stepping outside the liberal paradigm this analysis of critiques of free-trade economics suggests that the intellectual dominance of the latter was no foregone conclusion. More specifically, the concept of Christian political economy has exerted a dramatic influence on our understanding of early nineteenth-century Conservatism in general and of 'Liberal-Toryism' in particular.[26] It used to be usual to construe 'Liberal-Toryism' as a pragmatic approach, during the 1820s and 1830s, to social and economic reform which was directed at forestalling popular radicalism and constitutional change.[27] Boyd Hilton offered a radically new and ideological interpretation which cast 'Liberal-Toryism' as a philosophy of 'laissez-faire' which was motivated mainly by evangelicalism. For Hilton, the evangelicalism of 'Liberal-Tories' like Lord Liverpool, Henry Goulburn and Sir Robert Peel predisposed them to forge conditions for minimal government and social and moral individualism. In this view, 'Liberal-Tories' aimed to free up the operations of God's market, and to strip away the impediments of social and economic paternalism.[28] This evangelical economics permitted 'Liberal-Tories' to conceive of economic fluctuations and inequalities as preordained, purgative and retributive processes.

---

[24] Hilton, *Age of atonement*, 36–70, 203–51; Waterman, *Revolution, economics and religion*, 171–215, 217–53.

[25] Harling, *The waning of 'Old Corruption'*. 9. Harling identifies consensus in the following: J. E. Cookson, *Lord Liverpool's administration, 1815–1822: the crucial years*, Edinburgh 1975; A. J. B. Hilton, *Corn, cash, commerce: the economic policies of the Tory governments, 1815–1830*, Oxford 1977; N. Gash, '"Cheap government", 1815–1874', in *Pillars of government and other essays on state and society c. 1770–c. 1880*, London 1986, 43–54; H. C. G. Matthew, *Gladstone, 1809–1874*, Oxford 1986.

[26] In keeping with historiographical convention this book uses the term 'Tory' before 1830 and 'Conservative' during and following 1830. Capitalisation denotes support for or association with the Tory/Conservative party.

[27] N. Gash, *Lord Liverpool: the life and political career of Robert Bankes Jenkinson, second earl of Liverpool*, Cambridge, Mass. 1984, 126–91, 217–47; Cookson, *Lord Liverpool's administration*, 1–17, 90–129, 215–28, 340–66.

[28] Hilton, *Corn, cash, commerce*, esp. pp. 307–14; 'Peel a reappraisal', *HJ* xxii (1979), 585–614 at pp. 606–11; *Age of atonement*, 203–51. On the application of Christian political economy to social policy see Mandler, *Aristocratic government*, 200–27, and 'Tories and paupers: Christian political economy and the making of the new poor law', *HJ* xxxiii (1990), 81–103.

INTRODUCTION

Thus, evangelical economics generated 'Liberal-Tory' policies which were designed to restrict economic growth to morally sound, durable enterprises and which saw no role for government in levelling out the inequalities and fluctuations of the nineteenth-century economy. Far from disputing Hilton's conclusions on the moral and religious origins of 'Liberal-Tory' economic thought and policy, this study explores another facet of Conservative economic discourse which flourished beside and frequently in opposition to evangelical free-trade liberalism. Through an analysis of the intellectual opposition of Conservatives to free trade this study reveals their responses to state intervention, to the market and to economic fluctuations and emphasises the importance of constitutional argument in economic discourse during the first half of the nineteenth century. By definition, as an intellectual history of the relationship between Conservatism and protectionism this study does not presume to offer a comprehensive account of early nineteenth-century Conservatism. Yet it is hoped that this survey of the depth and character of opposition to free-trade liberalism within an identifiably Conservative intellectual milieu does go some way towards explaining the depth of the ideological cleavage of 1846.[29] Indeed, unless due attention is given to the critics of 'Liberal-Toryism' the emergence in the late Victorian period of an activist and 'radical' Conservatism can only be viewed as an unprecedented phenomenon.[30] Thus, while this study does not attempt to draw specific intellectual links between Conservatism in the first and second halves of the nineteenth century, it does suggest that the integrated political, economic, imperial and social discourse of Conservatives during the former period foreshadowed the substance and scope of Edwardian Conservatism.

A more general impact of Hilton's revisionism was to refocus attention on the social and economic dimensions of early nineteenth-century Conservatism. Effectively, Hilton overturned Norman Gash's assertion that the nineteenth-century Tory party 'was a constitutional and religious, not a social and economic party'.[31] Despite Hilton's emphasis on the importance of analysing the social and economic elements of nineteenth-century Conservatism, Gash's paradox has been explicitly endorsed by J. J. Sack.[32] Sack has argued persuasively that 'right-wing' associational activity in early

---

[29] The intellectual history of nineteenth-century Conservatism remains fractured: on 'High' Toryism see D. Read, *Peel and the Victorians*, Oxford 1987, 54–5, 86–7; on 'Romantic Toryism' see D. Eastwood, 'Robert Southey and the intellectual origins of Romantic Conservatism', *EHR* civ (1989), 308–31, and 'Ruinous prosperity: Robert Southey's critique of the commercial system', *The Wordsworth Circle* xxv (Spring 1994), 72–6; on the intellectual foundations of 'Liberal' Toryism see Hilton, *Age of atonement*, 126–7, 223, 234–5.

[30] E. H. H. Green, 'Radical Conservatism: the electoral genesis of tariff reform', *HJ* xxviii (1985), 667–92, and *The crisis of Conservatism: the politics, economics and ideology of the British Conservative party, 1880–1914*, London 1995, esp. pp. 317–33.

[31] Hilton, *Age of atonement*, 236; N. Gash, *Reaction and reconstruction in English politics, 1832–1852*, Oxford 1965, 131.

[32] J. J. Sack, *From Jacobite to Conservative: reaction and orthodoxy in Britain, c. 1760–1832*, Cambridge 1993, 37.

nineteenth-century Britain was dominated by constitutional and religious questions but has also reintroduced an unhelpful dichotomy between socio-economic philosophies and constitutional-religious identities.[33] What printed discussions of agricultural protection and of monetary and imperial policies suggest, however, is that economic and constitutional argument were not rigidly separate but were interactive and mutually influencing. Thus, one major aim of this study is to analyse the integration of constitutional and political elements within Conservative political economy.[34] A second purpose is to dispute the common assumption, endorsed by Sack, that 'it is difficult and unhelpful to discuss a general or consistent right-wing view of sophisticated economic matters'. This assumption was itself grounded on another pervasive premise, that 'Not for the only time, the Right (and especially the press) appeared to *feel* such matters rather than offer a measured intellectual *analysis* of them.'[35] Historiographically, this assumption first took root in free-trade histories of the fall of protection. Variously, opponents of economic liberalism were cast as economic ignoramuses and reactionaries. In particular, the protectionism of Conservatives was often explained either as a product of blatant self-interest or as a reflex motivated by political pique.[36] In keeping with recent rejections of socio-economic determinism in the history of class formation, this study resists the temptation to reduce ideas to their apparent economic determinants.[37] Self-evidently, the rise of a commercial and manufacturing economy did not generate an uncontested intellectual hegemony for free-trade liberalism. By the same token, recognising the colonial, agricultural, and commercial interests which propelled protectionism invalidates neither the social, moral and constitutional languages of protectionists, nor the broader economic claims they made. For in the constitutional context of the period, 'interest' was simultaneously an accepted mode

---

[33] For Sack, conservative nomenclatures and collectivities identified predominantly with loyalism, monarchism, the Established Church and constitutional conservation: ibid. 30–155. (The term 'right-wing' is Sack's.)

[34] In his analysis of conservative constitutionalism R. B. Smith has allowed constitutional and economic categories to interact. See his observations on the relationship of liberty, feudalism and commerce in eighteenth-century 'conservative' thought: *The Gothic bequest: medieval institutions in British thought, 1688–1863*, Cambridge 1987, 71–96.

[35] Sack, *From Jacobite to Conservative*, 180.

[36] Contemporary condemnations of the corn laws as a class monopoly are reprinted in F. W. Hirst, *Free trade and other fundamental doctrines of the Manchester School*, New York 1968: 'Joseph Hume's speech on the corn laws, May 17 1833', esp. pp. 123–5, and 'Speech of W. J. Fox in reply to Cobden's address at Covent Garden, 28th Sept. 1843', at pp. 162–72; J. Morley, *The life of Richard Cobden*, London 1908; A. Prentice, *History of the Anti-Corn-Law League*, 1st publ. London 1853, ed. W. H. Challoner, London 1968, ii. 418–33.

[37] G. Stedman-Jones, 'Rethinking Chartism', in *Languages of class: studies in English working-class history, 1832–1982* Cambridge 1983, 90–178; D. Wahrman, *Imagining the middle class: the political representation of class in Britain, c. 1780–1840*, Cambridge 1995, 1–18, 410–11; J. Lawrence, *Speaking for the people: party, language and popular politics in England, 1867–1914*, Cambridge 1998, 68.

of understanding social and economic groupings, and a legitimate impulse to political action.[38] In tangible ways property was the emblem of political fitness, and 'interest' was the focus of political representation. Revealingly, an anonymous commentator of 1852 expected commercial policy to be 'consistent with the exigencies of the State, subservient to every great interest of the nation, and established on the broad principle of justice to all classes of community'.[39] Thus, in an early nineteenth-century context, divining social and economic determinants for economic arguments can neither negate those ideas nor furnish sufficient intellectual provenances for them.

Many histories of nineteenth-century economic policy have cast protectionism as a philosophy which rejected the growth of a manufacturing and commercial economy and have tended to treat it as a mere foil for 'enlightened' economic liberalism.[40] Most notably, R. W. Stewart reduced the economic argument of Conservative protectionists to a set of romantic and reactionary reflexes.[41] Though he did not dismiss protectionist economic thought, T. L. Crosby was less concerned to delineate economic arguments than to analyse the formation, activities and political impacts of agrarian pressure groups.[42] It should not therefore be surprising that pejorative approaches to protectionism still lurk in more general 'political' histories of the nineteenth century.[43] Similarly, economic historians have only relatively recently begun to question the deeply embedded assumption that free trade brought prosperity and economic growth to nineteenth-century Britain.[44] D. McCloskey even suggested that 'free trade did not cause British

---

[38] Ibid. 90–6.
[39] Anon. [W. W. N.], 'Justice to John Bull'; or, the fallacies of the existing policy called 'free trade': addressed to the 'pupils' of the 'Manchester School', and to the working portion generally of 'John Bull's family', by one of the latter class, London 1852, 5.
[40] A. Brady, William Huskisson and Liberal reform: an essay on the changes in the economic policy in the twenties of the nineteenth century, Oxford 1928, 5. D. G. Barnes included protectionist argument but couched it in a teleology of repeal in A history of the English corn laws, London 1930, 185–271. C. R. Fay granted that protectionists 'fought a good case on weak ground' but sketched mainly the arguments of repealers in The corn laws and social England, Cambridge 1932, 102, 88–108. In presentations of repeal as a great instalment of social reform, the confinement of protection to a class monopoly, was axiomatic: A. A. W. Ramsay, Sir Robert Peel, London 1928, esp. pp. 218–40, 288–348; G. Kitson-Clark, Peel and the Conservative party: a study in party politics, 1832–41, 2nd edn, London 1964, 148–9, 400–1.
[41] R. W. Stewart, The politics of protection: Lord Derby and the protectionist party, 1841–1852, Cambridge 1971, 46–7.
[42] T. L. Crosby, English farmers and the politics of protection, 1815–1852, Hassocks 1977, 26–56, 154–86.
[43] See, for example, E. Biagini, Liberty, retrenchment and reform: popular Liberalism in the age of Gladstone, 1860–1880, Cambridge 1992, 95–8, and J. P. Parry, The rise and fall of Liberal government in Victorian Britain, London 1993, 163–5.
[44] See the counterfactual analysis in D. N. McCloskey, 'Magnanimous Albion: free trade and British national income, 1841–1881', Explorations in Economic History xvii (1980), 303–20, and his 'Reply to Peter Cain', ibid. ix (1982), 208–10; A. Marrison, British business and protection, 1903–1932, Oxford 1996, 1–7.

growth; indeed, it may have retarded it'.[45] Notwithstanding such revisionism protectionist thought remains neglected by historians of the first half of the nineteenth century to the extent that it is often assumed that there was no serious intellectual opposition to free trade during this period.[46] The fullest account of British protectionist thought remains Derek Walker-Smith's brief presentation of the arguments of Peel's critics during the 1840s as an appropriate set of responses to contemporary social and economic fluctuations.[47] This interpretation was revived and expanded in Angus Macintyre's study of Lord George Bentinck which presented protection as a broadly coherent set of alternatives to free-trade liberalism and which suggested that the opposition of Conservatives to the policies of Sir Robert Peel had some ideological roots.[48] Indeed, as a study of the 'ideas and values' of protectionism from the end of the Napoleonic period to the mid century this study responds to Macintyre's prompt: 'Until this mass of material is further investigated, we will not know how widely diffused protectionist ideas and values were, nor how broad was the evident gap between those who accepted and those who rejected free trade.'[49]

Elevating the ephemeral: pamphlets, journals and political culture

The 'mass of material' referred to by Macintyre was the prolific economic and political journalism of the first half of the nineteenth century. This serious genre of pamphlet and periodical literature was a distinctive feature of British intellectual culture in this period. As W. E. Aytoun put it, 'This branch of composition is peculiar to our own age, in which periodical literature is so marked and eminent a feature.'[50] When it is combined with a thorough analysis of parliamentary debates, a sustained reading of these sources offers a survey of the public debate on political economy which flourished beyond the pages of the formal economic treatise. As Disraeli noted in 1852:

> although an anonymous publication was no authority, there were publications of that kind of such high character, as the Edinburgh and Quarterly Reviews for example, to which many cabinet ministers of both sides had been contributors, that it might fairly be adduced not as evidence of any fact,

---

[45] McCloskey, 'Magnanimous Albion', 320.
[46] See, for instance, F. Trentmann, 'The transformation of fiscal reform: reciprocity, modernisation, and the fiscal debate within the business community in early twentieth-century Britain', *HJ* xxxix (1996), 1005–48 at p. 1005.
[47] D. Walker-Smith, *The protectionist case in the 1840's*, Oxford 1933 repr. New York 1970, 9–14, 20–2, 26–8, 31–6, 66–72.
[48] A. Macintyre, 'Lord George Bentinck and the protectionists: a lost cause?', *TRHS* 5th ser. xxxix (1989), 141–65.
[49] Ibid. 157.
[50] W. E. Aytoun, 'Alison's political essays', *BEM* lxvii (May 1850), 650–21 at p. 650.

but certainly as evidence of the belief of well-informed circles on particular circumstances.[51]

It is essential to treat such sources systematically and not to dismiss them as ephemeral supplements to other categories of evidence.[52] This monograph is therefore based on a sustained reading of the Conservative journals – *The Quarterly Review*, *Blackwood's* and *Fraser's* – together with the pamphlets and parliamentary debates of the first half of the nineteenth century. These texts were explicitly partisan, they frequently cross-referenced each other and they insisted on locating economic argument in the specific contemporary context of debates on public policy. Formally and substantively, periodicals and pamphlets contextualised political economy and sank precise chronological roots. The sources therefore guard against excessive historiographical abstraction and discourage the construction of artificial intellectual interfaces. Essays and reviews on economic questions were seldom merely theoretical responses to 'the state of the art'. They were printed beside political or literary essays and usually engaged with key thinkers within defined contemporary policy contexts. The formal characteristics of political and economic journalism in nineteenth-century Britain legitimate this attempt to break down the artificial 'economic', 'social', 'constitutional', 'moral' and 'political' categories which have frequently been imposed on Conservative thought.

Before surveying the content of this 'mass of material' it is first necessary to examine in greater detail some contemporary perceptions of serious economic journalism during the first half of the nineteenth century. It is of course highly implausible that nineteenth-century print-media did exercise, 'a greater influence over the manners and opinions of civilised society, than the united eloquence, of the bar, the senate and the public'.[53] What is clear is that editors, commentators and politicians did weigh these sources as important elements of an integrated political world which was not confined behind the walls of Westminster. It is essential therefore to examine these contemporary attitudes towards the influence of the serious periodical press – that is to say, to historicise the question of 'influence'. By doing so it becomes clear that the print-media did not merely offer representations of or reflections on politics but were themselves components of the political world of nineteenth-century Britain.[54]

It is of course notoriously difficult to establish reliable circulation figures for reviews, magazines and pamphlets during this period because, unlike

---

51 B. Disraeli, *Lord George Bentinck: a political biography*, 3rd edn, London 1852, 273.
52 Parry, *Democracy and religion*, 47–9; Sack, *From Jacobite to Conservative*, 2–3, 8–29; Wahrman, *Imagining the middle class*, 9–13.
53 This claim was made in Anon., *The periodical press of Great Britain and Ireland: or an inquiry into the state of the public journals, chiefly as regards their moral and political influence*, London 1824, 1.
54 This approach is admirably employed in A. Jones, *Powers of the press: newspapers, power and the public in nineteenth-century England*, Aldershot 1996.

newspapers, they were not subject to the stamp tax. There are, however, a number of reliable estimates of circulation based on print orders and sales figures which suggest that *Blackwood's*, the *Quarterly* and *Fraser's* were widely read. Morris Milne has estimated the average monthly print run of *Blackwood's* at 6,000–7,500 during 1817–46 and the average quarterly print run of the *Quarterly* at 9,200 for the same period.[55] These aggregate figures have been supported by the estimates of Scott Bennet and Joanne Shattock on sales and print orders but it is agreed that they mask a more nuanced reality.[56] Shattock has shown that popular or controversial numbers of the *Quarterly* were increasingly reprinted and were frequently pirated in America. Both journals circulated in America and the colonies and from 1843 *Blackwood's* also appeared in a colonial edition.[57] It is generally agreed that the heyday of the review was the 1820s and that by the 1840s magazines like *Blackwood's* and *Fraser's* were rising in relative popularity.[58] What figures for production and sales cannot offer is an adequate estimate of how many people actually read nineteenth-century periodicals. It was customary of course for newspapers to 'review' periodical publications thus diffusing the content of the latter amongst a wider readership.[59] It is highly likely that each copy of a journal was read by multiple readers and was not confined to the individual purchaser. Typically, the Brontë household regularly borrowed its journals: 'We see the *John Bull*; it is a high Tory, very violent. Mr Driver lends us it, as likewise *Blackwood's Magazine*, the most able periodical there is.'[60] Beyond informal lending the periodical was the staple of circulating libraries and book societies which constructed more formal networks of multiple readership. Indeed, in 1841 the publishing firm of Saunders, Otley and Co. could boast of

---

[55] M. Milne, 'The politics of *Blackwood's*, 1817–1846: a study of the political, economic and social articles in *Blackwood's Edinburgh Magazine*, and of selected contributors', unpubl. PhD diss. Newcastle 1984, 33–5.
[56] S. Bennet, 'Revolutions in thought: serial publication and the mass market for reading', in J. Shattock and M. Wolff (eds), *The Victorian periodical press: samplings and soundings*, Leicester 1982, 225–57, 236, 239; J. Shattock, *Politics and reviewers: the* Edinburgh *and the* Quarterly *in the early Victorian age*', Leicester 1989, 11–12.
[57] Ibid. 98, 160–1; J. J. Barnes, *Authors, publishers and politicians: the quest for an Anglo-American copyright agreement, 1815–1854*, London 1974, 30–48; M. Milne, 'The management of a nineteenth-century magazine: William Blackwood and Sons, 1827–47', *Journal of Publishing History* i (1985), 24–33.
[58] A. Ellegård, 'The readership of the periodical press in mid Victorian Britain', *Göteborgs Universitets Årsskrift* lxiii (1957), 27–8; Shattock, *Politics and reviewers*, 19.
[59] W. E. Aytoun's, 'British agriculture and foreign competition', *BEM* lxvii (Jan. 1850), 94–136, provoked a massive response in the newspaper press. The national scope and character of this response was detailed in 'Appendix to *Blackwood's Magazine* no. 412: opinions of the press', ibid. lxvii (Feb. 1850), 1–122. B. Disraeli praised this article in a letter to his sister, 1 Jan. 1850, in *Lord Beaconsfield's correspondence with his sister, 1832–1852*, London 1886, 238. On the dangers of selective reviews in newspapers see Anon., *The periodical press of Great Britain and Ireland*, 208.
[60] Charlotte Brontë, cited in L. Brown, *Victorian news and newspapers*, Oxford 1985, 27–8. On multiple readership see also Thompson, *The people's science*, 6.

their subscription scheme for private book clubs that, 'The best Periodical Works will be included.'[61] It cannot be assumed therefore that the majority of *readers* of nineteenth-century periodicals and pamphlets were necessarily their owners or buyers.[62] Whilst periodicals were by their nature 'tracts for the times' the contemporary practices of binding and indexing elevated the 'ephemeral'. In the collections of individuals and of private and circulating libraries, binding and indexing transformed periodicals and pamphlets into resources for posterity.[63]

This elevation of the ephemeral is perhaps best demonstrated by contemporary attitudes to the 'influence' of the serious periodical press. While it cannot be assumed that editors and journalists succeeded in representing or moulding public attitudes they nevertheless strove to define their public and to negotiate a balance between guiding and reflecting public opinion.[64] The familiar notion of the press as a mirror to the public mind was implicit in the certainty with which editors identified 'niche' markets for their publications. In 1817 William Blackwood targeted his new magazine at Tory readers who were opposed to the liberalism of the *Edinburgh Review* announcing his intention to conduct *Blackwood's* on 'avowed and determined principles'.[65] The primacy of politics in *Blackwood's* was recognised by one French commentator in 1857: 'Ce recueil est le premier qui ait fait une place à la politique: il a été crée au moment ou le rétablissement de la paix generale, en ranimant les espérances des whigs, fit sentir au parti tory la nécessité de défendre par la presse la prépondérance qu'il possédait encore dans le Parlement.'[66] J. G. Lockhart was similarly confident in the assumptions he made about the relationship between the *Quarterly* and its readers: 'Our chief readers and chief *purchasers* are the Parson & the Squire – & to them we must look first, after our own consistency & character, which however are identified with their cause.'[67] If, for commercial reasons, editors presupposed a certain readership they also considered themselves to be in the business of opinion forming. Par-

---

61 [Saunders, Otley and Co.], *Hints for the formation of reading and book societies in every part of the United Kingdom with an improved plan for rendering them more extensively available and efficient*, London 1841, 16. See also Jones, *Powers of the press*, 184–7, and A. Aspinall, *Politics and the press, c. 1780–1850*, London 1949, 26.
62 This distinction was made for newspapers in Anon., *The periodical press of Great Britain and Ireland*, 24–5.
63 On the binding and indexing of newspapers see Jones, *Powers of the press*, 69–70.
64 See Lawrence's caution regarding the capacity of Victorian political parties to influence their public: *Speaking for the people*, 61–2, 67–8.
65 M. Milne, 'The "veiled editor" unveiled: William Blackwood and his magazine', *Publishing History* xvi (1984), 101. *Fraser's Magazine* was modelled on the political and stylistic character of *Blackwood's*: 'Fraser's Magazine: introduction', in *The Wellesley index to Victorian periodicals, 1824–1900*, Toronto 1972, ii. 303–19 at p. 304.
66 M. Cucheval Clarigny, *Histoire de la presse en Angleterre et aux États-Unis*, Paris 1857, 253.
67 J. G. Lockhart to J. W. Croker, 26 Feb. 1846, in 'Some unpublished letters of John Gibson Lockhart to John Wilson Croker', ed. A. L. Strout, *Notes & Queries* clxxxix (22 Sept. 1945), 124.

ticularly on questions of politics and political economy, the Tory journals sought to combat the diffusion of Whig-Liberalism, Philosophic Radicalism and 'orthodox' economics with a closely defined partisan opposition.[68] In *Blackwood's* this editorial stance was often expressed in explicitly didactic essays on economic and political liberalism.[69] Similarly Lockhart insisted that his review was more than a mere mirror of opinion: 'The Q. R. must not be the reflection merely of a few people's private views, hopes and fears. We must, I think, consider it as bound up in the interests of the Tory party and look *how*, without absolutely compromising our own personal consistency, it may be possible for us to serve the cause.'[70] The Tory 'cause' invoked by Lockhart was, of course, that of constitutional defence.

Editors and journalists commonly perceived the Tory periodical press itself as an organ of constitutional defence. By amplifying a reasonable and respectable register of Conservative public opinion editors and writers believed they were combating democratic forces.[71] Such positions were based on the assumption that the popular press was increasingly democratic and dangerously influential, the 'fourth estate' of British politics.[72] Thus the journalist Archibald Alison articulated the commonly held view that the 'immense circulation' of the popular press overpowered the influence of property on public opinion. He maintained that 'the only real antidote to the press is to be found in the press itself': 'An established press, to fight the battle of Conservative principles, against the incessant attacks of anarchy, is necessary in the political world, for the same reason that an established church and established schools and universities are in the moral.'[73] Writing in 1859 another *Blackwood's* journalist, E. S. Dallas, rejected the idea that the press constituted an additional 'fourth estate' in British politics. He nevertheless insisted that the press was an integral component of the political system: 'It is the merest fallacy to regard the press as in any sense a fourth estate; it is but an extension of the third. It has a constituency as real and an election as genuine

---

[68] On Philosophic Radicalism and Whiggism see Fontana, *Rethinking the politics of commercial society*, 112–46.

[69] See, for instance, T. De Quincey, 'Ricardo made easy; or, what is the radical difference between Ricardo and Adam Smith?: part I', BEM lii (Sept. 1842), 338–53; 'Ricardo made easy; or, what is the radical difference between Ricardo and Adam Smith?: part II: with an occasional notice of Ricardo's oversights', ibid. (Oct. 1842), 457–69; and part III, ibid. (Dec. 1842), 718–39.

[70] Lockhart to Croker, 12 Jan. 1835, in 'Some unpublished letters', *Notes & Queries* clxxxv (9 Oct. 1943), 222.

[71] Lockhart to Croker, 26 March 1840, in 'Some unpublished letters', ibid. clxxxvi (4 Nov. 1944), 207.

[72] Croker discussed the idea of the press as a 'Fourth estate' in 'M. Guizot on democracy', QR lxxxv (June 1849), 308–10. Croker imported H. Brougham's unease at the influence of the press into Conservative discourse: H. Brougham, *Political philosophy*, London 1843, iii. 116–23.

[73] A. Alison, 'The influence of the press', BEM xxxvi (Sept. 1834), 373–91, 377, 383. See also Aspinall, *Politics and the press*, 234.

as any that the House of Commons can boast.'[74] Indeed Dallas maintained that by 1859 the press had created a 'public opinion' which was 'true to reason' and immune to democratic delusion.[75] Thus editors and journalists saw their Conservative journals as participants in the political process and not merely as publications which orbited 'politics proper'.

The attempts of politicians to harness the Conservative journals suggest that they too viewed them as an integral components of their political world. It was of course the explicit partisanship of much periodical and pamphlet literature which facilitated and encouraged the efforts of politicians to influence the press. One contributor to *Fraser's* was firmly of the view that the press was essential to the prosecution of party politics: 'Independently of cause and creed, a party depends very greatly on the talent alone of its press', and, 'Without an influential press, the Tories must be powerless; and their press cannot be influential if it be not duly supported by its party.'[76] Like the newspaper press, therefore, periodicals and pamphlets were caught up in an intricate web of influence and information-mongering.[77] Famously, the *Quarterly's* John Wilson Croker claimed to serve as a 'conduit' for the ideas of premiers and cabinet minsters; 'they supplied the *fact* and I supplied the *tact*, and between us we used to produce a considerable effect'.[78] It was common for editors and journalists to elicit the less direct support of key Conservative politicians. As Milne has shown, William Blackwood regularly sent copies of the magazine to the Tory ministers Liverpool, Sidmouth and Canning and was delighted when Wellington ordered a full set on becoming prime minister.[79] Canning, Huskisson and Disraeli were among the Conservative politicians who took active if sporadic parts in promoting the Conservative press.[80] Disraeli figured in the nexus of journalists and politicians who persuaded Lockhart to become editor of the *Quarterly* in 1826. In collaboration with John Murray the proprietor of the *Quarterly*, Disraeli was also directly involved in the promotion of the shortlived Tory *Representative* in 1826, and

---

[74] E. S. Dallas, 'Popular literature – the periodical press', BEM lxxxv (Jan. 1859), 180–95 at p. 184.
[75] Ibid. at pp. 194–5.
[76] R. B. Seeley (?), 'On political parties (no. 1)', FM v (May 1832), 448–62 at p. 461, and 'On parties (no. 3)', ibid. vi (Sept. 1832), 205–15 at p. 213.
[77] On the politicisation of the nineteenth-century press see Aspinall, *Politics and the press*, passim. See also T. Morley, ' "The arcana of that great machine": politicians and *The Times* in the late 1840s', *History* lxxiii (1988), 38–54'. On Conservatives and the press see Sack, *From Jacobite to Conservative*, 8–29.
[78] Cited in Aspinall, *Politics and the press*, 200. On the politics and politicking of J. W. Croker and W. Maginn see Sack, *From Jacobite to Conservative*, 20–9. On Lockhart, Croker and S. L. Giffard see R. B. McDowell, *British Conservatism, 1832–1914*, London 1955, 13–55.
[79] Milne, 'The "veiled editor" unveiled', 101.
[80] See, for instance, George Canning's close involvement in the establishment of both the *Anti-Jacobin* and *The Quarterly Review*: Sack, *From Jacobite to Conservative*, 14. On Huskisson's forays into journalism see below p. 93 n. 18.

was proprietor and principal writer of the *Press* between 1853 and 1856; both ventures were attempts to revivify Conservative journalism.[81] The importance of serious journalism in supporting the Conservative cause was recognised in political circles as Disraeli indicated to his sister in 1850: 'I received Professor Aytoun to breakfast on Saturday. . . . It is the fashion now to fete him, in gratitude for the protection articles in "Blackwood", of which he is the author.'[82] The periodical press of the first half of the nineteenth century should not therefore be relegated to the status of mere commentary. It is perhaps neither necessary nor possible to draw continuous and systematic connections between writers, editors and politicians. What is clear however is that contemporaries perceived the periodical press as an influential and integral participant in a partisan political world.

In assessing the distinctiveness of the Conservative periodicals as a genre it is essential to make some observations on their character and content. As a serious review which appeared each quarter, the *Quarterly* was designed and received as a heavyweight counterbalance to the Whig-Radical *Edinburgh Review*. It is tempting perhaps to draw too stark a distinction between the *Quarterly*'s identity and that of the monthlies *Blackwood's* and *Fraser's*. Admittedly the literary character of the magazines was more pronounced, they did not formally 'review' books and the authorial tone was often less temperate than that of the *Quarterly*. All the same the public image of the magazines cannot be dismissed as Shattock has done as 'one of at best rollicking high spirits, literary pranks, and generally "light" articles'.[83] The 'political' essays and articles in the magazines were frequently as penetrating and analytical as the formal 'reviews' in the *Quarterly*. Indeed all three publications fielded writers of high calibre who cannot be dismissed as irresponsible jobbing hacks.[84] Robert Southey and John Wilson Croker were the stalwart contributors of 'political' articles to the *Quarterly*. Archibald Alison, the Revd George Croly and Professor W. E. Aytoun together performed the same function for *Blackwood's* while William Maginn shouldered the bulk of the 'political' burden for *Fraser's*.[85] It was not uncommon for writers to contribute to more than one periodical publication. For instance the Revd Edward Edwards wrote extensively for *Blackwood's* on social and political questions but also contributed to the *Quarterly*. Similarly, John Galt penned numerous articles on colonial questions for both *Blackwood's* and *Fraser's*. The consider-

---

[81] Shattock, *Politics and reviewers*, 45–53. On the *Representative* episode see A. Andrews, *The history of British journalism, from the foundation of the newspaper press in England, to the repeal of the Stamp Act in 1855*, London 1859, ii. 167, and S. Koss, *The rise and fall of the political press in Britain, I: The nineteenth century*, London 1981, 89–91.

[82] *Lord Beaconsfield's correspondence with his sister*, 246. Disraeli's editor at *The Press*, was another *Quarterly* journalist D. T. Coulton: Koss, *Rise and fall*, 90.

[83] Shattock, *Politics and reviewers*, 6.

[84] See biographical appendix.

[85] It is revealing to note that 'social', 'economic' and 'partisan' and 'constitutional' articles were all conventionally classified under the heading 'political'.

able degree of autonomy afforded by editors to their contributors perhaps accounts for the high levels of authorial loyalty, and therefore substantive continuity, enjoyed by all three publications.

It would be a mistake to view the anonymity of much nineteenth-century periodical writing as an impediment to their use in reconstructing the intellectual history of the period. On the face of it the convention of keeping the identity of authors secret makes the task of identifying the intentions of and influences on writers very difficult. In practice, of course, scholars have established the authorship of most anonymous contributions to nineteenth-century periodicals.[86] Despite this fact, the convention of anonymity perhaps exposes periodical and pamphlet writing to charges of irresponsibility and impermanence. But contemporaries justified anonymous authorship in periodicals as a way of throwing the authority and reputation of the entire publication behind an article.[87] As E. S. Dallas explained in 1859,

> It is essential to the organisation of the press that it should be secret. A great public journal must of necessity be the work of a considerable number of hands ... and although an organ of opinion thus constituted can never attain perfect consistency, yet without the anonymous it would be impossible to reach even that degree of harmony which is at present attainable – that continuity of thought and sentiment which is its life and power.[88]

This determined effort at creating and maintaining a cohesive identity is an important element in grasping why and how 'continuity of thought and sentiment' on questions of political economy was sustained in several publications across half a century. Interestingly, in his defence of the public utility of anonymous authorship Dallas went beyond a publication's cohesive and corporate identity. He maintained that anonymity was fundamental to the representative functions of serious journalism:

> No doubt the member of Parliament is an exponent of principles as well as of individuals; and the literary organ, in the discussion of opinions and the advocacy of interests, has also to do with individuals. The one implies the other; yet directly, as we have said, the parliamentary representation is of individuals, the journalistic representation is of classes, interests, subjects, opinions – in one word, abstractions, things which do not exist except in thought ... The anonymous is the corner-stone of class journalism – it is the postulate of the English system.[89]

---

[86] Fetter, 'The economic articles in the *Quarterly Review* and their authors', 45–64; 'The economic articles in the *Quarterly Review*: articles, authors and sources', 150–70; and 'The economic articles in *Blackwood's Edinburgh Magazine*, and their authors', 85–107, 213–31; *Wellesley index*, i, ii. 303–19.
[87] Brown, *Victorian news*, 108.
[88] Dallas, 'Popular literature – the periodical press', 182–3. On anonymity and the corporate voice see also Shattock, *Politics and reviewers*, 15.
[89] Dallas, 'Popular literature', 183–4.

Dallas therefore maintained that when an author relinquished his name he consciously shelved egotistical writing and entered the public sphere of 'representative' journalism. In several senses, then, this contemporary perception of the convention of anonymous journalism informs our understanding of the distinctiveness and value of periodicals as historical sources.

Aside from questions of circulation, influence and authorship, some key characteristics of the form and content of periodical publications make them highly rewarding for historians of nineteenth-century ideas. It would be shortsighted to dismiss their 'political' and 'economic' content simply because nineteenth-century periodicals were miscellanies in which political economy formed only one small facet. Precisely because their publications ranged the entire gamut from religion to travel writing did editors rely on 'political' articles to establish substantive cohesion and continuity.[90] When periodicals are viewed in the context of the nineteenth-century press as a whole, it is clear that readers looked to them for serious analysis. Daily and weekly newspapers were chiefly concerned to 'report' news. Thus reviews magazines and pamphlets provided the lengthy analysis which newspapers could not offer.[91] It should not be surprising therefore that William Spence insisted on the high intellectual status and distinctiveness of periodicals in 1815:

> If a foreigner were to inquire into where he was to look for the opinions of our most eminent living economists, he would doubtless be referred to three quarterly publications called Reviews, but in reality collections of essays or treatises on the interesting questions of the day, in which under mask, our ablest writers on different sides, more effectually and extensively lead the taste and opinions of the public, than they could do by detached publications in their own persons.[92]

The periodical press was therefore recognised by contemporaries as a valuable source of 'political-economic' debate and offers invaluable perspectives to the historian of ideas. By connecting up the economic controversy in periodicals, pamphlets, books and parliament as contemporaries did, it is possible to construct a historicised account of the public discourse on political economy.

---

[90] Shattock, *Politics and reviewers*, 92.
[91] On the 'division of labour' between periodicals and newspapers see Andrews, *The history of British journalism*, i, and Brown, *Victorian news*, 108.
[92] W. Spence, *The objections against the corn bill refuted; and the necessity of this measure to the vital interests of every class of the community demonstrated*, 4th edn, London 1815, 27.

INTRODUCTION

Characterising Conservative political economy

The debates on central policy questions in explicitly partisan texts form the foundation of this essay on the intellectual history of nineteenth-century Conservatism. It is possible to trace a remarkably consistent and distinctively Conservative set of approaches to agricultural protection, currency and banking policies, and the empire across half a century. This discourse blended political and constitutional debate with economic and social commentary. Many Conservatives did not merely attempt to define the causes of the wealth of nations but also debated government's capacity to influence the durability and social consequences of economic change. Methodologically, Conservatives tended to elevate 'history' and 'experience' over the abstract theorising of 'orthodox' political economy. 'Economic' criteria of balanced development, centring on the mutual consumption of classes and interests in home and colonial markets, reinforced and expressed the Conservative aim of achieving social and political stability without conceding constitutional reform. Of course, criticism of the free market was neither a necessary nor an exclusive characteristic of Conservative thought. Yet if we are to appreciate why criticism of free trade came to be predominantly identified with Conservatism by the middle of the nineteenth century it is essential to analyse the ideological character of the economic argument adumbrated in Conservative texts during the preceding half-century. The remainder of this introductory chapter will therefore summarise the book's chief arguments.

Part I is chiefly concerned to challenge the idea that protectionism was marginal in Conservative argument and in political debate more generally. Indeed, the apparently mundane question of food policy provoked debate on the boundaries of intervention and on the functions of parliament and the executive in the immediate aftermath of the Napoleonic wars. By challenging free traders' explanations of successive economic depressions Tory protectionists debated the extent of government's capacity to stabilise economic change. The financial implications of corn law reform were frequently juxtaposed against statements of the pre-eminent needs of the state in the determination of financial policy. Constant concern that the economic policies of governments did not arbitrarily alter relative property values intruded a constitutionalist dynamic into economic argument. By focusing on the impact of corn law reform on the living standards of the labouring classes, Tories debated the functions of property and government in welfare and social order. In a context of popular radicalism, this discourse therefore framed resistance to free-market theories and policies as a set of strategies for constitutional conservation. After the Great Reform Act of 1832 protection gained new constitutional significance for Conservatives. Justifications of agricultural protection were reworked within specific Conservative interpretations of the 1832 Reform Act. These arguments glossed parliamentary reform as a revolutionary transformation not only of the franchise but also of the electoral pressures on the tariff. Thus the constitutional significance of protection in nineteenth-century Conservatism was not confined to maintaining the economic and political pre-eminence of land. Rather, the protective tariff was conceived as a means of forestalling a popular fiscal politics. That is to say, fiscal policy was presented as a way of sustaining a balanced representation of a range of interests within the reformed constitution while harnessing property of all descriptions behind a revivified Conservative party. Together, the growth of manufacturing populations, working-class protest, and the severity of depressions during the thirties and forties re-emphasised the representation of agricultural protection as a responsible food policy and refocused public attention on the capacity of government to influence economic change through protective tariffs. Because it rooted economic stability primarily in trade between domestic and colonial producers, protection appealed to Conservatives as a strategy for economic, social and political cohesion. Conservatives therefore mounted sweeping challenges to the Anti-Corn-Law League's apparent reduction of the 'Condition of England Question' to the panacea of corn-law repeal.

Insisting that debates on monetary and banking reform were not merely technical questions, Part II rethinks their economic, social and constitutional relevance in Conservative discourse from the Napoleonic period to the mid-century. In debates on convertibility, small notes and deflation, Tories searched out the boundaries and functions of monetary legislation. During 1810–11, 'bullionism' was no dogmatic category in Conservative thought, but was itself an arena of debate. For many Tory texts did not present monetary policy as a strategy for restricting economic change. They assumed that beyond the stabilisation of both prices and the foreign exchanges the projected resumption of cash payments would not be excessively deflationary and would prove to be economically anodyne. Monetary debate, then, was couched in constitutionalist languages which were concerned with the intrusion of legislation onto the terrain of relative property values. It follows that the critiques of the resumption of cash payments which appeared after 1819 also focused on the constitutional implications of a monetary deflation which originated with legislation. The redistributive, albeit unintended, consequences of a deflationary monetary policy were considered as arbitrary threats to the constitutional relationship between the state and property holders. Simultaneously Conservative texts debated the effects of excessive deflation on the constriction of credit, of consumption, and of production. These arguments also debated the social and economic impact of banking and monetary reform on the localities. It followed therefore that Conservative texts explored the potential of different banking and monetary policies to reverse these distributive consequences. Naturally, these arguments were also filtered through broader debates on financial policy and on the roles of institutions in precipitating or moderating commercial and financial crises.

In part III this study reveals the empire as a defining and integral component of Conservative political economy in the first half of the nineteenth century by analysing Conservative approaches to a range of central issues in imperial policy. Conservatives competed for the patriotic mantle of imperialism by exposing the anti-imperialism of free-trade theory as well as the ambiguous position of some Whigs and Radicals on imperial questions. In their defences of the East India Company's monopoly many Conservatives challenged the imperial prescriptions of free-trade economists and Utilitarian reformers. Alternative historicist and constitutionalist approaches vindicated the fusion of sovereign and commercial functions in a company chartered by parliament. Those who justified monopoly confronted the abstractions of liberal political economy and Utilitarianism with an imperialism which was defined and limited by locality, experience and history. Following the loss of the Company's monopoly in 1813, Conservative texts approached the issues of Indian administration and the remaining monopoly over the China trade with broadly similar arguments. They tended to reject emigration as a mere panacea for domestic pauperism. Instead they emphasised the political and social importance of exercising the duties of property within the domestic poor law. Yet, this perspective on emigration emphatically did not preclude attempts to search out the long-term economic, social and constitutional significance of colonialism for the metropolitan state. It followed that Whig and Radical imperial reformism was confronted by the ideological challenges of Conservatives in the thirties and forties. These responses increasingly presented the empire as an arena where government could influence metropolitan social and economic change through the fiscal instruments of imperial protection and preference. The Great Reform Act injected political and constitutional urgency into Conservative arguments for the continued representation of imperial interests in preferential tariffs. In this context, the Whig-Radical reforms of Canadian governance during the 1830s provoked Conservative responses which threw the onus of retaining imperial integrity on preference and protection rather than on political and religious liberalism.

By allowing the intrusion of political and constitutional questions into economic discourse, this study traces a recognisably Conservative political economy over half a century. Yet it also seeks to establish that 'political economy' was not simply synonymous with free-trade liberalism in the first half of the nineteenth century. This is not an examination of how protection worked and whether it failed, but an exploration of its justifications. In debates on agricultural, monetary and imperial policy, protectionists contested the legacies of Adam Smith and engaged critically with the ideas of David Ricardo, with the changing intellectual incarnations of Ricardianism, with Richard Cobden, and with the Anti-Corn-Law League. After 1846 protectionists continued to question free trade and its applications to public policy and posed broad and demanding intellectual problems for free-trade political economy. In their approaches to the corn laws and to the empire protectionists presented free trade as an exacerbation of the manufacturing economy's central weakness; a tendency to produce beyond the means of consumption. Protection was offered, largely though not exclusively by Conservatives, as a solution to the problem of 'sustainability' in its nineteenth-century incarnation; how to achieve stable economic change which would not destroy the established social, moral and constitutional structures of early nineteenth-century Britain. By spreading national income and employment dependencies over a range of producing interests, protection was submitted as a strategy for avoiding the risks of over-specialisation. Moreover, by identifying domestic and colonial producers as secure consumers, the policies of protection and preference were viewed as ways of counteracting the severity of periodic slumps.

This protectionist emphasis on consumption was also mediated as a question of social and political cohesion. The protectionism of Conservative prints contributed to wider debates on the political and social consequences of the perceived distributive characteristics of the British economy. By resisting Ricardian theories on the relationship of wages with profits many Conservatives offered socially cohesive alternatives which identified the interests of labour with those of capital. By presenting domestic and imperial producers as interests bound by mutual consumption, protectionists confronted the tendency of free-trade argument to express the relationship of economic sectors in antagonistic terms. Increasingly, the economic, social and political desiderata of protection were complemented by approaches to monetary and banking policy which stressed the distributive benefits of monetary liquidity. Similarly, the connections made by contemporaries to other debates on questions of financial and fiscal policy suggest that protectionism was neither an abstract philosophy nor an insulated discourse. Far from rejecting the importance of manufacturing and commercial wealth protectionists placed the emphasis on moderating the social costs and dramatic fluctuations of contemporary economic experience. In doing so they challenged both the substance and boundaries of free-trade political economy.

PART I

PROTECTION IN PRINT

2

Debating the Corn Laws, c. 1814–1830

It is tempting to view the 1820s as the moment when Britain resumed the continuous thread of liberalisation which had begun with the reforms of Pitt and was to culminate in the Gladstonian minimal state.[1] Most persuasively, this liberalisation has been explained in terms of the readjustment by a propertied polity to the qualitatively new problems posed by the massive public indebtedness of an increasingly commercial and manufacturing economy.[2] Most recently, the rolling back of the early nineteenth-century state through free trade and retrenched expenditure has been presented primarily as a political strategy and only secondarily as a set of purely financial or economic initiatives.[3] The retreat of the state from intervention in the socio-economic sphere through reduced taxation and the liberalisation of the tariff has from various perspectives been identified as a defining component of the nineteenth-century liberal orthodoxy.[4]

The historiographical consensus on the contours of public policy has perhaps diverted attention away from serious consideration of intellectual and political opposition to this 'liberal' orthodoxy. While few historians would now dismiss protectionism as the 'whining of lame dogs for exceptional treatment', it is still presented chiefly as the lobbying of vested interests against the retreat of the state from 'economic favouritism'.[5] By embracing the broader political, financial and socio-economic dimensions of protection this chapter reveals a rich seam of opposition to the politics of retrenchment

---

[1] C. R. Fay, *Great Britain from Adam Smith to the present day: an economic and social survey*, London 1929, and *The corn laws*, passim; Brady, *William Huskisson and Liberal reform*, esp. pp. 1–20, 168–72; Barnes, *English corn laws*, 118–25, 130–2, 158–9, 170–1, 175–6.
[2] A. W. Acworth, *Financial reconstruction in England, 1815–1822*, London 1925; W. D. Jones, *Prosperity Robinson: the life of Viscount Goderich, 1782–1859*, London, 1967, 65–109; Cookson, *Lord Liverpool's administration*, 1–17, 90–129; N. Gash, 'After Waterloo: British society and the legacy of the Napoleonic wars', TRHS 5th ser. xxviii (1978), 145–57; Hilton, *Corn, cash, commerce*, 3–30, 69–97, 127–201.
[3] N. Gash, ' "The state of the nation" (1822)', in *Pillars of government*, 43–54; Harling, 'Rethinking "Old Corruption" ', and *The waning of 'Old Corruption'*, 136–96.
[4] But see the account of the comparative strength of British protection 1846–1860 in J. V. Nye, 'The myth of free-trade Britain and fortress France: tariffs and trade in the nineteenth century', JEcH li (1991), 23–46 at pp. 24–7, 35–7.
[5] Fay, *Great Britain from Adam Smith to the present day*, 47–8. On protection and vested interests see Hilton, *Corn, cash, commerce*, 3–15, 98–101, 127–32; Crosby, *English farmers*, 26–56; D. Spring and T. L. Crosby, 'George Webb Hall and the Agricultural Association', JBS ii (1982), 115–31.

and freer trade. Protectionists interpreted the social and economic experience of post-Napoleonic Britain with arguments which cannot be confined in the old-fashioned concepts of 'mercantilism' and 'physiocracy'.[6] Notwithstanding their engaged responses to free-trade theory, protectionists offered more than alternative economic theories: they offered an alternative view of how public policy could influence the direction and durability of economic and social change. Agricultural protection was simultaneously presented as a coherent food policy for a growing industrial population and as a way of placing manufacturing advance on the secure and socially-cohesive foundation of the home market. Protection was also projected as a responsible financial strategy which would militate against the tendency of post-war deflation to magnify the burden of public and private debts while maintaining a financial core of taxable property. Beside the arguments of Radicals and retrenchers there flourished a competing discourse on the 'fiscal legitimation' of the early nineteenth-century state which emphasised two key points: the need to preserve the financial capacity of the post-war state to pay for a military establishment and to redeem the interest on the national debt while maintaining an equitable balance between the taxes paid by different forms of property. Notions of fiscal 'equitability' and 'balance' were, indeed, hotly contested since one person's perception of 'balance' was another's definition of 'bias'. Yet it was this contestation which forged an essentially political discourse focused more on perceptions of the balance of taxation than on the quantifiable incidence of taxes.

Of course, protection did not become the distinctive concern of Conservatives until the later 1830s. In parliament the cross-party consensus was protectionist in 1815 and individual Whigs were prominent defenders of the corn laws throughout the 1820s.[7] Yet, within a historiography which has privileged 'Liberal-Toryism' it is important to understand the prominence of protection in Tory economic discourse. Even if Tory ministers were reaching towards a distinctive form of economic liberalism and were seeking to withdraw the state from social and economic intervention, the more general purchase of such 'Liberal-Toryism' remains questionable.[8]

Protectionist expositions, 1813–15

Historians have long understood that the corn-law debates of 1814–15 were not polarised between 'protection' and 'free trade' but were focused on the

---

[6] E. F. Heckscher, *Mercantilism*, 1st publ. 1935, repr. London 1994, i. 19–30; ii. 112–72; L. Magnusson, *Mercantilism: the shaping of an economic language*, London 1994, 21–59.
[7] It should be noted that the protectionist Whigs, C. C. Western and J. C. Curwen, were marginalised in their parliamentary party on the question of protection.
[8] On the evangelical dimension to the 'Liberal-Tory' approach to the retreat of the state see Hilton, *Corn, cash, commerce*, 303–14, and *Age of atonement*, 203–51.

construction and purposes of protection.[9] The 1815 corn law rested on an autarchic consensus that self-sufficiency in food could be secured by ensuring high prices and secure markets for domestic agriculture. Indeed in the parliamentary debates of 1813–15 there were so few advocates of free trade in corn that one MP took it 'for granted that no-one now entertains the remotest idea of an entirely free trade in corn'.[10] The corn laws of 1814 and 1815 did not merely re-establish the legislative protection which high wartime prices had nullified, they completely re-fashioned it. The act of 1804 had established a bounty on exportation up to 48s., had prohibited exportation above 54s. and had constructed three scales of import duties. The act of 1814 abolished this bounty while the 1815 corn law absolutely prohibited foreign imports up to a certain price beyond which foreign corn was admitted duty-free.[11] This protectionist consensus was not based on an outdated emphasis on the economic importance of agriculture but responded to the demands of post-Napoleonic statecraft. Protectionists stressed the political imperative of sustaining both self-sufficiency in food and the taxable prosperity of British agriculture. Although their political economy engaged with the theories of Malthus and Ricardo it also responded to the Britain's economic experience of population growth and indebtedness. Protectionism in post-war Britain cannot be reduced to a sectional or reactionary strategy for it was presented as a policy for economic change which was sustainable in political, social and economic senses.

During the immediate aftermath of war, the necessity and feasibility of self-sufficiency in food were central planks of protectionist argument. The autarchic consensus was driven by two imperatives, one strategic and one ideological. The first was the insecurity of the peace. Both Malthus and William Jacob insisted on determining systems of trade according to contemporary international relations not abstract economic theory. For Jacob, Adam Smith's political perspective was anachronistic: 'Can we now be guided by principles deduced from a state of affairs such as that which existed in 1773 before the first war with America, the Revolutions of France, or before the late Continental System had been created?'[12] The second imperative was debate aroused by Malthus's theory of population; given the relative powers of increase of population and food, unchecked population growth would

---

9   Hilton, *Corn, cash, commerce*, 15–30 (Hilton revised interpretations of the 1815 law as a producers' law); Barnes, *English corn laws*, 117–56 at pp. 141–9; Fay, *The corn laws*, 135–55.
10 G. Rose, House of Commons (12 May 1813), Hansard xxvi. 694–5.
11 On abolition of the corn bounty see *Report of the select committee appointed to enquire into the corn trade of the United Kingdom* (1813), repr. Hansard xxv, appendices lvi–lxv, lxii. On the 1815 law see Barnes, *English corn laws*, 117–18, 134, 141.
12 W. Jacob, *Considerations on the protection required by British agriculture, and on the influence of the price of corn on exportable productions*, London 1814, 13; T. R. Malthus, *The grounds of an opinion on the policy of restricting the importation of foreign corn*, London 1815, esp. pp. 15–16.

inevitably outstrip food supplies.[13] Although in 1814–15 Malthus was a powerful advocate of protection and self-sufficiency, his *Essay on the principle of population* was not interpreted unproblematically as a mandate for agricultural protection.[14] Following W. T. Comber, George Ellis engaged with the Malthusian idea that the political and moral evils of society were attributable to the inevitable excess of population over a deficient means of subsistence. Whereas 'Population Malthus' was read as an advocate of 'discouragements to the further increase of the species', Ellis viewed 'population as a means of increasing wealth', considered 'depopulation and decline as synonymous', and allowed no necessary disparity between the produce of God's earth and human reproduction.[15] Sir Humphry Davy's *Elements of agricultural chemistry* and Sir John Sinclair's promotion of agricultural improvement threw expertise behind the assumption that legislation could tailor the means of subsistence to the rate of population growth.[16]

The necessity of national self-sufficiency was underlined by William Jacob as early as 1814; regardless of international politics, foreign sources could not be relied upon for any significant proportion of food supply. Jacob concluded from a comparison of census data with the returns of the Board of Agriculture that Britain could not always feed herself. Yet the dearth of 1800–1 had established that Europe could not reliably supply the deficiency.[17] European imports had yielded 'one eighth of wheat, or six weeks' supply, and one fortieth, or less than two weeks' supply, of other corn' and had placed almost insupportable demands on shipping capacity.[18] Thus, within the autarchic consensus, protectionists debated the best route to national self-sufficiency. Jacob's autarchic idea was mainly a metropolitan one which threw the onus on marginal land in the British isles: 'the subsistence of our people depends, if not wholly, at least principally, on retaining in cultivation those lands which,

---

[13] Idem, *An essay on the principle of population or a view of its past and present effects on human happiness; with an inquiry into our prospects respecting the future removal or mitigation of the evils which it occasions*, 2nd edn, London 1803, ed. D. Winch, Cambridge 1992, 13–29.
[14] Idem, *Observations on the effects of the corn laws and of a rise or fall in the price of corn on the agriculture and general wealth of the country*, London 1814. Of course Malthusianism and protectionism were not mutually inconsistent: Winch, *Riches and poverty*, 288–322.
[15] G. Ellis, 'Comber on national subsistence', QR x (Oct. 1813), 157–75 at p. 158; W. T. Comber, *An inquiry into the state of national subsistence, as connected with the progress of wealth and population*, London 1808. See also J. Weyland, *The principles of population and production, as they are affected by the progress of society; with a view to moral and political consequences*, London 1816, 21–4, 81–106, 105–6.
[16] T. Young, 'Davy's *Agricultural Chemistry*', QR xl (July 1814), 318–31 at p. 318; Sir H. Davy, *Elements of agricultural chemistry, in a course of lectures for the Board of Agriculture*, 2nd edn, London 1814, 3–30, 375–479. On Sir John Sinclair see Jacob, *Considerations*, 15.
[17] Lodged more recently in the public memory was the scarcity of 1812: Malthus, *Observations*, 26–7.
[18] Jacob, *Considerations*, 34, 31. Jacob's central objection to relying on European imports was the generality of harvest conditions on the continent (pp. 37–53).

if deprived of the capital they employ, would be of little or no value'.[19] The protection of marginal producers was presented as fundamental to securing national subsistence. Indeed John Weyland believed that discontinuing encouragement to production on inferior soils would destroy the population's natural tendency to 'keep *within the powers* of the soil', undermining 'public happiness, industry, and prosperity'. Since this tendency would apply only where the productive energies of the soil were not unnaturally depressed (say by imports), protection was for Weyland the mark of a 'moral and well-governed state'.[20]

It followed that Ireland was drawn firmly within the protectionist idea of the nation. The full integration of Irish agriculture into the domestic supply was lauded as a consolidating benefit of the Act of Union in the post-war world. As Sir Frederick Flood put it, 'Great Britain and Ireland were now one, and engaged in a common cause; formerly they pulled opposite ways, but now he trusted the same wealth would entwine the rose, the leek, and the shamrock.'[21] While some English protectionists did condemn the report of the select committee of 1813 as an 'Irish fix' many embraced Ireland in their economic idea of the nation.[22] If William Elliot celebrated Ireland as 'a most fruitful and abundant granary for the British empire' others offered a more extended view of the political economy of the metropolitan empire.[23] Both Sir John Newport and William Huskisson believed that by fostering Irish grain production the Westminster parliament could build a stable and permanent market for British manufacturing industry.[24] Corn-law reform was therefore perceived as a constructive tool of British post-Napoleonic statecraft.

The achievement of self-sufficiency in foodstuffs was not perceived as a

---

[19] Idem, *A letter to Samuel Whitbread, Esq. M.P, being a sequel to 'Considerations on the protection required by British agriculture, to which are added remarks on the publications of a fellow of University College Oxford: of Mr. Ricardo, and Mr Torrens*, London 1815, 6, 23–4. For Ricardo's critique of cultivating marginal land see below pp. 41–2.
[20] Weyland, *The principles of population and production*, 21–2, 232, 105. Malthus responded in *An essay on the principle of population*, 5th edn, London 1817; Waterman, *Revolution, economics and religion*, 173.
[21] Sir F. Flood, House of Commons (17 Feb. 1815), Hansard xxix. 826.
[22] *Report of the select committee* (1813), pp. lv–lvii. The full integration of Ireland in the British grain market was rejected by some English protectionists: House of Commons (20 May 1814), Hansard xxvi. 994–5. John Lockhart rejected such narrow English protectionism: ibid. (6 June 1814), 1071.
[23] William Elliot, House of Commons (3 Mar. 1815) ibid. xxix. 1230. See also Jacob, *Considerations*, 118–20; Lord Sheffield (John Baker-Holroyd), *A letter on the corn law and on the means of obviating the mischiefs and distress which are rapidly increasing*, 2nd edn, London 1815, 35–7; Anon., *Considerations upon the corn bill; suggested by a recent declaration from a high authority, that it was calculated 'To throw the burden from those upon whom it ought to rest, to those upon whom it ought not'*, London 1815, 39–40.
[24] Sir J. Newport and W. Huskisson, House of Commons (23 Feb. 1815), Hansard xxix. 822, 2022, 1040. See also Huskisson's speech on Parnell's resolutions in *The speeches of William Huskisson, with a biographical memoir, supplied to the editor from authentic sources*, London 1831, i. 295, 297–8.

mere practical and administrative problem. For the post-war debates on food policy ventilated important issues concerning the role of the state in the economic arena. The 1815 corn law's provisions for warehousing corn aroused protectionist controversy over the state's intrusion in the buying and selling of grain.[25] Although they insisted that the provision of subsistence was ultimately a function of legislation both Jacob and Lord Sheffield feared the exposure of the state to popular pressure during scarcity when warehouses would effectively become public granaries.[26] Appropriately, both authors appealed to Edmund Burke's *Thoughts and details on scarcity*, invoking his fear of the state's vulnerability to popular pressure, corruption and excessive power.[27] Others, however, eschewed Burke's squeamishness about state intrusion. Typically, George Booth saw warehousing laws as the fulfilment of the state's duty to provide subsistence during scarcity, stabilising supply, steadying price and effectively mediating between producer and consumer.[28] Such intervention in the corn market signified more than an expression of government's social and economic duties. Reconciling the interests of producer and consumer was essentially a political function: 'It is, in short, by a well conducted regimen, to infuse that salutary temperance into the political constitution, which, like that of the natural body, may alike secure us from the delirium of fever, as from the supineness of lethargy.'[29]

The dominance of food policy did not emasculate theoretical and economic features of protectionist argument. Frequently, these dimensions of protectionism have been loosely reduced to an unthinking 'physiocracy'.[30] 'Physiocracy' in turn has been read as a reactionary agrarian philosophy which was repulsed by manufacturing and commercial advance. A brief analysis of the ideas of William Spence suggests that this notion of physiocracy is unhelpful in understanding British protectionism. Spence

---

[25] F. J. Robinson, House of Commons (23 Feb. 1815), *Hansard* xxix. 805–6. The 1815 corn law extended bonded warehousing, and attempted to make London an entrepôt for the re-export trade. The act allowed free warehousing for domestic corn at all times: Hilton, *Corn, cash, commerce*, 13, 25–6.

[26] 'It is an imperative duty of every country to take all possible precautions, that the people subject to its government shall be abundantly supplied with all the necessaries of subsistence': Jacob, *Considerations*, 1.

[27] Jacob quoted Burke extensively ibid. 108–12. See also Sheffield, *A letter on the corn laws*, 35–7; E. Burke, *Thoughts and details on scarcity originally presented to the right hon. William Pitt in the month of November, 1795*, London 1800, 2, 9, 27–8, 45–6.

[28] G. Booth, *Observations on lowering the rent of land, and on the corn laws*, Liverpool 1814, 22–3. See the account of William Huskisson in Hilton, *Corn, cash, commerce*, 25–6, and W. Chapman, *Observations on the effects that would be produced by the proposed corn laws on the agriculture, commerce, & population of the United Kingdom*, London 1815, 6–10.

[29] Sir F. P. Eliot ['Falkland'], *Three letters on the financial and political situation of the country, in the year 1815; being a continuation to those of the preceding year*, London 1815, 496.

[30] Hilton suggested that protectionists forced physiocratic influences on the 1815 corn law: *Corn, cash, commerce*, 3, 28. See also R. L. Meek, *The economics of physiocracy: essays and translations*, London 1962.

repulsed James Mill's attempt to impose the pejorative label 'physiocrat' on him.[31] Spence surveyed physiocracy as a set of responses by Quesnay, Turgot and Mirabeau to the specific fiscal, economic and political problems of *ancien régime* France; their policy recommendations – internal free trade in corn, freedom of export, concentration of the fiscal burden in direct taxes on landowners – were applicable only to historical France. Spence also regretted the presentation of physiocracy as the thinking of an 'agricultural sect' which was opposed to manufacturing and resisted such polarisation of economic discourse in Britain:[32] 'The case, however, seems very different in Europe, and an attention to the facts will prove, directly in opposition to the opinion of the Economists, *that in Britain, agriculture has thriven only in consequence of the influence of manufactures; and that the increase of this influence is requisite to its further extensions.*'[33] For Spence the dominant antagonism in Britain was not between the domestic productive sectors (agriculture and manufactures), but between productive economic activity and mere exchange, or, commerce.[34] Despite the republication of Mirabeau's *Oeconomical table* in Britain in 1815, it is unlikely that French physiocracy exerted any meaningful influence on British protectionist discourse.[35]

British protectionism was no narrow agrarian philosophy in 1815 but was sensitively attuned to the distinct financial and fiscal condition of post-war Britain. Protectionists frequently argued that any significant reduction of agricultural protection would tend to be deflationary. Deflation, it was argued, would be redistributive, and would cramp economic activity in general.[36] Protectionists maintained that since the nominal value of debts would not adjust to lower real prices, the real burden of debts would be

---

31 W. Spence, *Britain independent of commerce; or proofs, deduced from an investigation into the true causes of the wealth of nations, that our riches, prosperity, and power are derived from resources inherent in ourselves and would not be affected, even though our commerce were annihilated*, 2nd edn, London 1807, was criticised by James Mill in *Commerce defended*, London 1808, 4, and by T. R. Malthus in 'Spence on Commerce', ER xi (Jan. 1808), 429–48. Spence subsequently refuted Mill's accusation of physiocracy in *Agriculture the source of the wealth of Britain; a reply to the objections urged by Mr. Mill, the Edinburgh Reviewers, and others, against the doctrines of a pamphlet entitled 'Britain independent of commerce', with remarks on the criticism of the monthly reviewers on that work*, London 1808, 5–11.
32 Idem, *Britain independent*, 10.
33 Ibid. 20, 24–5 (Spence's emphasis).
34 Idem, *Agriculture*, 28–36, 48–60. Spence invoked B. Franklin, 'Papers on subjects of general politics', in *The works of Benjamin Franklin*, London 1806, ii. 382–468 at p. 409 on this point.
35 *On the corn laws; being a digest from the oeconomical table: an attempt towards ascertaining and exhibiting the source, progress, & employment of riches, with explanations, by the friend of mankind, the celebrated marquis de Mirabeau: digested from the English translation as printed for W. Owen*, trans. 1766, repr. London 1815. R. Preston referred to Mirabeau in *An address to the fundholder, the manufacturer, the mechanic and the poor; on the subject of the corn laws*, London 1815, 5, 7. Francis Horner alleged that Preston had misread Mirabeau: House of Commons (23 Feb. 1815), Hansard xxix. 1030–2.
36 Anon., *A letter to the earl of Liverpool, on the probable effect of a great reduction of corn*

increased by the lower corn prices which freer trade might bring. This would effectively redistribute wealth from debtor to creditor interests throughout the economy: 'The real question is, whether a sudden reduction of the price of agricultural produce will not occasion a rapid and enormous increase of our national debt, a violent reflux of our paper circulation, and, consequently, a dangerous shock to our credit, public and private.'[37]

Given the state of credit and currency in post-war Britain, a deflationary corn-law reform was viewed by many as a dangerous prospect in constitutional, economic and financial senses. As Lord Liverpool's anonymous Correspondent observed: 'Violent transitions of property strike at the root of civil order and economy; they derange the whole frame of society, and sap the very foundations of good faith and morality.'[38] It was feared that the contraction of productive economic activity caused by reduced means of payment, constricted credit, and increased burdens of private debt, would diminish the tax base.[39] Simultaneously deflation would magnify the real burden of the public debt and force the government to increase the weight of taxation on the diminished means of the producing classes.[40] Protectionism in 1815 was not therefore an abstract philosophy but was rooted in the precise conditions furnished by the public and private indebtedness of post-Napoleonic Britain.

The specificity of British protectionism was also expressed in debates on the relationship between protection and the condition of the labouring classes. Protectionists emphasised the social imperatives behind maintaining 'high' corn prices. For Malthus, protection helped perpetuate the contemporary combination of a 'low price of precious metals' with a 'high price of corn and labour', which, though detrimental to manufacturing capitalists, benefited the labouring classes by extending their purchasing power over commodities.[41] More commonly, protectionists contended that grain importation would be detrimental to the labouring classes, not because of any direct influence of the price of corn on wages but because of the rural unemployment which would ensue from decultivation, and the consequent pressure exerted on the general labour market.[42] As George Booth put it, freer corn trade

---

prices, by importation; upon the relative condition of the state and its creditors, and of debtors and creditors in general, London 1814.
[37] Ibid. 95. See also Preston, *Address to the fundholder*, 22–3.
[38] Anon., *A letter to the earl of Liverpool*, 101, 106. On the constitutionalist languages of monetary debate see below ch. 4.
[39] Anon., *An address to the two houses of parliament on the importance of the corn laws to the national revenue*, London 1815, 5–6, and Preston, *Address to the fundholder*, 53.
[40] Anon., *An address to the nation on the relative importance of agriculture and manufactures, and the means of advancing them both to the highest degree of improvement of which they are capable; together with remarks on the doctrines lately advanced by Mr. Malthus on the nature of rent, and the relation it has to the amount of national income; and a prefaratory letter to C. M. Talleyrand Perigord, prince of Benevento, on the late exposé of the financial state of the French nation*, London 1815, 29–33, esp. p. 30; Malthus, *The grounds of an opinion*, 39–40.
[41] Idem, *Observations*, 30–1; *The grounds of an opinion*, 24–5.
[42] W. Spence, *The objections against the corn bill refuted; and the necessity of this measure to the*

would, 'according to the novel, but fashionable phrase, *demoralize* a great portion of the people'.[43]

Protectionists could therefore argue that the diminution of protection would incur social costs which could not be compensated by any gain to manufacturing or commercial competitiveness. This position was articulated in a theoretical controversy over the influence of the price of corn on wages. Even before David Ricardo published his *Essay on the influence of a low price of corn on the profits of stock*, protectionists denied that the corn laws were impeding the rate of manufacturing profit by artificially sustaining the price of corn.[44] Malthus's denial of any direct relationship between the price of corn and labour aimed to refute Smith's theory of value not Ricardo's. To Malthus, Smith's contention 'that the price of corn immediately and entirely regulates the prices of labour and all other commodities' was 'contrary to all experience'.[45] By invoking Sir F. M. Eden's findings on the wide range of commodities in working-class consumption, Malthus could show that a significant portion of wages were unaffected by the price of corn. Moreover, by appealing to the behaviour of corn prices and wages between the reigns of Edward III and Elizabeth, Malthus contended that there was no demonstrable correlation between them.[46] Applied to policy, Malthus's observations on corn and wages were designed to show that corn laws did not, through this mechanism at least, pervert the course of capital allocation: 'corn and labour rarely keep an even price together; but must often be separated at a sufficient distance, and at a sufficient time, to change the direction of capital'.[47]

While Malthus responded to Smith's emphasis on capital allocation, William Jacob anticipated free-trade criticisms of the influence of agricultural protection on the internal rate of profit in manufacturing. Like Malthus, Jacob denied any dominant relationship between corn and wages: 'the price of labour, like every other commodity, is regulated by its own abundance or scarcity'.[48] But, for Jacob, the importance of a 'market theory' of wages was that it isolated agricultural protection from the rate of profit in manufacturing. He pointed out that manufacturing profits were squeezed chiefly by outgoings in fixed and circulating capital, not wages or the price of food: 'that portion of labour which depends on the price of the subsistence of the labourer, is one quarter, or twenty-five *per cent*, on the price at which the

---

vital interests of every class of the community, demonstrated, 4th edn, London 1815, 10–11; Jacob, *Considerations*, 126–7.
[43] Booth, *Observations on lowering the rent of land*, 17; cf. Malthus, *Observations*, 28.
[44] D. Ricardo, *An essay on the influence of a low price of corn on the profits of stock; shewing the inexpediency of restrictions on importation: with remarks on Mr Malthus's two last publications*, 2nd edn, London 1815.
[45] Malthus, *Observations*, 9.
[46] Ibid. 5, 12n. See also Sir F. M. Eden, *The state of the poor*, 1st publ. 1797, ed. A. G. L. Rogers, London 1926, repr. London 1966.
[47] Ibid. 8.
[48] Jacob, *Considerations*, 146. See also Spence, *The objections*, 10–11.

goods are sold when finished'.[49] So Jacob could maintain that a dramatic differential between British and foreign corn prices could affect manufacturing profit rates and competitiveness in foreign markets to a very minor extent. Together, the limited influence of corn prices on wages, and the minimal pressure of agricultural protection on manufacturing profits, featured prominently in Jacob's response to what became Ricardian orthodoxy. Jacob offered a combined critique of Ricardo, West and Torrens which hinged on the proposition first elaborated in 1814, 'That the corn on which the labourers in our manufactories are fed, is much the smallest part in the composition of our exported manufactures.'[50] Though protectionists did not engage in detail with the theories of diminishing returns and rent in 1815,[51] by disputing the necessary links between corn and wages, wages and profits they challenged the foundations of Ricardianism at its genesis.

Such theoretical tussles were mere details in a larger debate about the direction and durability of the British economy. Even in 1815, British agricultural protectionism did not reject industrialisation though some protectionists did view the concentration of population, urban re-settlement, and the transformation of work by manufacturing industry as socially and morally undesirable.[52] The real question was a 'macroeconomic' one: should public policy encourage the concentration of national resources on manufacturing industry, or on retaining sectoral balance in the economy? Malthus framed the issue thus:

> The question, as applicable to this country, is not whether a manufacturing state is to be preferred to one merely agricultural, but whether a country the most manufacturing of any ever recorded in history, with an agriculture however as yet nearly keeping pace with it, would be improved in its happiness, by a great relative increase to its manufacturing population and a relative check to its agricultural population.[53]

For many of its supporters agricultural protection was fundamental to a balanced and stable economic modernity; the secure growth of manufactures was predicated on a thriving agricultural sector. Since food importation would cause domestic decultivation, protectionists could present freer trade

---

[49] Jacob, *Considerations*, 138. For his general argument see pp. 137–41.
[50] Idem, *A letter to Samuel Whitbread*, 56. Jacob engaged with E. West, *Essay on the application of capital to land*, London 1815, with R. Torrens, *Essay on the external corn trade*, London 1815, and with Ricardo, *Essay on the influence of a low price of corn*.
[51] Jacob's critique of West's 'theory of diminishing returns' merely observed that in marginal cultivation, an absolute surplus was more significant than the long–run behaviour of *rates* of return: *A letter to Samuel Whitbread*, 332. His critique of Ricardo reaffirmed (pp. 34–5) the importance of marginal production in subsistence.
[52] Jacob, *Considerations*, 143n.
[53] Malthus, *Observations*, 29.

as the contraction of manufacturers' securest markets.[54] William Spence pointed out that lower bread prices would be small compensation to merchants and manufacturers suffering the consequences of either lower agricultural profits or decultivation: 'a saving of a few pounds a year in flour, is a wretched consolation for a daily declining consumption and bankrupt customers'.[55] Thus Lauderdale looked to the 1815 corn law for the relief of manufacturing distress: 'Far from burthening the manufacturer, it would relieve him by relieving the farmer; for from the prosperity of the farmer, the labourer would be employed, the shopkeeper would thrive, and would create a demand – the most material and safest demand on the manufacturer for his commodities.'[56]

By focusing on the home market protectionists addressed the problem of sustaining economic growth in a manufacturing economy. William Jacob attempted to expose the wrongheadedness of seeking manufacturing advance on the basis of competitiveness in foreign markets. He pointed out that in 1810 over half of British manufactures were exported to protected colonial markets not to competitive foreign markets.[57] Even if cheaper corn could make manufactures more competitive, there could be no guarantee that foreign states would not impose import duties. Thus Jacob concluded that 'Excess of capital directed to the manufacture of exportable productions, is fraught with consequences highly detrimental to general wealth; by producing more goods than the wants of foreign nations spontaneously require, we are induced to overload the few markets open to all, as well as those in which we have a monopoly.'[58] So, not only was reliance on competitive foreign markets seen as relatively insecure, it was also thought to encourage speculative production beyond the means of consumption, and consequently, economic depression and social suffering. In this light, the new Ricardianism of reducing corn prices, reallocating capital away from the land to manufactures, raising the rate of profit in manufacturing, and boosting competitiveness in foreign markets, was a manifesto for the 'misapplication of the national capital'.[59] Protectionists provided an alternative vision of secure and proportionate manufacturing advance which was rooted in domestic popula-

---

[54] Idem, *The grounds of an opinion*, 34–5; Booth, *Observations on lowering the rent of land*, 6–9.
[55] Spence, *The objections*, 12. See also G. Webb Hall, *Letters on the importance of encouraging the growth of corn and wool, in the United Kingdom of Great Britain and Ireland*, London 1815, at p. 8, letter ii, 'To the editor of the Farmer's Journal' (20 Jan. 1815), and p. 34, letter vi, 'To the Right Hon. The Mayor of London' (12 Aug. 1815).
[56] Lauderdale, House of Lords (15 Mar. 1815), Hansard xxx. 203.
[57] Jacob, *Considerations*, 131–6.
[58] Idem, *A letter to Samuel Whitbread*, 9.
[59] Ibid. 16. Jacob pointed to speculative production for South American markets during the American war (pp. 10–13).

tion growth and agricultural expansion: 'These, indeed, are the real, the substantial increase of public wealth.'[60]

Ricardo exposed: protectionist perspectives on depression, 1816–25

The agricultural depressions of 1816 and 1822 and the commercial depression of 1825 impacted dramatically on British economic discourse. Denying that depression was the product of either over-extended cultivation or the corn-law subsidy, protectionists reaffirmed the possibility of self-sufficiency in food and looked to wider monetary and economic causes of depression. By lobbying for additional protection they did not merely advocate a sectional cause. For in their responses to the reports of the two parliamentary committees on agricultural distress which were published in 1821 and 1822 protectionists engaged closely with the intrusion of Ricardo's theories into the 'mainstream'.[61] These responses exposed the gap between Ricardian theory and economic reality. In the protectionist reading of contemporary economic experience Ricardo's totems of diminishing returns and rent could neither explain the suffering of 1816 nor account for the commercial depression of 1825.

The protectionist discourse of these years has in general been understood in terms of the 'politics of relief'.[62] That is to say corn-law defence has been described as one weapon in an extensive armoury designed to protect farmers' incomes: in this view inflationary monetary reform, retrenched taxation and protection were all means to the same pecuniary end. Yet by reducing post-war protectionism to the 'contingency politics' of agricultural relief we lose sight of the variegation and sophistication of contemporary economic discourse.[63] While the Ricardian agricultural report of 1821 may have influenced policymakers it also served to strengthen the protectionist response.[64] This response combined proposals for monetary and fiscal reform with protection in a cohesive approach to the economic and political implications of fiscal legislation. Adumbrated against the apparent liberalisation of commer-

---

[60] Ibid. 19. See also Preston's observation that Ricardianism suited only those manufacturers dependent on foreign markets: *An address to the fundholder*, 23.
[61] *Report from the select committee to whom the several petitions complaining of the depressed state of the agriculture of the United Kingdom were referred* (1821); *Report of the select committee appointed to inquire into the allegations of the several petitions which have been presented to the House in the last and present session of parliament, complaining of the distressed state of the agriculture of the United Kingdom* (1822).
[62] Crosby, *English farmers*, 26–56; Hilton, *Corn, cash, commerce*, 98–106.
[63] Ibid. 127–32, 140–5. On the 'Liberal-Tory' politics of retrenchment see Harling, *The waning of 'Old Corruption'*, 136–96.
[64] Hilton argued that the government abandoned autarchy: *Corn, cash, commerce*, 106–12, and looked to an economy geared towards manufactured exports (p. 126). On the direct influence of Ricardo on William Huskisson see ibid. 117–25.

cial policy during the 1820s this broad protectionist response offers an important perspective on Tory economic discourse. While Tory ministers may have reached toward a 'liberal' formula of retrenchment, 'sound money' and freer trade, they were not supported by the bulk of Tory public opinion. The seeds of the ideological rupture of 1846 may well have germinated in the 1820s.

In their response to the depressions of 1816 and 1821–2 protectionists vehemently denied that domestic over-production was the cause. Naturally, free traders offered the most powerful indictments of over-production: David Ricardo attributed the 1821 depression to low agricultural prices consequent on a succession of good harvests, importations from Ireland, and the perpetuation of extended cultivation by the 1815 law.[65] In response some protectionists interpreted abundance as evidence that domestic agriculture could demonstrably provide sufficient food at moderate prices.[66] Others blamed over-supply on the misuse of the warehousing clauses of 1815 not on domestic over-production.[67] In a critique of the agricultural report of 1821 John Ellman maintained that the warehousing of foreign corn in London had facilitated speculative stockpiling which had distorted prices.[68] He also argued that fraudulent and erroneous computation of the corn averages had allowed vastly excessive foreign importations between August 1818 and February 1819 despite an adequate harvest in 1818. In this view the cause of the agricultural depression was maladministration of the legislation of 1815 not over-production.[69] This emphasis on the direct agency of the state in the manipulation of the corn market perhaps helped to win the more protective corn law of 1822 in the teeth of Ricardian 'logic'.[70]

The debate on the role of over-supply in the depressions of 1816 and 1821–2 had several consequences for the broader question of agricultural protection. Perceptions of domestic abundance may account for the absence of a

[65] D. Ricardo, *On protection to agriculture*, 4th edn, London 1822, in *The works and correspondence of David Ricardo*, ed. P. Sraffa, Cambridge 1951, iv. 201–26, esp. pp. 259–60, 263. On 'over-production' see also the Revd A. Crombie, *Letters on the present state of the agricultural interest, addressed to Charles Forbes., Esq. MP.*, London 1816, 27–47 (letter ii).
[66] Anon., *A view of the causes of our late prosperity, and of means which have been proposed for our relief*, Exeter 1816, 21–2. See also R. Preston, *Further observations on the state of the nation*, London 1816, 20–1, 41–2.
[67] Ibid. 7, 9.
[68] Ellman founded the metropolitan committee of the 'Agricultural Association': Crosby, *English farmers*, 31–4. He gave evidence to the 1821 Committee on agricultural distress: Hilton, *Corn, cash, commerce*, 104. See also S. Farrant, 'John Ellman of Glynde in Sussex', *AgHR* xxvi (1978), 77–88.
[69] J. Ellman, *Considerations on the propriety of granting protection to the agriculture of the United Kingdom; with remarks on the report of the select committee of the House of Commons thereon*, London 1821, 9–12, 15, 18–20. See also W. Burrell and C. C. Western, House of Commons (22 Feb. 1821), *Hansard* n.s. iv. 1151, 1155.
[70] The 1822 law excluded foreign wheat when British prices were below 70s./qtr. When domestic prices were between 70s. and 80s./qtr, a duty of 12s. would be levied on foreign wheat. At 80s.–85s., the duty would be 5s., and above 85s., 1s. The scale could not operate until domestic wheat prices reached 80s. See Barnes, *English corn laws*, 174, and Hilton,

serious discussion of imperial supply beyond Ireland and reaffirmed confidence in Britain's capacity to feed a growing population under the 1815 corn law. Indeed, Lord Liverpool argued that abundance in 1821–2 vindicated the incorporation of Ireland into domestic supply during 1813–15.[71] Denying the culpability of overextension and monopoly, many protectionists looked to monetary policy and to the weight of taxation for explanations of distress.[72] As early as 1816, protectionists blamed the post-war contraction of circulation and credit for the agricultural depression.[73] As chapter 4 shows in more depth, it was widely maintained that deflation not only redistributed wealth from debtors to creditors but also cramped consumption throughout the economy.

This search for alternative monetary and fiscal explanations should not however lead us to over-emphasise the significance of retrenchment in protectionist argument. Of course, agriculturists' involvement in campaigns for reduced taxation and government expenditure cannot be ignored.[74] But many protectionists opposed the reduction of public expenditure if this meant that the state would break faith with the public creditor.[75] Tellingly, John Galt appropriated William Pitt's 'system of preservations of institutions and classes as against yielding all up to individuals' in an argument against the pressure for retrenchment by altering the terms of payment to the nation's creditors.[76] For Galt such an expedient would have been tantamount to the abuse of power by a landed polity: 'Who in fact, have created the

---

Corn, cash, commerce, 149–56. Among advocates of increased (albeit temporary) protection in 1822 were R. Torrens, *A letter to the right honourable, the earl of Liverpool, on the state of the agriculture of the United Kingdom, and on the means of relieving the present distress of the farmer, and of securing him against the recurrence of similar embarassment*, London 1816, 33; *Substance of the speech of the marquis of Londonderry, delivered in the House of Commons, on Friday, the 15th day of February, 1822, on the subject of the agricultural distress of the country, and the financial measures proposed for its relief*, London 1822, 82–3; Ricardo, *On protection to agriculture*, 263.

[71] *The speech of the earl of Liverpool, delivered in the House of Lords, on Tuesday, the 26th day of February, 1822, on the subject of the agricultural distress of the country, and financial measures proposed for its relief*, London 1822, 49–50.

[72] See below esp. pp. 102–4.

[73] Anon., *A view of the causes of our late prosperity*, 17–18. See also Anon., *England may be extricated from her difficulties consistently with the strictest principles of policy, honour and justice, by a country gentleman*, London 1816, 56–7, and Anon., *Remedies proposed as certain, speedy and effectual, for the relief of our present embarrassments, by an independent gentleman*, London 1816, 10–16, 31. The latter author appealed (pp. 32–3, 16) to Preston, *Further observations*, and to David Hume, 'Of public credit', London 1752, in *Hume*, ed. K. Haakonssen, Cambridge 1994, 166–78.

[74] Stanhope, House of Lords (21 Feb., 1822), *Hansard* n.s. vi. 555; Barnes, *A history*, 158–61; Crosby, *English farmers*, 57–80; Hilton, *Corn, cash, commerce*, 127–69 at pp. 135–40, 145–9.

[75] Anon., *A view of the causes of our late prosperity*, 41–72, and Anon., *England may be extricated from her difficulties*, 56–7.

[76] J. Galt, 'Bandana on the abandonment of the Pitt system: letter III', *BEM* xiii (May 1823), 515–18 at p. 516.

national debt? The landed interest.... Why, they themselves, by their commissioners, raised these loans at the *fair* rate of *interest of the day*.'[77] This reflected his general rejection of 'self-interested' protectionism: for him the 'politics of relief' reduced the landed interest to social 'drones'.[78]

Galt's fiscal argument contributed to a continuous current of Tory fiscal discourse which emphasised the financial capacity of the state (for expenditure on the military establishment and the national debt), the fiscal responsibilities of property and the need to maintain equitability in the incidence of tax on the different forms of property. Though not exclusively the preserve of Tories this current of fiscal argument was consistently opposed to the reformist consensus on retrenchment. Far from rejecting the property tax many protectionist tracts of 1816 sought to redirect and reaffirm it. For protection and property taxation were presented as mutual necessities for the early nineteenth-century fiscal state:

> The finance minister must be sensible that a property tax is the only means of supporting the credit of the country, or rather of preserving the appearance of the ability of paying the public creditor and the establishment.... It is absurd however and impracticable to impose any new tax on him [the landowner] without ... giving them [the tenantry] an ability to pay rents founded on a calculation that wheat is worth 10s. per bushel as an average price.[79]

In parliament also, some protectionists rejected retrenchment as a solution to agricultural distress and advocated the fiscal option of an 'equitable' property tax combined with protection: given the burden of the national debt, the financial interest of the state lay in sustaining a profitable and taxable agricultural sector, or, 'to stamp such a value on the produce of the soil ... as can alone enable that taxation to be paid'.[80] Indeed, when he presented a petition to parliament in 1821, T. S. Gooch insisted that agriculture was entitled to 'that protection which its value in the state demanded', sustaining his claim with evidence from the property tax returns.[81] Such arguments did not, however, imply that protectionists harked back to a narrow and 'physiocratic' idea of agriculture as the fount of wealth and taxes for 'wherever income is, it represents property'.[82] Hence, Curwen's proposals for a reformed property tax

---

77 Idem ('T. E.'), 'On the agricultural distresses', ibid. xii (Oct. 1822), 436–40 at p. 436.
78 Galt maintained that agricultural lobbying for retrenchment and relief threatened to create a self-interested caste: 'Bandana', and 'Hints to the country gentlemen: letter I', *BEM* xii (Oct. 1822), 482–91. See also J. Lockhart, House of Commons (8 May 1822), *Hansard* n.s. vii. 424–6.
79 Preston, *Further observations*, 30, endorsed in Anon., *Remedies proposed as certain*, 32–3. See also Anon., *Three letters of Paul Silent to his country cousins*, 2nd edn, London 1816, 11–31 at pp. 15–27, 43.
80 Ellman, *Considerations on the propriety*, 46.
81 T. S. Gooch, House of Commons (7 Mar. 1821), *Hansard* n.s. iv. 1141–2. See also H. G. Bennet and H. Bankes, House of Commons (30, 31 May 1820), ibid. n.s. i. 676, 722.
82 Galt, 'On the agricultural distresses', 439.

were framed around the principle of 'a fair and modified income tax, by which the expense would be fairly shared between all descriptions of property, instead of pressing exclusively on the land'.[83] In this way protectionists presented direct taxation and protection as opposite sides of the same fiscal coin. In doing so they established a permanent strain of fiscal argument which persisted up to 1852 in Tory fiscal discourse. In an intellectual sense therefore, direct taxation was no automatic corollary of the 'liberal' alternative of freer trade and retrenchment.

The conjunction of the property tax with protection was also expressed in economic justifications of direct taxation. John Galt viewed the retention of direct taxation as crucial to preventing over-capitalisation and over-production and boosting consumption. The key to sustaining economic advance lay, for Galt, in maintaining an increasing proportion of the population as consumers not producers. He therefore diagnosed the depression of 1821-2 in the following terms: 'Our present situation is a superabundance of capital, and a want of the means of employing it – and this has been caused by a reduction which has taken place in the amount of taxation.'[84] So Galt believed that direct taxation *especially* constituted, 'a fund which will allow the community to maintain a larger portion of the population unproductive'.[85] In Galt's view, the balancing function of direct taxation operated principally through government expenditure. Forming the state's income, direct taxes facilitated public expenditure which could envigorate consumption throughout the economy.[86] Thus protectionist approaches to taxation show that property taxation and protection were not perceived to be mutually inconsistent.

Protectionist argument was distinguished by responses to the intrusion of Ricardian theory during 1821-2. David Ricardo served on the committee of 1821, opposed the appointment of another committee on agricultural distress in 1822 and published *On protection to agriculture* as a pre-emptive exposition on the 1822 report.[87] Notwithstanding the doubts of historians protectionist contemporaries were convinced of Ricardo's influence on the policy debate:

> But Mr. Ricardo has placed himself, or rather has been placed by his advocates, at the head of a new school of political economy.... The progress which this school has made in the propagation of its doctrines, has of late been most extensive, so that it can boast among its élèves my Lord Liverpool, the Marquis of Londonderry, Mr. Vansittart, and more especially Mr. Huskisson.[88]

---

[83] J. C. Curwen, House of Commons (30 May 1820), *Hansard* n.s. i. 670. Curwen's fiscal argument placed him at odds with most fellow Whigs.
[84] J. Galt, 'Hints to the country gentlemen: letter II', BEM xii (Nov. 1822), 624-35 at p. 626.
[85] Ibid. 625.
[86] Ibid. 629. See also D. Robinson on local direct taxation: 'The poor laws', BEM xxiii (June 1828), 923-36 at p. 930.
[87] P. Sraffa, 'Note on "Protection to agriculture" ', in *Works*, iv. 203-5.
[88] S. Turner, *Considerations upon the agriculture, commerce, and manufactures of the British*

In order to analyse how contemporaries understood Ricardianism it is first necessary to outline some elements of Ricardo's economics. His central argument was that the declining rate of profit in agriculture was dragging down the rate of profit in manufacturing and could even hasten a stationary state.[89] His inter-related theories of 'rent' and 'diminishing returns' were fundamental to these general propositions. For Ricardo, rent was not a cost of production but was rather a surplus taken from the produce of the land after all costs of production had been repaid and profit had accrued at the average rate. Rent arose as a consequence of the progress of cultivation and agricultural capitalisation: the more fertile land first cultivated would, intrinsically, command no rent. Once worse land came into cultivation rent would accrue on the land first cultivated.[90] The core of Ricardian theory – that rent rose with every application of capital to existing land or cultivation of new, less fertile land – went something like this. Since the cost of producing the same portion of corn would be progressively higher both on less fertile land newly brought into cultivation and on land to which more capital had been applied than it would on the notional fertile 'land first brought into cultivation', the rate of profit on the former lands would be lower than on the latter. As profits had a tendency to equalise, the rate of profit on the land first cultivated would fall to the lower rate despite high nominal prices. The difference between the 'original' rate of profit on the better land and its new rate would be taken as rent on the better land leaving prices at the higher levels demanded by the cost of production on less fertile lands.[91] Thus, Ricardo could maintain two key points. Firstly, the progressive increase of rent was a function of the operation of diminishing returns to capital invested in agriculture at an advanced or extended state of cultivation. Secondly, the interests of landlords was necessarily opposed to that of every other class in society.[92]

Ricardo believed that diminishing returns and rent reduced the rate of profit in manufacturing by keeping food prices high: 'Profits then depend on the price, or rather, the value of food.'[93] As the price of labour was principally determined by the price of food, high wages reduced the portion of the manufacturing and commercial product which could be taken as profit.[94] Ulti-

---

empire; with observations on the practical effect of the bill of the right. hon. Robert Peel, for the resumption of cash payments by the Bank of England; and also upon the pamphlet lately published by David Ricardo, Esq., entitled, 'Protection to agriculture', London 1822, 1–2; Gordon questioned Ricardo's parliamentary influence in *Political economy in parliament*, esp. pp. 3–5, 25–6, 65–70, 80–101, 131–54. On Ricardo's influence on ministers see Hilton, *Corn, cash, commerce*, 121, 304–5.
89 Ricardo, *An essay on the influence of a low price of corn on the profits of stock*.
90 Ibid. 3–7, 15.
91 This is usually termed the 'theory of diminishing returns': ibid. 8–12, 13.
92 Ibid. 20.
93 Ibid. 27.
94 Ibid. 21–2

mately, therefore, high food prices could extinguish the incentive to invest hastening the stationary state and capital flight.[95] As Ricardo's response to the agricultural report of 1822 showed, he indicted protection as encouragement to diminishing returns, rent and high food prices. By this logic, manufactures and commerce could be liberated from the agrarian incubus only by importing foreign food at lower prices: forcing decultivation of domestic marginal land would narrow the margin of diminishing returns and reduce rents.[96] Yet, in spite of this theoretical indictment of protection, Ricardo was forced to admit in 1822 that agricultural depression was the product of low not high prices.[97] As high food prices were central to Ricardo's argument that agriculture was retarding the rate of manufacturing advance, the gap between theory and experience seemed unbridgeable to protectionists.

Many responses to Ricardo were general and 'philosophical' focusing on the political implications of his ideas not their theoretical significance. Indeed Ricardo's theoretical method was rejected by thinkers who elevated 'history' and 'experience' over *a priori* reasoning. One essay of 1818 erected the territorial constitution against Ricardo's contention that the interest of landlords was always opposed to that of every other class in the community. Not only did land lie at the foundation of the British polity but the interests of labour and capital were historically linked by 'an invisible Adamantine chain' and were not necessarily mutually opposed.[98] William Stevenson questioned the general validity of doctrinal political economy as a guide to what he called 'social wealth'. He maintained that the political economists conflicted on the definitions of value, price, wages, capital and rent. Stevenson also pointed out that since the 'economists' could not even agree on the relationship between production and consumption their conclusions could not be read as guides to policy.[99] Moreover, because Ricardian political economy derived its conclusions from theory not observation, it could not legitimately claim the methodological mantle of Baconian science.[100]

Yet protectionist prints also engaged directly with the different components of Ricardian theory.[101] Thomas Hopkins and Samuel Turner offered

---

[95] Ibid. 25–6. On the 'corn theory' of wages and its relation to the rate of profit see Ricardo, *On protection to agriculture*, 236–8.
[96] Ibid. esp. pp. 235–40, and idem, *An essay*, 28–36.
[97] Idem, *On protection to agriculture*, 255–61.
[98] Anon., 'Ricardo and the Edinburgh Review', BEM iv (Oct. 1818), 58–62.
[99] W. Stevenson, 'The political economist: essay II', ibid. xv (June 1824), 643–55, contrasted the theories of Quesnay, Smith, Say, Ricardo, Sismondi and Malthus, and used the phrase 'social wealth' (p. 643). Stevenson's 'The political economist: essay II: part II', ibid. xvi (July 1824), 34–45, analysed their views on policy.
[100] Idem, 'The political economist: essay III: part I', ibid. 202–14; 'The political economist: essay III: part III', ibid. xvii (Feb. 1825), 207–20.
[101] See also the critique by the free trader N. Senior in 'Report on the state of agriculture', *QR* xxv (July 1821), 466–504.

systematic critiques of Ricardo's *On protection to agriculture*.[102] Fundamentally, both writers maintained that rent was not a surplus but was rather a legitimate cost of production, determined by demand for the land's produce. This position had two consequences. Firstly, since rent was a component of price it could not also be its consequence. Thus, the proportion of the agricultural product accruing as rent could not increase with higher agricultural prices.[103] Secondly, the extension of cultivation onto marginal land could not originate rent. Indeed, Hopkins maintained that marginal cultivation tended to diminish rents on better lands by adding to supply and therefore reducing the intensity of demand for their produce.[104] As Hopkins summarised, 'land in cultivation pays a rent, not because lands of inferior fertility are taken into cultivation, nor because successive portions of capital employed in the same land, obtain a diminished quantity of produce, but because the land is scarce'.[105] Protectionists also targeted the theory of diminishing returns. Turner attacked Ricardo's assumption that the cost of production on poorer soils regulated agricultural prices by pointing to the absence of empirical evidence even on the proportion of land identified as 'poor'. Not only was Ricardo's teleology of cultivation (progressing from fertile to infertile) inherently questionable, it also ignored the benefits of enclosure, fertilisation and the division of labour in overcoming absolute levels of fertility.[106] Further, Sir John Sinclair maintained that the price of wheat on marginal lands was forced to fall to that of better lands and not *vice versa*. He added that by confining his theory of agricultural profits in an arable paradigm Ricardo had ignored the role of other commodities in maintaining profits on corn-producing mixed farms.[107]

Beyond such theoretical contestations protectionists prosecuted the macroeconomic message and policy prescriptions of Ricardianism. By challenging Ricardo's central proposition that the dominant influence on wages was the price of food protectionists attempted to sever the connection between the state of agriculture and rate of manufacturing advance.[108] As Malthus re-emphasised in 1823, the prices of all commodities, labour included, were chiefly determined by supply and demand not the cost of production or sub-

---

102 T. Hopkins, *Economical enquiries relative to the laws which regulate rent, profit, wages and the value of money*, London 1822; Turner, *Considerations*, 3–15.
103 Hopkins, *Economical enquiries*, 7–11, 13, 18, 39.
104 Ibid. 34.
105 Ibid. 36.
106 Turner, *Considerations*, 8–12. See also Ellman's critique of attitudes to marginal cultivation in the 1821 report in *Considerations on the propriety*, 21–2, and M. Attwood's response in the House of Commons (7 May 1822), Hansard n.s. vii. 380, praised by T. Lethbridge at p. 402.
107 Sir J. Sinclair, *Address to the owners and occupiers of land, in Great Britain and Ireland*, Edinburgh 1822, discussed in Barnes, *A history*, 175–6.
108 Turner, *Considerations*, 18. Hopkins emphasised the superior influence of culture and the state of the labour market in determining wages: *Economical enquiries*, 57–8.

sistence.[109] The focus for criticism was Ricardo's assumption that 'the difficulty of production on the land is the regulator of profits, to the entire exclusion of the cause stated by Adam Smith, namely the relative abundance and competition of capital'.[110] Further, by rejecting Ricardo's view that wages and profits necessarily related inversely, protectionists could sidestep his agrarian interpretation of the origins of the stationary state.[111]

It follows that advocates of agricultural protection also rejected Ricardian interpretations of the commercial and manufacturing depression of 1825. As early as 1824 Malthus maintained that the recent fall in manufacturing profits could not be attributed to the performance of agriculture. Supply and demand had made corn cheap allowing Malthus to observe that, 'Under these circumstances with a falling price of labour, the doctrines of the new school teach us that profits ought to rise.'[112] Though no direct influence can be demonstrated protectionist writers shared Malthus's diagnosis that declining profits were due to the 'the competition of capital', not to the performance of agriculture.[113] For, like Malthus, protectionists rejected 'Say's law', 'which teaches that all increase of demand depends upon increase of supply, and diminution of demand on diminution of supply'.[114] Unlike Malthus, however, protectionist prints maintained that free-trade theory and policy neglected the necessity of protecting domestic consumption. As early as 1821, M. Fletcher had rejected elements in the reports of the select committees on foreign trade which had advocated importation of raw produce, specialisation in manufacturing and increased reliance on foreign markets.[115] In this vein, David Robinson argued that the commercial reforms of the 1820s pointed towards a ruinous political economy of cheapness.[116] Not only would this

---

[109] T. R. Malthus, 'Tooke on high and low prices', *QR* xxix (Apr. 1823), 213–39, esp. at p. 223. Malthus reviewed Thomas Tooke's *Thoughts and details on the high and low prices of the last thirty years*, London 1823.
[110] T. R. Malthus, 'Political economy', *QR* xxx (Jan. 1824), 297–334 at p. 320. This was a critical review of the Ricardian, *Essay on political economy: supplement to the Encyclopedia Britannica*, vi, pt i, Edinburgh 1823. See also Hopkins, *Economical enquiries*, 99–101, 103.
[111] D. Robinson, 'The repeal of the combination laws', *BEM* xviii (July 1825), 20–31 at pp. 24–5, and 'The combinations', ibid. (Oct. 1825), 463–78 at pp. 470–2.
[112] Malthus, 'Political economy', 324.
[113] Ibid. 328.
[114] Idem, 'Tooke on high and low prices', 230. See also D. Robinson, 'Free trade', *BEM* xvii (May 1825), 551–63 at p. 563; J.-B. Say, *A treatise on political economy; or the production, distribution, and consumption of wealth*, trans. C. R. Princep, London 1821, i. 162–82. On Say see W. J. Baumol, 'Say's (at least) eight laws, or what Say and James Mill may really have meant', *Economica* xliv (1977), 145–62, and Gordon, 'Say's law', 438–46.
[115] M. Fletcher, 'Freedom of commerce', *QR* xxiv (Jan. 1821), 281–302 at pp. 284–8. Among texts reviewed by Fletcher were the *First report from the select committee of the House of Lords, appointed to inquire into the means of extending and securing the foreign trade of the country* [1820], and the *Report from the select committee of the House of Commons, appointed to consider of the means of maintaining and improving the foreign trade of the country* [1820].
[116] Robinson, 'Free trade', 551–63. On the commercial reforms see Hilton, *Corn, cash, commerce*, 173–201, and Jones, *Prosperity Robinson*, 65–109.

increase the risk of production beyond the means of consumption but by inducing the competition of capitals it would also drive domestic producers from both production and consumption.[117] At base the protection of agriculture, commerce and manufactures was offered as a strategy for keeping demand up to the productive capacity of the British economy. Thus protectionism cannot be cast solely as a self-interested philosophy. For, against the Ricardian panacea, it was presented as an alternative route to a stable economic future for nineteenth-century Britain.

Poverty and protection: maintaining the corn laws, 1826–30

During the later 1820s protectionists combined their theoretical critiques of Ricardian political economy with sweeping indictments of the social consequences of freer trade. The corn laws gained new significance in the debates on the social, economic and political threats posed by the distributive characteristics of British economic change. Concerns about food supplies and social order drove the government to emergency strategies: the release of bonded corn in 1825 and 1826, the dispatching of William Jacob to survey the state of the corn trade in June 1825, and the corn bill of 1827. The next major instalment of reform – the sliding scale of 1828 – shifted the principle of the corn law from prohibition to protection by integrating foreign corn firmly into the ordinary domestic supply.[118] Yet the direction of public policy should not lead us to assume that protectionism was on the intellectual defensive after 1826. Not only were the responses of protectionists to freer trade persistent and engaged, they also broached the deeper issue of the social, political and economic responsibilities of fiscal legislation. By presenting protection as a solution to the economic instability which threatened both social cohesion and political peace protectionists identified a distributive instrument for the early nineteenth-century state. In this way protectionists addressed their 'Condition of England Question': how could government alleviate the social and political tensions generated by economic change while defending the propertied constitution?

Even if the reform of 1828 can be located on a 'high road' to corn-law repeal, it cannot be assumed that, intellectually, the case for self-sufficiency was exhausted.[119] Indeed protectionists interpreted the empiricism of the government's official expert, William Jacob, as a reaffirmation of a protec-

---

117 Robinson, 'Free trade', 554–7. See also his 'The silk trade', BEM xviii (Dec. 1825), 736–50, for an application of this analysis to the liberalisation of the silk trade. For Robinson's approach to the financial and commercial crisis of 1825 see below pp. 112–13.
118 Hilton, *Corn, cash, commerce*, 272–4, 281–2, 287, 294.
119 Hilton noted an 'early, dramatic and little-noticed reversal of policy', and concluded that 'the important break in official thought on agricultural protection between 1815 and 1846 occurred before 1821': ibid. 109. In this reading the 1828 law was the 'first step' in applying this policy: ibid. 292.

tionist approach to self-sufficiency and as a refutation of free trade. Jacob's, *Report on the trade in foreign corn, and on the agriculture of the north of Europe* (1826) has been interpreted as evidence that Britain's exclusion of foreign corn (except at scarcity prices), contracted European supply and stymied effective food policy: if in 1814 Jacob's belief that foreign corn was scarce had pointed to a policy of protection, by 1826 the compass had swung round to progressively freer trade.[120] Yet far from underlining the 'irrationality' of protection Jacob's 1826 report was understood by many to bolster the case for a protective corn law. Thus J. R. McCulloch's Ricardian interpretation of Jacob's report was only one view which did not represent the wide range of positions in the discourse on food policy.[121] To McCulloch Jacob's report urged the reduction of the British corn law as an incentive to European production which would reverse diminishing returns in domestic agriculture and prevent both the progressive erosion of profit rates in manufacturing and distortion in capital allocation. Yet Jacob himself denied such arguments; prices were determined by supply and not *vice versa*. Thus he demonstrated from a survey of imports from Dantzig that supply from the Vistula basin remained broadly static regardless of changes in British prices and legislation. Jacob showed that even the intense French and British demand during 1791–1801 had not succeeded in attracting more than twelve days' consumption annually from the Vistula basin.[122] Thus Jacob concluded that changes to the British tariff could not liberate extensive European grain supplies. Further, Jacob denied any necessary relationship between corn prices and wages in manufacturing industry. As he deduced from observations in western Prussia, 'I have no reason to think that hitherto the low price of Corn has had the effect of lowering the price of manufacturing labour, in any degree approaching to the depression which the products of the soil have experienced.'[123] So, by elevating locality and experience over theory, Jacob's first report severed the Ricardian connection between agricultural performance and manufacturing profit rates.

---

[120] Ibid. 274, 293–4, 299–300. Hilton refuted Fairlie's argument that protection was 'rationally based': S. Fairlie, 'The nineteenth-century corn law reconsidered', *EcHR* 2nd ser. xviii (1965), 562–75, and 'The corn laws and British wheat production, 1829–76', ibid. xxii (1969), 88–116.

[121] J. R. McCulloch, 'Abolition of the corn laws', *ER* xliv (June 1826), 319–59. John Wilson observed that this piece was identical to McCulloch's, 'Price of foreign corn – abolition of the corn-laws', ibid. xli (Oct. 1824), 55–78, itself reprinted in the *Scotsman* (28 Jan. 1826): *Some illustrations of Mr McCulloch's political economy*, Edinburgh–London 1826, 6–35. D. Robinson repeated Wilson's exposé in 'The corn laws', *BEM* xxi (Feb. 1827), 169–81 at p. 169.

[122] W. Jacob, *Report on the trade in foreign corn, and on the agriculture of the north of Europe: to which is added, an appendix of official documents, averages of prices, shipments, stock on hand in the various exporting countries, &c., &c. &c.*, London 1826, 115–23. See also his *Report presented to the Lords of the committee of his Majesty's Privy Council for trade respecting the agriculture and the trade in corn, in some of the continental states of Europe*, London 1828, 98–106.

[123] Idem, *Report on the trade in foreign corn*, 114–15.

Contemporaries were aware that Jacob's empirical survey could not necessarily be read as an argument for a freer corn trade: protectionists competed legitimately, then, for Jacob's intellectual mandate. Indeed David Robinson wielded Jacob's evidence as a weapon against the entire Ricardian edifice: 'Yet the Report strikes at the very keystone of the new system; it demolished in the most triumphant manner, the "abstract" truths which form the basis of the new Political Economy, and it proves, unanswerable, that free trade in corn would be very destructive.'[124] Robinson challenged McCulloch's inference from Jacob's evidence that the smallness of foreign supply did not threaten British agriculture.[125] Similarly, Harvey Wyatt amplified Jacob's suggestion that under free trade capital in continental corn-producing countries might be reallocated to manufacturing and might reduce corn available for export and raise prices.[126] Another protectionist condemned the free trader W. W. Whitmore's comments on Jacob's first report as the reading of a 'theorist' and 'ultra-economist', and revived Jacob's scepticism about the British tariff's influence on foreign supply.[127] Applying Jacob's assessments of prospective importations, he questioned whether an annual importation of 600,000 quarters, 'would be at all likely to remove the difficulties under which manufactures and commerce at present labour'.[128] Ricardian readings of Jacob's first report were also rebutted in parliament where protectionists underlined the importance of maintaining national self-sufficiency in food: 'the growth of the United empire is adequate to the demand in ordinary years, and might be increased to an incalculable extent'.[129] In this view the achievement of self-sufficiency in food remained a sovereign function of the nation state in the post-Napoleonic era.[130]

In their response to the reform of 1828, therefore, protectionists uniformly reaffirmed that self-sufficiency remained both possible and desirable.[131] Many maintained that a prohibitive protection was the most effective mechanism

---

124 D. Robinson, 'Jacob's report on the foreign trade in corn, &c', BEM xx (Aug. 1826), 359–85 at p. 359.
125 Idem, 'The corn laws', 170.
126 H. Wyatt, An address to the owners and occupiers of land on the importance of an adequate protection to agriculture, London 1827, 31, 33; Jacob, Report on the trade in foreign corn, 115.
127 Anon., Observations on the corn laws, addressed to W. W. Whitmore, Esq. MP. in consequence of his letter to the electors of Bridgenorth, London 1827, 22–3, 21; W. W. Whitmore, A letter to the electors of Bridgenorth, upon the corn laws, London 1826, 50–3.
128 Anon., Observations on the corn laws, 7.
129 C. C. Western, House of Commons (23 May 1828), Hansard xix. 901. On Irish supply see Col. Wood, House of Commons (2 May 1826), ibid. xv. 806, and T. Lethbridge, House of Commons (1 Apr. 1827), ibid. xvii. 176.
130 Redesdale, House of Lords (22 Feb. 1827), ibid. xvi. 629–30, and his 'Resolutions on the corn trade' (29 Mar. 1827), ibid. xvii. 120–8.
131 The 1828 corn law repealed those of 1815, 1822 and 1827, increased colonial preference, replaced a prohibitive tariff with a protective sliding scale of duties, and retained the principle of a 'renumerating price' to domestic growers: Barnes, English corn laws, 201–2.

for price and supply management in the interests of both producers and consumers.[132] They agreed on a guaranteed remunerating price around the mid 60s. mark and on the need for a permanent settlement of corn legislation.[133] Yet the protectionist discourse fractured around the question of moving from a prohibitive law to an open principle of protection. In his response to Huskisson's bill of 1826, David Robinson rejected the sliding scale on the grounds that it left domestic farmers prey to fraud and erroneous computation of the corn averages. More significantly, he maintained that the 'open' sliding scale would reverse the principle of protection: 'In plentiful years it will admit foreign corn in ruinous abundance, when you wish it to be prohibited; and in deficient years it will prohibit such corn when you wish it to be admitted.'[134] William Jacob's own criticism of the legislation of 1828 was rather different. He maintained that the 1815 law had proved insufficiently protective because it was prohibitive; an 'open' law would annihilate the accumulations at ports and warehouses of cheap foreign corn which damaged domestic producers once the ports were opened. Jacob disputed the principle of the 1828 law which looked to increased reliance on foreign supply and the decultivation of domestic marginal lands:

> We must look to our own supply, if not quite exclusively, at least chiefly.... It can only be by due and real protection that the British farmer can be enabled to supply the wants of the community; and, if for want of such protection, he should fail considerably in his annual produce, the void cannot be filled up except at a cost very far beyond what such protection, expended on the domestic cultivators, would amount to.[135]

While they sometimes differed from Jacob on points of detail most protectionists shared his continued commitment to the basic desideratum of self-sufficiency.

These apparently arcane arguments about the state of European grain sup-

---

[132] Anon. [Atticus], *Observations on the corn laws*, London 1827, 10–15, invoked Joseph Lowe, *The present state of England in regard to agriculture, trade and finance; with a comparison of the prospects of England and France*, London 1822, on price stability. See also D. Robinson 'On the corn laws: no. II', BEM xxi (Mar. 1827), 274–310 at pp. 274–8.

[133] G. Higgins, *An address to the Houses of Lords and Commons, in defence of the corn laws*, London 1826, 23–9; Anon., *Thoughts on the policy of the proposed alteration of the corn laws*, London 1827, 6; R. Wilmot Horton (poss. with E. Edwards), 'The corn laws', QR xxxv (Jan. 1827), 269–83 at pp. 272–3.

[134] D. Robinson, 'The condition of the empire', BEM xxvi (July 1829), 97–119 at p. 109. Robinson claimed that Lord Malmesbury and Squire Western concurred in his 'The rejected corn law', ibid. xxii (Aug. 1827), 240–9 at pp. 241–2, 247.

[135] Jacob, *Report presented to the Lords*, 98, cited by John Barton in *In defence of the corn laws being an inquiry into the expediency of the existing restrictions on the importation of foreign corn with observations on the present social and political prospects of Great Britain*, London 1833, repr. in *John Barton: economic writings*, ed. G. Sotiroff, Regina, Sask. 1962, ii. 5–136 at p. 41.

plies and the mechanics of protection masked a much broader debate on the validity of Ricardian political economy for the social and economic condition of Britain 1826–30. Protectionists responded to the general proselytisation of Ricardo's ideas during the late twenties.[136] By challenging the theories of his chief disciple, J. R. McCulloch, David Robinson hoped to puncture Ricardo's influence on opinion and policy, 'bringing the reasoning of one side into visible, direct, full and decisive conflict with the other'.[137] Thus protectionist writers reiterated in more detail those objections to Ricardo's views on rent, diminishing returns and the rate of profit in manufacturing industry which had first surfaced around 1822.[138] What distinguished the theoretical argument of protectionists after 1826 was a sharpened approach to the 'corn theory' of wages and the Ricardian relationship between wages and manufacturing profits. As Alexander Macdonnell wrote, 'The relation between wages and profits forms the pillar of their system. If its base can be proved unsound, all argument for an unaltered distribution of industry, and the removal of restrictions on commerce, according to their own admission, falls to the ground.'[139] From a comparative analysis of the living standards of French and British labourers, Macdonnell concluded that higher wages in England were not attributable to agricultural performance or to indirect taxation. Rather, 'five-eighths' of the difference between living standards in Britain and France was due to qualitative cultural factors which dictated the relatively high level of the 'natural rate' of wages in Britain.[140] More conventionally, David Robinson emphasised the relatively low proportion of labourers' wages expended in corn, the role of machinery in diminishing the pressure of the cost of subsistence on profits, and the pre-eminent influence of supply and demand for

---

136 Examples of Ricardian prints are Anon. *The corn laws considered, in their effect on the labourer, tenant, landlord &c., &c.*, London 1826, 9–10, 23–9, on diminishing returns; H. Drummond, *Cheap corn best for farmers proved in a letter to George Holme Sumner, Esq. M. P. for the county of Surrey, by one of his constituents*, London 1826, on rent; J. S. Mill, 'The corn laws', *Westminster Review* iii (Apr. 1825), 394–420.
137 Robinson, 'The corn laws', 169. For denunciations of McCulloch's essays in *The Edinburgh Review* see Anon., *Remarks on certain modern theories respecting rents and prices*, Edinburgh 1827, 1–4, 80–96, and Anon., *Thoughts on the policy of the proposed alteration of the corn laws*, 26–9, 34–8.
138 L. Mease, 'Letter on Ricardo's theory of rent', *BEM* xxi (Jan. 1827), 74–9; E. Edwards, 'On agriculture and rent', *QR* xxxvi (Oct. 1827), 391–437 at pp. 404–7; D. Low, 'On the theory of rents', *BEM* xxi (Mar. 1827), 311–14; D. Robinson, 'Political economy II', ibid. xxvi (Oct. 1829), 671–87 at pp. 678–9.
139 A. Macdonnell, *Free trade; or an inquiry into the expediency of the present corn laws; the relations of our foreign and colonial trade; the advantages of our navigation system; the propriety of preventing combinations among workmen; and the circumstances which occasion a derangement of the currency: comprising a general investigation of the alterations lately adopted, and still further meditated in the commercial policy of the country*, London 1826, 219–20.
140 Ibid. 10–28, endorsed by R. Wilmot Horton, 'Taxation and expenditure', *QR* xxxv (Jan. 1827), 283–315 at p. 295.

labour on wages.[141] Protectionist critiques of the theoretical foundations of Ricardian policy prescriptions were confident, persistent and engaged.

This emphasis on the social implications of Ricardian theory was part of a much broader discourse on the durability of manufacturing advance and the inequalities of economic change. While Ricardians identified agriculture as the incubus which preyed on manufacturing profits protectionists argued that the competition of capital within the manufacturing sector was the most powerful single factor in reducing manufacturing and commercial profits.[142] Yet the most powerful element in the protectionist challenge to Ricardo was the widely-diffused argument that the inexorable fluctuations of the manufacturing economy were due to failures in demand for manufactured goods. In the Ricardian view such crises of 'under-consumption' were impossible. As Alexander Macdonnell noted, Say, Ricardo, McCulloch and James Mill all assumed that 'extensive production leads to extensive consumption'.[143] Macdonnell therefore amplified the concern of the political economists Malthus and Sismondi with the problem of demand and insisted that the will and capacity to consume was a decisive influence on accumulation in any economy.[144] Similarly, David Robinson intensified his critique of 'Say's law' for which he substituted an alternative axiom: 'The means of consumption must flow from, but they must govern, production. The consumption of manufactured goods must govern the production of them, and such production must govern that of raw produce.'[145] For Robinson the 1829 depression was only explicable as a crisis of consumption: the commercial reforms of the 1820s had undermined the domestic means of consumption by destroying the capacity of domestic producers to consume and introducing foreign competition in domestic markets.[146]

If freer trade was condemned as the factor which undermined the sustainability of manufacturing advance, protection was presented as the bedrock of balanced and permanent economic change. The policy of protection had, 'prohibited one body from buying what would ruin another: it prohibited the nation, as a whole, from buying what practically it could neither consume nor sell again – from destroying its own market and ruining itself'.[147] In this view the protection of agricultural incomes furnished the state with an important instrument within a wider 'under-consumptionist' approach to sustaining

---

141 Robinson, 'On the corn laws: no II', 281, and 'The condition of the empire', 115–16. On mechanisation see Anon., 'The corn laws', *QR* xxxvii (Mar. 1828), 426–47 at pp. 439–40.
142 Macdonnell, *Free trade*, 213; Robinson, 'On the corn laws: no. II', 304; Robinson, 'Political economy II', 671.
143 Macdonnell, *Free trade*, 103–4, 105. On Sismondi see below pp. 78–9.
144 Macdonnell, *Free trade*, 131.
145 Robinson, 'Political economy II', 672.
146 Idem, 'The condition of the empire', 103.
147 Idem, 'Agriculture', *BEM* xix (Mar. 1826), 287–313 at p. 294.

economic advance.[148] By discouraging over-specialisation and protecting a range of employment and income dependencies, government could help maintain demand and iron out economic fluctuations.[149] Sectoral balance in economic change was perceived as fundamental to the project of keeping production proportioned to consumption: 'Production, it may be said, is encouraged; but the fundamental axiom of political economy is, that to give factitious encouragement to one mode of production over another is faulty, and instead of increasing, must diminish, the aggregate productiveness of the country.'[150] Agricultural protection was not projected as a sectional philosophy but rather as a pre-condition of balanced and stable economic change in early nineteenth-century Britain.

The general protectionist concern with the balance and character of economic development was also expressed in debates on the inequalities of economic change. If at one level protectionists challenged the distributive consequences of Ricardianism for the economy, at another they questioned its impact on living standards and social cohesion. Specifically, protectionists insisted that it was necessary for social reasons to insulate Britain from the general European grain market. Agricultural protection was seen to defend the high relative value and high relative living standards of British as compared with European labour.[151] The relative cheapness of foreign corn was presented as the product of the extreme poverty of European peasant producers not the superior fertility or better cultivation of foreign soil.[152] Therefore it was argued that freer trade in corn would tend to level British living standards down to a European minimum.[153] The precise operation of this mechanism was open to debate. One anonymous reviewer endorsed Edward Cayley's appropriation of a corn theory of wages for protectionism: if wages related directly to corn prices, then the high prices ensured by protection could sustain high corn wages and extend purchasing power for other commodities.[154] But most protectionists focused on the domestic decultivation, reduced living standards and increased competition for work which foreign

---

[148] Mease, 'Letter on Ricardo's theory of rent', 78; Macdonnell, *Free trade*, 290–1, 299–301; Robinson, 'The condition of the empire', 106–7.

[149] Idem, 'Mr Huskisson's speech in defence of free trade', *BEM* xix (Apr. 1826), 474–88 at p. 480.

[150] Lord Elgin, 'Causes and remedies of pauperism in the United Kingdom', *QR* xliii (May 1830), 242–77 at p. 257. See also Robinson, 'Mr Huskisson's speech', 478, and 'Agriculture', 292.

[151] Suttie, 'Letter from a Scottish freeholder on the effects of the introduction of foreign grain upon the condition of the labouring population', *BEM* xxi (Jan. 1827), 1–8 at pp. 2–3.

[152] Robinson attributed excessive European production to serfdom: 'Jacob's report', 364–8; 'The corn laws', 172–3 and 'The taxes', *BEM* xxvii (Mar. 1830), 487–500 at pp. 495–6.

[153] Anon., *The high price of bread shown to be the result of commercial prosperity, not the cause of national distress; and the dangers of a free trade in corn pointed out: by a warning voice*, London 1827, 32–5, 40, 64–7.

[154] Anon., 'The corn laws', 429–30, used evidence from Edward Cayley's, *Corn trade, wages, and rent*, London 1826.

competition would bring.[155] The high relative wages and a high money price of bread which characterised the protective system were cast as symptoms of a progressive civilisation: 'not only an evidence of commercial prosperity, and the general ease and comfort of society; but as these must depend upon greater or less degrees of civilisation and freedom, it is a test by which we can estimate the advances of both, and of man himself to a more perfect state of social happiness'.[156] Alexander Macdonnell emphasised the importance of relatively high wages in establishing the sociological foundations of economic and social 'progress' in a protected economy. The economic imperative of a deep and broad domestic means of consumption necessitated high relative wages for the labouring population.[157] Yet this would also encourage the growth of an open middle class and the extension of the 'emulative' and 'accumulative' impulse to every class in society.[158] In short, protection was widely seen to forge the sociological underpinnings of a 'well-established prosperity'.

This concern with living standards and social 'progress' can only be fully understood when it is situated beside the broader contemporary discourse on poverty and its relief. The later 1820s were years of financial and intellectual crisis for the old poor law which culminated in the widespread social distress of 1829–30. In this context agricultural protection was presented as a focused response to the social crisis facing rural Britain. In the later 1820s a number of protectionist writers identified the unemployment caused by agrarian reforms as the origin of rural poverty. Sir Francis Palgrave, Robert Southey, Edward Edwards and Lord Elgin all interpreted rural poverty as a historical consequence of enclosure and mechanisation.[159] These interpretations generated rural solutions which depended on the protection of agriculture: the reconstruction of rural society through allotment systems and the domestic resettlement of the urban and rural poor in 'home colonies'.[160] Of course, such agrarian solutions rejected Ricardo's priority of relocating labour and capital

---

[155] Robinson, 'On the corn laws: no II', 287; Higgins, *An address to the Houses of Lords and Commons*, 6–7.

[156] Anon., *The high price of bread*, 194. See also Robinson, 'On the corn laws: no. II', 279–80.

[157] Macdonnell, *Free trade*, 61, 113–17.

[158] Ibid. 132; Wyatt, *An address to the owners and occupiers of land*, 6.

[159] See Palgrave's response to the *Report of the select committee appointed to inquire into the wages of labour* (1825) in 'The poor laws', QR xxxiii (Mar. 1826), 429–55 at pp. 432–7, and Southey's review of *Reports of the select committee on emigration from the United Kingdom* (1828), in 'Emigration report', ibid. xxxviii (Mar. 1828), 539–78, esp. pp. 549–57. See also E. Edwards, 'Conditions of the English peasantry', ibid. xli (July 1829), 240–84 at pp. 240–7, and Elgin's response to *Report from the select committee of the House of Commons, on that part of the poor-laws relating to the employment or relief of able-bodied persons* (1828), in 'Causes and remedies of pauperism in the United Kingdom', 252–3.

[160] See Sir Walter Scott, 'On planting waste lands', QR xxxvi (Oct. 1827), 558–600, and E. Edwards, 'Cultivation of waste lands', ibid. xxxviii (Oct. 1828), 410–41 at pp. 429–35. On 'home colonisation' see below pp. 169–70. On the destruction of 'commoning economies' see J. Neeson, *Commoners: common right, enclosure and social change in England, 1700–1820*, Cambridge 1993, 158–84.

to manufacturing: debates on rural poverty and agricultural protection were inextricably connected. David Robinson linked his defence of the corn laws to his advocacy of 'home colonisation' in preference to colonial emigration. A protected and extended domestic agriculture could employ the poor, and 'would be infinitely more advantageous to the State, than their being sent to any of the Colonies'.[161] Thus, not only did protectionists reject Ricardian indictments of 'waste', they also presented its protection as a valid response to rural poverty and as one element in a general defence of the principles of the Old Poor Law.

By debating protection in distributive terms protectionists evolved and addressed a 'Condition of England Question'. They identified social and economic inequalities and interpreted these as consequences of erroneous legislation thus formulating a 'Question' which was ideological and political: how could government influence the moral and social consequences of economic change? For William Johnstone the moral, social and economic crisis facing modern Britain derived from extreme polarisation of wealth: 'while such misery exists among the poor, there never was a time in which the luxury of the rich was carried to a more extravagant degree'.[162] He believed that this inequality did not originate with manufacturing *per se* but rather with its inadequate distribution of the product identifying 'a change from the abundant disbursement of capital among the working classes in exchange for their labour, to a very curtailed disbursement'.[163] Johnstone focused on two sources of this change: government policy and the changing nature of capitalism. Since 1815 governments had abandoned high borrowing and spending together with inflationary monetary policies and had replaced these with retrenchment, freer trade and deflation. These policies, combined with mechanisation and concentrated production, drove a wedge between capital and national wealth on the one hand, and labour on the other: 'the connection which formerly subsisted between the employment of capital in manufactures, and the employment of the people, was now unnecessary ... and the capitalist found that he could increase his own wealth, and the wealth of the country, while the people were left in idleness and starvation'.[164]

But, inequality was also perceived as an ideological phenomenon, in origin and effect. David Robinson argued that Ricardianism had exacerbated and sanctioned the polarisation of wealth. The desideratum of competitiveness

---

[161] Robinson, 'On the corn laws: no. II', 310, and 'The surplus population of the United Kingdom', BEM xxi (Apr. 1827), 377–91 at p. 381. See also E. Edwards, 'Home colonies', QR xli (Nov. 1829), 522–50.

[162] W. Johnstone, 'The state and prospects of the country', BEM xxvi (Sept. 1829), 464–573 at p. 465.

[163] Ibid. 466.

[164] Ibid. See also idem, 'Our domestic policy: no. I', ibid. (Nov. 1829), 768–74; 'Our domestic policy: no. II', ibid. (Dec. 1829), 940–7; 'Domestic policy: no. III', ibid. xxvii (Jan. 1830), 90–6; E. Edwards, 'The influence of free trade upon the condition of the labouring classes', ibid. (Apr. 1830), 553–68 at p. 564.

and cheapness had necessarily squeezed the share of labour, and the idea of comparative advantage and specialisation seemed to have influenced reforms which threatened significant employment dependencies.[165] But to Robinson, the Ricardian relationship between wages and profits destroyed more than the mutuality of labour and capital: 'By making high profits the *sine qua non* of national wealth, and low wages that of high profits, it in reality makes the grand principle of civil government, to keep the mass of the human race in the lowest stages of indigence and suffering.'[166] Thus protectionists articulated their critiques of free trade in political and ideological terms. Fundamentally, the 'fierce and eternal conflict' between labour and capital, which had apparently arisen as a consequence of economic liberalisation, was seen to threaten the existence of a propertied polity.[167]

These formulations of the origins and political implications of the polarisation of wealth led free trade's critics to focus on the restorative possibilities of protectionist legislation. If the causes of social crisis lay in economic legislation then reform could win more positive functions for the state. Critics of free trade presented protection as a public policy which would generate wealth that was balanced in both sectoral and social terms and would therefore lay the foundations of political stability. Thus protectionists combated the divisive language of Ricardianism with a socially cohesive alternative. For critics of free trade isolated a range of distributive strategies for government which were ultimately designed to legitimate and sustain a propertied polity. It was therefore argued that by maintaining mutual demand between classes and sectors in the home market agricultural protection could bind together the different interests which comprised the nation:

> The landowners, farmers, and working classes, husbandry, manufacturing and trading, must ... prosper and suffer together.... Upon them the small manufactures and traders depend almost wholly.... Upon all these the more opulent manufacturers and traders mainly depend. The middle classes exist principally through good prices of agricultural produce and good wages. Without such prices there can be no farmers worthy of the name; and of course the gigantic part of the middle classes which the latter form, must be destroyed.[168]

For Robinson, to abandon protection was tantamount to destroying the social

---

[165] Robinson, 'The condition of the empire', 107–8, and 'Political economy III', ibid. xxvi (Nov. 1829), 789–808 at pp. 791–2.

[166] Idem, 'Political economy I: to the heads of the University of Oxford', ibid. (Sept. 1829), 510–23 at p. 511. 'What effect have the doctrines touching on capital and labour had among the labouring classes?: they have caused labour to make war on capital': idem, 'Mr McCulloch's Irish evidence', ibid. xix (Jan., 1826), 55–76 at p. 74.

[167] Idem, 'Political economy I', 523; Johnstone, 'The state and prospects of the country', 469–70, and 'Domestic policy: no. III', 92–3; J. Galt, 'Thoughts on the times', BEM xxvi (Oct. 1829), 640–3.

[168] D. Robinson, 'Political economy IV', ibid. xxvii (Jan. 1830), 22–47 at p. 29. See also Edwards, 'The influence of free trade', 562.

compact, to 'root out the feelings and regulations which give being and weal to society, and replace them with those that brutalise and destroy it'.[169]

Protectionists also looked to other elements of fiscal policy as ways of addressing the problem of distribution. In keeping with the debates of 1816–22 there was no necessary inconsistency in advocating both protection and direct taxation in the later 1820s. A striking emphasis of debate during these years was the presentation of direct taxation as a distributive corollary of protection. As David Robinson proposed, 'Having given these great advantages to the agriculturists, impose a property tax in Britain and Ireland to raise ten millions annually; impose it for twelve years, to be reduced one-fourth in every third year, and take off twelve millions of duties.'[170] In this view, severing the connection between protection and revenue did not necessitate the abandonment of protection's economic functions. Rather, by enabling parliament to rescind duties on a range of imported commodities (not otherwise manufactured in Britain), a property tax was seen to consolidate the economic and political functions of protection.[171] Hence, Elgin identified the main impediment to 'the effective demand for labour' as 'the misdirection of taxation'. With the proviso of protection, Elgin advocated shifting the burden of taxation onto property.[172] Given the conviction of protectionists that Britain was suffering a social, moral and political crisis of distribution this insistence that the taxation of property should be a corollary of its protection represented an ideological and political response to their 'Condition of England Question'.[173] Thus nineteenth-century debates on direct taxation cannot be understood simply in terms of a nascent Gladstonian trilogy of free trade, retrenchment and financial probity guaranteed by property taxation. For, in the contexts of 1816, 1822 and 1829–30 protectionists advocated the direct taxation of property in opposition to freer trade and retrenchment. By the fourth decade of the nineteenth century, protection was clearly identified beside a property tax as a distributive option for a responsive and stable state.

---

[169] Robinson, 'The condition of the empire', 99. See also Johnstone, 'Our domestic policy: no. III', 90–6.

[170] Robinson, 'The condition of the empire', 117.

[171] Ibid. J. W. Croker (or J. Miller) presented direct taxation as compensating for consumption lost through landlord absenteeism especially from Ireland: 'Internal policy', QR xlii (Jan. 1830), 228–78 at p. 240.

[172] Elgin, 'Causes and remedies', 252, 255.

[173] For Edwards and Robinson property taxation enforced the 'social' (as opposed to 'natural') rights of landed property: Robinson, 'Mr. McCulloch's Irish evidence', 55–76; E. Edwards, 'Irish absentees', QR xxxiii (Mar. 1826), 455–73 at pp. 470–1. These were critiques of J. R. McCulloch's justifications of absenteeism offered to the select committee of the House of Commons appointed to inquire into the state of Ireland (1825) and his 'Absenteeism', ER xliii (Feb. 1826), 54–76, and the Scotsman (12 Jan. 1822). See also Wilson, Some illustrations of Mr McCulloch's political economy, 58–62.

3

Protectionism and Conservatism, 1830–1847

Between the Great Reform Act and the repeal of the corn laws in 1846 protectionism became increasingly identified with Conservatism and the Conservative party.[1] Indeed in 1846 the Conservative party was shattered by the clash between free trade and protection. This schism has usually been understood in one of two ways. Historians have either presented the crisis of Conservatism as a conflict between the different constituency interests which underpinned the changing complexion of electoral support for the party.[2] Or they have presented it as an ideological clash between the modernised economic liberalism of Peel and the reactionary protectionism of his backbenchers: a failure of political education.[3] Most recently this ideological rupture has been glossed as the final battle between the 'disinterested Conservatism' of Peel and the unreconstructed Conservatism of vested interests.[4] It is implicit, of course, in all these approaches that protection was a lost cause in political and economic terms by the 1840s. As Robert Stewart once wrote, 'The Tories looked about them at the poverty and ugliness of London and Manchester, recoiled in fear and disgust from the Satanic Mills, and strove to keep England a green and pleasant land.'[5]

Yet if we are to explain why and how the relationship between protectionism and Conservatism was cemented during the 1830s and why the schism of 1846 went so deep, protection cannot be dismissed as a 'lost cause'.[6] While protectionism was kept alive in the Whig party by the contributions of pro-

---

[1] I would like to thank the *English Historical Review* for permission to use material from A. Gambles, 'Rethinking the politics of protection: Conservatism and the corn laws, 1830–1852', *EHR* cxiii (1998), 928–52.
[2] C. Schonhardt-Bailey, 'Linking constituency interests to legislative voting behaviour: the role of district economic composition in the repeal of the corn laws', in J. A. Phillips (ed.), *Computing parliamentary history: George III to Victoria*, Edinburgh 1994, 86–118, and 'Interests, ideology and politics: agricultural trade policy in nineteenth-century Britain and Germany', in A. Marrison (ed.), *Free trade and its reception, 1815–1960*, London 1998, i. 63–81.
[3] I. Newbould, 'Sir Robert Peel and the Conservative party, 1832–1841: a study in failure?', *EHR* cxlviii (1983), 529–57; R. W. Stewart, *The politics of protection: Lord Derby and the Protectionist party 1841–52*, Cambridge 1971; N. Gash, *Sir Robert Peel: the life of Sir Robert Peel after 1830*, 2nd edn, London 1986, 562–615.
[4] Harling, *The waning of 'Old Corruption'*, 228–66.
[5] Stewart, *The politics of protection*, 46–7.
[6] Walker-Smith, *The protectionist case*, 7–84; Macintyre, 'Lord George Bentinck and the protectionists', 141–65.

tectionists like E. S. Cayley it was increasingly pushed to the fringes of Whiggery: by 1839 the Whig leadership was committed to a low-fixed duty in corn and the report of the select committee on import duties of 1840 was a blueprint for free trade. Thus the identification of protection with Conservatism was increasingly distinct. It will be shown here that far from being the emblem of an outdated Conservatism, protection was perceived by many Conservatives as a crucial component in the electoral and intellectual revival of the party after the constitutional crisis of 1828–32. Following the Great Reform Act protection gained a new significance as an economic instrument with which governments could represent and balance propertied interests within the reformed constitution. Indeed it appeared to many Conservatives that the reform of 1832 had transformed both the nature of representation and the electoral pressures on the tariff through the primacy of the sectional interests of urban manufacturers and creditor interests in the reformed political nation. This transformation of fiscal politics gave protection a new significance in Conservatism as an alternative fiscal politics. The protectionism of Conservatives must therefore be located within a specific Conservative construction of the 1832 Reform Act's impact on the British polity. This 'politics of protection' was reinforced by economic justifications which were mounted in constitutional and political languages. Conservatives met the challenge of Richard Cobden and the Anti-Corn-Law League with a public philosophy of protection as a viable panacea for food policy, stable and sustained manufacturing advance and balanced economic development; in the mutuality of economic interests lay the foundations of social and political cohesion. They responded to the protest of Chartists and Leaguers with sweeping indictments of free-trade political economy as a divisive and contracted philosophy of society and of the social and economic responsibilities of government. Political protest was explained as a direct consequence of a social and economic crisis of distribution which free-trade political economy seemed to compound. Thus protection was simultaneously offered as a restorative political language and as a practical intervention of government which could sustain employment dependencies and relative living standards. Until the autumn of 1845 most protectionists believed that Peel shared their commitment to protection as a policy for social cohesion, economic stability and political peace. Thus, when Peel relinquished protection he rejected a Conservative political economy which fused together political and constitutional positions with economic and social arguments.

Rethinking the politics of protection

Three principal emphases have dominated historical approaches to the 'politics of protection'. By concentrating on agrarian pressure groups some historians necessarily conceptualised the politics of protection as a set of responses to the fluctuating demands of interested constituencies.[7] More ideological approaches to the Conservative party's split in 1846 have generally erected a 'modernised' Conservatism, which had adapted to the Reform Act of 1832 against a retrograde and reactionary protectionist alternative.[8] Most recently, Philip Harling's study of the propertied polity's self-legitimation during 1779–1846 identified corn-law repeal as a consummation of the state's retreat from a sectional politics of interest: that is to say, by relinquishing the monopolistic corn law Peel confirmed the neutrality of the state and insulated the propertied constitution from the odium of corruption.[9] Yet all three approaches to 'the politics of protection' stand in need of some modification. Intellectual elements in protectionism confirm that its politics cannot be confined exclusively to the demands of rural electorates. Neither was economic liberalism a necessary component of Conservative acceptance of constitutional reform. For in print as in parliament protection was perceived as a vital feature of a revivified Conservatism which was directed at harnessing property behind constitutional conservation within the reform of 1832. Protectionists consistently exposed the substance and form of the repeal agitation as quintessentially sectional. Repeal itself was presented as the identification of the state with the specific interests of manufacturing exporters and only ostensibly with those of the consumer. According to the protectionist *telos* repeal was an inevitable consequence of the transformation of fiscal politics by the Reform Act of 1832. Politically, then, repeal was cast as the ultimate concession to a self-interested urban electorate. Protectionists represented the repeal of the corn laws as a constitutional concession which relinquished the tariff as a tool for the balancing of economic interests; the abandonment not the embodiment of a contested ideal of impartiality.

At one level, the relationship between constitutional conservatism and agricultural protection seems simple: protecting agriculture preserved the landed basis of the British constitution.[10] George Croly's biography of Edmund Burke, published in *Blackwood's* during 1833–4, was a detailed justification of the 'territorial constitution'.[11] Unlike owners of commercial or manufacturing property, possessors of 'real' property held 'sufficient interest

---

[7] For T. L. Crosby, the experiences of agricultural constituencies determined the rise and fall of Conservative protectionism: *English farmers and the politics of protection*, 81–189.

[8] Brady established a tenacious antagonism between 'liberal' and 'unreconstructed' Conservatism in *William Huskisson and Liberal reform*, 5. N. Gash conceived politics in general between 1832 and 1852 as a struggle between reformers and reactionaries: *Reaction and reconstruction*. For Newbould, the polarity was between pragmatic Peelism and 'Ultra-Toryism': 'Sir Robert Peel and the Conservative party', 529–57.

[9] Harling, *The waning of 'Old Corruption'*, esp. pp. 248–54. Parry has also suggested that a major significance of corn-law repeal was the distancing of the state from economic vested interests: *The rise and fall of Liberal government*, 165–6.

[10] H. Thompson, *Free corn ruinous to England*, 4th edn, London 1839, 5–6, 13, 19.

[11] G. Croly, 'Edmund Burke: pt I', BEM xxxiii (Mar. 1833), 277–97; 'Pt II', ibid. (Apr.

in the settled constitution of things to make change a serious loss to themselves'.[12] Conservatives justified the dominance of landed property in the unreformed constitution in terms of the virtues and rights of property ownership: 'the share of each individual of the government ought to be proportioned to his stake, and the degree in which his interest and feelings are identified with the weal of his fellow subjects'.[13] Thus the political rights conferred by property were constructed as social rights determined by convention, not individual rights drawn from abstract theory.[14] Specifically, the reform of the borough franchise had overthrown a mechanism by which talent was harnessed to the state and commerce, shipping and the colonies were virtually represented.[15] In this reading the enfranchisements of 1832 gave the individual a 'worthless vote' and deprived 'vast divisions of population and property of representation in respect of their special interests'.[16] Thus the principle of 'individual representation' was considered to threaten the transformation of British politics into a constant clash of population and property.

Thus Conservative readings of the Great Reform Act as a 'revolution' did not rely on an exclusively 'landed' notion of the propertied constitution. Indeed, Archibald Alison thought that the Tories had missed a pressing opportunity to pass a Conservative measure of parliamentary reform:

> by a concession of reform to the higher classes in the great towns the ferment might have been lessened; and by such allies the Conservative party in the country materially strengthened. The Tories missed it, confounding reform in Parliament with increase of democratic power, and refusing to grant it even on principles which would have diminished that formidable force.[17]

As early as 1832 Tories were urging that the dual project of Conservative party regeneration and constitutional defence could be achieved by harnessing the interests of urban property.[18] By competing for the wealthy and edu-

---

1833), 597–620; 'Pt III', ibid. xxxiv (July 1833), 25–46; 'Pt IV', ibid. (Sept. 1833), 317–43; 'Pt V', ibid. (Oct. 1833, pt i), 485–502; 'Pt VI', ibid. (Nov. 1833), 739–61; 'Pt VII', ibid. xxxv (Jan. 1834), 27–48; 'Pt VIII', ibid. (Feb. 1834), 273–90; 'Pt IX', ibid. (Apr. 1834), 508–25; 'Pt X', ibid. xxxvi (Aug. 1834), 228–39; 'Conclusion', ibid. (Sept. 1834), 322–40.
12 Croly, 'Edmund Burke: pt VI', 756.
13 R. B. Seeley (?), 'On political parties (no. II)', FM i (June 1830), 603–20 at p. 603.
14 Croly, 'Edmund Burke: pt V', 490; 'Conclusion', 330–1, 338; J. G. Lockhart, 'Coleridge's Table-talk', QR liii (Feb. 1835), 79–103 at p. 101; A. Alison, 'Experience of democracy: the prospects of the constitution', BEM xl (Sept. 1836), 293–308 at pp. 304, 307–8; G. Croly, 'William Pitt: no. VII', ibid. xxxviii (Sept. 1835), 356–69 at pp. 358–9.
15 Idem, 'Edmund Burke: pt III', 37–8; 'Part VI', 742–6; Anon., 'The present balance of parties in the state and the results of the Reform Bill', FM v (Apr. 1832), 294–316 at pp. 315–16.
16 Seeley (?), 'On political parties (no. II)', 611; Croly, 'Edmund Burke: pt VIII', 287–8.
17 A. Alison, 'The progress of social disorganisation: no. III: the prostration of government', BEM xxxv (Apr. 1834), 526–46 at p. 546.
18 Idem, 'Duties of the Conservative party', ibid. xxxii (July 1832), 139–43 esp. pp. 140–1; R. B. Seeley, 'On parties (no. III)', FM vi (Sept. 1832), 205–15 at pp. 213–14.

cated urban electorate, and breaking down the impediments in social life between 'the ranks' and 'the intermediate classes', Alison believed the Conservative party could confound the Whigs with the ten-pounders.[19] Thus fiscal policy, and specifically protection, was identified as a key element in the electoral revival of Conservatism. As William Maginn put it, 'we want chiefly 1, a distinct recognition that there is a right and wrong in religion . . . and 2, an abandonment of the ruinous quackery of the economists'.[20]

The ideological significance of protection for the revival of Conservatism must therefore be understood in terms of Conservative responses to the Great Reform Act. If 1832 represented an open ended 'revolution' then one immediate consequence was the transformation of fiscal politics. The Whigs' retrenchments of the 1830s were explained as inevitable financial concessions to an urban middle-class electorate. Appropriating the duke of Wellington's version of the financial history of the reformed parliament's first session, William Johnstone feared that the financial power of the state would be neutered by Whig populism.[21] This view became prominent in many critiques of Whiggism which contributed to the intellectual reconstruction of Conservatism during the 1830s.[22] Typically J. W. Croker politicised financial debate by employing a specific version of recent financial history: the sound 'Tory' policy of William Pitt had been perverted by Whig retrenchments which were thought to have emasculated the state's capacity to service the national debt and to afford expenditure on the military and on the Church.[23] Fundamentally, this transformation of financial politics was interpreted as a consequence of the Great Reform Act. As Alison summarised, 'The Reform Bill has practically vested the administration of affairs, and especially the finan-

---

[19] A. Alison, 'Hints to the aristocracy: a retrospect of forty years from the 1st January, 1834', BEM xxxv (Jan. 1834), 68–80 at pp. 74–80.
[20] W. Maginn, 'The state and prospects of Toryism: January, 1834', FM ix (Jan. 1834), 1–25 at p. 25.
[21] W. Johnstone, 'The duke of Wellington on the finances of the country', BEM xxxii (Sept. 1832), 375–80 at pp. 375–6. Johnstone extracted (pp. 376–8) part of Wellington's critique of Althorp's budget: I. Newbould *Whiggery and reform, 1830–41: the politics of government*, London 1990, 106–7.
[22] A. Alison, 'The British finances', BEM xxxi (Apr. 1832), 598–621; 'On the financial policy of Mr Pitt and his successors', ibid. xxxiv (Aug. 1833), 179–95 at pp. 180–7; 'Whig and Tory finance', ibid. xlvi (Oct. 1839), 494–504; Croly, 'Edmund Burke: pt IX', 517.
[23] Ostensibly Croker reviewed *Corrected report of the speech of Lord John Russell at the dinner given at his election for Stroud, on Friday, 28th July, 1837, and an account of the proceedings*, London 1837, and Anon., *Domestic prospects of the country under a new parliament*, London 1837: 'Lord John Russell's Speech at Stroud', QR lix (Oct. 1837), 519–64. On Pitt contrasted with Petty see pp. 526–8; on 'irresponsible' retrenchment see pp. 532–3 (and also A. Alison, 'The Whig dissolution', BEM l [July 1841], 1–31); on damage done to establishments by Whig financial policy see pp. 19–20; for a statistical comparison of Whig and Tory financial performance see pp. 8–9.

cial concerns of the nation, in the masses of the people; . . . the government has had no alternative but to live on from day to day.'[24]

Thus fiscal discourse was acutely politicised during the 1830s. Conservatives argued that the balance of interests embodied in Whig budgets was distorted by the prominence of urban interests in the reformed constitution. Thus Archibald Alison condemned successive Whig budgets for abandoning the principle of balancing interests.[25] Thus Conservatives argued that the transformation of fiscal politics by the reform of 1832 made a constitutional case for reappropriating executive control over the tariff's financial and protective functions. Croker therefore opposed the Whigs' initiative to make the corn law an 'open' question in 1834 because of its constitutional consequences; as the Great Reform Act had replaced the virtual representation of interests with direct representation an 'open' corn question exposed the state to a direct clash of conflicting interests.[26] In this view the Whig's commitment to a low fixed duty after 1839 and Peel's repeal of the corn laws in 1846 were merely the fiscal companions of constitutional reform.[27]

Protection therefore gained a new profile in the Conservative project of forestalling democracy. For Conservative commentators the re-institution of sound finances through Peel's income tax was a constitutional riposte to the Whigs' erosion of the state's financial power and a re-identification of the duties of property with the interests of the state.[28] In 1842 Peel's income tax was supported by many protectionists and was not understood as a device which facilitated freer trade.[29] Parliamentary opposition to Peel's tax was led by Cobden and Hume not by protectionists. For, from the free-trade perspective, Peel's income tax was the fiscal price of protective subsidies.[30] Many Conservatives understood the fiscal settlement of 1842 as a protectionist one

---

[24] Alison, 'Whig and Tory finance', 502.
[25] Idem, 'On the financial measures of a reformed parliament: no. I: the Whig budget', BEM xxix (June 1831), 968–76 at pp. 971–6; 'The Whig dissolution', 4, 19; 'The first session of the reformed parliament: Ireland – West Indies – East Indies – domestic and foreign policy of ministers', ibid. xxxiv (Nov. 1833), 776–804 at pp. 779–81.
[26] J. W. Croker, 'On the corn laws', QR li (Mar. 1834), 279–83. This was an appendix to R. Southey's article, 'The corn laws', ibid. 228–83.
[27] J. W. Croker, 'The budget and the dissolution', ibid. lxviii (June 1841), 238–80, at p. 244; T. De Quincey, 'Sir Robert Peel's position on next resuming power', BEM l (Sept. 1841), 393–409 at pp. 393, 402; C. Neaves, 'Prospects under the Peel ministry', ibid. (Oct. 1841), 537–46 at pp. 537–40, 512; J. W. Croker, 'Whig tactics', QR lxxv (Mar. 1845), 519–32 at p. 523, and 'Ministerial resignations', ibid. lxxvii (Dec. 1845), 298–321 at pp. 300–1.
[28] Idem, 'Policy of Sir Robert Peel', ibid. lxx (Sept. 1842), 485–531 at p. 490. See also De Quincey, 'Sir Robert Peel's position on next resuming power', 409, and 'Sir Robert Peel's policy', ibid. li (Apr. 1842), 537–52 at p. 552.
[29] See Viscount Sandon, House of Commons (13 Apr. 1842), Hansard 3rd ser. lxii. 389–400.
[30] R. Cobden, House of Commons (18 Apr. 1842), ibid. lxi. 703–8; Sir W. Clay, House of Commons (21 Mar. 1842), ibid. 963; J. Hume, House of Commons (25 Apr. 1842), ibid. lxi. 1083–4.

which responded to a Whig/Radical fiscal politics of concession. Through the instrument of protection, the fiscal representation of interests could be reappropriated for the executive, from 'the people'. This concept of the fiscal representation of interests was fundamental to how Conservatives understood the functioning of political parties and the propertied constitution. As R. B. Seeley explained, 'Political party, of necessity, takes its creed in the main from the interests of those divisions which sustain it. Community of interests connects the Crown, aristocracy, Church and Agriculture; the Tory party flows from them, and it combats for their benefit as the means of promoting its own.'[31] In his response to Peel's 'Tamworth Manifesto', Croker took a broader view of the 'wide variety of rights and interests which are mingled and combined in what we call the Constitution'. Beside the crown and the Church, Croker's list embraced land, manufactures, public credit and colonies.[32] If the constitution was defined as the interests which comprised it, then protecting those interests equated with constitutional defence. Thus Conservatives viewed the fiscal protection of national interests as a mode of constitutional defence which rebutted the numerical logic of 1832.[33] Together with sound finances, protection was presented as a strategy which would identify all propertied interests permanently with constitutional conservation.[34]

It is therefore essential to recognise this constitutional and political context if we are to understand the protectionism of Conservatives during the 1830s and 1840s. Some Conservatives recognised that the party's bid for urban commercial, manufacturing and creditor interests would necessarily influence the representative balance of the tariff. As Alfred Mallalieu observed in 1836, 'The great and now all-powerful body of manufacturing and mercantile classes, three fourths of the intelligence and wealth of which are with us, have not fought the up-hill fight of Conservatism on behalf of party, but of country.'[35] Many protectionists therefore accepted that protection was a territory for the re-negotiation and re-balancing of interests by an active executive.[36] Thus, in 1841 protectionist writers urged Peel to reconsider the

---

[31] R. B. Seeley (?), 'On political parties (no. 1)', *FM* v (May 1832), 448–62 at p. 452.

[32] J. W. Croker, 'Sir Robert Peel's address', *QR* liii (Feb. 1835), 261–87 at pp. 274–5; Neaves, 'Prospects under the Peel ministry', 544–5.

[33] Anon., *Letter to the duke of Buckingham, on the corn laws by a practical farmer: 'live and let live'*, London 1839: 'If the Ministers consent to the ruin of the agriculture of this empire... the mob will carry all before it' (p. 9).

[34] Alison, 'Whig and Tory finance', 499–502, and 'The Whig dissolution', pp. 1–4. See also Neaves, 'Prospects under the Peel ministry', 541–3. One prominent opponent of the income tax was Sir Richard Vyvyan: *A letter from Sir Richard Vyvyan Bart., M.P., to his constituents upon the commercial and financial policy of Sir Robert Peel's administration*, London 1842, 13–15.

[35] A. Mallalieu, 'Foreign policy – foreign commerce – and the Prusso-Germanic customhouse league', *BEM* xxxix (Jan. 1836), 49–79 at p. 78.

[36] Croker urged the abandonment of dogmatic positions in the protection debate: 'The

balance of the corn tariff. G. C. Holland's suggestions for reform of the corn laws were underpinned by his conviction that 'the nature of the reciprocal relations uniting interest to interest, and class to class, presents one of the most difficult inquiries in the whole range of political economy'.[37] Similarly D. Salomons accepted that corn-law reform was impelled by the need to achieve an equitable balance of interests; as corn prices had fallen between 1828 and 1841 a portion of the existing protection had become excessive. In their capacity as consumers therefore, urban interests could legitimately demand measured reform.[38] It follows that Peel's tariff reforms of 1842 were celebrated by protectionists as a judicious re-balancing of the interests of producers and consumers. Indeed it was Cobden who condemned the budget of 1842 as 'a scandal to England and Christendom'.[39] Thus Croker spoke for the protectionist consensus when he described the 1842 budget as 'the best combination and adjustment of all interests that our position admits, and the fairest promise of permanent protection to the farmer, and permanent plenty to the people'.[40]

Yet there was no necessary progression from reformist protectionism to free trade. Although Christopher Nevile did embrace the repeal of the corn laws in 1846 other reformers remained protectionists.[41] J. W. Croker and Samuel Warren reiterated the rigid distinction between Conservative fiscal policy and a Whig politics of concession. Warren observed that by recognising an urban consumer interest the fiscal settlement of 1842 had adapted Conservatism to the 'totally new political exigencies of the times . . . out of the elements of democracy to arrest the progress of democracy'.[42] Yet he could also insist that the settlement of 1842 represented a *'formal recognition of the principle of agricultural protection'*, rejecting a Whig fiscal politics which 'arrayed the agricultural and manufacturing interests in deadly hostility against each other'.[43] In retrospect Conservatives resisted attempts to construe the 1842 corn law as an instalment of free trade insisting instead that it was the 'maintenance of a fair and rational protection for domestic inter-

---

budget and the dissolution', 248. See also J. Gladstone, *The repeal of the corn laws; with its probable consequences briefly examined and considered*, London 1839, 10.
[37] G. C. Holland, *Suggestions towards improving on the present system of the corn-laws; inscribed by permission, to the right hon. Sir Robert Peel, Bart.*, London 1841, 22.
[38] D. Salomons, *The corn laws: their effects on the trade of the country considered, with suggestions for a compromise*, London 1841, 10–11; C. Nevile, *The sliding scale, or a fixed duty*, London 1842, 32–3.
[39] R. Cobden, House of Commons (24 May 1842), Hansard 3rd ser. lxiii. 718.
[40] Croker, 'Policy of Sir Robert Peel', 528. See also De Quincey, 'Sir Robert Peel's policy', 542, and the Revd C. Nevile, *The new tariff*, London 1842, 7.
[41] Idem, *Corn and currency, in a letter to A. Alison, Esq.*, London 1846, 3–29.
[42] S. Warren, 'Position and prospects of the government', BEM lv (Jan. 1844), 103–32 at p. 108.
[43] Idem, 'Great Britain at the commencement of the year 1843', ibid. liii (Jan. 1843), 1–23 at p. 5 (Warren's emphasis).

ests'.[44] Thus many Conservatives contemplated free trade late in 1845 as the relinquishment of a political strategy.[45] In this reading corn-law repeal was more than a surrender to the un-constitutional methods of the Anti-Corn-Law League: It also marked the moment when an essentially Conservative fiscal polity was transformed.[46] By retreating from the task of balancing interests Peel was understood to have exposed the interests which comprised the state to the tyranny of numbers.[47]

The identification of protection as a distinct Conservative cause after 1841 was not determined simply by the demands of the party's rural constituency. True, Conservative responses to parliamentary reform had re-emphasised the particular functions of land in the propertied constitution. But the constitutional relevance of protection was not restricted to preserving landed wealth. During the 1830s protectionist commentaries urged the Conservative party to embrace urban creditor, commercial and manufacturing interests. Beyond electoral benefits this was a strategy of constitutional preservation designed to establish the Conservative party as a broad bulwark against democracy. For, albeit prematurely, Conservatives identified a rolling consequence of 1832 as the transformation of fiscal politics: the neutering of the state through retrenchments demanded by a middle-class electorate, and the subversion of the representation of a range of interests in the tariff by freer trade. Thus 'sound finances' and protection were partly constitutional categories for Conservatives. Protection allowed a Conservative executive periodically to re-balance the representation of interests in the tariff and to tie propertied interests to the state. As one journalist predicted, Peel's abandonment of protection in 1846, 'would simplify or remove many of the intricacies of government'.[48]

The 'public economics' of protection

The politics of protection was reinforced by a protectionist economics which was not exclusively identified with the land. Protectionists challenged the basic free-trade point that the corn law epitomised 'class legislation' by elaborating a public political economy of protection. Established protectionist arguments were revitalised in response to the Whig commitment to a low fixed duty after 1839, to the campaigns and arguments of the Anti-Corn-Law League and, ultimately, to repeal. Theoretical critiques of free trade were

---

44 Croker, 'Whig tactics', 524.
45 Idem, 'Ministerial resignations', 319–21.
46 B. Disraeli, House of Commons (4 May 1846), *Hansard* 3rd ser. lxxxvi. 86.
47 J. W. Croker, 'Close of Sir Robert Peel's administration', *QR* lxxviii (Sept. 1846), 535–80 at pp. 549–52, 554–5, 569. Croker went on to present repeal as possible destruction of the constitutional functions of 'real' property in 'Agriculture in France – division of property', ibid. lxxix (Dec. 1846), 202–38 at pp. 237–8.
48 Anon., 'The late and present ministry', *BEM* lx (Aug. 1846), 249–60 at p. 253.

refocused on Ricardo's disciples J. R. McCulloch and Perronett Thompson, on the reformism of Poulett Thomson and James Deacon Hume at the Board of Trade, and on Richard Cobden's qualitatively new ideology of free trade. A new empiricism was injected into presentations of protection as a viable food policy and as a strategy for stable economic change: the protectionist response to the panacean pretensions of free-trade economics was thorough and engaged.

In print and in parliament, protection continued to be justified as the responsible food policy of an active executive. By defining the preservation of a stable core of domestic supply as a 'duty of government' protectionists sought to rid agriculture of the odium of unjustifiable monopoly. Free trade was cast as an irresponsible reliance on importation which would not only ruin producers, but would damage the interests of consumers. Thus protectionists rejected the sanguine assumption that British agriculture had nothing to fear from a low fixed duty or from corn-law repeal. They re-emphasised the insecurity of foreign food supplies which were subject to common European harvest conditions and doubted the feasibility of extensive supply from the USA.[49] Various authors engaged with J. R. McCulloch's predictions of the average price of grain imported under his proposed low fixed duty.[50] In parliament Sir John Walsh indicted Ricardian political economy as a ruinous recipe for the 'decultivation' of Britain.[51] Idiosyncratically, Thomas De Quincey followed the logic of Ricardo's theory of diminishing returns through to absurd lengths: foreign cultivation would ultimately reach a stationary state unless foreign economic diversification intervened in turn increasing demand for limited food supplies.[52] In a technical sense protectionists defended the advantages of the sliding scales of 1828 and 1842 in ensuring stability of price and supply, and in striking a balance between the

---

[49] Sir J. Graham, House of Commons (6 Mar. 1834), *Hansard* 3rd ser. xxi. 1225–6; Falmouth, House of Lords (11 June 1840), ibid. liv. 1020; A. Alison, 'Free trade and protection: the corn laws', BEM lv (Mar. 1844), 385–400 at p. 385; Barton, *In defence of the corn laws*, 46–50; Southey, 'On the corn laws', 259–60.

[50] J. R. McCulloch, *Statements illustrative of the policy and probable consequences of the proposed repeal of the corn laws, and the imposition in their stead of a moderate and fixed duty on foreign corn when entered for consumption*, London 1841, 7–16; Sir J. C. Dalbiac, *A few words on the corn laws, wherein are brought under consideration certain of the statements which are to be found in the third edition of Mr. McCulloch's pamphlet on the same subject*, London 1841, 4–7; G. Taylor, *An enquiry into the principles which ought to regulate the imposition of duties on foreign corn, in answer to 'Statements illustrative of the policy and probable consequences of the proposed repeal of the existing corn laws', by J. R. McCulloch, Esq.*, London 1842, 27–9.

[51] Sir J. Walsh, House of Commons (9 Feb. 1846), *Hansard* 3rd ser. lxxxiii. 584–5; Southey, 'On the corn laws', 265–6; A. Alison, 'The corn laws', BEM xliv (Nov. 1838), 650–64 at pp. 651–2.

[52] T. De Quincey, 'Dilemmas on the corn law question', ibid. xlv (Feb. 1839), 170–6 at pp. 173–6; 'Sir Robert Peel's position on next resuming power', 400; (with S. Warren), 'Anti-Corn Law deputation to Sir Robert Peel', ibid. lii (Aug. 1842), 271–82 at p. 280.

interests of producers and consumers.[53] The general protectionist contention was that the alternative of a low fixed duty would exacerbate the extremes of prices and would be unenforceable during scarcity.[54] Thus protectionists generally embraced the sliding scale of 1842 as a refinement of food policy while free traders vilified it.[55] Hence protectionists condemned the use of the Irish famine as a pretext for annihilating what they saw as the successful food policy of 1842; not only was Ireland a net exporter of grain, but in December 1845 domestic corn prices were falling with corn to spare in the warehouses.[56] The problem of food supply evoked positive approaches to agricultural improvement and productivity which also served to identify agricultural protection with public interests. This responded to the persistence of Ricardian assumptions in economic discourse particularly in the prints of the Anti-Corn-Law League.[57] As Thomas de Quincey put it 'Worse quantities of soil are continually neutralised by improved skill or science in agriculture.'[58]

Thus, protectionists eulogised the community of agricultural improvers as a virtuous one.[59] The diffusion of the research of J. F. W. Johnston and Justus Liebig on agricultural chemistry in the protectionist periodicals gave techni-

---

[53] D. Robinson, 'The corn law and a fixed duty', ibid. xxvix (Apr. 1831), 645–51; Southey, 'On the corn laws', 230; A. Mallalieu, 'The corn law question', *BEM* xxxv (May 1834), 792–801 at p. 793.

[54] G. C. Holland, *An analysis of the address of F. H. Fawkes, Esq., to the landowners of England*, 2nd edn, London 1841, 26. Peel invoked the authority of Thomas Tooke and Joseph Lowe against a low fixed duty: *The speech of the right honourable Sir Robert Peel, Bart. in the House of Commons, on Mr Villiers' motion on the corn laws*, 2nd edn, London 1839, 41–3. See also Lowe, *The present state of England*, 134. The latter was also a source for E. S. Cayley (12 Mar. 1839), *Hansard* 3rd ser. xlvi. 396–7.

[55] Croker, 'Policy of Sir Robert Peel', 525–8; G. Croly and J. F. W. Johnston, 'Things of the day II', *BEM* li (Mar. 1842), 398–416 at pp. 414–15; R. Cobden, House of Commons (24 May 1842), *Hansard*. 3rd ser. lxiii. 718.

[56] Croker, 'Ministerial resignations', 299, 309–12. This article in part reviewed E. S. Cayley, *Letters to the right honourable Lord John Russell, MP., on the corn laws*, London 1846. For free traders' use of the Irish pretext in debate see Morley, *The life of Richard Cobden*, i. 362.

[57] G. P. Scrope, 'Jones on the doctrine of rents', *QR* xlvi (Nov. 1831), 81–117 at pp. 81–97. Revd R. Jones, *An essay on the distribution of wealth and on the sources of taxation*, London 1831, i. 1–14, 185–329; [Maydwell], *Maydwell's analysis of Cobden's addresses, with remarks on Mr Greg's speech at the great League meeting at Manchester*, London 1843, 36; Revd A. Crombie, *A letter to Lieut. Col. Torrens M. P. in answer to his address to the farmers of the United Kingdom*, London 1832, 5–10; R. Torrens, *Address to the farmers of the United Kingdom, on low rates of profit in agriculture and in trade*, London 1831. Of course George Poulett Scrope was a Whig MP not a Conservative. He found his intellectual home, however, in the Conservative *Quarterly* and explicitly distanced himself from Whig policy on banking and the poor law: see, for example, G. P. Scrope, House of Commons (2 Aug. 1833), *Hansard* 3rd ser. xx. 295. Some Conservative journalists appealed to Scrope as an authoritative critic of the Whigs: see p. 122 n. 18.

[58] De Quincey, 'Ricardo made easy; or, what is the radical difference between Ricardo and Adam Smith?: part II: with an occasional notice of Ricardo's oversights', 466.

[59] G. Webb Hall, *The connexion between landlord and tenant, and tenant and labourer, in the*

cal teeth to the argument that soil fertility was neither fixed nor necessarily diminishing.[60] The improvement of domestic agriculture was widely canvassed as an alternative to free trade, not its corollary.[61] If scientific agriculture could be presented as an explicit riposte to the application of Ricardian political economy to the corn laws it also represented a patriotic commitment to autarchy impelled by the need to feed a growing manufacturing population.[62] In parliament the marquess of Granby invoked the demographic thought of Archibald Alison as an argument for a national food policy of self-sufficiency.[63] As Croker observed in 1843, 'The first duty of a nation – like that of a family – that looks to strength, honour, or even existence, is to take care that it shall be able to *feed itself*.'[64]

Beyond food policy protectionists disputed the panacean economic benefits claimed for free trade in corn. Although the free-trade case diversified during the 1830s Ricardo's argument that repeal would liberate the rate of profit in manufacturing industry, persisted.[65] As in the 1820s, critiques of Ricardianism hinged largely on the relationship between corn prices and wages, and between wages and profits.[66] Thus, Alfred Mallalieu went to the heart of the Ricardian critique of the corn laws: as corn prices made up only a small proportion of wages manufacturers would require a reduction in corn prices of over 60 per cent to meet their competitiveness aims through a

---

cultivation of the British soil; their rights, their duties, and their interests, London 1841, 24; Lord George Bentinck, House of Commons (27 Feb. 1846), Hansard 3rd ser. lxxxv. 339–42.

60 J. F. W. Johnston's, *What can be done for British agriculture?*, London 1842, was 'reviewed' in Croly and Johnston, 'Things of the day II'; J. F. W. Johnston, 'Science and agriculture', BEM li (June 1842), 738–55; 'The practice of agriculture', ibid. liii (Apr. 1843), 415–32; 'Practical agriculture – Stephen's book of the farm', ibid. lvii (May 1845), 298–314; W. Gregory, 'Liebig on agricultural chemistry', QR lxix (Mar. 1842), 329–45, and 'Liebig's Animal chemistry', ibid. lxx (June 1842), 98–128. These articles reviewed Gregory's translation of Liebig's, *Organic chemistry, in its applications to agriculture and physiology*, London 1842.

61 *Report of the proceedings at a meeting of the landowners, farmers, and others resident in the county of York, interested in the welfare of British agriculture, for the establishment of the Yorkshire protective society*, London 1844, 17–18, 33.

62 W. Buckland, 'Agriculture', QR lxxiii (Mar. 1844), 477–509 at pp. 478–81. Among other texts Buckland reviewed the *Journal of the Royal English Agricultural Society*, London 1839–43.

63 Marquess of Granby, House of Commons (11 May 1846), Hansard 3rd ser. lxxxvi. 331; A. Alison, *The principles of population and their connection with human happiness*, London 1840. See also Southey, 'On the corn laws', 256, and W. E. Aytoun, 'The Scottish harvest', BEM lviii (Dec. 1845), 769–84 at p. 780.

64 J. W. Croker, 'Policy of ministers', QR lxii (Sept. 1843), 553–93 at p. 560.

65 For example T. S. Smith, *On the economy of nations*, London 1842.

66 G. P. Scrope, 'The political economists', QR xliv (Jan. 1831), 1–52 esp. pp. 27–32. Scrope targeted J. R. McCulloch's, *Principles of political economy with a sketch of the rise and progress of the science*, 2nd edn, London 1830, ch. iv, and bemoaned the influence of Ricardian theory on the *First report of the committee on artisans and machinery* (1824). On Scrope see above p. 66 n. 57.

reduction of the wages bill.[67] Beside the established protectionist position that wages were determined principally by labour market conditions, refutations of the long-term price effect of corn law repeal were suggestive.[68] Protectionists argued that the project of liberating profit rates by reducing wages would in the long term be counter-productive; by diminishing consumption, and effectively reducing the share of wages while increasing that of capital, repeal would compound problems of production beyond the means of consumption and would reduce competitiveness and profits.[69]

A defining feature of Richard Cobden's economics was the conviction that the corn laws contracted foreign markets for British manufactures via a range of non-Ricardian mechanisms: the encouragement of foreign manufactures and tariff barriers by the corn law, the uncertainty of a reciprocal commerce reliant on irregular demand for foreign corn, and the monetary fluctuations institutionalised by irregular trade.[70] At one level, protectionists countered with empirical denials that manufacturing exports would increase with corn importations. Mallalieu used official returns to show that as imports from foreign corn-producing nations had advanced so manufacturing exports to those countries had declined between 1814 and 1830.[71] In parliament Cayley offered detailed empirical evidence to sustain his view that far from increasing foreign consumption of British manufactures, free trade in corn would reduce Britain 'to the condition of a pyramid inverted on its apex – vibrating, reeling, tottering to our fall'.[72] Similarly, Alison employed a distinctive history of trade during the 1830s to demonstrate that corn importations correlated with periods of manufacturing decline.[73] Like Cayley, Croker urged against tying manufacturing exports to a corn trade whose fluctuations

---

[67] Mallalieu, 'The corn law question', 798.

[68] Anon., *How much would the four-pound loaf be lowered by the repeal of the corn laws?*, London 1844, 4–6.

[69] Anon., *Public economy concentrated; or a connected view of currency, agriculture, and manufactures*, Carlisle 1833, 26–36; A. H. Moreton, *Thoughts on the corn laws, addressed to the working classes of the county of Gloucester*, London 1839, 8, 22; Anon., *Cheap corn, but no bread: or the results of free corn trade*, London 1835, 18–23; J. H. Renny, *Reflections upon the corn laws and upon the their effects on the trade, manufactures, and agriculture of the country, and on the condition of the working classes*, London 1841, 73–6.

[70] See Peel's summary of Cobden's case against the corn laws: *Speech of the right honourable Sir Robert Peel*, London 1839, 32–3. For Cobden's confidence that repeal would instantly liberate trade between Britain and the United States see Morley, *The life of Richard Cobden*, i. 200–1, and for a brief summary of Cobden's theory of trade see ibid. 346–7; ii. 334–5.

[71] Mallalieu argued that exports to Prussia had declined by one-seventh while imports had tripled between 1814 and 1830. The relativities of British trade with Russia and the USA had altered in similar proportion: Mallalieu, 'The corn law question', 795–6.

[72] Cayley invoked the arguments of the *BEM* author James McQueen, House of Commons (12 Mar. 1839), *Hansard* 3rd ser. xlvi. 418, 415–16.

[73] Alison, 'The corn laws', 655–6; 'The anti-national faction', *BEM* xlvii (Apr. 1840), 544–52 at pp. 547–50; 'Free trade and protection', ibid. lv (Feb. 1844), 259–68 at pp. 261–2.

were determined by harvest conditions not by the corn law.[74] Thus protectionists viewed the prospect of relying on poor foreign agrarian economies for permanent markets for British manufactured goods as economic suicide.[75]

By arguing that the corn law did not inhibit manufactured exports protectionists attempted to demonstrate that the trade barriers of foreign nations were not retaliatory responses to British protectionism. Cobden's critics instead constructed the protective policies of European nations as patriotic and responsible.[76] Just as Britain had fostered all her producing interests under a protective umbrella, so European nations had pursued constructive policies of protection after the Treaty of Vienna. Similarly, British protectionists amplified the legitimacy of national protection in the New World. The ideas of the American presidential candidate Henry Clay were widely lauded by British protectionists as evidence of the essential patriotism of shielding domestic producers.[77] Thus, protectionists challenged Cobden's assumption that free trade was the natural condition of nations with an alternative notion of international relations where the distinct and differing interests of nations was axiomatic. Protectionists insisted that there existed no natural or automatic reciprocity between nations. The establishment of genuine reciprocity required the traditional mechanism of commercial negotiations not unilateral alterations to the British tariff.[78] Thus, in parliament protectionists claimed the legacy of William Huskisson for this traditional commercial policy not free trade.[79] Similarly, many protectionists viewed Peel's commercial treaties as more significant components of commercial policy than his unilateral alterations to the tariff: sound commercial policy consisted in engineering mutual bargains through the agency of the foreign

---

74 Anon., *A counterplea for the poor, shewing that the cause of their distress is not attributable to the corn laws by the poor man's friend: in a reply to a pamphlet by the Hon. and Rev. Baptist Noel*, 3rd edn, London 1841, 16–17; Dalbiac, *A few words on the corn laws*, 20–1; Croker, 'The budget and the dissolution', 270–2.
75 Anon., *A few words on the repeal of the corn laws*, London 1846, 22–5; P. Miles, House of Commons (9 Feb. 1846), *Hansard* 3rd ser. lxxxiii. 554.
76 Alison, 'The anti-national faction', 550–1; D. Bain, *The egregious and dangerous fallacies of the Anti-Corn-Law League; or, the protection of agriculture not a question with landlords but for the whole kingdom*, Edinburgh 1843, 21–2; G. G. Day, *The farmers and the League; the speech of Mr George Game Day, of St Ives, at Huntingdon, January 27, 1844, on the occasion of forming an Anti-League Association for the county of Huntingdon*, 5th edn, London 1844, 12–13.
77 Sir H. Douglas, House of Commons (6 June 1842), *Hansard* 3rd ser. lxiii. 1287–8; Vyvyan, *A letter from Sir R. Vyvyan to his constituents*, 50–2n.; A. Williams, *The law or the league: which?: a letter to Robert Palmer, Esq., MP*, London 1843, 18–21.
78 Cobden was no 'reciprocist' in the 1840s: Morley, *Life of Cobden*, ii. 326, 329–31, 336n.; Cobden's pacifism was based on harnessing the self-interest of nations in a multilateral free trade system: ibid. i. 112–19.
79 Sir J. Graham, House of Commons (6 Mar. 1834), *Hansard* xxi. 1229–31; J. C. Herries, House of Commons (5 Apr. 1841), ibid. lvii. 905.

office.[80] Whereas Cobden emphasised the moralising and pacifying influence of free trade, protectionists contended that the bargaining power preserved by a protective tariff could be used as leverage in international relations thereby preventing hostilities.[81]

Not only did protectionists strike at the root of Cobden's idea of trade, they also offered an alternative vision of the practical, multilateral consequences of corn law repeal. To the extent that foreign trade could be reduced to a straightforward barter of goods for grain, protectionists stressed the inherent instability of making the foreign export trade reliant on the state of the harvest.[82] More commonly, protectionists maintained that grain-producing nations would prefer gold to manufactures as an equivalent; if repeal could not guarantee foreign markets for British manufactures, neither could it stabilise international bullion flows. Given Britain's gold standard this could only exacerbate monetary crises.[83] Since the value of the British currency was fixed, the capacity of repeal to dispel the great incubus on foreign purchasing power – the prohibitively high relative value of the pound – was perceived to be limited.[84] In multilateral terms, protectionists insisted that repeal would force Britain to purchase grain with gold and to re-purchase gold from a third nation with manufactures. Since the third nation's demand for British manufactures would be finite and could not correspond identically with the bullion value of grain imports it was considered that repeal would inevitably destabilise manufacturing industry, commerce and the monetary system.[85]

Fundamentally, protectionists rooted stable and secure manufacturing advance in home and colonial markets. Arguments first articulated in the 1820s were reworked in response to the perceived threat to the home market posed by the repeal campaign. Variously, protectionists exposed the folly of sacrificing certain domestic markets for uncertain foreign ones.[86] As G. C. Holland put it, 'The broad basis of home consumption, on which the inter-

---

[80] A. Mallalieu, 'Commercial policy: Spain', *BEM* liii (May 1843), 673–92, esp. pp. 673–6; R. Peel, House of Commons (25 Apr. 1843), *Hansard* 3rd ser. lxviii. 960–3; A. Mallalieu, 'Commercial policy: Russia', *BEM* liii (June 1843), 807–26; S. Warren, 'Position and prospects of the government', ibid. lv (Jan. 1844), 103–32 at p. 118; B. Disraeli, House of Commons (1 Apr. 1840), *Hansard* 3rd ser. liii. 385.

[81] Mallalieu linked trade policy inextricably to the resolution of the Eastern Question: 'Foreign policy and foreign commerce', *BEM* xxxix (Feb. 1836), 145–5. In national security terms Mallalieu compared relinquishing protection to surrendering the Royal Navy: 'Commercial policy: Europe', ibid. liv (Aug. 1843), 243–55 at p. 254.

[82] Taylor, *An enquiry into the principles*, 13–15, and G. Taylor (possibly the same person), 'Census of 1841', *QR* lxxvi (June 1845), 11–38 at pp. 17–18.

[83] Sir H. Douglas, House of Commons (13 Feb. 1846), *Hansard* 3rd ser. lxxxiii. 843.

[84] Renny, *Reflections upon the corn laws*, 64, 66–7, 93, 96–8, 106.

[85] E. S. Cayley, *Letters to the Right Honourable Lord John Russell, M.P., on the corn laws*, London 1846, 23–4; Anon. ['Cincinnatus'], *Remarks on the Anti-Corn-Law mania, in a letter to his grace the duke of Buckingham*, London 1846, 6.

[86] Anon. ['Veritas'], *A plea from the poor, versus many canting pleas for the poor; showing the*

ests of all classes can alone permanently repose, is overlooked in the eagerness to grasp a remote good.'[87] Protectionist defences of the home market were armed with empirical demonstrations of the relative size and macroeconomic status of agriculture. Using statistics derived from Antonio Pablo Preber, Archibald Alison observed 'how much superior the agricultural interest of the state still is to the manufacturing notwithstanding the enormous increase of manufactures of all sorts in late years'.[88] Alison presented a highly favourable estimate of agriculture's relative importance in national capital and employment dependencies, but, using 1835 as a typical year, he also contended that considerably more than two-thirds of manufactures were produced for a domestic market centring on agriculture. In parliament and in print protectionists invoked J. Marshall's warning that 'mistaken notions almost universally prevail, in regard to the greater or lesser extent and importance of each great branch of Population and occupation'.[89] Marshall's evidence was appropriated as a challenge to a free-trade language of statistics which inflated the importance of modernised manufacturing and underestimated artisanal manufactures and agriculture.

The character of protectionist empiricism was dictated by the Anti-Corn-Law League's demand for an economic policy which favoured manufactured exports.[90] This alternative protectionist language of statistics relied heavily on attempts to demonstrate the superior value of domestic and colonial over foreign markets. Mallalieu concluded that foreign trade in 1834 was 'equal to one-seventh only of the Home consumption'.[91] Similarly, in 1840–1, Alison employed Porter's figures on shipping to demonstrate the absolute and rela-

---

ignorant and absurd notions of anti-protection and free-trade mania being advantageous to the commercial polity of the British nation; but, on the contrary, particularly injurious to the working classes; in reply to pamphlets written by J. R. McCulloch, Esq., W. W. Whitmore, Esq., and Rev. B. Noel, M. A., London 1841, 8–9; J. Almack, *Character, motives and proceedings of the Anti-Corn law leaguers, with a few general remarks on the consequences that would result from a free trade in corn; dedicated to W. R. Greg*, London 1843, 74–6; Anon., *An address on the corn laws: by a protectionist*, London 1846, 11.

87 Holland, *Suggestions towards improving on the present system*, 31.

88 Alison, 'The corn laws', 658; A. L. R. P. de V. M. Preber, *Taxation, revenue, expenditure, power, statistics, and debt of the whole British empire; their origin, progress, and present state; with an estimate of the capital resources of the empire, and a practical plan for applying them to the liquidation of the national debt*, London 1833, iii, pt ii, 300–2, 350–1.

89 E. S. Cayley, House of Commons (12 Mar. 1839), *Hansard* 3rd ser. xlvi. 378; W. Maginn, 'On national economy (no. VIII): on the corn laws – Colonel Thompson's and Mr Booth's pamphlets', FM viii (Aug. 1833), 222–31 at p. 227; J. Marshall, *A digest of all the accounts relating to the population, productions, revenues, financial operations, manufactures, shipping, colonies, commerce, &c. &c, of the United Kingdom of Great Britain and Ireland*, London 1834, i. 9–90, and tables 10–11.

90 Alison, 'The corn laws', 660.

91 Mallalieu, 'The corn law question', 801. Mallalieu extended this argument into the 1840s: 'Commercial policy – ships, colonies and commerce: no. I', BEM liv (Sept. 1843), 406–14, and 'Commercial policy – ships, colonies and commerce: no. II', ibid. (Nov. 1843), 637–49.

tive decline of commerce with European nations and the concentration of British commercial expansion in colonial trade.[92] Alison's purpose, of course, was to hijack the empiricism of 'the great free-trade apostle' for protectionism.[93] Having established that 'the total amount of . . . manufactures exported . . . is somewhat less than one-third of the total, produced', Alison concluded that domestic agriculture constituted the primary market for British manufactures.[94] Likewise James McQueen's computation of the comparative superiority of domestic and colonial over foreign markets was employed by E. S. Cayley as an argument for the formation of a Protectionist League.[95] Free-trade empiricism was widely challenged by a protectionist language of statistics.

Protectionist statistics were designed to substantiate the central point that corn-law repeal would undermine the durability of manufacturing advance by undermining the home market. As Sir James Graham observed in 1834, 'the ultimate effect would be the total destruction of the manufacturing interest of the country by destroying the home market. He did not undervalue the foreign market . . . but the zeal to extend it should not lead to the destruction of the home market, which would be fatal to the prosperity of all'.[96] This was no mere debating ploy. For, as advocates of agricultural protection stressed repeatedly, stable economic development could be achieved only through maintaining balanced expansion in all sectors.[97] By facilitating the mutual consumption of domestic agriculture, manufactures and commerce, protection was considered to balance powers of production with consumption in the home market. This notion of 'sustainability' was of course adumbrated within specific economic and ideological contexts: the manufacturing depressions of 1836, 1839 and 1842, and the Anti-Corn-Law League's advocacy of specialisation in manufacturing.

From various perspectives, protectionists explained periodic manufacturing slumps in terms of the nature of manufacturing capitalism. Some pointed to a historical trajectory 'pregnant with instances of decay'.[98] As John Barton had in 1833, so Disraeli located the decline of the Sussex iron industry in a general sketch of European manufacturing history which rejected the tele-

---

[92] Alison, 'The anti-national faction', 545, and 'The Whig dissolution', esp. pp. 14–15; G. R. Porter, *The progress of the nation in its various social and economical relations from the beginning of the nineteenth century*, London 1836–43, sections iii and iv; *Interchange, and revenue, and expenditure*, London 1838, 92–178, esp. pp. 98, 102, 104–5.
[93] Alison, 'The Whig dissolution', 15.
[94] Ibid. 27–8.
[95] E. S. Cayley, *Reasons for the formation of the Agricultural Protection Society, addressed to the industrious classes of the United Kingdom; published by the Society*, London 1844, 15. See also J. McQueen, *Statistics of agriculture, manufactures and commerce, drawn up from official and authentic documents*, Edinburgh–London 1850, 17–23.
[96] Sir J. Graham, House of Commons (6 Mar. 1834), *Hansard* xxi. 1235.
[97] Buckland, 'Agriculture', 144, and W. E. Aytoun, 'Ministerial measures', BEM lix (Mar. 1846), 373–84 at p. 379.
[98] Anon., *Public economy concentrated*, 27.

ology of progress assumed by the Anti-Corn-Law League.[99] Combining such historicism with theoretical analysis, G. P. Scrope identified an inherent propensity of British mechanised manufactures to produce beyond the means of consumption. For Scrope, therefore, the relative advance of British manufactures had established powers of production superior to those of any other nation, and impelled a trade policy which would balance production with consumption.[100] Thus Adam Smith's argument that falling rates of profit were primarily due to competition between capitals was frequently reiterated in the protectionist cause during the 1830s and 1840s.[101] Even the free trader Robert Torrens admitted that the principal problem of British manufactures was not the corn law but the effect of foreign competition combined with the expansion of British productive power beyond available markets.[102]

Defending the corn laws against free-trade imputations of responsibility for manufacturing depression evoked specific analyses of the fluctuations of the 1830s and 1840s. One strain of protectionist argument rejected pathological views of manufacturing decline. Commenting on the depression of 1836, Mallalieu noted that the competitiveness problems of manufacturing were not general but were concentrated in low value cottons.[103] Similarly, in 1839, Peel rebutted the notion that British manufactures were suffering a general decline in competitiveness.[104] Thus protectionists read the manufacturing depression of 1842 mainly as a consequence of production beyond the means of consumption. Thomas de Quincey's account of Britain in 1842 employed a critique of Ricardo's explanation of the decline of seventeenth-century Holland. Ricardo had likened the impact of corn importation on Dutch commercial profits to the effect of the nineteenth-century British corn

---

99 Barton, *In defence of the corn laws*, 38–9, reiterated in Southey, 'On the corn laws', 268; *The speech of Mr Disraeli, in the House of Commons, on Friday, 15th May, 1846*, London 1846, 24–5, 29–30; B. Disraeli, House of Commons (15 May 1846), *Hansard* 3rd ser. lxxxvi. 553–68.
100 In his 'The political economists', 22–4, Scrope aimed to refute the Ricardianism of James Mill's, *Elements of political economy*, London 1821. Scrope was a Whig who believed in the 'rational encouragement' of efficient cultivation and chose to publish in the protectionist and Conservative *Quarterly Review*: see above p. 66 n. 57.
101 Ibid. 20–1. Southey cited Kirkman Finlay's evidence to this effect in the *Report of the select committee on manufactures, commerce, and shipping*, in 'On the corn laws', 269–70. See also Anon., *A counterplea for the poor*, 15. On Smith see below pp. 153–4.
102 R. Torrens, *A letter to the right honourable Sir Robert Peel, Bart. MP, on the condition of England and on the means of removing the causes of distress*, London 1843, 17–22.
103 A. Mallalieu, 'The cotton manufacture', BEM xxxix (Mar. 1836), 407–24 at p. 424. On 'early socialist' connections between the character of production and economic stability in the 1830s see Thompson, *The people's science*, 165–8.
104 *Speech of the right honourable Sir Robert Peel*, 7–11; S. Jackson, *Commercial distress temporary; arising from natural and periodical causes, and not from the effects of the corn laws; letter I: addressed to the right hon. Earl Fitzwilliam*, London 1839, 13–4. See also Anon. ['Britannicus'], *Corn laws defended; or, agriculture our first interest, and the mainstay of trade and commerce*, 24–5; Anon. ['Cincinnatus'], *Remarks on the Anti-Corn-Law mania*, 7, 9.

law on manufacturing profits missing the fundamental point, 'that the consumption of a nation must be maintained in some sufficient ratio to its scale of production; precisely because it was not in Holland of the seventeenth century, did rapid accumulation proceed too rapidly'.[105] Maintaining a prosperous agricultural sector was therefore offered as a guarantee against commercial and manufacturing decline.[106] Simultaneously, protectionists interpreted Peel's comments on the 1842 depression within the concept of balancing production with consumption. By emphasising the locality and specificity of depression, Peel was seen to explain it as a product of production beyond the means of consumption in localities still adapting to the productive powers of mechanisation.[107]

Yet by refocusing the causes of depression on manufacturing protectionists did not reject the reality of industrialism nor the economic importance of the manufacturing sector. For protection was seldom offered purely as an agrarian device. Indeed, a thriving and diverse manufacturing sector was identified as a vital component of a balanced economy. Thus Cayley invoked David Hume's emphasis on the relative security to be gained by encouraging a range of manufactures as against specialisation.[108] And Alfred Mallalieu's rhetoric regaled free-trade theorists for neglecting the benefits of protecting infant industries: 'Were general restrictive imposts on foreign manufactures no protection? was the virtually prohibited importation of the cotton fabrics of India no boon? of India root and branch sacrificed for the advancement of Manchester?'[109] Beyond the infant industry argument, protectionists condoned fiscal encouragements of domestic manufacturing industry. Samuel Warren, for example, interpreted Peel's reduction of duties on raw materials in 1842 as 'a safe, effective, and permanent stimulus to trade and commerce'.[110] Ultimately, the free-trade settlement of 1846 was presented as the destruction of mutual domestic markets. As Aytoun observed,

Where the different industrial classes of a nation purchase from each other,

---

[105] De Quincey, 'Ricardo made easy; or, what is the radical difference between Ricardo and Adam Smith?: part II', 465–6; D. Ricardo, *On the principles of political economy and taxation*, London 1817, repr. in *Works of David Ricardo*, i. 290n.

[106] See Bain on depression in Paisley, *The egregious and dangerous fallacies of the Anti-Corn-Law League*, 16–17.

[107] De Quincey and Warren, 'Anti-Corn-Law deputation to Sir Robert Peel', 275–80; Sir R. Peel, House of Commons (9 Feb. 1842), *Hansard* 3rd ser. lx. 207.

[108] Cayley, *Reasons for the formation of the Agricultural Protection Society*, 18. Cayley possibly invoked D. Hume, 'Of commerce', 1st publ. 1752 repr. in *Hume*, 93–104.

[109] Mallalieu, 'Commercial policy: Russia', 809. See also his 'The cotton manufacture', 417.

[110] Warren, 'Position and prospects of the government', 111. Croker perceived Peel's reduction of duties on foreign ores as effective protection for the consumer and for domestic metal manufacturers: 'Policy of Sir Robert Peel', 516–17. Croker also noted that the tariff of late 1845 still offered protection (albeit inoperative) to British manufactures: 'Ministerial resignations', 312.

there is a mutual benefit – when either deserts the home market and has recourse to a foreign one, the benefit is totally neutralized. There is no greater fallacy than the proposition, that it is best to buy in the cheapest and sell in the dearest market.[111]

To protectionists the free-trade panacea of cheapness stood to undermine stable, secure and balanced economic development.

In their quest to present protection as a public policy not a sectional strategy, protectionists also challenged the financial promises of free trade.[112] From various perspectives, protectionists challenged the central free-trade proposition that by stripping away indirect taxes consumption would be liberated and the yield from revenue taxes raised. David Robinson rejected Sir Henry Parnell's view that freer trade would liberate consumption. Robinson believed that small gains to individual consumers would be offset by the contraction of government expenditure necessitated by reduced tax yields.[113] Others defended the economic effects of a tax burden concentrated on indirect forms. At least before the corn laws were repealed, Archibald Alison defended indirect taxation principally because, though voluntary, its wide incidence could sustain a responsible financial policy. Moreover, indirect taxes did not, in Alison's view, press on the origin of economic enterprise – accumulation by small proprietors.[114] Croker questioned the desirability and efficiency of Whig tariff reductions, observing that, 'Not only must the habit of *consumption* be extended, but the power of *producing* must also be enlarged – and both are the work of time.'[115] Protectionists agreed on the direct financial effects of repealing the corn laws: by diminishing the capacity of agricultural producers to pay taxes, repeal would neuter the financial power of the state. Thus the repeal campaign intensified protectionist arguments for the equalisation of the burdens of direct taxation between different forms of property.[116] Such 'equalisation' was justified as effective financial policy and as a political response to the transformation of the balance of taxation by

---

111 Aytoun, 'Ministerial measures', 381.
112 Sir Henry Parnell, *On financial reform*, 3rd edn, London 1830, esp. pp. 94–6; *Report of the select committee on import duties* (1840); 'This Report was the Charter of Free Trade': Morley, *Life of Richard Cobden*, i. 255.
113 D. Robinson, 'Sir H. Parnell on financial reform', BEM xxx (Sept. 1831), 457–74 at pp. 459, 461–3, 470–2. See also Croly on government expenditure: 'Edmund Burke: part III', 29.
114 Alison, 'On the financial policy of Mr Pitt and his successors', 182–4, 190–2. See also his 'The British finances', 598–621, and Vyvyan, *A letter from Sir Richard Vyvyan*, 26.
115 Croker, 'The budget and the dissolution', 248. See Stewart, *The politics of protection*, 41, for critiques of Peel's claims for the financial efficiency of tariff reduction by W. E. Gladstone (1845) and Bentinck (1847).
116 Anon., *Letter to the duke of Buckingham, on the corn laws*, 12–14; J. Bell, *A vindication of the rights of British landowners, farmers and labourers against the claims of the cotton capitalists to a free trade in corn*, London 1839, 29; Croker, 'The budget and the dissolution', 260.

corn-law repeal.[117] Many protectionists applied this Conservative fiscal politics to analyses of the political and financial implications of a deflationary repeal of the corn laws. As John Bell put it, 'to lower the value of labour, however, is virtually to increase the value of money. If wages, through the influence of a free trade in corn, should fall one-third, the national debt would be in effect, increased to the extent of one third'.[118] Corn-law repeal was therefore condemned as a redistributive instrument which was politically unacceptable: 'This cannot fail to increase the burden of the national debt and promote a far greater change in the pecuniary relations of every class of society than the return to cash payment at a former period.'[119] Thus protection appealed to constitutional Conservatives who resisted the intrusion of the state into the realm of relative property values.

Thus defenders of the corn laws constructed a public economics of protection. This challenged the Anti-Corn-Law League's explicit identification of public interests with those of manufacturing exporters.[120] If at one level agricultural protection was presented as a legitimate function of the executive in food policy, at another it was cast as the means of influencing stable, durable and balanced economic change through legislation. As Charles Newdegate put it, 'By Protection, he understood a principle ... not implying prohibition, but the regulation of trade. He considered the maintenance of protection as much a part of the function and duty of Government as protection of the person.'[121] The sophistication of protectionist economic argument confirms that the debate provoked by the corn laws was no polarised battle between the 'dying forces of feudalism' and the 'lusty youth of industrialism'.[122] Lord George Bentinck's economic expositions in parliament during 1846 possessed a vital and engaged provenance in print.[123] This ensured that economic discourse during 1830–46 was not 'intellectually a suburb of Manchester'.[124]

---

[117] On direct taxes as a *quid pro quo* for protection see W. F. P. Napier, *Observations on the corn law, addressed to Lord Ashley*, 2nd edn, London 1841, 6; Almack, *Character, motives and proceedings*, 88; W. J. Lushington, *Six letters addressed to the agriculturists of the county of Kent, on the doctrines of the Anti-Corn-Law League, and the subject of free trade*, London 1843, 24–7.
[118] Bell, *A vindication of the rights of British landowners*, 23. See also Alison, 'The Whig dissolution', 30, and Anon. ['Britannicus'], *Corn-laws defended*, 26. A free trader also warned Peel that 'he would ultimately have to reduce the price of everything to the continental level': G. F. Muntz, House of Commons (20 Feb. 1846), *Hansard* 3rd ser. lxxxiii. 1312–18.
[119] Anon. ['F. C.'], *Present condition and future prospects of the country, in reference to free trade and its recent application*, London 1846, 34, and Anon., *Brief considerations with reference to the corn laws and on the theory of protection generally*, London 1846, 5.
[120] Morley, *Life of Richard Cobden*, i. 153.
[121] C. N. Newdegate, House of Commons (20 Feb. 1848), *Hansard* 3rd ser. lxxxiii. 1293.
[122] Harold Macmillan in his preface to Walker-Smith, *The protectionist case*, p. vii.
[123] A. Macintyre, 'Lord George Bentinck and the protectionists', 154.
[124] The phrase was coined by Walker-Smith: *The protectionist case*, 13.

The moral economy of protection

'religion, virtue, loyalty, patriotism, deeply-rooted associations, social affections, local attachments, are of infinitely greater value than mere commercial theories . . . Your cheapest market principle dreams of profit and profit alone. Your theory is to consider man as a machine by which you are to make a profit': E. S. Cayley, House of Commons (11 May 1846), *Hansard* lxxxvi. 412.

It is striking that protectionists have usually been left out of the historical roll-call of critics of 'laissez-faire' ideas in nineteenth-century Britain. Christian political economists, 'Romantic Conservatives', working-class radicals and proto-socialist thinkers have all taken their places as moralists who rejected or modified 'laissez-faire' attitudes. Although they offered a sustained rejection of free trade as a normative philosophy of society and government, protectionists have been neglected. To them the repeal of the corn laws was more than the alteration of the tariff because free trade was the symbol of a pernicious and divisive social philosophy. To protectionists free trade seemed to reduce political economy and the science of government to a theory of wealth creation. Its ascendancy was perceived as part product and part symptom of the political influence of manufacturing and creditor interests after the Reform Act of 1832. The diffusion of free-trade ideas was seen to threaten both social cohesion and the political legitimacy of the propertied constitution. The moral economy of protection appealed in particular to Conservatives as a restorative political language which responded to free-trade ideas and to contemporary economic experience. For protectionists debated the 'Condition of England Question' as a moral, social and political crisis of distribution. While free-trade economists seemed to compound the crisis of distribution, protectionists presented their ideas as responsive and restorative alternatives. By guarding the employment and living standards of labour, protection offered distinct distributive solutions to the 'Condition of England Question'. By assuming definite economic, social and political functions for commercial legislation protection offered to Conservatives a coherent response to the problems of governing the first industrial nation.

Protectionist critiques of free trade stretched beyond economic theory to question the fundamental purpose of political economy. Though a free trader G. P. Scrope maintained that political economists after Adam Smith had contracted the boundaries of their discipline to a science of mere wealth creation.[125] In Scrope's view this had limited debate on the purposes of public policy, blurring the distinction between 'the circumstances which promote the happiness of a community from those which merely add to its stock of marketable wealth'.[126] Likewise, John Barton identified the glaring weakness of Perronet Thompson's mathematical definition of national wealth as the

---

[125] Scrope, 'The political economists', esp. pp. 1–6.
[126] Ibid. 47.

absence of any necessary correlation between the growth of capital and 'national happiness'.[127] Barton recalled his own tussle with David Ricardo over the social impact of mechanisation as evidence of the fundamental disjunction between 'social happiness' and wealth creation in free-trade political economy.[128]

Revealingly, British protectionists identified J. C. Simonde de Sismondi as a more appropriate guide to the civil government of an industrial society.[129] Sir Francis Palgrave surveyed Sismondi's progression from mathematical definitions of wealth to the broad 'moral economy' of his mature oeuvres:

> The fundamental position of Sismondi' matured theory is, that the writers of the Smith School have not really treated upon political economy at all. . . . They have applied themselves entirely to *chrematistics* – a hard and Aristotelian, yet apposite term – i.e. *the science of the increase of riches*. Chrematistic writers, having considered wealth in the abstract, and not in relation to man and society, wholly pervert the direction which their studies ought to receive.[130]

Palgrave endorsed Sismondi's reading of the consequences of this flawed philosophy: the policy prescriptions of unlimited competition and non-intervention in trade and commerce.[131] In his response to Sismondi, Archibald Alison identified protection as the means of constructing a political economy beyond chrematistics.[132] In this view only legislative intervention could moderate 'the ruinous pursuit of wealth' by addressing the consequences of free trade: the social polarisation of wealth, production beyond the powers of consumption and the unbalanced development of economic sectors.[133] Indeed, Alison respected Sismondi as a co-thinker who insisted that the separation of political economy and civil government from the study of history would hasten the decline of European civilisation.[134] This

---

[127] Barton, *In defence of the corn laws*, esp. pp. 70–7.
[128] Ibid. 75–6. For Barton's criticism of Ricardo's assumption that capitalisation necessarily increased the demand for labour see *John Barton: economic writings*, pp. xi, xvi.
[129] Idem, *In defence of the corn laws*, 76–7, cited from J.-C.-L. Simonde de Sismondi, *Nouveaux principes d'economie politique, ou de la richesse dans ses rapports avec la population*, 2nd edn, Paris 1827, ii. 317–18. In 1822 Sismondi wrote favourable reviews of Barton's *Observations on the circumstances which influence the Condition of the labouring classes of society*, London 1817, and also his *An inquiry into the causes of the progressive depreciation of agricultural labour in modern times*, London 1820: *John Barton: economic writings*, i. p. xvii.
[130] F. Palgrave, 'Life and works of Sismondi', *QR* lxxii (Sept. 1843), 299–356 at p. 349. Palgrave was perhaps referring to Aristotle's distinction between natural exchange and unnatural trade: *Aristotle: the politics*, ed. T. J. Saunders, London 1981, i. 80–8 at pp. 85–7.
[131] Palgrave, 'Life and works of Sismondi', 349–50.
[132] A. Alison responded to J. C. L Simonde de Sismondi's, *Études des sciences sociales*, Paris 1837, in 'Sismondi', *BEM* lvii (May 1845), 529–48.
[133] The phrase was Alison's: ibid. 536. On the moral and social consequences of free trade see pp. 537–9, 545–6.
[134] Ibid. 547. See also idem, 'The Roman Campagna', ibid. lix (Mar. 1846), 337–55 at

philosophical response to free-trade political economy was widely shared in protectionists tracts which condemned the reduction of public policy to mere chrematistics and looked to a broader protectionist political economy for moral and social safeguards.[135]

Protectionists also condemned the Anti-Corn-Law League's transformation of the terms of social and economic debate. The League was exposed as an inevitable consequence of the transformation of fiscal politics after 1832.[136] Its emergence marked the ascendancy of a new fiscal politics dominated by urban consumers and manufacturers which was expressed in the divisive and destructive political language of the League's propaganda. Conservative journals based this interpretation on close analysis of the League's *Anti-bread tax circular*.[137] Croker believed the League's texts were 'revolutionary' and destructive because they ranged the interests of the urban middle and working classes against the aristocracy and rural society in its entirety.[138] Similarly De Quincey and Warren condemned Peel's receipt of a deputation from the Anti-Corn-Law League in 1842, as a dangerous endorsement of a revolutionary class politics.[139] The protectionist response to the League was not therefore restricted to the narrow question of repeal itself. As Mallalieu observed, 'the distinction and disjunction of interests ... is the work of the League alone, which, having originated the senseless cry of "class interests" would seem doggedly determined to establish the fact, *per fas nefas*, as the means of founding and perpetuating class divisions'.[140] In this way protectionists attempted to expose the political language of the League as destructive of both social and political cohesion.

Within these general terms protectionists combated the League's distributive justifications of repeal. They focused on the central proposition that

---

pp. 344–9, and 'The fall of Rome: its causes at work in the British empire', ibid. lix (June 1846), 692–718 at p. 706.
135 Anon., *Brief considerations with reference to the corn laws*, 14, 28–9, 36–7, 40; Anon. ['F. C.'], *Present condition and future prospects*, 5, 21, 31.
136 Critiques of the League's 'undue' electoral influence abounded in protectionist tracts: J. W. Croker, 'Anti-Corn-Law agitation', QR lxxi (Dec. 1842), 244–314 at p. 314; Anon., *An address on the corn laws*, 26.
137 Croker analysed, 'the ephemeral spawn of incendiary tracts, advertisements and placards, with which the Anti-Corn-Law Associations inundate the country': 'Anti-Corn-Law agitation', 244.
138 On the League's class-language see ibid. 259, 268–9. Croker's article was endorsed by Almack in *Character, motives and proceedings*, 63, and by R. Davies in *A defence of the agricultural interest, comprising, also, a refutation of the statements of the Anti-Corn-Law-League: addressed to the landed proprietors, &c., &c.; to which is added a letter to Lord John Russell*, London 1846, 44.
139 De Quincey and Warren, 'Anti-Corn-Law deputation to Sir Robert Peel', 271–2. The following responded to the League's agricultural campaign of 1843 with analysis of specific League texts: Lushington, *Six letters*, 23–8; *Maydwell's analysis of Cobden's addresses*, esp. pp. 14–57.
140 Mallalieu, 'Commercial policy – ships, colonies and commerce II', 637.

corn-law repeal would raise real wages. As early as 1833 an influential protectionist tract had maintained that British manufacturing competitiveness was achieved chiefly by reducing wages and therefore exacerbated a social and economic crisis of distribution.[141] Distributive reality seemed to confirm the essential opposition of the interests of labour and capital in Ricardian economic theory.[142] So Croker could expose the wage reductions which had sparked off the 'plug riots' of 1842 as a consequence of the manufacturers' predictable response to the reduction of the corn law in 1842.[143] Most notably, John Almack and Sir George Game Day juxtaposed the material claims made in the League's propaganda against its 'corn theory' of wages.[144] By establishing the centrality of a direct relationship between wages and corn prices in the League's texts, protectionists attempted to undermine free trade's distributive promises. If corn and wages related directly, then repeal could at best keep real wages static. Even Robert Torrens conceded in 1843 that, 'The abolition of the Corn Laws will be utterly inoperative, as far as regards the removal of the causes which are depressing money wages. All that their abolition . . . could accomplish, would be, to prevent *real* wages from falling in a greater proportion than *money* wages.'[145] Thus protectionists attempted to shed the odium of class oppression by pinning it on the League as the instrument of manufacturing capitalism.

Historians have tended to assume that protectionists also based their social justification of protection on a 'corn theory' of wages.[146] That is to say, if wages related directly to corn prices then the corn law was effectively a wages subsidy. This reading of protectionist argument emanates perhaps from the caricature of protection which Peel offered in 1847.[147] Yet, consistent with their responses to Ricardo in the 1820s, protectionists commonly denied a direct relationship between wages and corn prices and stressed that repeal

---

[141] Anon., *Public economy concentrated*, 48–50, 54–6, reiterated by Southey in, 'On the corn laws', 276.

[142] G. P. Scrope projected McCulloch's theory of wages and profits as pernicious and divisive social philosophy: 'The political economists', 27–30.

[143] Croker, 'Anti-Corn-Law agitation', 291–3. See also R. Sowler, 'The League's revenge', BEM lii (Oct. 1842), 542–50 at pp. 547–8, and Lushington, *Six letters*, 19. The 'early socialist' John Gast also made this point in the 1830s: Thompson, *The people's science*, 137.

[144] Almack, *Character, motives and proceedings*, 30–47, who concluded (p. 53) that 'The Anti-Corn Law league, is, properly speaking, an "*Anti-Labour League*"'. See also Day, *The farmers and the League*, esp. pp. 25–6. Maydwell endorsed earlier renditions by both Almack and Day: *Maydwell's analysis of Cobden's addresses*, 60. Day's argument and evidence was cited by Warren in 'Position and prospects of the government', 125.

[145] Torrens, *Letter to the right honourable Sir Robert Peel*, 29, referring at p. 4 to 'recent numbers' of *QR* and *BEM*'. These were probably Sowler, 'The League's revenge', and 'The revolt of the workers: the employer and the employed', BEM lii (Nov. 1842), 642–53, and Croker, 'The Anti-Corn-Law agitation'.

[146] Macintyre, 'Lord George Bentinck and the protectionists', 156; Hilton 'Peel: a reappraisal', 599–600.

[147] In his *Letter to the electors of Tamworth* (July 1847), Peel underlined three justifications of protection – high relative British taxation, the 'special burdens' of land over manufac-

would reduce wages through its impact on the labour market.[148] Such labour-market positions were employed extensively against the Anti-Corn-Law League in the 1840s. Archibald Alison and others added a new empirical dimension to protectionist emphasis on the importance of agriculture as an employment dependency, presenting the Anti-Corn-Law League as an 'anti-national faction'.[149] In parliament, J. C. Colquhoun and Howard Douglas maintained that repeal would reduce the general condition of labour by glutting the labour market.[150] Similarly G. C. Holland and W. F. P. Napier argued that corn-law repeal would reach beyond the margins of agriculture to damage the entire labouring class; highly productive farms would be forced to reduce wages in order to compete driving the rural unemployed to seek urban employment.[151] Others emphasised the essential immobility of rural labour, challenging free traders' confidence in the reallocation of labour to manufacturing after repeal.[152]

In sum, the cheapness promised by the League was presented by protectionists as a blueprint for pauperisation and demoralisation. In 1833, John Barton had attempted to demonstrate direct relationships between corn prices and the social and moral condition of the population, rural and urban. Using mortality rates as a crude index of well-being and morality Barton had challenged the belief that low corn prices were unquestionably desirable.[153] Barton had argued that low prices simultaneously fostered improvident marriages in rural districts and depravity and dissipation in towns. By these mechanisms, low corn prices generated higher average mortality rates than did high ones.[154] Barton's influence reached beyond Robert Southey's amplification of his views in 1834 because the Agricultural Protection Society injected a more concise version of his 1833 pamphlet into the debates of 1844.[155] The new version incorporated the census of 1831 into a general

---

tures, and the direct variation of wages with food prices: Lord Mahon and E. Cardwell (eds), *Memoirs by the right honourable Sir Robert Peel*, London 1857, ii. 102–3; Walker-Smith, *The protectionist case*, 62.
148 Anon., *Public economy concentrated*, 22–4; Barton, *In defence of the corn laws*, 10, 67; C. Putt, *Observations on the corn laws, or bread for thirty millions of inhabitants; without the importation of a single grain of corn: without loss to the farmer, the landlord, or the fundholder*, London 1840, 7, 11–12, 15, 20–1, 32.
149 Alison, 'The corn laws', 659, and 'The anti-national faction', 552; G. Taylor, 'Population of Great Britain and Ireland', *QR* liii (Feb. 1835), 56–78, 63.
150 J. C. Colquhoun, House of Commons (12 Feb. 1846), *Hansard* 3rd ser. lxxxiii. 764, and H. Douglas, House of Commons (13 Feb. 1846), ibid. 842.
151 Holland, *An analysis of the address of F. H. Fawkes, Esq.*, 6–7; Napier, *Observations on the corn law*, 1–2. See also Anon., *British industry or foreign labour; a few words addressed to the working classes*, London 1846, esp. pp. 2–4.
152 Barton, *In defence of the corn laws*, 38–9, cited in Southey, 'On the corn laws', 266–7; Napier, *Observations on the corn law*, 9–12; *Speech of Mr. Disraeli*, 14–15, 26–7.
153 Barton, *In defence of the corn laws*, preface.
154 Ibid. 10–31, 127–9.
155 Southey, 'On the corn laws', esp. pp. 112–13. Although no direct influence can be in-

analysis of mortality rates at 'low', 'middle' and 'high' corn prices. Decennial averages revealed a concentration of mortality in the low category and a dramatic falling off in the high. Comparative evidence from the Poor Law Commissioners' continental surveys was employed to confirm Barton's findings for Britain:[156] 'a low price of corn is injurious to the labourer, and constantly accompanied by poverty, increased disease, and death. Surely this is *"a great fact,"* if a fact at all'.[157] Thus protection was defended as a legislative instrument which could preserve the real living standards of the British labouring classes. Consistently, protectionists elevated 'ability to buy' over nominal cheapness. By protecting the incomes of domestic producers in all sectors and preserving their domestic markets, it was argued that protection could sustain the living standards of British labour.[158] For protectionists, then, the economics of 'under-consumption' also constituted a strategy for social cohesion.

Protectionist perceptions of the 'Condition of England Question' as a crisis of distribution were also mediated in comparative terms. It was widely argued that the equalisation of British and European corn prices would be tantamount to the voluntary erosion of real wage relativities. Protectionists made high nominal food prices a corollary of Britain's relative advancement: 'Every gradation . . . towards a higher numerical value of provisions, is, in every community, the proof and the measure of its progress towards greater civilization; and that value, whatever it may be, constitutes the *scale of maintenance* so different in every country.'[159] By this reasoning corn-law repeal could be presented not only as the lowering of the 'scale of maintenance', but also as the surrender of control over British living standards. Contentiously, 'The Poor Man's Friend' attempted to demonstrate the superiority of British living standards from a comparison with average wages and hours worked in France, Switzerland, Austria, Tyrol, Saxony and Bonne. He concluded that the 'unnatural competition' inaugurated by corn-law repeal would drive British wages down to uniformly lower European levels.[160] Equalisation of European corn prices was therefore projected as the generalisation of European poverty. As E. S. Cayley opined 'The object of the repeal of the corn

---

ferred, both Peel and Alison questioned the social and moral desirability of low food prices: *Speech of the right honourable Sir Robert Peel*, 29; Alison, 'The Whig dissolution', 30. See also J. Barton, *The influence of the price of corn on the rate of mortality*, London 1844, in *John Barton: economic writings*, ii. 139–46. A committee of the London Statistical Society (including the Leaguer John Bowring) refused to publish *The influence*: ibid. p. xiii.

[156] Ibid. 140–2, 144.

[157] Ibid. 145. For similar conclusions see Anon., *Public economy concentrated*, 32–3, 50; Mallalieu, 'The corn law question', 800.

[158] Dalbiac, *A few words on the corn laws*, 1; Anon. ['Britannicus'], *Corn-laws defended*, 27–8; *Speech of Mr Disraeli*, 12, 13–15.

[159] Anon., *The farmers of England: foreign corn, the cost price of producing wheat in some foreign countries*, London 1841, 10–11.

[160] Anon., *A counterplea for the poor*, 14–15. See also Anon., *Cheap bread and its consequences*, 4–6, and Anon., *Guilty or not guilty?: being an inquest on the Conservative parliament and ministry*, London–Plymouth 1842, 9.

laws, is to reduce English and Continental wages to a level, and it is almost inferred in the argument that the corn-laws produce the difference.'[161] Thus protection was presented as a buffer against the Europe-wide levelling of social conditions. From the protectionist point of view, the high prices attributed by free traders to the corn law emanated from a more fundamental differential 'between the natural range of prices on the continent and in England'.[162] Protecting this disjunction was tantamount to preserving sovereignty over British living standards.[163]

Not only did protectionists question the social promises of repealers, they also challenged the League's construction of the 'Condition of England' debate. It was widely maintained that the League reduced social discourse to a monocause. Samuel Jackson condemned the intellectual impoverishment of working-class minds by the League's 'Bread-tax' campaign of 1839: 'Advantage has been taken of their necessities to infuse into their minds one idea, and this not an idea of cause and effect, but of cause only.'[164] Protectionists refocused debate about the condition of manufacturing society on the character of manufacturing capitalism. Jackson understood economic fluctuation, the principal destroyer of stable living standards, as a consequence of the profit motive.[165] Since it pushed production beyond the means of consumption for profit, human nature was the cause of economic depressions. For Alfred Mallalieu, the profit motive also ensured that employers made economic depressions fall heaviest on labour: 'Will they, in adverse circumstances undertake beneficially to dispose elsewhere of the superfluous provision, and prevent, on behalf of the poor, a depression of labour-wages, as for the wealthy orders they have stayed their advance?'[166] The factory system was presented as the most obvious consequence of the profit motive. The transformation of production from hand to power looms had, 'The Poor Man's Friend' maintained, destroyed the home as the locus of work.[167] He invoked John Marshall's evidence that concentrated production was hastening the physical 'dwindling down' and moral 'degeneration' of the manufacturing working classes.[168] So, by challenging the confinement of social debate to the corn laws, protectionists combated the League's class idiom: 'the landlords are

---

[161] Cayley relied on the evidence of Jacob and W. R. Greg, House of Commons (12 Mar. 1839), *Hansard* xlvi. 413. See also his *Letters to Lord John Russell*, 25–6.
[162] Anon., *Upon the probable influence of a repeal of the corn laws upon the trade in corn*, London 1846, 40.
[163] Croker, 'Ministerial resignations', 307–8; Disraeli, House of Commons (20 Feb. 1846), *Hansard* lxxxiii. 1344.
[164] Jackson, *Commercial distress temporary*, 33.
[165] Ibid. 22.
[166] Mallalieu, 'The cotton manufacture', 421.
[167] Anon., *A counterplea for the poor*, 5–7.
[168] For the terms see ibid. 6. Marshall explained the increase of pauperism and crime as a consequence of the transformation of working-class morality by the factory system's destruction of domestic industry: *A digest of all the accounts*, i, tables 9, 46–9. A. Mallalieu targeted

called a bread-taxing oligarchy, a handful of swindlers; despicable, base, sordid, detestable'.[169] Thus, the League's language of class was combated with an alternative pejorative language of 'millocracy'.[170]

Strikingly, protectionists did not search out solutions in a return to a rural arcadia but rather in the moralisation of manufacturing capitalism. This served to re-direct the terms of debate on the condition of manufacturing society away from the essential materialism of the repeal campaign. Robert Sowler rooted the improvement of the moral and material condition of the labouring classes in the moralisation of labour relations:

> The tie of master and workman, of employer and employed, . . . is getting closer and more important with every onwards movement of society; and in large towns . . . the welfare of the whole community, the peace and happiness of rich and poor alike, will soon be dependent upon the way in which these two classes discharge their several duties towards each other.[171]

For Sowler, repeal was a distraction from effective employer philanthropy. This rested instead on improving factory and domestic conditions, public health reforms, recreational facilities, reduced reliance on female employment and most importantly, in providing for the moral and religious education of the workforce.[172] Although some protectionists recognised the efforts of 'moral' manufacturers like John Fielden to improve the condition of the working classes by endorsing the 'Ten Hours' campaign, factory reform *per se* was not prominent in the printed discourse on protection.[173] Religious and moral education was consistently elevated over corn-law repeal and the length of the working day.[174] For Archibald Alison, repeal was one of 'num-

---

Baines's and Ure's emphasis on the benign and edifying effects of the factory system in 'The cotton manufacture and the factory system': *BEM* xl (July 1836), 100–21 at pp. 119–20. See also A. Ure, *The philosophy of manufactures: or, an exposition of the scientific, moral, and commercial economy of the factory system of Great Britain*, London 1835, and E. Baines, *History of the cotton manufacture in Great Britain*, London 1835.

[169] Almack, *Character, motives, and proceedings*, 3. His *Cheap bread and low wages* (printed for the Agricultural Protection Society), London 1844, summarised the 1843 pamphlet. See also Davies, *A defence of the agricultural interest*, 44.

[170] G. C. Holland publicised the term widely in *The millocrat: letters to J. G. Marshall in answer to his letter to Lord Fitzwilliam, on the state of the manufacturing classes*, London 1841. See also Almack, *Character, motives, and proceedings*, 8, and Napier, *Observations on the corn law*, 13.

[171] Sowler, 'The League's revenge', 549.

[172] Idem, 'Revolt of the workers: the employer and the employed', 647–53. Some protectionists would have added the reform of the urban poor law to Sowler's list, for example Bell, *A vindication of the rights of British landowners*, 47–8.

[173] Manufacturing and commercial philanthropists were praised in: Mallalieu, 'The cotton manufacture and the factory system', 113–18; Anon., *Thoughts on the corn laws*, 12–13; Almack, *Character, motives and proceedings*, 5–12, 19–20; Lushington, *Six letters*, 22.

[174] Anon., *A counterplea for the poor*, 11–12; A. Mallalieu, 'The ministry and the people, the workhouse system, the factory system, and the ten hours bill', *BEM* xli (June 1837), 836–54 at pp. 839, 852–3.

berless philanthropic delusions'.[175] Alison identified the 'real balm for an ulcerated nation' in the identification of philanthropy with both social stability and the state and advocated the effective establishment of philanthropy in a programme of national education executed by the Established Church.[176] Within this context the social benefits of the corn law – protection of domestic markets for produce and labour, self-sufficiency in food and stability in real and relative living standards – were seen to regulate social conditions without transforming either the profile or character of the British state.

---

[175] A. Alison, 'Lessons from the past', ibid. 1 (Sept. 1841), 275–87 at p. 286.
[176] Ibid. 287.

PART II

CURRENCY, BANKING AND CONSERVATIVE DISCOURSE

4

The Politics of Convertibility and Deflation, 1809–c. 1830

'Religion, constitution and currency, are in fact the three links which bind together the members of a great community. Destroy any one of them, and you ruin the whole': Sir J. Sinclair, House of Commons (15 May 1811), *Hansard* xx. 168.

In their early nineteenth-century context money, credit and banks were not arcane subjects which were confined to the technical sphere of the 'experts' but were debated in general terms in parliament and in print. So generalised was monetary debate in 1811 that Sir John Sinclair could claim that, 'it has been so ably discussed in the debates in this House, and has been so fully treated of, not only in an endless succession of pamphlets, but in daily, weekly, monthly, quarterly, and every other species of periodical publication, that it seems to be in great measure exhausted'.[1] While public interest in monetary questions did not persist at the fever pitch of 1811, Sinclair was wrong to suggest that the subject was 'exhausted'. The changing contexts of war finance, public indebtedness and reconstruction after 1815 and the economic and financial fluctuations of the 1820s sustained public interest in the character of banking and currency policy. The central points of controversy centred on whether money was merely a neutral means of exchange or an important influence on economic and social conditions. What was the socio-economic impact of legislation affecting the supply of money and the availability of credit? How did this affect the relative positions of different propertied interests? Could monetary policy therefore be viewed as an interface between the state and private property and as an instrument through which governments could influence economic and social conditions?

In common with the historiography of economic discourse and policy more generally, the history of monetary debate has usually been written in terms of the ineluctable evolution of a mid Victorian orthodoxy.[2] Indeed, it has been assumed that 'In the mid-Victorian period the classical triptych of liberal political economy – laissez faire, free trade and the gold standard – had

---

[1] Sir J. Sinclair, House of Commons (15 May 1811), *Hansard* xx. 158.
[2] Fetter, *The development*; A. Feaveryear, *The pound sterling: a history of English money*, 2nd edn, Oxford 1963; Sir J. Clapham, *The Bank of England: a history*, Cambridge 1944, 1–112; Hilton, *Corn, cash, commerce*, 31–66, 87–97, 202–31, 232–68; M. Collins, *Money and banking in the UK: a history*, London 1988, 9–30.

stood virtually unchallenged and, in the eyes of many, unchallengeable.'[3] While historians have explored the ideas of critics of the orthodoxy in the last quarter of the nineteenth century relatively little attention has been directed at their antecedents.[4] Where critics of the monetary component of the 'classical tryptych' have been recognised, this has often served mainly to expose the precocity of nineteenth-century anticipations of more recent monetary theorising.[5] Alternatively, nineteenth-century monetary debate has been painted as a dualistic tussle between the advocates and opponents of the gold standard, or, 'two contrary theories respecting the influence of bank issues'.[6] In this binary intellectual world, proponents of the gold standard (bullionists) believed that both prices and the state of the foreign exchanges could be regulated by proportioning bank issues to the size of gold reserves.[7] At the opposite pole critics of the gold standard denied that the quantity of bank issues exerted any influence over prices or the state of the exchanges and maintained that banks should be free to issue notes and credit according to the needs of commerce.[8] Yet this dualistic perspective on early nineteenth-century monetary debate runs the risk of reducing a rich discourse to mere technical tussles. Between bullionism and 'anti-bullionism' lay a range of positions on the technical questions of convertibility and the relationships between the size of the money supply, domestic prices and the state of the exchanges. More importantly this public debate ranged far beyond technical questions of monetary theory to explore the constitutional, social and economic implications of changing the value of money and the availability of credit through the agency of legislation.

It would, of course, be simplistic to suggest that nineteenth-century monetary debate slotted into neat partisan categories.[9] Yet in response to a historiography which has identified the gold standard as a defining component of

---

[3] E. H. H. Green, 'Rentiers versus producers?: the political economy of the bimetallic controversy c. 1880–1898', *EHR* ciii (1988), 588–612 at p. 608. See also Hilton, 'Peel: a reappraisal', 612–14, and Harling, *The waning of 'Old Corruption'*, 9–10.

[4] Ibid. See also A. C. Howe, 'Bimetallism, c. 1880–1898: a controversy re-opened?', *EHR* cv (1990), 377–91; E. H. H. Green, 'The bimetallic controversy: empiricism belimed or the case for the issues', ibid. 673–83; Howe, *Free trade and Liberal England*, esp. pp. 199–204. On early nineteenth-century critics see A. Briggs, 'Thomas Attwood and the economic background of the Birmingham Political Union', *CHJ* ix (1948), 190–216.

[5] D. P. O'Brien, *Thomas Joplin and classical macroeconomics: a reappraisal of classical monetary thought*, London 1993.

[6] J. S. Mill, *Principles of political economy with some of their applications to social philosophy*, 1st publ. London 1848, ed. W. J. Ashley, London 1909, iii. 652, 651–76.

[7] Among prominent bullionists were J. Wheatley, D. Ricardo and H. Thornton: Fetter, *The development*, 47, and H. Thornton, *An enquiry into the nature and effects of the paper credit of Great Britain*, 1st publ. London 1802, ed. F. A. Hayek, London 1939, 141–60, 193–211, 260–76.

[8] On Thomas Attwood see Fetter, *The development*, 75–6. See also Mill's summary of 'anti-bullionism' in *Principles*, 652.

[9] See Hilton's warning in *Corn, cash, commerce*, 59–60, and D. Robinson, 'The country banks and the Bank of England', *BEM* xxiii (Feb. 1828), 197–213 at p. 208.

the free-trade political economy of Victorian Britain and has concentrated on Liberal political philosophies it is important to explore the intellectual character of opposition to the orthodoxy. Until relatively recently the ideological significance of monetary debate in Tory economic discourse remained relatively neglected. Monetary policy during the 1820s was glossed as an administrative category which was somehow insulated from politics and ideas or identified as the characteristic of an enlightened 'Liberal-Toryism' which was to flow unimpeded into Gladstonian Liberalism.[10] More recently, Boyd Hilton's account of economic policy in the 1820s offered a more sophisticated reading of monetary debates and outlined the importance of currency reform in moulding commercial, agricultural and financial policy.[11] He suggested that the return to the gold standard was motivated by a desire to 'eliminate abhorrent fluctuations', to 'vet and prune' exports rather than indiscriminately to expand them, and to 'stimulate' 'sound' economic activity which was not based on speculation.[12] Subsequently, he presented bullionism as a defining component of the Christian political economy which underpinned 'Liberal-Tory' economics; mechanistic structures would allow the retreat of the state from the economy freeing up the operation of a divine economic state of trial which would moralise economic life.[13] Since this is neither a study of policy formation nor of the motivations of key political actors it does not question these conclusions on the intellectual roots of policy but explores the intellectual character of Tory opposition to this 'Liberal-Tory' bullionism. Though the Tory journals were often divided on technical points they consistently challenged the deflationary consequences of bullionist policy and sought out positive functions for monetary and banking legislation by applying distinctive political and constitutional languages to monetary questions.

As Timothy Alborn has demonstrated it is hugely rewarding to conceptualise debates on monetary and banking policy as essentially political discourses about the location, nature and legitimacy of financial power in early nineteenth-century Britain. Alborn has shown how monetary reformers presented the return to the gold standard as a blow against 'Old Corruption' which prevented financial interests from gaining at the public's expense and which therefore restored political legitimacy to monetary policy.[14] These

---

[10] Acworth, *Financial reconstruction in England*, 91–114, and Brady, *William Huskisson and Liberal reform*, 21–40.
[11] Hilton, *Corn, cash, commerce*, 30–66, 87–97, 132–5, 156–61, 202–31, 232–68.
[12] Ibid. 60. Of course Hilton did not present bullionism exclusively in ideological terms but also emphasised administrative and political contexts: ibid. 48, 65, 87–92, 210–15, 227–31.
[13] Ibid. 307–14, and idem 'Peel: a reappraisal', 600–4, 606–14. On the influence of evangelicalism on 'Liberal-Tory' monetary, social and economic thought see idem, *Age of atonement*, 125–31, 206, 218–36, 244–6, 248–51.
[14] Alborn, *Conceiving companies*, 55–63. On 'early socialist' bullionism see Thompson, *The people's science*, 175–82, 210–13.

largely Whig and Radical political languages also intruded political debates on franchise extension and on the relative merits of 'direct' and 'virtual' representation into the discourse on banking reform.[15] Yet beside this Whig/Radical idiom there flourished a vibrant Tory discourse on monetary and banking policy. In the Tory journals debate centred on the legitimacy of altering the relative positions of debtors and creditors through monetary legislation and on determining the precise influence of monetary policy on social and economic conditions. Whereas defenders of the gold standard tended to assume that monetary policy was economically anodyne and politically neutral, its critics contended that the palpable redistributive consequences of bullionist legislation needed at the very least to be made explicit. For many defenders of the pre-1832 constitution debates on monetary and banking policy were largely about maintaining the vitality of the propertied polity by confining the unconscious and unaccountable incursions of the state into the realm of relative property values.

Cash and the constitution: debating the gold standard, 1810–19

The Bank of England's suspension of cash payments in 1797 signalled the temporary relinquishment of the gold standard by the legislature. On the understanding that cash payments would be resumed six months after peace had been settled, parliament agreed to the suspension as a war measure.[16] This did not, however, preclude continued debate on the question of the standard which culminated in the *Report of the select committee on the high price of gold bullion* of 1810.[17] Although the report's recommendation that cash payments should be resumed within two years was rejected by parliament in 1811 the report laid the intellectual foundations for subsequent monetary policy. The grounds for resuming cash payments in 1819, for restricting the activities of country banks in the late 1820s and for imposing a restrictive charter on the Bank of England in 1844 differed little from the bullionist position of 1811. Yet the dominance of bullionism over monetary policy did not foreclose vigorous intellectual debate on monetary theory, on the socio-economic functions of monetary policy and on the political and constitutional implications of changing the value of money. Critics of bullionism rejected the view that monetary policy was neutral and consequently debated the functions of monetary legislation in explicitly constitutional languages.

The bullionist position of 1810 was founded on a number of related theoretical propositions. In common with other advocates of a convertible currency bullionists believed that bank notes were merely the representatives of

---

[15] Alborn, *Conceiving companies*, 62–3, 65–6.
[16] 37 Geo. III. c. 45
[17] *Report from the select committee on the high price of gold bullion*, PP 1810–11 (52) ii, repr. in E. Cannan (ed.), *The paper pound of 1797–1821*, London 1919, 1–71.

coin which possessed intrinsic value; the mechanism of convertibility distinguished 'real' money from mere credit currency which was sustained by commercial confidence. What differentiated bullionists from other supporters of a convertible currency were the precise connections they drew between the suspension of the gold standard, the depreciation of the value of the pound and the adverse state of Britain's foreign exchanges. By comparing how much gold the pound sterling could command at the mint with how much it could procure in the market bullionists concluded that the value of the pound had depreciated since 1797. The fundamental proposition of the bullionists was 'That the Fall which has thus taken place in the Value of the Promissory Notes of the Bank of England, and in that of the Country Bank Paper which is exchangeable for it, has been occasioned by too abundant Issue of Paper Currency, both by the Bank of England and by the Country Banks.'[18] To bullionists therefore, Britain's adverse foreign exchange position was explained by the 'overissue' of bank notes and consequent depreciation of the currency: 'the extraordinary degree, in which the Exchanges have been depressed for so long a period, has been, in a great measure, occasioned by the depreciation which has taken place in the relative value of the Currency of this Country, as compared with the Money of foreign countries'.[19] Their solution to the problem of adverse foreign exchanges was therefore to put an end to overissue and depreciation by returning to the gold standard and obliging banks to issue notes in strict proportion to their gold holdings.[20] When he advocated the resumption of cash payments in 1819 Robert Peel invoked these related theoretical positions in his argument for the restoration of a metallic currency.[21]

Yet even in 1811 bullionism did not exert a stranglehold over monetary thought in Britain. Indeed many advocates of a convertible currency rejected the precise bullionist argument for returning to the gold standard. Writing in the *Quarterly*, William Greenfield produced a nuanced theoretical critique of bullionism.[22] Drawing heavily on the writings of Henry Thornton, Greenfield was sceptical of the theories of depreciation and overissue upon which bullionism rested: 'Those gentlemen content themselves with proving *synthetically*, we had almost said, with *asserting*, that a redundance of currency

---

[18] F. Horner's resolutions on the *Report from the select committee on the high price of gold bullion*, House of Commons (6 May 1811), *Hansard* xix. 831; G. Ellis, W. Huskisson and G. Canning, 'Huskisson on the depreciation of the currency', *QR* iv (Nov. 1810), 414–53 at p. 416. On the depreciation of sterling on the Hamburg exchange between 1809 and 1811 see Fetter, *The development*, 27.
[19] F. Horner's resolutions on the *Report from the select committee on the high price of gold bullion*, House of Commons (6 May 1811), *Hansard* xix. 831.
[20] Ellis, Huskisson and Canning, 'Huskisson on the depreciation of currency', 434–5.
[21] Robert Peel invoked Horner's resolutions of 1811 in House of Commons (24 May 1819), *Hansard* xl. 678.
[22] W. Greenfield, 'The high price of bullion', *QR* iii (Feb. 1810), 152–61.

must occasion depreciation; whereas it would be at least equally interesting to trace the actual steps by which this consequence is brought about.'[23] Thus Greenfield adopted Thornton's point that 'overissue' was not always the cause of depreciation and therefore that monetary contraction was not always an appropriate response to either the problem of depreciation or an adverse foreign exchange position.[24] Greenfield also observed that disparity between the market and mint price of gold could be caused by other factors such as an adverse exchange position resulting from heavy importations of raw produce. This raised fundamental doubts about the omnipotence of the size of the money supply over the state of the exchanges.[25] Similar scepticism about the bullionist theory of foreign exchange was voiced in parliament by Alexander Baring who insisted that it was the state of trade not 'overissue' which dominated Britain's foreign exchange position.[26] Clearly, bullionist theory could not command the support of all advocates of a convertible currency in 1811.[27]

Yet the most sweeping critiques of bullionist theory were mounted by those who rejected the gold standard altogether. In parliament in 1811 George Rose insisted that gold itself was a commodity which fluctuated in value and which therefore defied any attempt to fix a stable formula for the convertibility of the pound.[28] Similarly in 1819 Lauderdale insisted that it was 'sporting with the commercial greatness and prosperity of the country' to attempt, effectively, to fix the value of gold through legislation.[29] As Horner noted in 1811 those who argued that it was impossible to fix a gold standard for the currency often appealed to philosophical theories of value.[30] Citing the monetary thought of John Locke in 1819, the Revd Edward Tatham argued that Lockean notions of value had been misappropriated by bullionists: 'there is no such *intrinsic, natural, settled* value of anything, as to make

---

[23] Ibid. 157 (Greenfield's emphasis). Greenfield drew heavily on H. Thornton, *Paper credit*, and on Sir P. Francis, *Reflections on the abundance of paper in circulation, and the scarcity of specie*, London 1810, and 'reviewed' D. Ricardo, *The high price of bullion, a proof of the depreciation of bank notes*, London 1810.

[24] Greenfield, 'The high price of bullion', 159, 161; Thornton, *Paper credit*, 143–6, 152–3, 259. For C. F. Peake, the distinction between Ricardo's neutral monetary economics and the 'active' system of Thornton was a seminal feature of Ricardianism: 'Henry Thornton and the development of Ricardo's economic thought', *HPE* x (1978), 193–212.

[25] The Bank directors, John Hill and J. C. Herries, among others also emphasised the influence of non-monetary factors on the state of the exchanges: Fetter, *The development*, 44, 46.

[26] A. Baring, House of Commons (8 May 1811), *Hansard* xix. 1058–9.

[27] See Castlereagh's observation, House of Commons (7 May 1811), ibid. 987.

[28] G. Rose, House of Commons (6 May 1811), ibid. 854.

[29] Lauderdale, House of Lords (21 May 1819), *Hansard* xl. 640. For similar positions see W. Heygate and H. Gurney, House of Commons (25 May 1819), ibid. 752–3, 762.

[30] Horner referred to 'Aristotelian theorists' in House of Commons (6 May 1811), ibid. 805.

any assigned quantity of it constantly worth any assigned quantity of another'.[31] In order to undermine the absolute theory of value upon which bullionism rested Tatham also cited Aristotle: 'A standing measure is a fixed and permanent thing, by which other things are exactly measured; but nothing is capable of being so *exactly measured* but the predicament of *Quantity . . . Value*, the subject of the measurement of money, is a *Quality*.'[32] Tatham's contributions were significant for more than their intellectual sources. For such emphasis on the exchangeable and mutable value of gold characterised critiques of bullionist orthodoxy and its deflationary consequences throughout the nineteenth century.[33]

It would be a mistake, however, to confine early nineteenth-century monetary discourse within the limits of theory. For one central point of contention between bullionists and their opponents was the influence of monetary policy over socio-economic conditions. Of course, it cannot be assumed that Britain's return to the gold standard was perceived by contemporaries as an aggressive bid to boost her manufacturing industry and share of foreign trade. Indeed, Hilton has suggested that 'Liberal-Tory' ministers especially viewed the act of 1819 as an explicitly deflationary measure: 'Convertibility would combat the challenge of manufacturing, commercial and financial wealth . . . it might even moderate the expansion of manufacturing industry and encourage a movement back to the land' and 'far from being a policy for growth, resumption was essentially deflationary, a policy to favour the official classes living on fees and fixed incomes, the fundholders and investing groups rather than the industrial wealth-creators whose lot it was periodically to borrow money'.[34] While Hilton's reading may account for the motives of certain Tory ministers it would be misleading to apply it to bullionism in general or to Tory monetary discourse more broadly.[35] Indeed, the economic idiom of 'Liberal-Tory' bullionism in 1810–11 was explicitly Smithian not restrictive. Canning, Huskisson and Ellis were chiefly concerned to distance their arguments for returning to the gold standard from the eighteenth-century 'mercantilist' tendency to conflate wealth with treasure.[36] Like

---

[31] E. Tatham, *On the scarcity of money and its effects upon the public; with the expedients by which they alone can be remedied and the nation saved from ruin*, 5th edn, Oxford 1819, 56 (Tatham's emphasis); J. Locke, *Some considerations of the consequences of lowering the interest and raising the value of money*, 1st publ. 1692, in *The works of John Locke Esq.*, folio edn, London 1714, ii. 21.
[32] Tatham, *On the scarcity of money*, 60 (probably Tatham's emphasis). The sense of Tatham's citation is given in *The politics of Aristotle*, trans. B. Jowett, Oxford 1885, i. 16–17.
[33] See below pp. 120–1. On the later nineteenth century see Green, 'Rentiers versus producers?', 590–3.
[34] Hilton, *Corn, cash, commerce*, 60 (on 'agricultural bullionists') and his *Age of atonement*, 223 (on the aims of Liberal-Tory ministers). On Peel in 1844 see ibid. 224–5.
[35] I am grateful to Dr Hilton for illuminating discussions on this point.
[36] Scholars of mercantilism have questioned the 'Midas fallacy' as a characterisation of mercantilism: Heckscher, *Mercantilism*, ii. 175–216, 238–61; Magnusson, *Mercantilism*, 26–8, 35–6.

Adam Smith these Tory politicians caricatured mercantilism in order to present 'Trade' as a mutual transfer of equivalents between nations which was unaffected by the medium of exchange: in this view, the return to gold was devoid of any economic function beyond the stabilisation of the money supply and the foreign exchanges.[37] Ellis and Canning explicitly rejected the idea that monetary policy could influence national prosperity in a scathing critique of the ideas of Sir John Sinclair.[38] By the same token they refuted John Hill's prediction that the return to gold would be significantly deflationary and would tend to transfer wealth to creditor interests.[39] Strikingly, Huskisson dismissed monetary policy as an 'artificial contrivance' which could not create wealth or affect its distribution:

> Resources of a far different character this country possesses in abundance. They are to be found in the immense and increasing produce of its territory: – in the unwearied extension of its manufacturing industry: – in the elastick and expansive force of its legitimate commerce: – all mutually aiding and fostering each other: – all fed and put in motion by capital, the genuine growth of progressive accumulation – and not the factitious result of any artificial contrivance.[40]

For Tories in 1810–11, bullionism was emphatically not a strategy for the retardation or manipulation of British economic change.

It was the critics of bullionism who contested the 'neutrality' of money and insisted that monetary policy exerted a profound influence on economic conditions. Most vividly, Sir John Sinclair maintained that the paper currency had underpinned the prosperity of the Napoleonic period:

> 'it possesses a species of magical influence on the internal prosperity of a nation. Even in the midst of a long and expensive war, we see its effects – industry abounds, – agriculture flourishes – commerce and manufactures have increased – money is procurable at a moderate rate of interest – the public revenue becomes every year more productive ... and every species of domestic

---

[37] Ellis, Huskisson and Canning, 'Huskisson on the depreciation of currency', 432–3. See also Huskisson's speech of 7 May 1811 repr. in *Speeches of William Huskisson*, i. 209–10. See also A. Smith, *An inquiry into the nature and causes of the wealth of nations*, ed. R. H. Campbell, A. S. Skinner and W. B. Todd, Oxford 1976, i. 429–51; ii. 548–50.
[38] G. Ellis and G. Canning reviewed Sir John Sinclair's, *Observations on the report of the bullion committee*, London 1810, in 'Sir John Sinclair's observations on the report of the bullion committee', *QR* iv (Nov. 1810), 518–36. See also their 'Sir John Sinclair's remarks, &c.', ibid. v (Feb. 1811), 120–38, 129–31.
[39] Idem, 'Tracts on the report of the bullion committee', ibid. 242–62. The reviewers' case (pp. 243–4) against the deflationary predictions in John Hill's, *An inquiry into the causes of the present high price of bullion*, London 1811, rested on the assumption that a reduction in the quantity of paper in circulation would lower the exchangeable value of gold thereby offsetting the deflationary effect of resuming cash payments at the 1797 parity.
[40] Ellis, Huskisson and Canning, 'Huskisson on the depreciation of currency', 451, cited from W. Huskisson, *The question concerning the depreciation stated and examined*, London–Edinburgh–Dublin 1810, 153.

improvement ... are multiplied to an extent, not to be equalled in any period even of our own history'.[41]

Given the extent of wartime taxation and the size of the public debt Alexander Baring insisted on the inflationary benefits of a paper circulation: 'To support such a system, we must give a fictitious value to property, and must have a fictitious medium of circulation for carrying it on.'[42] More commonly Tory critics of the Bullion Report condemned the proposed return to gold as a suicidal erosion of state power. The suspension of cash payments insulated the domestic circulation from the vagaries of war and freed the government to export bullion in subsidies to allied governments or in exchange for raw produce.[43] Indeed Vansittart declared himself 'anxious that the arm of government should be strengthened rather than crippled'.[44] Thus the supposed 'neutrality' of money was vigorously contested in early nineteenth-century monetary discourse.

These debates on the 'neutrality' of money were inextricably connected to a constitutionalist discourse on the implications of monetary policy for the relationship between the state and private property in a propertied polity. For bullionists the monetary standard was an emblem of the authority and legitimacy of government expressed in the *'permanent* laws of the realm which regulate our coinage and determine our legal tender'.[45] In Huskisson's view the suspension of cash payments had, albeit temporarily, suspended a symbol of the British state's good faith and authority. Moreover, the depreciation of the value of sterling which had taken place during the suspension of cash payments had 'produced the total subversion of property'.[46] Though the redistributive consequences of the depreciation had been unintentional, Huskisson insisted that this was illegitimate in a propertied polity.[47] Thus the resumption of the gold standard at the parity of 1797 was justified as a measure which would prevent the continuous readjustment of relative property values under the aegis of legislation and would re-confine the prerogatives of legal tender within the accountable structure of parliamentary

---

41 Sir J. Sinclair, House of Commons (15 May 1811), *Hansard* xix. 160. Sinclair appealed (p. 159) to the monetary thought of David Hume. On Hume see below p. 104.
42 A. Baring, House of Commons (8 May 1811), *Hansard* xix. 1060.
43 Castlereagh, House of Commons (7 May 1811), ibid. 1010; Sinclair (15 May 1811), ibid. 159. G. Rose applied such arguments in a direct critique of Huskisson's rejection of the concept of the balance of trade (6 May 1811), ibid. 857.
44 N. Vansittart, House of Commons (7 May 1811), ibid. 966.
45 Huskisson, *The question concerning the depreciation*, 13, cited in Ellis, Huskisson and Canning, 'Huskisson on the depreciation of currency', 422; Horner, House of Commons (6 May 1811), *Hansard* xix. 831–2.
46 Ellis, Huskisson and Canning, 'Huskisson on the depreciation of currency', 448, and also pp. 422–3. See Horner's resolution no. 7 repr. in *Speeches of William Huskisson*, i. 184–5; Huskisson's speech of 7 May 1811, ibid. 188–91, 197–8.
47 Huskisson, *A question concerning the depreciation*, 10–11, 13–15, 18–20, 128–32.

legislation.[48] As Robert Peel insisted in 1819, 'That House had too long transferred its powers. On them devolved the duty to attend to the pecuniary and commercial interests of the country.'[49] In this light the resumption of cash payments at the 1797 parity was presented as a defence against the constitutional implications of simply devaluing the pound by adopting a lower standard. Such *legislative* devaluation of sterling was rejected by bullionists as a measure which would arbitrarily alter contracts between individuals and foist a redistributive profile on the state. Huskisson even appealed to the authority of John Locke on this point:

> The Standard once settled by publick Authority, the **Quantity** of Silver establish'd under the several Denominations, . . . should not be altered, till there were an absolute necessity shewn of such a Change, which I think can never be . . . . The reason why it should not be changed is this; Because the publick Authority is Guarantee for the performance of all legal Contracts.[50]

The legal tender of 1797 was thus projected as a legitimating pledge and guarantee of the authority of the state as expressed through public observance of the law. Bullionists believed that the alternatives of devaluing sterling or continuing the suspension breached the boundaries of parliamentary action in arbitrarily altering relative property values.

Critics of the return to gold challenged this bullionist appropriation of the constitutional high ground. In parliament Vansittart presented an alternative constitutionalist reading of the suspension of cash payments and proposed 'a general Resolution stating the right of the sovereign to regulate the legal current coin of the Kingdom'.[51] This resolution met with a torrent of bullionist opposition in parliament and in print.[52] Building on George Canning's argument of 1811 that Vansittart had proposed the encroachment of the powers of the executive into the prerogatives of private property, Edward Copleston published a refutation of Vansittart's resolution in 1819: 'it contains the plainest implication of the Sovereign's right to the property of his

---

[48] See also G. Ellis, 'Comber on national subsistence', *QR* x (Oct. 1813), 157–75 at p. 171. On Huskisson's constitutional defence of resumption in 1821 see Hilton, *Corn, cash, commerce*, 94, and *Speech of the Right Hon. W. Huskisson in the House of Commons, Tuesday, the 11th of June, 1822 on Mr Western's motion concerning the resumption of cash payments*, London 1823, 13–24, 50–1.

[49] R. Peel, House of Commons (24 May 1819), *Hansard* xl. 689.

[50] J. Locke, *Further considerations concerning raising the value of money; wherein Mr Lowndes's arguments for it in his late report concerning 'An essay for the ammendment of the silver coins'*, are particularly examined, 1st publ. London 1695, folio edn, London 1714, 69 (Locke's emphasis); 'Huskisson on the depreciation of currency', 438. For other bullionist appeals to Locke see Ellis and Canning, 'Sir John Sinclair's remarks, & c.', 128, and 'Tracts on the report of the bullion committee', 261.

[51] N. Vansittart, House of Commons (7 May 1811), *Hansard* xix. 957 approved *pro forma* (13 May 1811), ibid. xx. 83.

[52] G. Canning, House of Commons (8 May 1811), ibid. 1080; H. Thornton, House of Commons (13 May 1811), ibid. 76–124.

subjects, which has ever been hazarded in modern times. . . . These doctrines struck at the root of all sound political economy, of our constitutional privileges, and of our public honour and good faith'.[53] Yet these bullionist responses emphasised only one aspect of Vansittart's constitutionalist argument against the resumption of cash payments. His principal objection to bullionism was 'that a fixed and invariable equivalency between our legal money and bullion, never has been established by our laws'.[54] In other words, by attempting to fix a permanent and unalterable monetary standard the legislature was trespassing beyond its customary territory. This constitutionalist position was reiterated in 1819 by the Revd Edward Tatham who also questioned the competence of the legislature to fix an absolute value for money. He cited John Locke to push home his point:

> it is very unfit and *inconvenient*, that gold or any other metal should be made current legal money at a *standing settled rate*. This is to set a price upon the *varying value* of things by law, which *justly* cannot be done; and it is, as I have shewed, as far as it prevails, a constant *damage* and *prejudice* to the country where it is practised.[55]

Tatham used Locke to underline the injustice he perceived in the Act for the Resumption of Cash Payments. By fixing the value of money at the 1797 parity he believed the legislature violated its duty to protect *all* property rights impartially and at a stroke transferred wealth to creditor interests. As Locke had stated in 1695,

> Whether the Creditor be forced to receive less, or the Debtor forced to pay more than his Contract, the damage and injury is the Same, whenever a Man is defrauded of his Due. And whether this will not be a publick failure of Justice, thus arbitrarily to give one Man's Right and Possession to another, without any fault on the suffering Man's side, and without any the least advantage to the Publick, I shall leave to be considered.[56]

Locke's point was that the redistribution of property occasioned by legislative changes in the value of money not only exceeded the due scope of the law, but undermined the idea of public justice which was central to the state's authority and legitimacy. The Tory tussle for the mantle of John Locke serves to underline the prominence of constitutionalist discourse in the monetary debate of early nineteenth-century Britain.[57]

---

53 E. Copleston, *A letter to the right hon. Robert Peel, MP. for the University of Oxford, on the pernicious effects of a variable standard of value, especially as it regards the condition of the lower orders and the poor laws*, Oxford 1819, 76. On Canning see ibid. 76–8.
54 N. Vansittart, House of Commons (13 May 1811), *Hansard* xx. 35.
55 Tatham, *On the scarcity of money*, 51 (Tatham's emphasis); Locke, *Some considerations*, 166.
56 Ibid. 70.
57 See also G. Rose, House of Commons (6 May 1811), 843–4, 857; Anon., *A letter to the earl of Liverpool* (1814), 20–1, 23–7.

A presumptuous resumption?: deflation, distress and debt, 1819–22

The controversy which surrounded the return to the gold standard in 1819 was not confined to the narrow focus of monetary theory but was rather an expansive discourse which interpreted the economic experience of contemporary Britain. In parliament and in print commentators debated whether monetary policy was responsible for the contraction of trade in 1819 and for the agricultural depression of 1822. While advocates of the return to gold assumed that a stable and supposedly 'neutral' monetary settlement would tend to diminish economic fluctuations critics of this monetary 'orthodoxy' rejected the basic assumption that monetary policy was neutral. Far from functioning as a mechanistic instrument for the management of money supply and the foreign exchanges the bullionism of 1819 was perceived by its critics as a viciously deflationary policy. Even before the resumption of cash payments came into effect its critics observed the impact which preparations for the return to gold were exerting on commodity prices: 'from the absence of coin, and the diminution of paper, the general currency has decreased *more than one-third*; and consequently, by increasing the value of the other *two-thirds* in proportion, it has sunk the commodities *more than one-third*'.[58] In parliament opponents of the return to gold predicted that the convertibility provisions of the act of 1819 would contract the domestic means of payment and cramp commercial activity.[59] They also insisted that by increasing the value of money at a stroke the legislature would swell the real burden of debts and taxes.[60] Thus monetary discourse during 1819–22 blended economic and constitutional languages which attempted to spell out the economic consequences of a deflationary monetary policy and to expose the constitutional implications of redistributive deflation for a propertied polity. Though it would be misleading to suggest that this monetary discourse fell neatly into partisan categories it is important to note the prominence of Tories in the ideological campaign against the redistributive consequences of deflation. For this was an issue which challenged the notion that the state could somehow retreat from economic intervention and which questioned the assumption that economic legislation was politically anodyne.

It is essential to appreciate that in an early nineteenth-century setting 'deflation' was more a discursive category than it was a measurable phenomenon. By denying that the act of 1819 had increased the value of the pound by more than 4 per cent the government heavyweights Londonderry and Liver-

---

[58] Tatham, *On the scarcity of money*, 6 (Tatham's emphasis).
[59] 'Petition from the merchants and manufacturers of Leeds for the continued restriction of cash payments', House of Commons (1 Feb. 1819), *Hansard* xxxix. 188–9. See also petitions from Halifax and Liverpool (2 Feb. 1819), ibid. 212–13, and from the merchants of London, House of Lords (21 May 1819), *Hansard* xl. 599.
[60] W. Heygate, House of Commons (25 May 1819), ibid. 753, and H. Gurney, ibid. 762. On monetary debates in parliament see Fetter, *The development*, 74–88, and Gordon, *Political economy in parliament*, esp. pp. 27–58, 91–112.

pool rebutted the view that monetary policy was responsible for the slump in commodity prices and blamed 'over-production' instead.[61] Meanwhile David Ricardo admitted that monetary factors had caused excessive deflation but identified the Bank's administration of the resumption as the root cause.[62] In parliament critics challenged these estimates with alternative assessments of the magnitude of the deflationary consequences of the resumption of cash payments ranging from 25–50 per cent.[63] The accuracy of these claims was less significant than the pervasive assumption that monetary legislation was transforming economic conditions and relative property values. Naturally, the debate on deflation intensified following the activation of the Act for the Resumption of Cash Payments in May 1821.[64] Edward Copleston emerged as a powerful critic of the deflation of 1819 though not of convertibility *per se*.[65] The significance of Copleston's criticism goes beyond its theoretical interest since it has been suggested that he was a powerful influence on the 'Liberal--Tory' urge to moralise economic activity using the mechanism of deflation.[66] Yet by 1822 Copleston was arguing that the scale of deflation after 1819 was the accidental and unintended result of flawed monetary theory. He explained the excessive deflation after 1819 in terms of basic mistakes in the bullionist theory of depreciation.[67] Copleston pointed out several flaws in the strategy of assessing the degree of Napoleonic depreciation by comparing the mint value of gold with the market value which the paper commanded. Firstly, he observed that abundant issues of bank notes could merely indicate the existence of prosperity not depreciation:

> if the wealth and traffic of the country are increasing, a greater quantity of money is wanted to answer the purposes of trade; and if only the same quantity is to be had, it will rise in value; or if a greater quantity is introduced, it will

---

61 *Substance of the speech of the marquis of Londonderry*, 24; *The speech of the earl of Liverpool*, 25–6.
62 Ricardo, *On protection to agriculture*, 222–35. Ricardo insisted that the deflation was no greater than 10%: House of Commons (7 May 1822), *Hansard* n.s. vii. 393.
63 E. Ellice [30–50%], House of Commons (16 May 1820), ibid. i. 193–4; A. Baring [25%], ibid. 195; H. G. Bennett [35%], (8 May 1822), ibid. vii. 436.
64 On the timing of the resumption of cash payments see Acworth, *Financial reconstruction*, 93, and Hilton, *Corn, cash, commerce*, 156–61.
65 E. Copleston, 'State of the currency', *QR* xxvii (Apr. 1822), 239–67. This was republished as a pamphlet in 1830: Waterman, *Revolution, economics and religion*, 194.
66 On the general influence of Copleston's 'evangelical political economy' on Liberal-Tories see Hilton, *Age of atonement*, 234–5. On Copleston's policy prescriptions in the two letters to Peel see ibid. 126–7, 223. See also E. Copleston, *A second letter to the right hon. Robert Peel, MP. for the University of Oxford, on the causes of the increase of pauperism and on the poor laws*, Oxford 1819, 1–13.
67 Copleston's *Letter* had not indicted either inconvertibility or overissue (beyond gold reserves, without reference to the state of the exchanges), *per se* but had explained depreciation as the consequence of the size of the overall money supply (i.e. notes and coin) relative to the volume of trade: Waterman, *Revolution, economics and religion*, 187.

not necessarily fall in value, unless its increase exceed in proportion the increase in demand.[68]

Secondly, he rejected the assumption that the difference between the mint and market price of gold was either the proof and measure of a depreciated currency or a sufficient explanation of the Napoleonic inflation.[69] He sustained this point by showing empirically the absence of correlation between the changing disparities of the mint and market prices of gold and fluctuations in the contract prices of a range of commodities purchased by the Royal Hospital, Greenwich, over the period 1797–1816. Finally, he observed that the bullionist criterion of depreciation was inapplicable to the period 1797–1819 since suspension itself had removed demand for gold as a commodity invalidating 'market price' as a useful component in the theory of depreciation.[70] In rejecting disparity between the mint and market price of gold as a definitive index of monetary depreciation, Copleston effectively pulled the intellectual rug from under the Bullion Report and its legislative embodiment of 1819. More importantly he attributed the excessively deflationary consequences of the resumption to error in the theoretical underpinnings of legislation thereby locating himself within an expansive discourse on the legislative causes of distress.

Whether they advocated a more relaxed gold standard, a bimetallic or an inconvertible paper system critics of the 1819 act maintained that monetary legislation was the basic cause of economic depression.[71] Many parliamentary commentators on the roots of the agricultural depression of 1820–2 indicted the agency of deflation in magnifying the burden of debts and taxes.[72] As Matthias Attwood observed, 'It was the attempt to discharge debts and maintain taxes, in a species of money in which it was found utterly impossible to contract or impose them.'[73] It was claimed that while this magnification of fixed outgoings fell heaviest on agriculturists its crippling weight extended to

---

[68] Copleston, 'State of the currency', 244. For similar criticism see Jacob, *Considerations*, 192–3; R. Wilson, *An enquiry into the causes of the high prices of corn and labour, the depression of our foreign exchanges and high prices of bullion, during the late war; and consideration of the measures to be adopted for relieving our farming interest*, Edinburgh 1815, 14–26; P. R. Hoare, *Thoughts on the alleged depression in agriculture*, London 1816, 16; J. Wright, *Remarks on the erroneous opinions which led to the new corn law; and also on those of the bullionists on a circulating medium; and pointing out the only protection to agriculture*, London 1823, 20.

[69] Copleston, 'State of the currency', 250.

[70] Ibid. 252–3.

[71] But see the following rejections of monetary interpretations of depression: Crombie, *Letters on the present state of the agricultural interest*, 12–25; J. Boyes, *Observations addressed to the right hon. Lord Stourton, occasioned by his two letters to the earl of Liverpool*, York 1821; Malthus, 'Tooke – on high and low prices', esp. pp. 214–18.

[72] J. C. Curwen, House of Commons (25 May 1820), *Hansard* n.s. i. 669.

[73] M. Attwood (7 May 1822), ibid. vii. 377. This speech on the report on agricultural distress was described by T. Lethbridge as 'one of the most able . . . he had ever heard in the House': ibid. 402.

all productive interests in the economy.[74] As Baring put it, 'No country before presented the continuance of so extraordinary a principle as that of living under a progressive increase in the value of money, and a depression of the productions of the people . . . by the operation of the altered currency, they had loaded themselves not only with an immense public debt, but also with an increased debt between individual and individual.'[75] Although much criticism of the monetary orthodoxy was articulated within the context of debates on agricultural distress it cannot be dismissed as mere 'currency mongering in place of high corn laws'.[76]

The swollen burden of debts and taxes was not perceived as the only mechanism by which monetary policy depressed economic activity. Indeed the Tory journals tended to emphasise the devastating contraction of the means of payment and credit as a pernicious consequence of the act of 1819. George Croly presented the return to gold as the final nail in the destruction of markets which had followed the end of the Napoleonic wars and the cessation of government expenditure:

> The return of peace had made the manufacturer poor; and when the buyer is poor, the seller cannot long keep up his old extortion. All prices were thus lowered. To this was added the cessation of the government contracts, acting equally on the manufacturer and the farmer. Thirty millions were deducted from the means of both. Lastly, came the return to cash payments, which extinguished another great sum of the circulation; and left of the entire not more than half.[77]

In this view the resumption of cash payments had crushed the means of payment by imposing a formula on the money supply which totally ignored the real demand of local economies for currency and credit. This contraction of notes and credit, it was argued, removed a fundamental precondition for sectoral symbiosis in economic change. As Tatham put it, 'Currency as it flows through a vast agricultural and commercial country is analogous to blood in the human body' and, 'Agriculture and commerce lie in equal ruins on every side, for want of capital, for want of markets, and for want of employment – and all for *want of money*, both in coin and paper.'[78] Thus Tory critics

---

74 E. Ellice, House of Commons (22 Feb. 1821), ibid. iv. 895–900, and A. Baring, ibid. 902.
75 Idem, House of Commons (19 Mar. 1821), ibid. 1318.
76 Hilton, *Corn, cash, commerce*, 135. See also Brady, *William Huskisson and Liberal reform*, 34–5.
77 G. Croly, 'Domestic politics', BEM xi (Feb. 1822), 242–9 at p. 248. John Galt shared Croly's estimate of the degree of deflation – roughly 50%: 'On the agricultural distresses', 436. Galt professed similar views on government expenditure: 'Hints to the country gentlemen', 491. For Lauderdale's underconsumptionist critique of restricted money supplies see Gordon, *Political economy in parliament*, 47–8.
78 Tatham, *On the scarcity of money*, 16–17, 49. See also Galt, 'Hints to the country gentle-

located their criticisms of monetary policy in distinctive underconsumptionist readings of Britain's experience of economic depression in the early 1820s.

If deflationary monetary policy was indicted with causing the depression of trade and agriculture it followed that inflationary monetary reform was presented as an essential piece of corrective and constructive economic legislation. Strikingly, two commentators (one explicitly and one plagiaristically) quoted the same section of David Hume's essay, *Of money*, as an authoritative statement on the benefits of an expansive money supply: 'When money begins to flow in greater abundance than formerly, every thing takes a new face; labour and industry gain life; the merchant becomes more enterprising, the manufacturer more diligent and skilful, and even the farmer follows his plough with greater alacrity and attention.'[79] In parliament advocates of inflationary monetary reform also appealed to the authority of Hume. As C. C. Western observed, 'It was a very remarkable circumstance, that those two great writers, Locke and Hume, in considering the consequences which they anticipated from increasing the standard of value of the currency by diminishing its amount, had exactly described the state of things which at present existed.'[80] Of course not all such appropriations of Hume's monetary thought were either identical or accurate. Indeed in his argument for the relaxation of the monetary settlement of 1819 Copleston was at pains to replicate Hume's own distinction between inflation and monetary liquidity in an attempt to distance himself from those who rejected a convertible currency outright.[81] Yet what united those critics of the settlement of 1819 who invoked the intellectual authority of David Hume was the conviction that monetary policy could not be conceived of as an anodyne sphere of financial adminstration. If monetary policy had contracted economic activity then remedial legislation could expand and revivify it.[82]

---

men: letter II', 629; Anon., *A view of the causes of our late prosperity*, 17–18; Anon., *England may be extricated from her difficulties*, 12–25; Anon., *Brief thoughts on the agricultural report by a musing bee within the hive*, London 1821, 6; D. Robinson, 'The meeting of parliament', BEM xx (Dec. 1826), 859–72 at p. 864.

[79] Copleston, 'State of the currency', 259. Strikingly, Copleston imputed a Humean position on the productive effects of depreciation to his 'Letters to Mr Peel' of 1819, ibid. 258; H. Mathews did not acknowledge Hume in 'Thoughts on the present political aspects of the times', BEM viii (Feb. 1821), 483–96 at p. 494; Hume, 'Of money', repr. in *Hume*, 115–25 at p. 118. Malthus had also invoked Hume on the productive benefits of monetary liquidity: *The grounds of an opinion*, 32.

[80] C. C. Western, House of Commons (11 June 1822), Hansard n.s. vii. 890.

[81] Copleston, 'State of the currency', 259. Though he rejected Hume's advocacy of statutory devaluation Hume's commitment to a metallic currency and emphasis on the process of increasing the money supply rather than any objective state of liquidity appealed to Copleston: *Of money*, 119.

[82] Bimetallism, doubling the number of dividend payments, and limited liability for country banks were all strategies, 'for relaxing that tension . . . under which the currency now labours: Copleston, 'State of the currency', 264. See also Lowe, *The present state of England*, 140–1, and A. Baring on bimetallism (19 Mar. 1821), Hansard n.s. iv. 1327–8. On inconvertibility see Croly, 'Domestic politics', 242–9.

The power of monetary policy to influence economic conditions and to adjust relative property values was also debated in constitutional languages. Indeed contemporaries perceived that by raising the value of money the government had effectively redistributed wealth from debtor to creditor interests and had encroached on the prerogatives of private property. In parliament Attwood condemned 'the violent manner in which their measures had affected the rights of property'.[83] Not only was this process seen to transgress the boundaries of state action, it was also perceived to have undermined government's essentially constitutional function of maintaining a balance between the interests of different forms of property (in this case between debtors and creditors) within the propertied polity. Defining the 'balance of interests' was of course quintessentially subjective. Indeed, it has been argued that the resumption of cash payments was partly motivated by a conviction that wartime fortunes made during the suspension of cash payments were somehow illegitimate. In this view the return to gold restored the 'real' wealth of creditors which had been eroded by inflation.[84] Yet this retributive idea cannot account for a range of Tory responses to redistributive deflation. George Croly, for instance, did not celebrate resumption as a moral indictment of indebtedness. Rather, he rejected resumption's arbitrariness in increasing the real burden of debts such as rents:

> in this diminution of the national apparent wealth, which for all its temporary purposes, was as real as if it had been gold or diamonds, all incomes have been diminished but those of the landlord. His rent stands in the old characters of high prices and war. He must have his pound of flesh. It is so written in the bond. The grand remedy then must be, the reduction of the general rental.[85]

For Croly legislation had effectively forced landowners to violate the spirit, if not the letter, of tenancy agreements.[86] In a connected context one critic distinguished the legitimacy of the state's claim over that property which had effectively pledged by consensual taxation from the general inviolability of private property: the 'first and original faith of civil society', was 'to the property of the citizen and not to the demands of the creditor of the state'.[87] By presenting deflation as a legislative distortion of the real and relative values of private property Tory critics offered essentially constitutional critiques of the return to the gold standard.

The resumption of cash payments was commonly condemned as a measure which transformed the balance of interests within the state. As Tatham had

---

[83] M. Attwood, House of Commons (7 May 1822), *Hansard* n.s. vii. 388.
[84] Hilton, *Corn, cash, commerce*, 59–65.
[85] Croly, 'Domestic politics', 248.
[86] See also Anon., *A letter to the right. hon., the earl of Eldon on the present state of the agricultural lessees, and their right to relief from the payment of rent*, London 1822, 45.
[87] Anon., 'Whig retrenchment – and plan for the reduction of the national debt', *BEM* xxiii (Mar. 1828), 341–50 at p. 349.

warned in 1819, 'It will unhinge all property, which is the cement of the state: it will stop the circulation of currency, which is the blood of the nation, and it will destroy that equilibrium by which the whole constitution is so admirably poised.'[88] Similarly, Samuel Turner identified the agrarian depression of 1822 as a consequence of the distortion of relative property values by monetary legislation: 'it is solely owing to some gross errors in political regulations, whereby this annual mass of wealth is not distributed in due proportions amongst the different classes of society according to their relative situations'.[89] Others viewed the resumption as a blatant, if unintended, elevation of the 'funded interest' over the agricultural, manufacturing and commercial interests which relied on credit.[90]

One corollary of such positions was a tendency to identify the interests of the suffering 'productive classes' with the financial needs of the state. For resumption was also seen to have increased the burden of public debt at a stroke: 'The state has hitherto been taxed with extravagance; let us not have to charge it with madness too; and add to the imprudence of borrowing when money was cheap, the folly of rendering it dear before we begin to repay.'[91] Notwithstanding their indictments of the redistributive effects of deflation, however, Tory prints offered various arguments against compensating for deflation by lightening the burden of public debt through reducing the rate of interest paid to holders of government stock.[92] Copleston's primary argument against such 're-composition' was that government, like private individuals, should be constrained from the arbitrariness of readjusting contracts:

> If, at the time of borrowing money, it [government] expressly declared that the then price of gold was immaterial to the contract, and that the intrinsic value of the sum borrowed was not at all affected by that circumstance; if, in pursuance of this principle, it compelled every creditor, public and private, to accept a payment of his due after the same rate – if individuals were forbidden, under severe penalties, to resort to that mode of adjusting the value of the money that passed between them – is it allowable, upon any principle of right or justice, for the same government, when it comes to discharge the debt, to plead the difference of value which it denied before?[93]

---

[88] Tatham, *On the scarcity of money*, 62. See also Anon., *A letter to the earl of Liverpool on agricultural distress; its extent, cause and remedy by an old Tory*, London 1822, 27.
[89] Turner, *Considerations*, 64–5. This was an explicit response to Londonderry's disclaimer of Feb. 15 1822: see n. 92 below.
[90] Anon., *A letter to the earl of Liverpool* (1814), 38, 79, 89, 95, 106; Boyes (despite his critique of the inconvertible system), *Observations to the right hon. Lord Stourton*, 26–8; Wright, *Remarks on the erroneous opinions*, 23–4.
[91] Anon., *A letter to the earl of Liverpool* (1814), 75. See also Hopkins, *Economical enquiries*, 104, and Johnstone, 'Our domestic policy: II', 943–4.
[92] See Londonderry's justification of the reduction of interest payments to public creditors: House of Commons (15 Feb. 1822), *Hansard* n.s. vi. 375.
[93] Copleston, 'State of the currency', 241.

While John Galt's critique of readjusting contracts differed from Copleston's he also appealed to constitutionalist notions of accountability and legitimacy. He observed that, above the poorest classes, the 'public creditor' ranged the entire social scale and frequently did not possess the parliamentary franchise: 'The great mass of public creditors had nothing on earth to do with ministers or their loans, or the contractors of these loans, for they have not, and have never had, representatives in Parliament.'[94] Despite his condemnation of the deflationary and redistributive consequences of the resumption of cash payments therefore Galt insisted that revising the terms of the national contract was tantamount to the abuse of power.[95] Moreover, for Galt, reducing interest payments to government stockholders threatened to undermine the positive distributive effects of the national debt's structure, in diffusing capital and distributing interest payments among small, often provincial, lenders.[96]

Unsurprisingly the magnification of the real burden of the public debt by deflation generated debate on how the interest and capital of the debt could be repaid.[97] Some Tory critics of deflation considered that the taxation of property was a legitimate response to a debt incurred and magnified by a propertied polity. Hence Galt advocated a flat income tax of 10 per cent for an unspecified but limited period payable by all forms of property.[98] For Copleston, property taxation was an instrument which could redress the redistributive action of monetary deflation. So, unlike Galt, he did wish government to differentiate between funds and land in the schedules of his proposed property tax:

> First, then, if a *perpetual* tax of 2 per cent. be laid on land, let there be a tax of 10 per cent. on funded property for five years. The revenue from the funds alone will be three millions. Secondly, in order to encourage still more the transfusion of wealth from money to land, let the landholder have the option of redeeming his 2 per cent. land tax upon advantageous terms, e.g. transferring to government stock producing one-tenth *less* than his annual tax.[99]

Clearly, Copleston responded to the redistributive effects of monetary policy with an explicit proposal for the corrective redistribution of wealth by the fiscal state. Other proposals for a one-off capital levy were condemned in Tory prints as strategies which would compound the transfer of property effected by the resumption. Richard Heathfield's plan for a capital levy of 15 per cent on the value of real property in order to redeem government stock met with vigorous criticism along these lines in *Blackwood's*. His reviewer

---

94 Galt, 'On the agricultural distresses', 437.
95 Tatham even suggested that since the middle classes were losing 'most' from deflation, they should be compensated with enfranchisement: *On the scarcity of money*, 49–50.
96 Galt, 'Hints to the country gentlemen: letter II', 626.
97 On the impact of deflation on the tax burden see Anon., *A letter to the earl of Liverpool* (1814), 35, 54–5, and Anon., *A letter to the earl of Liverpool* (1822), 13, 19.
98 Galt, 'On the agricultural distresses', 438–40.
99 Copleston, 'State of the currency', 265.

objected that the scheme would dramatically tighten the already acute pressure on credit by forcing owners of real property to borrow in order to pay their levy.[100] This reviewer also condemned Heathfield's fundamental assumption that debt redemption was the responsibility of 'real' property: 'debt has been contracted in defence of the rights and liberties of all classes of the community'.[101] Moreover, as one critic subsequently commented, paying off the fundholders could kill off a mechanism which converted capital into revenue and raised the level of demand in the economy.[102] Clearly, financial and monetary policy were perceived as inter-connected interfaces between the state and private property in early nineteenth-century Britain.

Technical debates on the monetary standard therefore comprised only one element in an expansive discourse on constitutional, economic and financial implications of deflation during the early 1820s. By attributing deflation and depression to legislation many critics rejected the notion that monetary policy was 'neutral' and searched out positive functions for it. Owing to the instrumentality of legislation such 'economic' debates were inseparable from a constitutionalist discourse on the legitimacy of the state's agency in the redistribution of property from debtor to creditor interests and in the effective transformation of relative property values. Subsequent debates on the possibility of adjusting for the impact of deflation on the real burden of the public debt through taxation reforms were conducted in similar constitutionalist languages.

Banking, community and crisis, 1825–30

During the second half of the 1820s bullionist policymakers reached beyond the mechanism of the gold standard in attempts to regulate the issue policies of provincial banks. Bullionists interpreted the commercial and banking crises of 1825 as consequences of the over-extension of credit by country banks.[103] This reading of contemporary economic experience generated the

[100] Anon., 'Elements for a plan for the liquidation of the national debt by Richard Heathfield', *BEM* vi (Jan. 1820), 441–8, 446–8. The reviewer argued that Heathfield's, *Elements of a plan for the liquidation of the national debt &c*, London 1819, reworked Archibald Hutcheson's scheme of 1717.
[101] Anon., 'Elements of a plan for the liquidation of the national debt by Richard Heathfield', 445. See also Anon., 'Whig retrenchment and plan for the reduction of the national debt', 349.
[102] Ibid. 342. The latter reviewed articles by J. R. McCulloch on the national debt in *ER* xlvi (Oct. 1827), 390–414, and xlvii (Jan. 1828), 59–86. Among further economic and sociological defences of the national debt and the sinking fund were the following: Sir F. P. Eliot ['Falkland'], *Letters on the political and financial situation of the country in the year 1814, addressed to the earl of Liverpool*, London 1814, 388–94; *Speech of the earl of Liverpool*, 41–6; W. Jacob, 'Thoughts on the funding system and its effects', *QR* xxxi (Mar. 1825), 311–27; J. Miller, 'Past and present state of the country', ibid. xxxii (June 1825), 160–97 at pp. 182–6.
[103] R. Peel, House of Commons (24 May 1819), *Hansard* xl. 683.

Banking Co-partnership Act of May 1826, the banning of notes under £5 in England and Wales, and an attempt to extend this restriction to Scotland.[104] It follows that critics of bullionism shifted their emphasis from the effects of deflation to the social, economic and constitutional consequences of banking reforms which contracted local money supplies. Indeed it was common in Tory monetary discourse to identify bullionist policy as the monetary root of the crises of 1825. Such interpretations of this crisis were frequently combined with indictments of freer trade and with protectionism. For banking reform was also debated in terms of its economic impact on the balance between production and consumption and on interaction between different interests or sectors within the economy. This continued challenge to bullionist monetary policy evinced a range of alternative positions on the economic and social significance of banking legislation.

The social morality of early nineteenth-century monetary thought has usually been confined within a bullionist paradigm. Indeed, before he denounced the excessive deflation of 1819 Edward Copleston maintained that inflation caused by an extended money supply was disproportionately damaging to the labouring classes since their incomes did not tend to adjust promptly to changes in the exchangeable value of money: a convertible and stable money supply was for Copleston a way of avoiding the social damage caused by inflation.[105] Yet this reading was not a normative Tory view of the social impact of monetary policy but was only one feature of a broader monetary discourse which offered numerous alternative readings of the social significance of banking and monetary reform. The effective 'metallisation' of the currency through the abolition of small notes was frequently debated as a question of distribution. Some defenders of an extensive circulation justified a coin currency of small denominations in social terms: the intrinsic value of coin would protect the labouring classes from the insecurity of holding notes during runs on the banks.[106] Others predicted ruinous social consequences for the abolition of small notes however. In parliament William Cobbett condemned the proposed legislation of 1826 as a further instalment of deflation which damaged the labouring classes insisting 'that the last sixteen years have witnessed four sudden changes in the value of money; that every change has been attended with great masses of ruin; that, at every change, the working classes have been sunk deeper and deeper into poverty and want'.[107] William Johnstone also argued that 'metallisation' would deprive the poorer

---

[104] Fetter, *The development*, 107–24; Hilton, *Corn, cash, commerce*, 220–31; Collins, *Money and banking*, 17–20; E. V. Morgan, *The theory and practice of central banking, 1797–1813*, Cambridge 1943, 87–90.
[105] Waterman, *Revolution, economics and religion*, 186–8.
[106] Macdonnell, *Free trade*, 374; T. Lethbridge, House of Commons (14 Feb. 1826), *Hansard* n.s. xiv. 358.
[107] W. Cobbett, House of Commons (20 Feb. 1826), ibid. 571–2. See also Folkestone on the depression in Paisley, House of Lords (4 May 1826), *Hansard* xv. 833.

classes of their means of payment and would tend to exacerbate the concentration of wealth and capital already fostered by free trade and the balance of taxation.[108] Others defended small notes using distinctive readings of the distributive characteristics of the British economy. For Sir Walter Scott the proposed extension of small notes legislation to Scotland threatened a system of paper credit which had facilitated economic activity and sustained entire communities: 'It is to be hoped that experimental legislation will pause ere consigning a race which is contented with its situation to banishment, because they only offer at present hardy virtues and industry to the stock of national prosperity, instead of communicating largely to national wealth.'[109] Scott maintained that the application of strict convertibility rules to the issuing policies of Scottish joint-stock banks would cause banks to pass on the burden of purchasing gold to the Scottish producing and employing classes.[110] He maintained, moreover, that imposing 'metallisation' and strict convertibility on Scotland would reduce the distributive scope of the paper credit currency to that of English convertible notes which, 'never circulate like blood to the heart, and from thence to the extremities, but are current within a limited circle'.[111]

David Robinson's critiques of 'metallisation' in England and Wales were conducted in similar terms to those of Scott for Scotland.[112] Robinson's position grounded on the perception of banknotes as representatives of both currency and credit.[113] Since credit was frequently used as capital in both agriculture and manufactures Robinson maintained that to contract the currency was effectively to limit available capital. By providing foci for idle capital Robinson maintained that country banks had aided the financing of the Napoleonic wars:

> they formed points throughout the nation, in which the money of all ranks and callings concentrated, the moment it was rendered idle. . . . Had it not

---

[108] W. Johnstone, 'Emigration', BEM xxiii (May 1828), 615–20 at p. 619, and 'Our domestic policy: II', 943–6.

[109] [Sir W. Scott], *A third letter to the editor of the Edinburgh Weekly Journal from Malachi Malagrowther, Esq., on the proposed change of currency and other late alterations, as they affect, or are intended to affect, the kingdom of Scotland*, London–Edinburgh 1826, 33–4, and also *A second letter to the editor of the Edinburgh Weekly Journal, from Malachi Malagrowther, Esq. on the proposed change of currency and other late alterations, as they affect or are intended to affect the kingdom of Scotland*, 3rd edn, Edinburgh 1826, 55–6.

[110] Idem, *A third letter*, 21.

[111] Idem, *Thoughts on the proposed change of currency and other late alterations, as they affect, or are intended to affect the kingdom of Scotland*, Edinburgh 1826, 33. This essay is identical to *A letter to the editor of the Edinburgh Weekly Journal, from Malachi Malagrowther Esq. on the proposed change of currency and other late alterations, as they affect or are intended to affect the kingdom of Scotland*, 3rd edn, Edinburgh 1826.

[112] D. Robinson, 'Letters of E. B. Waverley Esq. to Mr Malagrowther Esq.', BEM xix (May 1826), 596–607.

[113] Idem, 'The country banks and the Bank of England: II', ibid. xxiii (Feb. 1828), 197–213 esp. pp. 198, 201–2, and 'Political economy: IV', 37.

been for these Banks, money would not have been found for carrying on the war; at any rate, government would have had to borrow at an almost double rate of interest, and in consequence, the taxes would have been at this moment many millions more than they are.[114]

Thus he could argue that a major social impact of a contracted metallic currency (combined with tighter credit) would be the reduction of both wages and employment.[115] Indeed Robinson insisted that 'notes... formed a gigantic source of employment for capital and labour' and their suppression 'forms an important part of that hateful and ruinous policy which this country is acting on, of grinding the middle and lower classes to powder, for the benefit of a comparatively few overgrown houses'.[116] Far from possessing a monopoly over social morality bullionism was condemned by many for the social costs of its impact on distribution within the British economy.

Corollary banking reforms – in particular, the extension of Bank of England branch banking – were debated in similar distributive terms. Provincial banks, whether Scottish joint-stock or English 'country', were defended as institutions which combined the interests of different social classes and economic interests. Scott's defence of Scottish banking was not dictated solely by his commitment to Scottish particularism but drew largely on such socio-economic positions. As Scottish banks rested chiefly on landed security Scott could view them as a socially cohesive interface between commerce, manufactures and agriculture.[117] Bi-weekly settlements between banks imposed a moralising structure of self-regulation, where financial property policed itself and matched private interest with public benefit.[118] More significantly for Scott, the extension of Bank of England branches threatened some unique services offered by Scottish banks. He asserted that the readiness of Scottish banks to offer small cash credits to the poorer classes had tended to reduce crime rates.[119] Robinson defended the vilified 'country' banks of England and Wales using a similar moral language of community. Unlike metropolitan banks or provincial branches of the Bank of England, country banks served the entire community.[120] Before the advent of savings banks the deposit facilities of country banks had not only fostered thrift but also the means of participation in economic change and in social advance-

---

114 Idem, 'The country banks and the Bank of England', 736.
115 Idem, 'Letters of E. B. Waverley Esq. to Mr Malagrowther Esq.', 604; 'The country banks and the Bank of England: I', 738, 741;'The country banks and the Bank of England: II', 205–7.
116 Idem, 'Political economy: IV', 37–8. See also E. D. Davenport, House of Commons (5 June 1828), *Hansard* n.s. xix. 1054.
117 Scott, *Thoughts on the proposed change of currency*, 33–6.
118 Idem, *A second letter*, 35–6. Huskisson rejected Scott's views on the relative security of Scotch banks: Hilton, *Corn, cash, commerce*, 222–3.
119 Scott, *A second letter*, 42–8.
120 Robinson, 'The country banks and the Bank of England: I', 735, 741–2, 750–1.

ment: 'The innumerable artisans, mechanics, and labourers, who leave their servitude and enter into business as masters, are in one way or another, mainly indebted to the country banks.'[121] For Robinson, then, the lending, depositing, and discounting policies of country banks were crucial to the growth of the 'middling classes' who in turn encouraged the diffusion of wealth, extended social gradation and provided a range of employments for the lower classes. He also defended country banks as institutions which united the interests of small market towns with those of surrounding rural districts: 'The bill currency forms, in a very large degree, the foundation of trade and manufactures, and indirectly it forms in a large degree that of agriculture. ... Upon the country banks, the bill-currency depends almost wholly for existence.'[122] Thus country banks were defended against bullionist banking reforms as mechanisms which mobilised demand within the domestic economy and as institutions which fostered social cohesion.[123]

Far from accepting the bullionist reading of the financial and commercial crisis of 1825 many commentators blamed bullionism itself. In the 'orthodox' bullionist interpretation the crisis was a direct consequence of speculative over-trading which had been encouraged by the issue and lending policies of country banks.[124] According to bullionist theory the adverse state of the exchanges could be reversed and commerce revived by contracting the domestic circulation.[125] Of course, some critics of bullionism simply blamed the Bank of England for the crisis.[126] Others offered more sweeping criticisms not only maintaining that monetary contraction was an inappropriate response to external drain but also arguing that such strategies would deepen the depression by depriving the nation of its domestic means of trade and payment.[127] Thus David Robinson attributed the crisis to a combination of commercial conditions with three features of public policy: the government's narrow definition of money, the clash between monetary policy and national debt management and the application of strict convertibility rules to bank issues.[128] Robinson maintained that the agricultural recovery of 1824 had mobilised the demand necessary for a general recovery but had also enlarged imports. Simultaneously government debt redemption strategies had poured capital into an already replete market. While some of this capital operated to

---

[121] Ibid. 738. Bank of England branches did not take small deposits: ibid. 750.
[122] Idem, 'The country banks and the Bank of England', 737.
[123] See also Turner, *Considerations*, esp. pp. 54–5.
[124] F. Robinson, House of Commons (10 Feb. 1826), *Hansard* n.s. xiv. 166–7, 168–93, and R. Peel, ibid. 286–302. See also Hilton, *Corn, cash, commerce*, esp. pp. 220–31.
[125] Fetter attributed the formalisation of this theory to James Pennington c. 1827: *The development*, 130–3.
[126] A. Baring, House of Commons (10 Feb. 1826), *Hansard* n.s. xiv. 205; M. Attwood, House of Commons (13 Feb. 1826), ibid. 302.
[127] Robinson, 'The letters of E. B. Waverley Esq. to Mr. Malagrowther Esq.', 603.
[128] Idem, 'Public distress', *BEM* xix (Apr. 1826), 429–46.

increase consumption most of it was channelled into speculation on high prices.[129] This capital swelled the existing superabundance created by the action of deflation on assets after 1819 and encouraged speculation.[130] When production and consumption reached equilibrium prices stabilised but speculative imports continued and eventually flooded the markets.[131] Distress spread from sector to sector and demands for accommodation pressurised the banks and precipitated failures. Commercial panic was generalised by bullionist policies of monetary contraction which were intended to reverse the exchanges and counteract the gold efflux but instead undermined the domestic means of trade.[132] This, Robinson argued, was the predictable consequence of a monetary settlement based on bullionism not on the needs of domestic commerce. Not only did monetary contraction directly reduce the domestic means of payment, it was also seen to annihilate the banks' capacity to accommodate legitimate enterprise by precipitating a general withdrawal of deposits.[133]

Such detailed indictments of bullionism as the cause of crisis in 1825–6 were accompanied by more general criticisms of the combined consequences of bullionist policies and freer trade. This connection between corn-law and currency reform was no new feature of Tory economic discourse. Indeed opponents of corn-law reform had frequently emphasised the instability inherent in combining a monetary system dependent on gold with a commercial system which encouraged more frequent international bullion transfers.[134] As M. Fletcher pointed out, imports of raw produce would tend to command specie not manufactured goods or other equivalents; deflationary pressures on British prices caused by such drains of bullion to foreign nations were not likely to re-attract gold until after monetary contraction had throttled domestic trade.[135] On the contrary, advocates of bullionism and free trade began to justify them as mutual necessities. Freeing up trade was presented partly as the removal of impediments to the action of monetary policy on the state of the exchanges.[136] Thus the commercial and banking crisis of

---

[129] Ibid. 429.
[130] On the significance of capital exports to finance South American mining speculation see Macdonnell, *Free trade*, 340; on the state of supply (therefore price) as the dominant influence on speculative imports see Robinson, 'The country banks and the Bank of England: II', 203–5.
[131] Idem, 'Public distress', 430, 439–40.
[132] Ibid. esp. pp. 441–6; Robinson, 'The letters of E. B. Waverley Esq., to Mr Malagrowther', esp. p. 603; Macdonnell, *Free trade*, esp. pp. 342–5.
[133] Robinson, 'The country banks and the Bank of England: II', esp. pp. 210–11.
[134] For example, Jacob, *Considerations*, 194; Anon., *An address to the nation on the relative importance of agriculture and manufactures*, 17–18; Preston, *Address to the fundholder*, 25.
[135] Fletcher, 'Freedom of commerce', esp. pp. 288–90.
[136] Anon., *On the relation of corn and currency*, London 1819, 1–3, 13, 27, 37, and Hilton, *Corn, cash, commerce*, 132–5, 280–1, 303. On the 1822 corn law as an attempt to adjust corn prices to compensate for deflation see Wright, *Remarks on the erroneous opinions*, esp. p. 28.

1825–6 rendered criticism of the holistic combination of a bullionist banking policy with freer trade all the more poignant. When Lord Redesdale defended his resolutions against the liberalisation of the corn trade in 1827 he made precisely such a connection between corn and currency: 'The experience . . . of the year 1826 justifies the assertion in the 13th Resolution . . . that it is most probable that foreign corn imported into this country will always be paid for in money, and not by a corresponding export of British manufactures, or other commodities.'[137] For many protectionists this fusion of freer trade with bullionist banking policy threatened ruinous consequences in the regular contraction of the domestic means of trade to meet external specie drains.[138] These combined critiques of the 'liberal' orthodoxy on corn and currency were firmly established features of Tory economic discourse long before the intellectual conflicts of the 1840s.

Banking reforms were also debated as questions of central/local relations in Tory monetary discourse. The fusion of monetary and constitutional questions was most pronounced in the public correspondence of Sir Walter Scott and J. W. Croker. According to J. G. Lockhart, Scott's monetary contributions 'produced in Scotland a sensation not, perhaps, inferior to that of Drapier's letters in Ireland; a greater one, certainly, than any political tract had excited in the British public since the appearance of Burke's Reflections on the French Revolution' forcing a response from J. W. Croker, 'the semi-official organ of Lord Liverpool's Government', in the *London Courier*.[139] Scott maintained that the proposed suppression of Scottish small notes was symptomatic of a general Westminster impulse to assimilate Scottish institutions.[140] For Scott, the imperial strength of the United Kingdom derived from the diverse identities of component nations not from their suppression through centralisation or coercion.[141] More specifically he suggested that the suppression of small notes was unconstitutional in its encroachment on the 'Scottish laws of private right'.[142] Croker contested Scott's constitutionalist

---

[137] *Observations upon the importation of foreign corn: with the resolutions moved by Lord Redesdale in the House of Lords, March 29, 1827; and his speech thereupon, May 15, 1827*, London 1828, 116–17. See also Redesdale, House of Lords (29 Mar. 1827), *Hansard* n.s. xviii. 120–8.
[138] Macdonnell, *Free trade*, 345; Robinson, 'The public distress', 445.
[139] J. G. Lockhart, *Narrative of the life of Sir Walter Scott*, London 1906, repr. London 1931, 514. Scott's intrusion into monetary debate was a direct consequence of his personal bankruptcy following the collapse of the publishing house of Constable in January 1826: ibid. 498–513. For wider recognition of the controversy between Malachi Malagrowther (Scott) and Edward Brawardine Waverley (Croker) see Grovenor, House of Lords (17 Mar. 1826), *Hansard* xiv. 1392, and *The Gladstone diaries*, ed. H. C. G. Matthew, Oxford 1978, vi. 238–39, 241.
[140] Scott, *Thoughts on the proposed change of currency*, 7–9, 13, 18. On reform of the suppression of small notes beside reform of the army and naval establishments, the Scottish judicature, stamp office and revenue boards see *A second letter*, 71–5.
[141] Ibid. 22, 27–8, 81. Scott suggested (pp. 23–5) a voting pact between Scottish and Irish MPs on the small notes question.
[142] Idem, *Thoughts on the proposed change of currency*, 52–3.

reading and invoked the Small Notes Act of 1765 to legitimate Westminster's intervention in the Scottish currency.[143] Identifying the currency as a totem of imperial sovereignty and identity Croker maintained that 'the framers of the Union admitted and established, both in *law* and *policy*, the *principle of assimilation*, ... when, in the process of time, a deviation from the similarity of currency took place in Scotland, the Imperial Parliament of 1765 stepped in to remove the most prominent difference'.[144] Though the public spat between Waverley and Malagrowther was specifically concerned with the character of the Union they did strike chords with more general defences of local liberties against the encroachments of banking reform. David Robinson presented Bank of England branches as structures which were 'armed by Government' and imposed on the provinces.[145] Indeed, the 'constitutionality' of bullionist banking reforms was not debated primarily as a jurisdictional question in Tory discourse. Rather, the intrusions of the centre into local banking liberties were challenged for their potential threats to the social and economic functions performed by local, independent institutions.[146] By threatening the essentially local underpinnings of 'the property and weal of the community', banking reforms were perceived not only to transgress the accepted boundaries of the central state but also to undermine some essential social and economic functions performed within existing 'permissive' legislation.[147] In recognising the social and economic significance of monetary and banking legislation, critics of 'bullionist' banking reform did not therefore seek to transform the economic and social profile of the early nineteenth-century state.[148]

---

[143] J. W. Croker, *Two letters on Scottish affairs from Edward Brawardine Waverley, Esq. to Malachi Malagrowther Esq.*, London–Edinburgh 1826, 41–3 (letter ii).
[144] Ibid. 44.
[145] Robinson, 'The country banks and the Bank of England: I', 739–40. For defences of provincial banks in Ireland and Wales see House of Lords (17 Mar. 1826), *Hansard* n.s. xiv. 1394–5, and E. J. Curteis, House of Commons (28 Apr. 1828), ibid. xix. 191.
[146] See the character of defences of the Scottish banking system in parliament: House of Commons (14, 16 Mar. 1826), ibid. xiv. 1358–60, 1381–88. On Wales see M. Attwood, House of Commons (22 May 1828), ibid. xix. 860. On Adam Smith's defence of Scottish banking see Alborn, *Conceiving companies*, 88–90.
[147] Robinson, 'The country banks and the Bank of England: II', 197, and 'The country banks and the Bank of England: I', 734.
[148] Idem, 'The country banks and the Bank of England: II', 211–13, and Macdonnell, *Free trade*, 370–3.

The assumptions and speculations of the Bullion Report chased plain everyday opinion from the field, and were hailed as matters possessing the truth of Divine Revelation; decisive experiment has since covered them with refutation.[149]

As David Robinson observed, far from dominating monetary debate during the first decades of the nineteenth century bullionism was consistently challenged. The 'Liberal-Tory' commitment to the gold standard was not permitted to extinguish a vibrant discourse which contested the notion that monetary policy was 'neutral'. Tory commentators were prominent in these debates on the constitutional, social and economic effects of altering the value and availability of money. Thus, in January 1830 one such reviewer rejected the idea that bullionism held a stranglehold over Tory political economy and offered an alternative reading of the latter's recent intellectual history.[150] Far from being unanimously welcomed as a measure of retributive and restorative justice the return to the gold standard had been widely condemned using conservative constitutionalist languages: the erroneous and excessive deflation of 1819 had illegitimately transformed relative property values and distorted the balance of propertied interests in favour of the funds.[151] Subsequent reforms were condemned for raising further the redistributive profile of the state and for institutionalising commercial and financial crises by compelling the contraction of domestic credit and currency in response to bullion efflux.[152] Moreover, through the banking reforms of the late 1820s the state was perceived to have trespassed on the local liberties of banks and on the distributive benefits these brought.[153] This description of the contours of contemporary public debate confirmed the importance afforded to the positive functions of monetary and banking policy in Tory economic discourse. If monetary policy was not 'neutral' then the impact of such legislation on the distribution of wealth and on the balance and sustainability of economic change needed to be made explicit. Thus monetary discourse contributed to a Tory political economy which was less concerned to identify the origins of economic growth than to underline the social and economic responsibilities of legislation within the constitutional context of a propertied polity.

---

[149] Robinson, 'The country banks and the Bank of England: I', 735. See also William Jacob's rebuttal of bullionism's intellectual status: *Considerations*, 191, and Croker (or Miller), 'Internal policy', 242–3.
[150] Ibid. 228–78.
[151] Ibid. 241, 245–50, 252, 254–5.
[152] Ibid. 260.
[153] Ibid. 259

5

The Limits of Economic Sovereignty, 1830–1847

'This was the whole secret of the *"fluctuations"* which had taken place in England for the last twenty-four years. It was all wretched nonsense to talk about *"overtrading"* and *"overpopulating"*, and *"overspeculation"*, and of twenty other Malthusian theories. These were the mere phenomena which a contracted currency presents': T. Attwood, House of Commons (30 May 1839), *Hansard* 3rd ser. xlvii. 1141.

The financial catastrophes of 1825–6 reverberated in British economic discourse and shocked policymakers into the realisation that a convertible currency could not guarantee stable monetary conditions. The restrictions which had been imposed on the independence of country banks in 1825–6 came into operation in 1829 aimed at encouraging provincial banks of issue towards the relative security of joint-stock formation. But after 1832 successive governments focused their search for an institutional framework for monetary stability on the Bank of England itself. The renewals of the Bank's charter in 1833 and 1844 raised demanding questions not only about the public accountability and public responsibilities of the Bank but also about the boundaries of legislation. Partly consequent on the Bank's failures to regulate itself during the 1830s, the renewal of her charter in 1844 attempted to formalise the public and private spheres of the Bank's activities by separating the public functions of the Bank's issue department from the profit-making sphere of banking.[1]

The intellectual history of banking during the thirties and forties has often been presented as a duel between the 'banking' and 'currency' schools which was fought somewhere remote from contemporary 'politics' and which resulted in reforms which laid lasting foundations for British financial institutions.[2] Of course, some historians have located these banking reforms within the broader context of nineteenth-century state formation but this 'political' aspect has usually been given a distinctively 'Liberal' twist.[3] Indeed, the insti-

---

[1] On banking policy between 1830 and 1847 see *British banking statutes and reports, 1832–1928*, ed. T. E. Gregory, Oxford 1929, i. pp. ix–lx; Clapham, *The Bank of England*, ii. 116–216; Morgan, *Theory and practice*, 100–42.
[2] See above pp. 89–91, and Fetter, *The development*, 129–33, 187–94. L. H. White has demonstrated the existence of a third ideological camp, 'the free banking school', in *Free banking in Britain: theory, experience and debate, 1800–1845*, Cambridge 1984, esp. pp. 51–76.
[3] J. K. Horsefield, 'The origins of the Bank Charter Act, 1844', in T. S. Ashton and

tutionalisation of bullionism in the Bank Charter Act of 1844 is customarily viewed as a defining feature of the mid-Victorian state.[4] More specifically, the bullionism of Robert Peel has been viewed as a central instrument of the restrictive, evangelical economic philosophy which motivated the economic reforms of his brand of 'Liberal' Conservatism.[5] As a corollary, historians have tended to neglect the monetary thought of Peel's critics and to assume that the settlement of 1844 was not seriously challenged in the economic discourse of Conservatives or in the wider public debate.[6] Yet if we step outside the paradigm of bullionist banking and monetary policy a richer and more varied intellectual landscape emerges. The institutional response of bullionists like Peel was vigorously contested by a range of critics who resisted the assumption that by stipulating reserve specifications and regulating the Bank's issue policy the legislature could create conditions for monetary stability. While some free traders insisted that banking, like commerce, should be unfettered by legislative regulation, a range of other critics (of varied partisan hues) identified important functions for the legislation which governed money and banks. Within this broad intellectual context a distinctively Conservative strain of monetary criticism challenged the hegemony of Peelite bullionism in Conservative economic discourse.

Increasingly, Conservative critics blended their critiques of bullionism with their criticisms of freer trade and of corn-law reform in particular. Of course, it would be crude to suggest any necessary fusion of 'anti-bullionism' with protectionism. Yet it remains helpful to situate the explicit intellectual connections drawn by contemporaries beside some broader assumptions about the origins of stable and balanced economic activity which underpinned both monetary and protectionist discourses. By identifying distributive implications both for readily available credit and for a domestic means of payment which was insulated from foreign exchange fluctuations Conservative critics underlined the fundamental importance of monetary and banking legislation. Monetary and banking policy were projected as instruments which would function in tandem with protection by creating conditions where consumption could meet production in the home market thereby moderating economic fluctuation and its social consequences. At the same time, tailoring currency and credit to the needs of domestic trade was per-

---

R. Sayers (eds), *Papers in English monetary history*, Oxford 1953, 109–125. Harling noted the lack of a recent history of relations between the state and the Bank: *The waning of 'Old Corruption'*, 5.

[4] Ibid. 9–11.

[5] Hilton, 'Peel: a reappraisal', 600–4, 606–14, and *Age of atonement*, 224–5. For contemporary observations of Peel's dogmatism on banking and currency see Croker, 'Close of Sir Robert Peel's administration', 161, and J. C. Colquhoun, *The effects of Sir R. Peel's administration on the political state and prospects of England*, 2nd edn, London 1847, 23.

[6] Stewart, *The politics of protection*, 115–18. Macintyre dealt briefly with monetary aspects of protectionism in, 'Lord George Bentinck and the protectionists', 150, 157 n. 48.

ceived as a strategy which could bind together the interests of the productive classes across the economy. This socio-economic discourse was shot through with essentially constitutionalist threads. The deflationary resumption of cash payments was perceived as an illegitimate intrusion of the state into the relative values of private property and resonated again in the context of the Great Reform Act. Erroneous monetary legislation was consistently identified as the root of commercial crisis and social distress and economic fluctuations periodically refocused the minds of critics on spelling out the social and economic functions of civil government. Bullionism and its applications were indicted in various ways with some measure of responsibility for the agricultural depression of the early 1830s and for the financial and commercial crises of 1836–7, 1839 and 1847. Thus, by identifying positive social and economic potential for 'anti-bullionist' monetary and banking reforms Conservatives offered strategies for the re-legitimation of legislation itself. Some critics perceived the social and economic influences of banking and monetary policies as a form of sovereignty over economic conditions which demanded regulation and assumed distinct social and economic responsibilities for government. Yet for others the defence of an independent Bank of England became a battle against the encroachments of the state on a private propertied establishment – a defence of the spirit of the 'old' constitution within the Reform of 1832.

The politics of deflation and contracted credit, 1830 – c. 1834

During the early 1830s policymakers focused on the policies and privileges of the Bank of England.[7] Of course, the public debate on monetary policy both followed and moulded the contours of this policy controversy. Yet the dominance of questions concerning the powers and responsibilities of the Bank did not emasculate continued debate on the origins and impact of monetary deflation and contracted credit. The Conservative periodicals shared with a range of other critics an insistence that economic fluctuations and social distress could be attributed to the deflationary and restrictive impact of legislation. What distinguished a distinctly Conservative strain of monetary criticism was the re-working of such arguments within particular readings of the causes and consequences of the Great Reform Act. For Conservative critics the strictly political purpose behind opposing bullionist monetary policy was to reclaim positive social and economic influences for legislation and to wipe out Radical claims that parliamentary reform was a necessary consequence of palpable misgovernment by a propertied oligarchy.

The identification of legislative roots for economic fluctuations was not an

---

[7] Clapham, *The Bank of England*, 116–30; Feaveryear, *The pound sterling*, 231–76. On the committee of secrecy to inquire into the Bank's charter in 1832 see *British banking statutes*, pp. xiii–xvi, 4–18.

exclusively Conservative intellectual phenomenon. Indeed an intense period of parliamentary petitioning on the culpability of monetary legislation culminated in Matthias Attwood's attempt to establish the legislative origins of successive depressions in parliament in 1833:

> The monetary system was screwed up in 1819; it was relaxed in 1824 and 1825, and distress prevailed when it was tightened, while prosperity followed its relaxation. The results up to 1818 and subsequent to 1823 were obviously the result of legislative interference with the money of the country; and, as it had produced, first distress, then prosperity, and now distress again, it was its duty [the House of Commons'] to look carefully to its own acts.[8]

In parliament and in print Conservatives were prominent supporters of Attwood's motion for a parliamentary inquiry into the economic consequences of monetary policy.[9] Again in 1835 and 1837 the Attwoods' most vocal supporters were Conservatives and some Whigs who openly rejected the monetary policy of the Whig government.[10] Critics of the reforms of 1819 and 1826 continued to estimate the degree of deflation at somewhere between 20 and 50 per cent. David Robinson maintained that the legislators of 1819 'never contemplated the possibility that they were effectuating an alteration in the value of money of from 30 to 50 per cent. Five per cent, they were told by such authorities as they referred to, was the extent of the alteration'.[11] Such estimates of the extent of monetary deflation may be inaccurate but as perceptions of the legislative origins of deflation they remain highly suggestive.

The case for attributing monetary deflation and contracted credit to legislation was bolstered by new geological and geographical perspectives on the exchangeable value of gold.[12] During the early 1830s critics of bullionism went beyond pointing out the futility of attempting to fix the value of gold to

---

[8] M. Attwood, House of Commons (22 Apr. 1833), *Hansard* 3rd ser. xvii. 392.
[9] Fetter suggested that Conservative voting on Attwood's motions presaged the schism of 1846: *The development*, 162.
[10] E. S. Cayley, House of Commons (1 June 1835), *Hansard* 3rd ser. xxviii. 265; Sir. G. Sinclair, House of Commons (2 June 1837), ibid. 1206.
[11] D. Robinson, 'The currency question', *BEM* xxvii (May 1830), 792–801 at p. 797. G. P. Scrope estimated deflation at 50% in 'The rights of industry and the banking system', *QR* xlvii (July 1832), 407–57 at p. 427. For slightly lower estimates see E. Edwards, 'Currency', ibid. xxxix (Apr. 1829), 451–75 at p. 460, and 'The effects of the variation of the currency', *BEM* xxvii (Jan. 1830), 59–71 at p. 62; J. Richards, House of Commons (22 Apr. 1833), *Hansard* 3rd ser. xvii. 435.
[12] Scrope debated William Jacob's, *An historical inquiry into the production and consumption of precious metals*, London 1831, in 'The rights of industry and the banking system', 421–5. Among Nilan's empirical sources for 'Distress of the country', 283–8 were John Miers, *Travels in Chile and La Plata*, London 1826, and Sir Henry George Ward, *Mexico in 1827*, London 1828. He probably also used either F. H. A. von Humboldt, *Personal narrative of travels to the equinoctial regions of the new continent during the years 1799–1804*, London 1814–29, or *Selections from the works of the Baron de Humboldt*, ed. J. Taylor, London 1824. On Scrope see above p. 66 n. 57.

argue that legislation itself had helped to increase the exchangeable value of gold. Edward Edwards observed that the resumption of cash payments had created a demand for gold which raised its exchangeable value worldwide.[13] While H. A. Nilan preferred to emphasise the decline of South American gold supplies, G. P. Scrope rejected the dominance of geology and reaffirmed the responsibility of legislation for a demand driven rise in the exchangeable value of gold.[14] He went on to suggest that economic fluctuations might be attributable to legislation which tied prices to a speciously 'fixed' gold standard: '*Price*, indeed, *being by law expressed in metal*, the price of metal itself cannot vary, however much its value in exchange for goods may sink or rise.'[15] Thus the Conservative periodicals embraced contemporary geology and geography not merely as topical guides to the extent of deflation but as empirical evidence for the legislative origins of deflation and its consequences in nineteenth-century Britain.

Criticism of the redistributive effects of the magnification of the real burden of debts through deflation remained prominent in Conservative economic discourse during the 1830s. Robert Southey drew on the reports of the Agricultural Committee of 1833 to argue that the chief source of agricultural distress was the insolvency of tenants caused by the continuing impact of deflation on fixed contracts.[16] Denying that agricultural depression was due to over-production Edwards isolated another lasting consequence of the resumption: 'its effect was to withdraw from the land a vast capital which, during the prosperous period of agriculture, had been vested in the improvement of the soil, – transferring it from the hands of the class of productive cultivators into the pockets of moneyed and non-producing capitalists'.[17] These long-term effects of the resumption were also indicted as sources of depression in the manufacturing sector. Scrope quoted from the Iron Masters' petition to Earl Grey of October 1831: 'In our humble opinion, the great cause which has been mainly instrumental in producing this depression in our respective trades, and among the productive classes of the country generally, is the attempt to render the rents, taxes, royalties, and other various engagements and obligations of the country, convertible *by law*, into gold at

---

13 Edwards, 'Currency', 464–6.
14 Nilan located the British resumption in a general post-Napoleonic return to metallic currencies: 'Distress of the country', *QR* xliii (May 1830) 278–304 at p. 288, and Scrope, 'The rights of industry and the banking system', 441. See also idem, *On credit currency, and its superiority to coin, in support of a petition to the establishment of a cheap, safe, and sufficient circulating medium*, London 1830, esp. pp. 13–15.
15 Idem, 'The rights of industry and the banking system', 421 (Scrope's emphasis).
16 Southey, 'On the corn laws', 236–8. W. Maginn also linked poverty directly to currency reform in 'The desperate system: poverty, crime and emigration', *FM* i (June 1830), 635–42, 641, and 'On national economy: no VII: "Free trade" – Col. Thompson's and Mr Booth's pamphlets', ibid. vii (July 1833), 103–12 at p. 112.
17 Edwards, 'Currency', 461.

£3.17.10½ per oz.'[18] As Sir Henry Willoughby maintained in parliament, 'It was true that the system which commenced in 1797, and continued up to 1819, was calculated to defraud creditors, persons of fixed incomes, and people of that description; but the error committed in 1819 defrauded debtors, manufacturers, and every individual connected with productive industry; and it was therefore an error of a much more dangerous character, and one that was followed by much more sweeping effects.'[19]

Commentators drew causal connections between monetary legislation and economic fluctuation in a number of ways. David Robinson had interpreted the monetary contraction of 1828–9 as a consequence of the government's national debt management in a capital market swelled by the deflation of 1819 and 1826.[20] His argument rested on the interchangeability of currency and capital. He maintained that in 1828 the capital market was swamped with redundant savings which had been deposited for want of opportunity to speculate. Robinson viewed this 'superabundance' partly as an effect of the act of 1819 but mainly as a consequence of reduced government borrowing in the convertible currency. He believed the banks' tendency to convert the idle money of capitalists into gold stimulated a general demand for the precious metal which encouraged capitalists to withdraw deposits in order to trade in gold and contracted the means of trade; 'the idle capital in its idleness, caused a scarcity of bills, and an excess of notes; it now reverses matters, and causes a scarcity of notes and an excess of bills'.[21] In less detail, Scrope also identified contraction of the means of trade as the key factor in the legislative origins of depression. For Scrope, the effective 'metallisation' of the currency by the laws of 1819 and 1826 was inherently restrictive:

> It has been attempted to make a greatly-diminished quantity of gold serve as a medium of exchange for a greatly-increased quantity of goods; to perform, in short, an operation, of which that executed by Procrustes was but a type, – to squeeze, clip, and cut down the full-grown commerce of Britain to fit the limits of its early and shrunken cradle.[22]

By connecting distress directly to legislation the Conservative periodicals debated monetary policy in essentially constitutional languages. At the heart of this discourse lay the perception that property had been redistributed by legislation. For Edwards, the act of 1819 distorted the relations of property within the polity; the resumption was, 'an act of barefaced robbery, as it enabled every creditor under the colour and sanction of the law, to exact a

---

[18] Scrope, 'The rights of industry and the banking system', 432. Idem, *The currency question freed from mystery*, London 1830, was summarised and cited in E. Edwards, 'Banking', QR xlii (Mar. 1830), 476–504 at pp. 499–505.
[19] Sir H. Willoughby, House of Commons (23 Apr. 1833), Hansard 3rd ser. xvii. 470.
[20] D. Robinson, 'The working of the currency', BEM xxv (Feb. 1829), 135–52.
[21] Ibid. 141.
[22] Scrope, 'The rights of industry and the banking system', 422. See also idem, *On credit currency*, 67–8.

pound sterling, measured by the present standard, for every depreciated pound note which he had lent'.[23] But beyond relations between creditors and debtors, one lasting consequence of the resumption was identified as a dissipation of general confidence in the established form of government. As Robinson expressed it, 'The consequences of those lamentable mistakes have done more to shake the attachment of the people to the established government, to produce a conviction of some defect in the organisation of the Legislature, than all the revolutionary efforts of the zealots in the miscalled cause of liberty at the commencement of Mr Pitt's war.'[24] Similarly Scrope believed that changes in the relative value of property had proved instrumental in destroying the political legitimacy of the propertied constitution:

> If we succeed in showing, that the unjust restrictions kept up by the present laws on the circulating medium of exchange, have had the effect . . . of silently but forcibly transferring a vast amount of property from the possession of one class to that of another, who had no right or title to it . . . it will be acknowledged that, until the laws which have perpetrated and continue to sanction this wholesale swindling are repealed, there is no safety for property; can there be any reliance on the stability of those other institutions, of which a confidence in the security of property is the indispensable foundation?[25]

Typically, Archibald Alison drew more precise connections between deflationary monetary policy and the Great Reform Act. To Alison it seemed that both 'the progress of social disorganisation' and 'the prostration of government' had been hastened by 'the fatal alterations in the monetary system, and the suppression of the small notes in 1826'.[26] The monetary reforms had increased the relative wealth and amplified the political voice of urban creditor interests, or, 'nearly doubled the strength of the town or democratic party, while it has reduced to a half the resources of productive and rural industry throughout the country'.[27] Thus, Alison contended that monetary reform had eroded the natural constituency of the Conservative party before 1832, had contributed to the distress which drove the lower classes to political radicalism, bolstered the electoral position of the Whigs and precipitated subsequent political, religious and fiscal concessions to urban 'democratic' interests.[28] Against a backcloth of popular radicalism and parliamentary reform, therefore, monetary reform was adumbrated as an essentially constitutional question in the Conservative periodicals.

---

[23] Edwards, 'The effects of variation in the currency', 63.
[24] Robinson, 'The currency question', 800.
[25] Scrope, 'The rights of industry', 419. See also J. Taylor, *A catechism of the currency*, 3rd edn, London 1836, pp. v–vi, viii.
[26] Alison, 'The progress of social disorganisation: the prostration of government', 526.
[27] Ibid. 533.
[28] Ibid. 534. Of course bank runs were employed during 1832 as weapons of political radicalism: Fetter, *The development*, 133–6. On the currency question and Thomas Attwood's 'Birmingham Political Union' see M. Brock, *The Great Reform Act*, London 1973, 58–9.

It follows that proposals for remedial legislation were also expressed in constitutional terms. As during 1819–22 most critics stopped short of advocating corrective strategies such as the legislative reduction of the terms of interest payable to the public's creditors but offered a wide range of proposals for remedial currency reform. Robinson urged the reinstitution of an inconvertible and unrestricted paper circulation while Scrope advocated a flexible standard which would alter with changes in the exchangeable value of gold and would isolate 'credit currency' from the ruinous social and economic consequences of sudden contraction.[29] While such proposals differed greatly in detail they were all designed to effect what Edwards called 'a *legitimate* diminution' in the exchangeable value of gold.[30] As Scrope observed, failure to reduce the standard would expose both the state and commercial confidence to the violent shock of another suspension of monetary legislation:

> Credit and confidence ... cannot exist in such an atmosphere of uncertainty as would prevail, were it once acknowledged that the only means whereby governments would or could lighten the evils of a continuous tendency of gold and silver to advance in value, were occasional *coups d'état* of this kind, by which the relations of every debtor and creditor in the state are violently, and without warning interfered with. Such a remedy were more injurious even than the disease.[31]

The purpose of currency reform in Conservative economic discourse was less to alter the profile of the state than to forestall the perceived constitutional and economic consequences of maintaining existing legislation.

If Conservative critics placed constitutional boundaries around the state's power to transform relative property values they nevertheless did assume some positive distributive functions for monetary legislation. Indeed, as one 'means of restoring *the happiness and prosperity of the people*', monetary reform was projected as a way of re-legitimating propertied government. In this vein Scrope challenged Owenite and Saint-Simonian ideological alternatives to free-trade Liberalism by offering a concept of 'social economy' in place of the competitive and individualistic orthodoxy.[32] That is to say, he attempted to shift the domain of political economy away from 'the means of increasing its [wealth's] aggregate amount', to a new intellectual territory where 'the welfare of the people is now universally acknowledged as the only legitimate

---

[29] Robinson, 'The working of the currency', 150; G. P. Scrope, *An examination of the bank charter question, with an inquiry into the nature of a just standard of value, and suggestions for the improvement of our monetary system*, London 1833, esp. pp. 26–9, and *Political economy for plain people applied to the past and present state of Britain*, 1st publ. 1833, 3rd edn, London 1873, 307–8.
[30] Edwards, 'Banking', 498.
[31] Scrope, 'The rights of industry and the banking system', 438.
[32] On Scrope's monetary response to 'Owenists' and 'Saint-Simonites' see 'The rights of industry', 409–15.

end of state policy'.[33] For Scrope, the problem of distribution was simultaneously the moralising core of political economy and the most appropriate measure of legitimate government: 'The problem is – what mode of distribution is most conducive to the happiness and permanent interests of the community, and by what legal arrangements can that mode of distribution be most securely provided?'[34] Strikingly, he identified 'the nature and extent of the *circulating medium*' as a more powerful distributive tool than 'the direction of *taxation*'.[35] Thus, for Scrope at least, monetary policy was pre-eminent in a political economy directed at distributing and sustaining the benefits of economic change and underpinning political stability: 'it is well understood now that the interest of the governor lies in the well-being of the governed; that political discontents have their origin in physical distresses; that the ease, the power, the wealth, and the glory, of a government depend on the prosperity of the nation it presides over'.[36]

In identifying distributive roles for monetary policy Scrope's political economy articulated social and economic positions expressed by other contributors to Conservative journals. In 1833 one anonymous commentator attributed excess capital, which he believed precipitated periodic slumps, to the combined effects of monetary and commercial laws which benefited capitalists at the expense of producers and consumers. Indeed, he posed a stark strategic choice for monetary policy, 'either the home trade and the acquirement of true wealth, or the foreign trade and hoarding of capital, which is merely nominal, must be preferred'.[37] Similarly, Scrope viewed the adjustment of currency and credit to the needs of trade as a mechanism which could balance up production to consumption. In order that demand could be 'effectual', Scrope insisted that consumers should be equipped with ready command over an adequate means of exchange. His insistence on revising the gold standard in line with changes in the exchangeable value of gold was directed at preventing the predictable coincidence of a 'high' value of money with 'over-production'.[38] Thus, beside his prescriptions for the standard, Scrope identified monetary liquidity as a duty of government which should be required, 'to apply whatever influence the legislature of states can exercise over that supply, (of money) to maintain it rather above than below the quantity required by the continually increasing supply of commodities in the general market'.[39]

---

[33] Idem, *Political economy for plain people*, pp. 17, xvii.
[34] Idem, 'The rights of industry', 415–16.
[35] Ibid. 416.
[36] Idem, *Political economy for plain people*, p. xix.
[37] Anon., *Public economy concentrated*, 80. Here the term 'capitalist' applied principally to fundholders and speculators.
[38] Scrope, *Political economy for plain people*, for example pp. 147, 175.
[39] Idem, *On credit currency and its superiority to coin*, 35. See also 'The rights of industry', esp. p. 456.

Monetary critiques in Conservative prints contributed to and were informed by a political economy which emphasised the interactions of the productive classes rather than division between the interests of different economic sectors, types of property or social classes. Scrope viewed a reflexive credit currency as fundamental to the balanced and integrated development of agriculture, manufactures and commerce: through monetary and banking reforms: 'the capital which now stagnates in the metropolitan money-market, would, by its agency, be spread over the whole surface of the country, and employed in small portions in promoting the various operations of productive industry'.[40] Such distributive characteristics would also generate political and social cohesion by binding together those 'productive interests' which were 'closely entwined and enlaced together, forming the warp and woof in the web of society'.[41] Indeed, Nilan also conceived of credit currency as a chain which connected producers in all sectors in mutual consumption and linked together the interests of landowners and manufacturers, agricultural labourers and factory workers.[42] Like protectionism, inflationary monetary reform figured in Conservative prints as a strategy for social and political cohesion.

Far from dominating the public debate bullionist approaches to banking and monetary policy were constantly challenged during the early 1830s. Criticism of the gold standard and of deflation persisted as distinctive characteristics of Conservative economic discourse. The distresses of 'the productive classes' were attributed partly to the long-term impacts of monetary legislation. This causal connection was identified as a significant contributor to the political, social and economic context from which the Great Reform Act emerged. The social, economic and constitutional consequences of fundamentally erroneous legislation were presented as important elements in the waning of confidence in the established form of government which was seen to have preceded the Reform Act of 1832. Thus the meliorative monetary reforms suggested by Conservative commentators were offered as strategies for the re-legitimation of legislative solutions to social and economic problems.

Locating economic sovereignty?: bank regulation, 1832–47

The renewal of the Bank of England's charter in 1833 entailed a sweeping survey of banking practice in the provinces and in the metropolis. Yet the

---

[40] Ibid. 444. Scrope attributed the original idea to David Hume: ibid. p. 428, and *On credit currency*, 33–4. In *A catechism*, 71, Taylor made a similar point but attributed it to Charles Davenant's *Discourses on the public revenues and on the trade of England*, London 1698, 161, 166. On the distribution of capital through monetary reform see also Nilan, 'Thoughts on the present distress', 297, 301–2.
[41] Scrope, *Political economy for plain people*, 205.
[42] Nilan, 'Thoughts on the present distress', 298–301.

financial crises of 1836–7 and 1839 shook public confidence in the Bank's capacity to regulate itself and provoked a vibrant debate on the stability of banks and commercial credit in general and on the public responsibilities of the Bank of England.[43] In legislative terms bullionists were forced to admit that the mechanism of convertibility itself was not a sufficient guarantee that banks of issue would manage currency and credit prudently. Thus bullionist positions on reserve specifications, issue policy and the relationship between the money supply and the state of the foreign exchanges were eventually formalised in the Bank Charter Act of 1844 and in the Scottish and Irish Banking Acts of 1845. It is limiting, however, to conceptualise the public debate in terms of the ineluctable victory of bullionist approaches to bank regulation.[44] For contemporaries reached beyond the technicalities of regulation to debate the nature, location and significance of the sovereignty over economic conditions which they perceived in banking legislation and practice. Questions raised by the Committee of Secrecy of 1832 were at first mediated in Conservative economic discourse as responses to the Great Reform Act and to Whig government. Yet the crises of 1836–7 and 1839 raised demanding questions about where institutional culpability for these commercial catastrophes was to be located. These debates drew on established assumptions about the social and economic significance of the behaviour of local banks and of the Bank of England. By attributing profound influences over social and economic conditions to local banks some Conservative commentators cast bank regulation as a question of sovereignty. Protecting local commercial conditions from foreign exchange fluctuations, or from the effects of the private business of the Bank of England, became a dominant desideratum in Conservative economic discourse. If at the start of the 1830s languages of Conservative constitutionalism had tended to reject the intrusion of the state into the territory of banking, by the decade's close they searched out appropriate modes of regulation and public accountability.[45]

The key questions raised by the 1832 Committee of Secrecy on the Bank of England's charter concerned the centralisation of banknote issues, the publication of the Bank's accounts and her monopoly over joint-stock formation in London.[46] Some Conservative responses to these questions were

---

[43] On the secret committee of 1832 on the Bank of England's charter and subsequent disatisfaction with the Bank's self–regulation see *British banking statutes*, esp. pp. xiii–xix, and Clapham, *The Bank of England*, ii. 121–30. On the partial responsibility of the Bank for the crises of 1836–7 and 1839 see ibid. 142–72.
[44] This modification of bullionism is usually described as the 'Currency School' position: Fetter, *The development*, 129–33. For a brief account of the 'Currency School' see *British banking statutes*, pp. xxi–xxiv, esp. Samuel Jones Loyd's evidence before the select commitee of 1840 at pp. 27–8, 32–3, 35–7.
[45] For a sustained discussion of Radical and Whig political languages of banking reform see Alborn, *Conceiving companies*, 7, 17, 53–82, 85–115.
[46] On the committee's debate on the publication of accounts see Clapham, *The Bank of*

moulded by a distinctive reading of the Great Reform Act and its constitutional consequences. Fundamentally, Archibald Alison conceived the preservation of the Bank's existing relationship with the state as one element in a wider strategy of constitutional defence. Although the Bank was a private institution, Alison believed it was, 'the greatest and most important establishment in the country' which had been exposed by the 1832 Reform Act to popular pressure and to a Whiggish impulse to centralise power. Though it was to prove unfounded, Alison's fear was that the Whigs would appoint a Royal Commission on the Bank in order to 'give themselves as great a control over *the fortunes and solvency of every mercantile or trading man in the Kingdom*, as the East India Commissioners, in 1784'.[47] Alison also objected to the publication of the Bank's accounts by invoking Rothschild's evidence to the committee of 1832. He argued that, in conjunction with self-regulation the publication of accounts would force the Bank to tie up a high proportion of its assets in gold reserves which in turn would restrict its banking business.[48] Following Rothschild, Alison also insisted that bank runs originated with 'little shopkeepers and people of that kind'.[49] As the information provided by compulsory publication was vulnerable to misinterpretation by the newspapers and the 'lower' classes, Alison contended that it risked exposing national credit to democratic elements. While advocates of publication tended to cite the Banque de France as evidence for the positive influence of public access to such information, Alison retorted that since the Banque did not issue notes of low denominations the French state was not exposed by the publication of its accounts to the uneducated whims of the lower classes.[50] Thus Alison's critiques of Bank regulation informed and drew on a more generally held idea that parliamentary reform had revolutionised the balance of representation and had substantively exposed the legislature to pressure from democratic elements.[51] Defending the interests of proprietors of Bank of England stock was for Conservatives part of a two-pronged strategy of constitutional defence:

England, ii. 126. The charter of 1833 (3 & 4 Will. IV. c. 98. viii) provided for a weekly confidential return by the Bank to the government, and a quarterly averaged summary of the Bank's accounts to be published in the *London Gazette*: *British banking statutes*, pp. xvi, 23.

[47] A. Alison, 'Revolutionary inroads – the Bank – the corn laws', *BEM* xxxii (Oct. 1832), 671–9 at p. 673 (Alison's emphasis). For Alison's general condemnation of Whiggery as 'democratic centralisation' see 'The first session of the reformed parliament', esp. pp. 799–801 on Whig commissions. For the constitutional ramifications of the East India debates of 1784 see p. 161 below.

[48] Alison, 'Revolutionary inroads', 673–5. On the self-regulatory 'Palmer Rule' see *British banking statutes*, pp. xi–xii, and Morgan, *Theory and practice*, 100–15.

[49] Alison, 'Revolutionary inroads', 675.

[50] Alison asserted that the lowest denomination of French Bank notes was equivalent to £30: ibid. 675–6.

[51] For a general summary of the perceived transformation of representation in 1832 see Croker, 'On the corn laws', 279–83. On its specific expression in banking reform see Croly,

identifying propertied interests with constitutional conservatism and with the Conservative party within the reform of 1832.[52]

Others offered different constitutionalist perspectives on the relationship between the Bank and the state. For Scrope the case for a government bank (to replace the chartered Bank of England) was grounded on an analysis of the effects of the Bank of England's private business on commercial cycles between 1814 and 1826.[53] He held that the Bank's issues had been regulated only opportunely by the 'public' principle of convertibility and that her primary consideration had been private profit. He proposed that a national bank, or national board of note issue, should assume the note-issuing functions of the Bank of England. This national bank would be directly accountable to the public for the socio-economic consequences of monetary policy. Indeed, Scrope believed that the monetary sovereignty conferred by legislative charter on the Bank of England was constitutionally dubious. The Bank's monopoly was, 'evidently a power over the public interests far exceeding that committed by the constitution to any one of the three estates of the realm'.[54] Scrope described the nature of this 'power over public interests' to the House of Commons:

> Its power was continually directed to alter prices, and its interest was frequently promoted by limiting the currency, and lowering the prices in all the markets of the country. Its power was infinitely greater than that possessed by the Legislature, and far exceeded in its extent and operation that power with which public opinion ever endowed any government.[55]

Thus he located responsibility for the influence of monetary policy in the legislature not in the private company it chartered. Scrope's indictment of the Bank affirmed the social and economic significance of banking policy and expressed this within an essentially constitutionalist idiom. In his response to the commercial and financial crisis of 1836-7, Alfred Mallalieu pointed to the social and economic influence of banking as grounds for the introduction of legislation which would locate monetary sovereignty in the executive.[56] He argued that 'the wielding of so tremendous an agency as a controlling power over the whole currency of the empire'[57] was a power which legiti-

---

'Edmund Burke: part III', 37, and Anon., 'The renewal of the Bank of England charter', *FM* vi (Sept. 1832), 231-5.
52 Alison, 'Duties of the Conservative party', 140-1; Johnstone, 'The duke of Wellington and the finances of the country', 380.
53 Scrope, *An examination of the bank charter question*, 44-50.
54 Ibid. 36.
55 Idem, House of Commons (28 June 1833), *Hansard* 3rd ser. xviii. 1316.
56 A. Mallalieu, 'Whig-Radical prosperity', *BEM* xli (Feb. 1837), 145-62, on joint-stock banks at pp. 146-7, 150-2, and on concentrating issue in the Bank of England at p. 155. Specifically, Mallalieu contended (p. 150) that careless lending facilitated production beyond the means of consumption.
57 Ibid. 161.

mately rested with the executive: 'we are not sure that it will not be found advisable to invest the Bank with even more of a national character – for the nation to enter into partnership with the Bank – to intervene direct by qualified representatives in the board of direction. The coinage of money is one of the highest royal prerogatives'.[58] Though he accepted the Bank's continuance as the government's banker, Mallalieu advocated the centralisation of note issue with the caveat of a ministerial power of veto if the Bank's decisions were considered to damage public interests. John Dickenson also debated the crisis of 1839 as a question of monetary sovereignty.[59] Reacting to a report of the Manchester Chamber of Commerce which indicted the Bank of England with responsibility for the commercial crisis of 1839, Dickenson pointed to the short-sighted lending polices of joint-stock banks.[60] Parliament, he argued, should frame and maintain the national circulation as an aggregate of existing local circulations.[61] By identifying parliamentary responsibility for monetary regulation, Dickenson effectively advocated the representation of local circulations in the national whole, not the centralisation of monetary authority as an end in itself. He sought to combine a controlling influence for government with the existence of independent local circulations which were insulated from foreign exchange movements:

> It is hardly necessary to point out how completely distinct a paper circulation of this kind is from a Government or national paper money. The issue of notes would be confined, as at present, to individual responsibility, and proportioned, of course, to commercial and local demand with exact precision, instead of being issued *ad libitum* for the necessities of the state.[62]

While these proposals differed in detail they shared the fundamental premise that monetary and banking policies exerted profound influence over social and economic conditions. The attempt to define this economic sovereignty and to identify an appropriate and accountable agency was a dominant characteristic of Conservative monetary discourse by the end of the 1830s.

---

[58] Ibid. 162.
[59] J. Dickenson, 'Banking and currency', ibid. xlix (Apr. 1841), 550–64.
[60] This report was probably J. B. Smith's *Report of the directors to a special general meeting of the chamber of commerce and manufactures at Manchester, on the effects of the administration of the Bank of England upon the commercial and manufacturing interests of the country*, London 1840. See also White, *Free banking in Britain*, 71.
[61] For contemporary assertions of the social and economic distress caused by the contraction of local circulations see Napier, *Observations on the corn law*, 31, and Renny, *Reflections upon the corn laws*, esp. pp. 76–7. The intrusion of banking debates into corn law prints was partly a consequence of debate generated by the select committees on banks of issue (1840, 1841): *British banking statutes*, pp. xvi–xix, 35–4, 49–50, 62–70.
[62] Dickenson, 'Banking and currency', 560. For a range of arguments for a domestic circulation attuned to local needs and secure from foreign exchange fluctuation see Taylor, *A catechism*, pp. viii, 92–5 (government bills); Mallalieu 'Whig-Radical prosperity', 155–6 (bimetallism); Alison 'The late commercial crisis – the work of the tyrant majority', *BEM* xlii (Aug. 1837), 210–25 at pp. 213, 225 (inconvertibility).

This concern with institutional frameworks did not emasculate continued debate on the question of the monetary standard. Indeed the persistent criticism of bullionism needs to be located within the broader context forged by the attempt of Conservatives and others to establish the sovereignty of monetary policy over social and economic conditions. While Mallalieu admitted the necessity of convertibility, he insisted on a bimetallic standard which would insulate the domestic reserve from bullion drains and would protect the socio-economic functions of the domestic money supply.[63] Similarly Dickenson's brand of convertibility was designed 'to provide for the country a secure and limited domestic circulation, independent of transactions with foreign countries, and not acted upon by the fluctuations of the exchanges'.[64] The fundamental purpose of insulating the domestic circulation from the fluctuations of the foreign exchanges fluctuation was to protect the social and economic functions of the domestic means of payment. These functions were spelled out in intellectual defences of the issue functions of local and provincial banks. Drawing on the arguments of Sir Walter Scott and G. P. Scrope, Edwards advocated a Scottish-style banking infrastructure of local institutions sustained by solid 'paid-up' capital which offered a credit currency, interest on deposits and cash advances.[65] Like Scott, Edwards defended local joint-stock banks as moral economies in microcosm; they enabled participation by all classes in local economies while small cash deposits encouraged the independence and self-sufficiency of the labouring classes.[66] For Edwards, joint-stock banks on Scottish lines achieved a moral symmetry of capital and labour: 'The system of banking which prevails in Scotland thus forms a link which directly connects the accumulated capital with the physical force of the country . . . but wherever these two elements are brought in contact, the result must be a vast increase in private comfort, as well as a vast accession of public wealth.'[67] Edwards went on to identify the cautious lending of joint-stock banks as a mode of capital policing: 'The managers of the Scottish banks thus constitute a species of social police – spies, impelled by the strong impulse of interest to watch with the most careful

---

[63] Mallalieu, 'Whig-Radical prosperity', 155–6.
[64] Dickenson, 'Banking and currency', 559.
[65] Edwards, 'Banking', 483–501. Edwards's advocacy of Scottish-style banking for the entire kingdom was influenced by the 'redoubted Malagrowther' (p. 478), and by Scrope's, *The currency question freed from mystery*. For a detailed contemporary account of Scottish banking see W. H. Logan, *The Scottish banker; or a popular exposition of the practice of banking in Scotland*, London 1838, 2nd edn, London 1844 [dedicated with permission to Sir Robert Peel].
[66] On the counter-cyclical importance of credit for agricultural and manufactures see Edwards 'Banking', 496–7. On Scottish banking and agriculture see J. Fullarton and J. W. Croker, 'Condition of the labouring classes: Wiltshire emigrants to Canada', QR xlvi (Jan. 1832), 349–89 at pp. 387–8.
[67] Edwards, 'Banking', 491. See also E. Edwards, 'The Bank of England', QR xliii (Oct. 1830), 342–66 at p. 354.

attention the conduct and proceedings of the classes engaged in productive industry.'[68] So not only did Scottish banks bind together the interests of capital and labour, Edwards thought they also 'policed' the supply side of the economy.

However, the banking legislation of 1844–5 moved towards unitary issue in England and Wales and attempted to impose bullionist policies on the Scottish and Irish banking infrastructure.[69] The Scottish Banking Act met with vigorous defences of the autonomy of local and provincial issuing banks both in print and in parliament.[70] The intellectual case for defending Scottish banks from the legislation of 1845 struck familiar chords; constitutionalist opposition to monetary centralisation, arguments for the moral utility of joint-stock banking, and explorations of the social and economic functions of independent local banks. In his attack on the legislation of 1845, W. E. Aytoun invoked Sir Walter Scott's response to the similar legislative initiative of 1826: 'CENTRALIZE and ASSIMILATE – these were the watchwords of the ministers of that day; and for ought that we can see, Sir Robert Peel is determined to persevere in the theory.'[71] In his objections to the restrictions on note issuing by private joint-stock banks in the metropolitan region of Ireland in 1839 one MP had objected to the suppression of provincial autonomy in similar terms asking, 'How could Gentlemen who had resisted a civil coercion bill for Ireland, support a mercantile coercion bill?... In the persevering with this measure, the Irish people would have one of the strongest arguments for a repeal of the Union.'[72] As for the moral and economic utility of the Scottish form of local autonomy, Aytoun presented joint-stock structure, the security of landed assets, and bi-weekly settlements between banks as safeguards for banking stability and as moralising processes in local economic activity.[73] The shareholding base of the Scottish banking structure made notes and credit the representatives of manufactures and landed wealth which in turn rendered banks accountable to property, 'almost every man of opulence in the country being a holder of stock to a greater or lesser amount'.[74] As Scott had done so Aytoun emphasised the social and economic benefits of the demand functions of monetary liquidity and diffused

---

[68] Ibid. 352. See also Scrope, 'The rights of industry and the banking system', 448. On joint-stock banks as 'subscriber democracies' see Alborn, *Conceiving companies*, 17, 85–7, 92–5.
[69] On the 1844 Act (7 & 8 Vict. c. 32) see *British banking statutes*, pp. xix–xxiv, 129–47. On the Scottish legislation of 1845 (8 & 9 Vict., c. 38) see S. G. Checkland, *Scottish banking: a history, 1695–1973*, London 1975, 454–8, and Fetter, *The development*, 194–7.
[70] For parliamentary defences of the Scottish system see House of Commons (5 June 1845), *Hansard* lxxxi esp. pp. 140–3, 149–58, 170–1.
[71] W. E. Aytoun, 'The Scottish banking system', *BEM* lvi (Dec. 1844), 671–86 at p. 672 (Aytoun's emphasis).
[72] D. Browne, House of Commons (19 Aug. 1839), *Hansard* 3rd ser. l. 392.
[73] Aytoun, 'The Scottish banking system', 683.
[74] Ibid. 678.

credit. He insisted that the proposed legislation threatened to extinguish the positive influence of Scottish banking on demand and distribution within the economy:

> In the event of any change which shall derange the present system of currency, the landowners and agriculturists of every class must prepare themselves for crippled markets, curtailment of the sales of their produce and consequently for a great reduction in the rent and value of land. This will apply equally to the fisheries, the distilleries, and the linen trade – to every branch, in short, of internal manufacture.[75]

Such socio-economic criticisms of the proposed suppression of banking autonomy in Scotland merely magnified long-established features of anti-bullionist argument in Conservative discourse. Indeed, in 1833 Baring had defended the autonomy of smaller provincial banks as institutions which 'gave accommodation which great establishments could not do – they went into petty details with the farmers and traders in their neighbourhood in a manner which the larger banks could not, and would not imitate – and they acted in that way much to the benefit of the country'.[76] By confining the liberties of local and provincial banks the legislation of 1844–5 was commonly viewed as intervention which would crush those chains of consumption and distribution which sustained and diffused economic development and helped to maintain political and social cohesion.

The public debate on bank regulation therefore reached far beyond mere technical controversies between the 'banking' and 'currency' schools during the 1830s and 1840s. By identifying powerful social and economic influences for monetary policy and banking practice critics of bullionism evolved a notion of 'economic sovereignty'; such power over the complexion of the national economy needed to be defined and accountable. In Conservative economic discourse this concept was at first articulated within distinctive representations of the meaning of the Great Reform Act and the character of Whig government. Yet, the crises of 1836–7 and 1839 directed Conservative constitutional languages away from confining the state towards an emphasis on recognising and locating the commercial sovereignty of banking and monetary policy in reforms of joint-stock banking and in tighter regulation of the Bank of England. Though the reforms proposed in Conservative prints differed widely the assumptions which underpinned them found consensus. Their central dynamic was not the dogmatic and restrictive 'currency principle' but the perception that legislation should allow banks to meet the local needs of trade and should insulate domestic, economic and social conditions

---

[75] Ibid. 685.
[76] F. Baring, House of Commons (28 June 1833), *Hansard*, 3rd ser. xviii. 1351. See also C. L. W. Sibthorpe, House of Commons (28 June 1844), ibid. lxxvi. 118, and J. S. Trelawny's views on the Irish Banking Act of 1845, House of Commons (16 June 1845), ibid. lxxxi. 624.

from the impacts of foreign exchange fluctuations. By focusing and confining the functions of policy thus, Conservative commentators defended the economic and social liberties of localities in constitutional languages. In effect this Conservative economic discourse incorporated the public debate on banking and currency into a more general socio-economic diagnosis which linked the political 'Condition of England' to a disease of maldistribution.

'Free trade and a fettered currency': gold, protection and the home market, 1844–7

' "Currency Reform", is to be seen placarded on all the streets of the kingdom, and in all the manufacturing cities of the kingdom, as an inducement to the public to purchase and read their papers': A. Alison, *Free trade and a fettered currency*, London 1847, 43.[77]

Undoubtedly it suited Archibald Alison's intellectual project to exaggerate the public's interest in the currency question in 1847. All the same, his characterisation of the public debate offers a welcome corrective to the pervasive historiographical assumption that Peel's monetary policy met with little serious opposition in the 1840s. A steady stream of pamphlets, journal articles and parliamentary speeches offered sweeping criticisms of Peel's monetary legislation. If, as Alison suggested, such positions did appeal to the public at large this was because they did not rely on arid technical arguments but instead debated the consequences of Peel's policies for the social distribution of wealth in Britain and for the durability of her economic advance. Of course Peel's Conservative critics need to be located within a fractured but broad critical discourse where positions on monetary questions were not dictated by party affiliation nor necessarily by attitudes to protection and free trade.[78] Yet it remains true that Conservatives took up the currency question as part of a distinctive nationalistic response to economic liberalism. In Conservative economic discourse the debate on monetary policy was fundamental to a wider controversy about whether Britain should move towards an open economy which was dependent on unrestricted international trade. While many free traders looked to the abolition of trade restrictions and to the gold standard as the foundations of Britain's economic pre-eminence, many protectionists eschewed this combination. Instead they insisted that Britain's economic future needed to rest on the security of a home market which could be insulated from the vagaries of foreign governments and from international

---

[77] W. E. Aytoun also claimed a broad consensus against the legislation of 1844–5, in 'Robert Peel and the currency', *BEM* lxii (July 1847), 113–28 at p. 119.
[78] C. Buller noted that free traders, notably the Political Economy Club, were among the most vocal critics of Peel's Bank Charter Act: House of Commons (13 June 1844), *Hansard* 3rd ser. lxxv, 849. Though he later changed his mind the protectionist Bentinck voted for the Bank Charter Act in 1844: House of Commons (10 May 1847), ibid. xcii. 622.

bullion movements. Thus Conservatives were prominent among those who engaged with what Thomas Arnold described as Peel's only principle: 'Peel has an idea about currency, and a distinct impression about it, and therefore, on that point I would trust him for not yielding to clamour.'[79]

Peel's Bank Charter Act of 1844 institutionalised bullionist principles in strict regulations which governed the Bank of England's policy on note issue, separated the Bank's issue department from her banking department and imposed rigid reserve specifications.[80] Historians have tended to assume that the most powerful criticisms of this legislation were mounted by the so-called 'Banking School' who maintained that within the constraints of convertibility banks should be permitted to apportion currency and credit according to the needs of trade.[81] Indeed such criticisms did penetrate Conservative economic discourse in the form of an article published in the *Quarterly Review* in 1847.[82] This article engaged systematically with the theoretical assumptions of the currency school as exemplified by Samuel Jones Loyd and Robert Torrens and applied by Peel.[83] Citing Thomas Tooke, Benjamin Hawes and John Fullarton, the reviewer argued that the principle of convertibility was not inconsistent with a credit currency expanding to the needs of commerce.[84] Using evidence from Tooke's *History of prices* the reviewer denied direct relationships between the national gold stock, commodity price levels and the state of the exchanges. In this critique, the automatic bullionist formula for regulating bank issues placed an unnecessary burden on bankers who regulated their issues according to the needs of legitimate trade.[85] Indeed from its 'entire adhesion to the doctrines of the currency school' the Bank

---

[79] Thomas Arnold to Archbishop Whately, 25 Nov. 1836, in *The life and correspondence of Thomas Arnold*, ed. A. P. Stanley, London 1844, ii. 57, cited by Croker in 'Close of Sir Robert Peel's administration', 551.
[80] For the terms of the Bank Charter Act (7 & 8 Vict., c. 32) see Clapham, *The Bank of England*, ii. 183–4, and *British banking statutes*, 129–47. For a general overview of debates surrounding it see Fetter, *The development*, 199–216.
[81] Ibid. 187–92.
[82] Anon. 'The financial pressure', QR lxxxi (June 1847), 230–73. Fetter suggested that this article was written by the Banking School theorist John Fullarton and was heavily edited by Lockhart and Croker: 'The economic articles in the *Quarterly Review*: articles, authors', 168.
[83] S. J. Loyd, *Thoughts on the separation of the departments of the Bank of England*, London 1844; R. Torrens, *An inquiry into the practical working of the proposed arrangements for the renewal of the charter of the Bank of England*, London 1844.
[84] J. Fullarton, *On the regulation of currencies; being an examination of the principles on which it is proposed to restrict within certain limits the future issues in credit of the Bank of England and of other banking establishments throughout the country*, London (Aug.) 1844, 2nd edn, London 1845; T. Tooke, *An inquiry into the currency principle; the connexion of the currency with prices*, 2nd edn, London 1844; B. Hawes, *Speech of Benjamin Hawes, Jun., Esq., in opposition to the second reading of the bank charter*, London 1844.
[85] The reviewer quoted Fullarton's *On the regulation of currencies*, beside details from the parliamentary committees of 1831–2 and 1840–1 as evidence that local banks did not issue beyond the needs of commerce: 'The financial pressure', 237–43.

Charter Act was identified as the root of the commercial and financial crisis of 1847: by separating the banking and issue departments of the Bank of England and by stipulating a fixed fiduciary issue the law effectively decreed that the banking department (and the commerce it sustained) would bear the initial burden of any gold efflux.[86] Though this technical 'Banking School' critique did penetrate Conservative economic discourse it was not the dominant voice. Drawing on themes which had first been raised in response to the bullion report in 1811, Conservatives offered distinctive criticisms of Peel's monetary policy which condemned the combined impact of deflation, contracted credit and freer trade on the distribution and durability of British economic change.

This Conservative and protectionist strain of monetary criticism also intersected with another set of prominent criticisms of Peel's banking legislation – those of the 'Birmingham School'. Briefly, this group of critics maintained that an inconvertible paper currency and an unrestricted banking system could meet the monetary needs of the economy.[87] In 1844 the Birmingham School consciously opened up divisions in Conservative economic discourse by republishing a pamphlet penned by Sir James Graham in 1826.[88] Though he was now Home Secretary in Peel's Conservative government Graham's condemnation of the resumption of cash payments had been so pronounced in 1826 that, 'It was chiefly on the question of currency that he was in disagreement with his own party – the Whigs.'[89] Of course the injection of these arguments into the public debate of 1844 served to amplify the arguments of Peel's Conservative critics. This provoked Peel to condemn the 'Gemini Tracts' as a volume which 'collects and repeats all the exploded fallacies on the subject of the standard of value and the currency'.[90] For Graham's argument that monetary deflation and agricultural protection were fundamentally incompatible and caused unnecessary social distress was identical to that of Peel's protectionist opponents.[91] Graham's republished pamphlet also mirrored those constitutionalist arguments which had characterised Conservative criticism of bullionism since 1811. Indeed Graham had viewed the redistributive effects of changes in the value of money as abuses of the socio-economic influence of monetary legislation and as a tyrannical incursion by the state into the sanctity of property: '*Here*, by law, we depreciated the currency, and by a solemn resolution of the House of Commons denied the fact of depreciation. *Here*, by law, we raised the value of money, and instead of

---

[86] Ibid. 259–60.
[87] On the 'Birmingham School' see Fetter, *The development*, 177–80, 212–14.
[88] Sir J. R. G. Graham, *Corn and currency, in an address to the landowners*, London 1826, repr. in *The Gemini letters*, London 1844. These in turn reprinted letters to the editor of the *Midland Counties Herald* written during 1843. On Graham's pamphlet see Hilton, *Corn, cash, commerce*, 270.
[89] A. B. Erickson, *The public career of Sir James Graham, 1792–1861*, Oxford 1952, 49.
[90] Sir R. Peel, House of Commons (6 May 1844), *Hansard* 3rd ser. lxxix, 726.
[91] Anon., *The Gemini letters*, no. iv (13 May 1843), 160–70.

avowing our purpose, and preparing for its effects, we mystified the intention and were blind to the result.'[92] By republishing Graham's pamphlet, therefore, the Birmingham School staked a claim for the representativeness of anti-bullionist positions in nineteenth-century monetary thought. In doing so they exposed the fractures wrought by the monetary question in Conservative economic discourse.

Although their arguments often intersected with those of the 'Banking' and 'Birmingham' schools, Peel's Conservative critics voiced a cohesive and distinctive strain of monetary criticism. Prominent Conservative commentators applied the familiar constitutionalist objections of 1819 to the act of 1844. By forbidding the foundation of any new banks of issue and by incarcerating the legislatively-fixed value of gold in new regulations Peel was thought to have pushed the state further beyond the boundaries of legitimate public authority. As a deflationary measure the Bank Charter Act was condemned for having exacerbated the redistribution from the productive to the creditor classes and therefore to have threatened further the relationship between property and the state.[93] Within such familiar constitutionalist languages Conservatives offered sweeping social and economic criticisms of Peel's banking legislation. They generally identified the fundamental structural flaw in the Bank Charter Act as the clause which stipulated that the Bank was obliged to contract the money supply in response to any external drain of gold. This, it was argued, was the legislative cause of the 'general monetary spasm and commercial crisis' which had occurred in 1825 and 1839 and would become systemic after 1844.[94] As Newdegate explained in his set-piece condemnation of the 1844 act in parliament, 'if you have fluctuation in the basis of any superstructure, and that basis is too narrow in proportion to the superstructure it supports, the fluctuation in the superstructure will be great in the ratio of its disproportion to the basis'.[95] His point, of course, was that monetary legislation threatened to institutionalise commercial fluctuations. Both Newdegate and Alison agreed that this amounted to a monstrous and arbitrary sovereignty over social conditions in Britain: 'under the present, a

---

[92] Compare Graham's position ibid. no. xvii (30 June 1843), 198, with E. S. Cayley, House of Commons (1 June 1835), *Hansard* 3rd ser. xxviii. 265, and C. N. Newdegate, House of Commons (13 June 1844), ibid. lxxv. 825. Newdegate expressly endorsed (p. 830) the ideas of the Birmingham School.
[93] Alison cited from Locke, *Some considerations*, 49, in his *England in 1815 and 1845, or, a sufficient and a contracted currency*, 1st edn, London 1845, 58. W. E. Aytoun drew heavily on Lord Ashburton's, *The financial and commercial crisis considered*, 3rd edn, London 1847 in 'Robert Peel and the currency', *BEM* lxii (July 1847), 113–28. Ashburton's pamphlet was also commended by A. Alison in *Free trade and a fettered currency*, London 1847, 26–7; Disraeli, *Lord George Bentinck*, 413.
[94] Alison, *England in 1815 and 1845*, 62. On Alison's interpretation of the 1837 crisis as a consequence of internal contraction designed to counteract external drain see his 'The late commercial crisis', esp. pp. 210–13.
[95] C. N. Newdegate, House of Commons (13 June 1844), *Hansard* 3rd ser. lxxv. 825.

fluctuation of sixpence on the value of a sovereign, is sufficient to reduce half the traders of the Kingdom to insolvency, and a third of the working classes to pauperism'.[96] As Newdegate warned the House of Commons, 'this Measure will again still higher raise the golden standard of our Currency above a sinking people'.[97]

By insisting that monetary legislation exerted powerful distributive influences over social and economic conditions, these critics rejected the 'laissez-faire' approach to social misery in which people and governments were powerless in the face of natural laws; 'Let us not deceive ourselves, therefore, nor ascribe to laws of nature the misery arising from the erroneous tendency of human institutions.'[98] In this perspective social unrest and wealth polarisation were identified as direct consequences of the legislative deflation imposed first by the act of 1819 and compounded by the Bank Charter Act of 1844.[99] Citing social statistics from Porter, Marshall and Moreau,[100] Alison argued that deflation adversely affected the social diffusion of wealth in several ways: it encouraged a fall in the money price of commodities followed by a disproportionately larger reduction in the wages of labour and simultaneously increased the real burdens of private debt, national debt and indirect taxation.[101] Similarly, Alison insisted that monetary and banking restrictions had hampered the development of those small capitals which he identified as the agent of socially-diffused wealth creation.[102] Opposition to Peel's deflationary and restrictive monetary policy was therefore conducted in social languages which dovetailed with Conservatives' social construction of protection. Indeed Newdegate made the connection in his sweeping critique of the Bank Charter Act: 'I say, that this system of one-sided free-trade, combined with a contraction of the Currency, is incompatible with the welfare of the country, and will produce a state of distress and misery among us that I cannot contemplate.'[103] Ultimately, both protection and monetary reform were presented as instruments for the diffusion and dis-

---

[96] Ibid. 63. See also Napier's description of monetary contraction as an 'enormous power, or screw' over working-class living standards in his *Observations on the corn law*, 7.
[97] C. N. Newdegate, House of Commons (13 June 1844), *Hansard* 3rd ser. lxxv. 825.
[98] Alison, *England in 1815 and 1845*, 20. See also C. N. Newdegate, House of Commons (12 May 1846), *Hansard* 3rd ser. lxxxvi. 427.
[99] Alison made specific claims for the direct correlations between economic distress and the rates of strikes and crime: *England in 1815 and 1845*, 13–14.
[100] Alison may have been referring to Porter's *The progress of the nation*, and may have used César Moreau's, *State of the trade of Great Britain with all parts of the world, 1697–1822*, London 1822. Alison drew on George Marshall's, *A view of the silver coin and coinage of Great Britain from 1662 to 1837*, London 1837.
[101] Alison estimated that by 1845 40% had been added to debts contracted before 1819: *England in 1815 and 1845*, 66. He added (pp. 88–9) that the return to the gold in 1819 had made the burden of indirect taxation – felt most acutely by the lower classes – insupportable. See also R. Wallace, House of Commons (24 June 1844), *Hansard* 3rd ser. lxxv. 1318.
[102] Alison, *England in 1815 and 1845*, 36–51.
[103] C. N. Newdegate, House of Commons (13 June 1844), *Hansard* 3rd ser. lxxv. 825.

tribution of wealth which bound together the interests of the productive classes. Both protection and opposition to the Bank Charter Act were, in part, strategies for the insulation of British living standards from the levelling impact of foreign competition and exchange fluctuations. The prominence of both strategies in Conservative economic discourse in the mid 1840s bears testimony to the persistence of a vibrant alternative to the *laissez-faire* assumption that the state could do little to alter social conditions in mid nineteenth-century Britain.

Opposition to the Bank Charter Act and to free trade were both facets of the economic nationalism which dominated the thinking of Peel's Conservative critics. In this alternative vision of Britain's economic future it was domestic and colonial not foreign markets which forged the securest foundations for stable and balanced economic advance. Indeed, both free trade and bullionism were condemned for their erosion of the fulcrum on which Britain's economic future was believed to turn – the home market. Within this broad context, Peel's critics elaborated a number of specific economic criticisms of the Bank Charter Act. The three chief targets for criticism in parliament and in print were the fixed fiduciary issue, the compulsion to contract the money supply in response to bullion drains, and the separation of the Bank's issue and banking departments. These clauses were considered to have left Britain bereft of an adequate means of trade, to have stymied the effective operation of the Bank as a lender of last resort and, worse, to have institutionalised commercial fluctuations. In print, Alison used anti-Malthusian methods to explain why the Bank Charter Act squeezed the monetary needs of the British economy. Whereas Malthus had maintained that population size was ultimately determined by the magnitude of natural resources, Alison approached the problem from the opposite premise: resources (whether food or money) could and should adjust to the needs of a growing population and economy.[104] By comparing his estimate of Britain's money supply in 1845 with the size of her population, her exports and her imports, Alison concluded that legislation had imposed a money supply which provided for less than half of the needs of the economy.[105] Similarly, Newdegate condemned the legislative compulsion to contract the money supply in response to any bullion drain: 'That clause was like ossifying the heart of the human frame, which, when any additional quantity of blood should be propelled through the veins, would inevitably result in the bursting of the smaller vessels.'[106] And as Alison commented, 'their only resource, on the occurrence of com-

---

[104] T. R. Malthus, *An essay on the principles of population*, 1st edn, London 1798, repr. London 1926, 1966, 13–14.
[105] Alison, *England in 1815 and 1845*, 65. Alison's definition of 'money' applied specifically to convertible notes. For a comparison of declining gold supply with increased rates of population growth see *Free trade and a fettered currency*, 68–71.
[106] C. N. Newdegate, House of Commons (24 June 1844), *Hansard* 3rd ser. lxxv. 1322.

mercial crisis, was to *contract the currency*, just as Dr Sangrado's was on every disease to bleed the patient'.[107]

If protection was presented as an economic strategy which safeguarded a domestic means of consumption so monetary contraction was condemned in Conservative economic discourse for constricting the home market. The combined effect of deflation and a contracted money supply was, Alison contended, the attrition of Britain's domestic market: 'Has not the home market been contracted as much and more than the foreign has been expanded?' and, 'the home market is crippled . . . by the decline of 50 *per cent*'.[108] Looking to Britain's foreign trade, Newdegate insisted in parliament that the act of 1844 would over-value sterling and impose damaging limits on foreign purchasing power over British manufactured exports. Using a pamphlet by A. Boucherett as an intellectual template, Newdegate urged that British manufacturers needed a devaluation of sterling not free trade in corn.[109] Thus, Peel's Conservative critics located their criticisms of his monetary policy within a coherent and expansive set of assumptions about the foundations of secure and stable economic advance.

It follows that such economic arguments against the Bank Charter Act were frequently fused with criticism of free trade in Conservative economic discourse. The integration of anti-bullionism with protectionism was, indeed, an established characteristic of the public debate.[110] From the 1820s free traders had maintained that the absence of tariff restrictions would ultimately regularise international trade and bullion transfers thereby stabilising monetary and credit conditions.[111] Against this protectionists insisted that the large imports of raw produce which inevitably would occur under the free-trade system would necessitate the periodic exportation of bullion in exchange. As the Bank Charter Act had stipulated that the domestic circulation was to be contracted in response to any bullion efflux, the combination of 'free trade and a fettered currency' was condemned as economic suicide. As Cayley had warned in 1839, 'The boors of Poland and Russia would not for a lengthened period be consumers to any material extent of our manufactures,

---

[107] Alison, *Free trade and a fettered currency*, 41.
[108] Idem, *England in 1815 and 1845*, 68, 87, and also his *Free trade and a fettered currency*, 41.
[109] C. N. Newdegate, House of Commons (13 June 1844), *Hansard* 3rd ser. lxxv. 826; A. Boucherett, *A few observations on corn, currency, and c. with a plan for promoting the interests of agriculture and manufactures*, London 1841, esp. pp. 7–9.
[110] See, for example, Anon., *Letter to the duke of Buckingham*, 2–3; Alison, 'The anti-national faction', 546–7, 549; Dalbiac, *A few words on the corn laws*, 53.
[111] See Peel's account of the Anti-Corn-Law League's use of bullionism in their opposition to protection in his speech against a low fixed duty on corn: *Speech of the right honourable Sir Robert Peel*, 32–3. See also Anon., *Corn and currency; or, how shall we get through the winter?*, London 1839, 8; Salomons, *The corn laws*, 32–44; Smith, *Economy of nations*, esp. p. 123. See also the Revd C. Nevile's explicit response to Alison in *Corn and currency, in a letter to A. Alison, Esq.*, London 1846, 3–5.

but would require gold in exchange for their corn.'[112] On the contrary protection prevented the need for huge food imports and guarded against bullion drains and monetary derangement.[113] Thus, the Bank Charter Act was commonly condemned as 'an Act for the more effectual transfer of panics from Agriculture to Commerce'.[114] In parliament and in print E. S. Cayley insisted that the manufacturing population would suffer from the combination of 'free trade and a fettered currency'.[115] Foreign exporters of food would take gold in preference to British manufactures causing contraction of Britain's money supply under the terms of the Bank Charter Act. Britain would then be forced to obtain gold from other foreign nations in exchange for manufactures in order to sustain both the basis of her currency and her manufacturing industry.[116] In this view the combination of 'free trade and a fettered currency' ransomed the future of the manufacturing sector and the entire system of currency and credit to an essentially limited foreign demand for manufactured goods.

These predictions that the combination of 'free trade and a fettered currency' would prove catastrophic for the British economy were reiterated in response to the repeal of the corn laws. Though the immediate cause of bullion efflux was harvest failure not free trade, the financial and monetary crisis of 1847 was interpreted as a predicted consequence of Peel's monetary and commercial policies. As W. E. Aytoun put it in 1847 'we must be left in absolute dependence for our circulation on the state of the harvest, or cripple labour at a season when employment is most urgently required'.[117] Alison explained the crisis of 1847 as a result of the legislatively compelled contraction of credit and currency in response to the payments in bullion for food imports.[118] He insisted that 'the whole of this loss . . . is to be *set down to the monetary laws*; no part of it, or at least a most inconsiderable part, is to be considered as arising from the visitation of Providence, or causes over which we

---

[112] E. S. Cayley, House of Commons (12 Mar. 1839), *Hansard* 3rd ser. xlvi. 393.
[113] Alison, 'Whig and Tory finance', 497–8.
[114] Idem, *England in 1815 and 1845*, 2nd edn, London (Aug.) 1845, 133. The first edition did not include this particular critique.
[115] Cayley, *Reasons for the formation of the Agricultural Protection Society*, 23–4.
[116] Idem in *Letters to Lord John Russell*, esp. pp. 23–4. For similar points see Anon. ['Cincinnatus'], *Remarks on the Anti-Corn-Law mania*, 6, and J. Gladstone, *Plain facts intimately connected with the intended repeal of the corn laws, its probable effects on the public revenue, and the prosperity of the country*, London 1846, 17–19.
[117] Aytoun, 'Robert Peel and the currency', 120. Aytoun cited (pp. 126–7) Alison's prediction of the operation of the Bank Charter Act during harvest failure. See Aytoun's combined critique of Peel's commercial and currency policies in 'Ministerial measures', esp. at p. 380, and Anon., *Upon the probable influence of the repeal of the corn laws*, 37–40.
[118] Alison, *Free trade and a fettered currency*, 20. Alison noted (p. 11) that during November and December 1846 American corn was paid for with three-month bills. Thus it was only during February 1847 that bills were presented for payment in specie, the gold drain accelerated and commercial crisis deepened.

had no control'.[119] To Alison and others it was clear that the severity of the 1847 crisis was attributable to the interaction of Peel's monetary, commercial and railway policies.[120] As Disraeli explained, Peel's Irish Railways Loan of March 1847 had converted floating capital into fixed capital at a time when his monetary legislation was already exerting insupportable pressure on the money market in response to food imports: 'By this law we are placed in this extraordinary position, that though trade is in danger of being destroyed for want of assistance of the bank, and though the bank is most willing and anxious to give trade that assistance, she is shackled by the operation of this law.'[121] The critical concept of 'free trade and a fettered currency' forged a holistic and distinctive critique of Peel's economic liberalism which persisted as a vibrant characteristic of Conservative economic discourse. As W. E. Aytoun opined in 1845, 'we think there are few commercial men in the country who will not agree with us in wishing that Sir Robert Peel had really accepted Mr Alison as the philosopher who is to instruct us on the currency'.[122]

Though, as Thomas Arnold had suspected, Peel did not yield up his 'idea about currency' to his critics, the persistence of a distinctively Conservative strain of monetary criticism remains suggestive. Peel's critics did not merely offer reflexive reactions but drew on a cohesive range of social, economic and constitutional positions against the application of bullionist principles to banking reform. The deflationary results of the return to the gold standard were perceived to have caused the state to alter the relative positions of propertied interests. During the 1830s such constitutionalist arguments were reworked within distinctive readings of parliamentary reform and Whig government. By attributing economic depression in the thirties and forties to the direct action of legislation, Conservative critics generated social and economic defences of local banking discretion which were ultimately designed to reclaim legitimacy for monetary legislation. Some viewed the defence of the Bank of England against further regulation by the state as an act of constitutional defence *per se*. But for others the debate on bank regulation took it for granted that money and banks exerted profound influences over social and economic conditions and raised important questions about the location and accountability of 'monetary sovereignty'. During the 1840s

---

[119] Ibid. 42.
[120] Ibid. 29–31 and esp. p. 54. See also Ashburton's observations on the effect of the operation of the Bank Charter Act on railway speculation: *The financial and commercial crisis considered*, 30–2.
[121] Cited from Bentinck's speech in the House of Commons, 30 Apr. 1847, in Disraeli, *Lord George Bentinck*, 418. Disraeli also invoked Henry Goulburn's speech in the debate on Irish Railways (30 Apr. 1847) (pp. 413–16), and referred (p. 420) to a letter from Bentinck to Mr Ichabod Wright (2 May 1847) outlining an anti-bullionist approach to monetary policy and public spending.
[122] Aytoun, 'Robert Peel and the currency', 128.

the concept of 'free trade and a fettered currency' fused protectionism and anti-bullionism by drawing on the common assumption that the state could insulate social and economic conditions in Britain from the dangerous vacillations of the foreign exchanges and from precarious dependence on foreign markets.

Thus, over four decades, Peelite bullionism was challenged in Conservative economic discourse by monetary positions which assumed definite influences for government in moulding the direction and durability of social and economic change. On the one hand legislative changes in the value of money and encroachments on the freedoms of banks were discussed in a constitutional and ethical language of restraint on the arbitrary powers of the legislature. On the other, monetary and banking policies were identified as mechanisms for manipulating and moralising the character of economic change without redrawing the institutional boundaries of state intervention. Most Conservative critics identified positive production and consumption benefits for an inflated and liquid monetary system. Such views were rooted in anti-Ricardian characterisations of stable economic change as resting on balance between the forces of production and consumption. Money and banks were seen as mechanisms which could magnify and diffuse consumption and reinforce the benign influence of protection on the social and economic complexion of the home market. While monetary policy was seldom abstracted from wider policy contexts in Conservative economic discourse it was invested with an independent social, economic and moral potency. By articulating debates on monetary and banking legislation as questions of the purposes of civil government Conservatives put the *political* back into political economy.

PART III

INCORPORATING EMPIRE

6

The Imperial Frontiers of Tory Political Economy, 1809–1830

Following the loss of the American colonies Britain embarked on a period of imperial consolidation which embraced North America, the West Indies, India and the Far East, the Mediterranean and even the creation of the United Kingdom of Britain and Ireland in 1801. This 'Second British Empire' rested, as C. A. Bayly has argued, on distinct strategic and ideological foundations, 'set in motion and powered by the ferocious reaction of the state and its military apparatus to external challenge and internal revolt'.[1] Indeed, this expansion of Britain's power and influence was a significant factor in her capacity to resist the economic warfare of Napoleon. It is striking, therefore, that the empire tends to be left out of many intellectual histories of economic thought and policy during the post-Napoleonic era.[2] This omission results, in part, from a fundamental assumption that until the late Victorian period contemporaries did not conceive of 'empire' as an overarching geopolitical phenomenon.[3] Yet intellectual approaches to the history of imperialism have perhaps been impeded by another more powerful factor: the tendency to conceptualise early nineteenth-century imperialism in terms of some totemic characteristics of the late Victorian empire, namely colonial self-governance and free trade. There is therefore a need, as Bayly has urged, to step outside the dominant Liberal teleology and to consider early nineteenth-century imperialism 'in its own right rather than as a plateau to the ascent of liberalism'.[4]

Unquestionably, 'the imperialism of free trade' has proved to be a tenacious feature of British imperial historiography. The work of Robinson and Gallagher revised Harlow's emphasis on the 'neo-mercantilist' characteristics of British imperial expansion and glossed this as a drive for markets by the first industrial nation.[5] More recently, the concept of 'free-trade imperialism'

---

[1] C. A. Bayly, *Imperial meridian: the British empire and the world, 1780–1830*, London 1989, 102.
[2] There are, of course, prominent exceptions including D. Winch, *Classical political economy and colonies*, London 1965, and more recently Brian Jenkins, *Henry Goulburn, 1784–1856: a political biography*, Liverpool 1996, esp. pp. 90–129.
[3] But see the imperial empiricism of Patrick Colquhoun's *Treatise on the wealth, power and resources of the British empire*, London 1815.
[4] Bayly, *Imperial meridian*, 11.
[5] V. T. Harlow, *The founding of the second British empire*, London 1952–64, i. 159–62,

has been relocated away from the market-driven impulse of manufacturing industry towards the different free-trade dynamic of portfolio capitalism.[6] While this notion of 'gentlemanly capitalism' may explain the interest of Victorian élites in the profits of empire it also tends to reaffirm the normative status of free trade in approaches to both empire formation and imperialism in the post-Napoleonic period. Of course other historians have focused on the essentially pacific and cosmopolitan concept of international relations which dominated the free-trade mind or they have emphasised the drive for retrenchment which pressurised military and imperial expenditure in nineteenth-century Britain.[7] Yet historians of economic thought have also been concerned to resolve the tension between 'free trade' and 'empire'. They have considered early nineteenth-century imperialism as a set of contradictions within free-trade liberalism and have attempted to explain the coexistence of imperialism with anti-imperialism within the classical tradition. Thus Donald Winch identified a transformation from classical scepticism to a temporary enthusiasm for the empire during 1776–1830 and explained this 'free-trade imperialism' as a coincidence of Philosophic Radicalism with under-consumptionist economics.[8] Bernard Semmel understood the liberal imperial paradox rather differently. He rejected the notion of an ideological high road to the free-trade internationalism of Richard Cobden and instead maintained that classical political economy never divested itself of 'mercantilist' and 'physiocratic' assumptions.[9] Still, these welcome perspectives on the 'imperial impurities' of classical economic thought were, by definition, contained within a free-trade paradigm.

The contortions of 'free-trade imperialism' suggest that it is time to reach outside liberal economics for an intellectual approach to the post-Napoleonic British empire. This chapter therefore explores the intellectual characteristics of another imperialism where naval muscle, the navigation code and the preferential tariff were all conceived as tools of British imperial statecraft.

179–81; R. Robinson and J. Gallagher, 'The imperialism of free trade, 1814–1915', EcHR 2nd ser. vi (1953), 1–15. For the influence of the latter on imperial historiography see Bayly, Imperial meridian, 9–10.

[6] P. J. Cain and A. G. Hopkins, 'The political economy of British expansion overseas, 1750–1914', EcHR xxxiii (1980), 463–90, and 'Gentlemanly capitalism and British expansion overseas, II: new imperialism, 1850–1945', ibid. xl (1987), 3–11; P. J. Cain and A. G. Hopkins, British imperialism: innovation and expansion, 1688–1914, London 1993, esp. pp. 3–104; L. E. Davis and R. A. Huttenback, Mammon and the pursuit of empire: the economics of British imperialism, Cambridge 1988, esp. pp. 30–57, 58–87, 162–82, 262–79.

[7] Ceadel, Origins of war prevention, 35–57, 103–7, 348–55; Harling, The waning of 'Old Corruption', 56–7, 136–7.

[8] For Winch, the underconsumptionism of Edward Gibbon Wakefield and the National Colonisation Society, was pivotal: Classical political economy and colonies, 73–168.

[9] Semmel, The rise of free trade imperialism, 138–9, 146–50. Semmel identified an imperialist 'agrarian critique' (p. 48) which opposed the alternative concept of 'trade empire' (pp. 48–75 esp. pp. 71–5). On physiocracy see above pp. 30–1; on mercantilism see above pp. 95–6.

For, in response to the ambiguities of free-trade liberalism an alternative imperial political economy was evolved largely in the pages of Conservative texts and journals. At the core of this imperial political economy lay the idea that 'national interests', defined by the distinctive historical experience of nations, dominated both international relations and international trade. The economic instruments of navigation laws, preference and protection were therefore presented as devices which suited Britain's historical circumstances and consolidated the political cohesion of her empire. This empire, in turn, was considered to be fundamental not only to the international power of the UK but also to the durability of her economic advance. Of course the integration of colonial and metropolitan conceptions of the imperial consolidation of the UK was never perfect.[10] Notable intellectual conflicts emerged between the cases for colonial emigration and 'home colonisation' and between the relative claims of colonial and domestic producers for preferential treatment by the fiscal state. But, notwithstanding such contradictions, a cohesive intellectual alternative to free-trade imperialism and cosmopolitanism emerged – an imperial political economy which continued to emphasise the fiscal forms of state power.

The empire was therefore no optional extra but was rather an integral feature of Tory economic discourse in the first half of the nineteenth century. Yet most discussions of Conservative economic policy and thought have been dominated by impressions of the inevitability of free trade. Admittedly C. R. Fay and A. Brady did identify a period of 'constructive' post-Napoleonic imperialism but, for both historians, this was a transitional phase sandwiched between 'High Protection' and 'Free Trade'.[11] Indeed Brady viewed Huskisson's commitment to imperial preference as anomalous; it symptomised the 'imperialist overriding the economist'.[12] From a different perspective Hilton's revision of the economics of 'Liberal-Toryism' placed the economic reforms of the 1820s and the debates which surrounded them in an essentially metropolitan matrix of intersecting policy pressures.[13] Commercial and tariff reforms reached in the direction of freer trade offering 'practical and gradual adjustments along traditional lines'.[14] In this reading the major imperatives behind tariff reconstruction were the corn laws, currency legislation, the fiscal needs of the state and the demands of economic interest groups, not imperial consolidation. While Hilton presented freer trade as pragmatic and cautious and challenged the assumption that free-trade theory dominated public policy he also suggested that the reforms of the British tariff consti-

---

[10] On the economic instruments of metropolitan imperial consolidation see A. Gambles, 'Free trade and state formation: the political economy of fisheries policy in Britain and the UK, c. 1780–c.1850', *JBS* (forthcoming).
[11] Brady, *William Huskisson and Liberal reform*, 132–67; Fay, *Great Britain from Adam Smith to the present day*, esp. pp. 43–58, 59–70.
[12] Brady, *William Huskisson and Liberal reform*, 136.
[13] Hilton, *Corn, cash, commerce*, esp. pp. 173–201.
[14] Ibid. 200.

tuted 'a process of purification, a sieve to ensure that newly won commerce was "natural", based on comparative advantage for example, and not a product of speculation or of a peculiar temporary situation'.[15] In this view the commercial and tariff reforms of the 1820s were driven ultimately by a specific economic morality not by the demands of colonial and imperial policy. By contrast C. A. Bayly identified 'the emergence of a constructive conservatism which mirrored the constructive imperialism of the wider British empire' during the period 1780–1830.[16] This concept of 'constructive conservatism' was essentially a philosophy of state power where strategic and political aims were expressed in imperial expansion. New ideological factors such as nationalism, 'the reinvented role of the Crown, the Church and the gentry', racialism, 'agrarian patriotism' and 'the church militant' were played out on a post-Napoleonic imperial stage within specific international contexts.[17] By examining the place of the empire in Conservative economic discourse this chapter suggests another intellectual interface between Bayly's 'constructive conservatism' and 'constructive imperialism'. Indeed, this exploration of the imperial dimensions of Tory economic discourse offers one step towards reintegrating the intellectual history of the British empire with that of the metropole in the early nineteenth century.[18]

Navigation, tariffs and trade: an imperial political economy

The concept of 'empire' lay at the heart of a 'constructive conservative' attitude to the political economy of the UK. Tory commentators appropriated distinctive imperialist positions in the public debate and engaged tenaciously with the financial and economic critiques of the empire which were tendered by some Radicals, Whigs and free traders. This Tory imperialist economics elevated history and experience over theoretical or abstract reasoning and rooted debates on imperial policy in the specific national and international circumstances of the post-Napoleonic era. The political phenomenon of 'imperium' was identified as a necessary feature of international relations and international trade both of which were thought to be determined by the distinct and historically-defined interests of nations. Within this intellectual setting the fiscal instruments of imperial policy – navigation laws, protection and preference – were construed as fundamental components of the sustained and stable progress of the British economy and of the political cohesion of the empire itself.

It would, of course, be wholly unjustifiable to claim that early nineteenth-

---

[15] Ibid. 179–80.
[16] Bayly, *Imperial meridian*, 11.
[17] Ibid. esp. pp. 102–5, 109–15, 133–60.
[18] On the periphery/metropole dichotomy in imperial historiography see Cain and Hopkins, *British imperialism*, esp. pp. 9–13, 50–1, 102.

century imperialism was exclusively a Tory phenomenon. All the same, Tory pamphleteers and journalists did attempt to appropriate the imperial high ground in contemporary economic discourse by impugning the imperial credentials of Whig and Radical prints. Numerous authors observed a dilution of the *Edinburgh Review*'s commitment to the empire in the transition from the intellectual dominance of Henry Brougham to that of J. R. McCulloch.[19] These Tory critics identified a new primacy of economic theory in Whig/Radical political economy which symbolised the apparent abandonment of history and experience for the certainty of abstraction. M. Fletcher applied this reading of Whig/Radical thought to the imperial question of the Navigation Laws: 'The *theorists* are beginning once more to find favour against the *experimentalists*: of old these followers of abstract principles were wont to overwhelm the opposition by the *ipse dixit* of Aristotle: now-a-days they attempt the same rational end by the use of the word *freedom* – free laws, free religion, free press, free trade.'[20] In response to Whig/Radical theorising Tories proffered essentially historicist approaches to the political economy of European empires. Such perspectives elevated social and economic circumstances over abstract principles of economic or political liberty in interpretations of Britain's recent imperial experience. Thus R. C. Wellesley understood the loss of the American colonies not as evidence of the inevitable victory of political and economic liberty over imperial thralldom but as the result of a prolonged historical process of social and economic maturation.[21] The inappropriateness of abstract liberal theories as templates for imperial practice was also emphasised in Tory attitudes to the decline of the French West Indian empire. Numerous commentators explained the French imperial crisis as a direct consequence of applying the 'unhistorical' principles of 1789 to the questions of slavery and colonial governance.[22] Indeed the influential James McQueen condemned the emancipation of the French slaves as a theoretically-driven intervention in the historical development of civil and economic liberty which could rest only on distinct moral, social and

---

[19] H. Brougham, *An inquiry into the colonial policy of the European powers*, Edinburgh 1803. On Brougham and colonies see Fontana, *Rethinking the politics*, 59–63; J. McQueen, *The West India colonies; the misrepresentations circulated against them by the Edinburgh Review, Mr Clarkson, Mr Cropper, &c. &c. examined and refuted*, London 1824, 1–6. J. Barrow engaged with the anti–imperialism of J. R. McCulloch and the ER in 'Political importance of our American colonies', QR xxxiii (Mar. 1826), 410–29 at p. 410. See also W. Maginn, 'MS. notes on the articles concerning Ireland, the West Indies &c., in the last number of the Edinburgh Review', BEM xvii (Apr. 1825), 461–71.
[20] M. Fletcher, 'The navigation laws', QR xxviii (Jan. 1823), 430–49 at p. 448 (Fletcher's emphases).
[21] R. C. Wellesley, 'Spain and her colonies', ibid. xvii (July 1817), 530–62 at pp. 534–7.
[22] M. Fletcher, 'Colonial policy', ibid. xxvi (Jan. 1822), 522–40 at p. 532; Wellesley, 'Spain and her colonies', 536; D. Robinson, 'Friendly epistle to John Bull, Esquire, from one of the old school', BEM xix (June 1826), 631–50 at p. 634.

economic conditions.[23] Thus Tory imperialists commonly held up the historicist yardstick of experience against the prescriptions of abstract liberalism for British imperial practice.[24]

This overtly historicist and experiential approach to interpreting recent colonial history was also applied to debates on British imperial policy. Here, the economic instruments of British imperialism – notably the Navigation code and the preferential tariff – were presented as necessary interventions in the regulation of international relations and trade. Britain's restrictive imperial shipping code remained on the statute book until 1849 but was substantially reformed in 1822 and 1828. Together with the 'Reciprocity of Duties Act' of 1823 these reforms were designed to open Britain's colonial trade to foreign nations while reaffirming the principles of imperial preference and reciprocity in foreign trade together with the strategic importance of Britain's mercantile marine. Foreign access to British colonial trade was strictly subject to the terms of mutual tariff bargains, lists of enumerated articles and adjudications of British Orders in Council.[25] While some Tory commentators received these reforms as evidence of the rolling progress of economic liberalism, others insisted that they had not shifted British policy beyond the boundaries of preference and protection.[26] William Jacob read Huskisson's commercial reforms as pragmatic modifications of the fiscal mechanisms of British imperial statecraft. Indeed his insistence that such commercial regulations were fundamental in disciplining post-Napoleonic international relations re-echoed Adam Smith's earlier concession on the strategic importance of the Navigation Laws.[27] The influence of free-trade cosmopol-

---

[23] See McQueen's reading of the St Domingo rebellion of 1791 in *The West India colonies*, 176–209. R. Wilmot Horton and C. R. Ellis reiterated McQueen's views in 'West India colonies', *QR* xxx (Oct. 1823), 574–5. (McQueen had dedicated his book to C. R. Ellis.) See also A. Alison, 'The West India question: introduction', *BEM* xxi (Feb. 1832), 412–23 esp. at pp. 419–20.

[24] J. G. Lockhart, 'Strictures on an article in no. lvi of the Edinburgh Review: no. II', ibid. ii (Oct. 1817), 90–6. See also Anon., 'Condition of the negroes in our colonies', *QR* xix (July 1823), 476–508 at pp. 495–6, endorsed by J. G. Lockhart in 'The West India controversy: no. III', *BEM* xv (Jan. 1824), 68–82 at pp. 68–9. See also Anon., 'The slave trade', *QR* xxviii (Oct. 1822), 161–79 at pp. 178–9, and *Speech of the right. hon. George Canning in the House of Commons, on the 16th day of March, 1824, on laying before the House the 'Papers in explanation of the measures adopted by His Majesty's government, for the amelioration of the condition of the slave population in the West Indies'*, London 1824, 5–8.

[25] B. Holland, *The fall of protection, 1840–1850*, 1st publ. London 1913, repr. Philadelphia 1980, 30–3; S. Palmer, *Politics, shipping and the repeal of the navigation laws*, Manchester 1990, 71. On the persistence of the principle of preference see W. P. Morrell, *British colonial policy in the age of Peel and Russell*, 2nd edn, London 1960, 166–7.

[26] For the 'discontinuity thesis' see D. Robinson, 'Mr. Huskisson's speech on the shipping interest: no I', *BEM* xxii (July 1827), 1–17; 'No II', ibid. (Aug. 1827), 135–61; 'The old system of trade and the new one', ibid. xxiv (Sept. 1828), 370–95. For the 'continuity thesis' see esp. W. Jacob, 'United States and the West Indies', *QR* xxxix (Jan. 1829), 215–48.

[27] Smith, *Wealth of nations*, 464–5.

itanism on early nineteenth-century attitudes to international relations was more dilute than has frequently been assumed.

This presentation of the economic devices of the navigation code and the preferential tariff as imperial instruments drew on a distinct set of assumptions about the economics of 'empire'. Imperialism, and specifically colonialism, were justified as expressions of the essentially 'nationalistic' character of international trade and as strategies for the avoidance of economic stasis. In elaborating such positions, numerous commentators exploited the imperial ambiguities of free-trade political economy. Adam Smith's observations on the relative value of domestic and foreign trade were harnessed as arguments for a protected and preferential colonial empire. Wielding an idea of domestic trade which embraced Britain's colonies one author questioned the scepticism shown towards the empire by a Ricardian writer:

> You are aware, Sir, that Dr Smith has said and *proved*, that capital employed in the home trade is more beneficially employed for the country than that which is invested in the foreign trade ... Smith remarks, that the interchange of commodities in the course of the home market replaces two *British* capitals with their profits, and that a similar interchange of commodities, by means of foreign trade, although it replaces two capitals with their profits, *replaces only one that is British.*[28]

This essentially nationalistic conception of trade was shared by commentators as diverse as M. Fletcher, J. G. Lockhart and A. Macdonnell who also appropriated Smith's views on exchange as intellectual justifications of a protected colonial trade.[29] These writers also invoked Smith's idea of the stationary state in their arguments for the superiority of colonial over foreign trade. Unlike the subsequent approaches of Malthus, West and Ricardo, Smith's concept of the stationary state emphasised the absence of sufficiently profitable 'vents' for capital and the consequent weakening of the impulse to accumulate.[30] Though he ignored Smith's caveat that abstractions of capital from the domestic economy caused allocative distortions Fletcher argued that, historically, the higher rates of return to capital exported to the New World had raised European profit rates.[31] Similarly, Alexander Macdonnell admitted the

---

[28] J. G. Lockhart and J. Wilson (probably), 'Tickler on the Scotsman', BEM v (Sept. 1819), 655–8 at p. 657 (author's emphasis); Smith, *Wealth of nations*, 607–9.
[29] Fletcher, 'Freedom of commerce', 281–302; J. G. Lockhart, 'The West India controversy: no. IV', BEM xvi (Dec. 1824), 682–98 at pp. 691–4; A. Macdonnell, *Considerations on negro slavery with authentic reports illustrative of the actual condition of the negroes in Demerara*, London 1824, esp. pp. 15–39.
[30] Smith, *Wealth of nations*, 105–15. On agrarian interpretations of the stationary state see above pp. 41–2.
[31] Fletcher, 'Colonial policy', 524. But note that Adam Smith also argued that higher rates of profit afforded by colonial monopoly perverted the natural course of capital allocation in the domestic economy. The syphoning of capital diminished competition in all other trades, subjecting British trade to an absolute and a relative disadvantage in every branch: *Wealth of nations*, 598–604.

superiority of trade with nearby foreign countries over a long-haul colonial trade for states in the early stages of commercial development. But for advanced commercial states like Britain, Macdonnell made colonial trade a fundamental mechanism for avoiding stasis: 'In the progress of time however, if the nation continue her frugality, all these channels of commerce are filled up, and the desideratum then becomes, not to procure, but to get a vent for capital. England has long passed this period; her monied men experience great difficulty in getting employment for their capital.'[32] By appropriating Smith's ideas these commentators neither attempted to represent his views accurately nor endorsed his economic thought as a whole. Rather, they adopted aspects of Smith's thinking on trade and on economic stasis as part of a historicist and nationalistic case for an imperial political economy.[33]

This imperial political economy was also justified in 'underconsumptionist' terms by Tory writers. Their defences of Britain's colonial empire as a set of secure and permanent markets for British trade and manufactures drew on the same fundamental economic assumption which underpinned their positions on protection and monetary policy. It was axiomatic in these commentaries that the British manufacturing economy and Ricardian economic theory were both afflicted by a structural imbalance between the forces of production and consumption. Many contributors to Tory journals refuted the assumption that 'extensive production leads to extensive consumption' and some employed Malthus's emphasis on the need to create conditions for the maximisation of demand in the British economy.[34] Strikingly, this Malthusian position was invoked by several Tory advocates of the economic benefits of Britain's colonial empire.[35] If the fluctuations of the British economy were understood largely in terms of periodic failures of demand it followed that the empire was frequently justified as a construct which might alleviate or avert such economic crises.[36] Indeed domestic and colonial markets were consistently identified as more secure foundations for productive industry than foreign trade. As Macdonnell observed in 1826, 'No trade dependent on the supply of foreign states with manufactures can ever be relied upon as perma-

[32] Lockhart, 'The West Indian controversy: no. IV', 691. This reference was part of a lengthy citation from Macdonnell, *Considerations*, 21.
[33] On Smith's ambiguous legacy see Semmel, *The rise of free trade imperialism*, 24–30, and E. Rothschild, 'Adam Smith and conservative economics', *EcHR* xlv (1992), 74–96.
[34] This was Macdonnell's summary of Say's Law, in *Free trade*, 104. See also T. R. Malthus, *Principles of political economy considered with a view to their practical application*, 1st publ. London 1820, ed. J. Pullen, Cambridge 1989, 29–50, 463–90.
[35] Direct references to Malthus included Fletcher, 'Colonial policy', 536, and Macdonnell (on unproductive consumers) in *Free trade*, 103–5, and *Considerations*, 23 (also cited in Lockhart, 'The West India controversy: no. IV', 693).
[36] See the imperial interpretations of the crisis of 1825, in particular Robinson, 'The meeting of parliament', esp. pp. 860–3; 'Friendly epistle to John Bull, Esquire', 647; 'The shipping interest', *BEM* xx (Sept. 1826), 442–68 at pp. 443–4.

nent and secure.'[37] The qualitative superiority of colonial over foreign markets was commonly identified in the range of finished 'high-value' manufactures bought by the colonies from metropolitan producers. As Robinson remarked:

> The colonies bought of us goods that had been again and again manufactured, – they bought of us not only cottons and woollens, but cottons and woollens manufactured into garments . . . in a word they were to us like resident customers. They bought of us the things that employed the greatest share of our labour, that left the largest profits, and that we otherwise, in many particulars could not have exported.[38]

Implicit in such emphases on the qualitative characteristics of colonial consumption was the idea that the colonies could influence Britain's economy away from specialisation in cheap and semi-finished textiles towards diversified and stable economic development.

The protection of Britain's colonial trade through tariff restrictions was therefore presented as a legitimate legislative influence on the stability and permanence of British economic change. Strikingly, the preferential treatment of colonial producers within the British tariff was frequently justified using such broad economic arguments. In parliament J. Marryat defended the preferential treatment of North American timber as one component of a coherent imperial political economy. Insisting that 'Justice and reciprocity, not liberality, ought to be the basis of our intercourse with foreign powers', Marryat rejected the application of free-trade principles to colonial trade.[39] He urged that, 'We are pursuing a wrong course, in attempting to increase the sale of our manufactures among the European powers. Most of them manufacture for themselves, and use every practical means to secure their own consumption to the industry of their own subjects.'[40] The preferential treatment of West Indian sugar was also justified as a legislative mechanism which could influence the stability of the metropolitan economy. One pamphleteer estimated that the annual average value of exports from the metropolis to the East Indies was less than half that to the West Indian colonies during 1818–23.[41] But, not only was West Indian consumption seen to be greater in crude terms, its intensity and range was considered superior in multiplying

---

[37] Macdonnell, *Free trade*, 265. See also Fletcher, 'Colonial trade', 526. For J. R. McCulloch's dismissal of the need for colonial trade see Winch, *Classical political economy and colonies*, 43–4.
[38] Robinson, 'The shipping interest', 454. See also A. Macdonnell, *Colonial commerce; comprising an inquiry into the principles upon which discriminating duties should be levied on sugar, the growth respectively of the West India possessions, of the East Indies, and of foreign countries*, London 1828, 29–30, and Fletcher, 'Freedom of commerce', 284.
[39] J. Marryat, House of Commons (29 Mar. 1821), *Hansard* n.s. iv. 1505.
[40] Ibid. 1504.
[41] The writer calculated the following annual averages from the annual official export values between 1818 and 1823: exports to the West Indies, £4,792,448; exports to the East

the number of metropolitan enterprises which were sustained by colonial consumption.[42] Clearly, Britain's preferential tariff was perceived as an instrument which could modify the direction and durability of British economic change.

It is important to emphasise, however, that these economic justifications of a colonial empire were never abstracted from their international and strategic contexts. Indeed the 'underconsumptionist' case for a protected colonial trade did not exclude more commonplace autarchic conceptions of the British empire. Thus, imperial preference was also justified as a legislative device which could secure national self-sufficiency in primary produce and thereby strengthen the resources which underpinned Britain's economic independence. The strategic advantages of cementing the partnership between 'old' and 'young' states through colonial trade was clearly perceived by contemporaries:

> A colonial intercourse with a European state is not an unnatural and forced one, but it is founded on diversity of climate and productions, mutual wants and dependence; nor will regulation, therefore, appear superfluous and unnecessary, if it defend us in our natural position, and secure what would, otherwise, be exposed to destruction or change.[43]

Yet such strategic conceptions of the economic devices used to protect colonial trade stretched far beyond the boundaries of autarchy. For the fiscal instruments of protection and preference were also understood to be political structures which bound together the diffuse elements of a far-flung empire. Thus, defenders of preference of colonial sugar and timber producers maintained that the tariff was essential to the integration and cohesion of what remained of Britain's empire in the west.[44] One defender of the West Indian sugar preference insisted that damaging West Indian producers would jeopardise the highly integrated shipping and trade networks of the West Indies and British North America which were crucial in counteracting the maritime power of the United States, and in penetrating South American markets and

---

Indies, £2,091,258: Anon., *A statement of the claims of the West India colonies to a protecting duty against East India sugar, dedicated to William Manning, Esq., MP.*, London 1823, 44. For a similar comparative approach see J. Marryat, *A reply to the arguments in various publications recommending an equalisation of the duties on East and West Indian sugar*, London 1823, 47–8, and McQueen, *The West India colonies*, 57.

[42] Marryat listed the range of imported articles necessary for the establishment of a West Indian sugar estate, from machinery, hardware, fuel and building materials, to clothing, food and furniture: *A reply to the arguments*, 16–17.

[43] Fletcher, 'Colonial policy', 529. See also Macdonnell, *Free trade*, 412–13; Fletcher, 'Freedom of commerce', 282; Anon., 'The history of Mauritius and the neighbouring islands, &c., &c.', *QR* v (Feb. 1811), 229–41 at pp. 229–34; Anon, 'Emigration to the Cape of Good Hope', *BEM* vi (Oct. 1819), 78–83 at p. 81; J. Barrow, 'The Cape of Good Hope', *QR* xxii (July 1819), 203–46.

[44] J. Marryat, House of Commons (5 June 1820), *Hansard* n.s. i. 1183.

resources.[45] Indeed, both John Galt and the pseudonymous 'Junius Colonus' viewed the timber and sugar preferences as integrated fiscal structures which reinforced the political integrity of the western empire.[46] Far from being viewed merely as a revenue tool, the preferential tariff was commonly cast as an instrument of imperial statecraft in Tory economic discourse.[47]

The empire was therefore an integral component of Tory economic debate not an eccentric addition. The imperial political economy of Tory journalists was, of course, consciously directed at the anti-colonialism they perceived in the arguments of free traders. Whereas the *Edinburgh Review* offered financial critiques of the costs and benefits of the empire the Tory journals responded with an alternative imperialist empiricism.[48] This alternative language of statistics measured the comparative value of foreign and colonial trade, the relative merits of reliance on foreign and colonial markets and the revenue yields from foreign and colonial imports.[49] While these Tory empiricists did challenge financial critiques of imperialism on their own terms, they nevertheless rejected the assumption 'that no colony is worth retaining, unless the mother-country derives from it a revenue equal to the expenditure upon it'.[50] For their imperial empiricism was merely an expression of a broader set of ideological positions on the character of British economic advance, the dynamics of international relations and the fiscal forms of state power. In an intellectual sense the 'high road to free-trade imperialism' was vigorously challenged in early nineteenth-century economic discourse.

---

[45] Anon., *A statement of the claims*, 29–32, 37–42. Macdonnell echoed this point in *Colonial commerce*, 71–2.

[46] Galt considered the reduction of duties on colonial timber and sugar together, as an issue of imperial integrity: 'The colonial question', 457. See also Anon. ['Junius Colonus'], 'British America: to the Right Honourable Sir George Murray, His Majesty's principal secretary of state for the colonies, &c. &c.', *BEM* xxvii (Apr. 1830), 604–7.

[47] See H. T. Colebrook's sweeping presentation of imperial preference as the cement of imperial unity in his *On import of colonial corn*, London 1818, 1–17, 116–24, 168–86, 209.

[48] John Barrow rejected the financial anti-colonialism of 'an itinerant professor of political economy' (presumably J. R. McCulloch writing in 'a recent number of a contemporary journal, in which these new lights are usually promulgated') and that of Joseph Hume in 'Political importance of our American colonies', 410, 427.

[49] Fletcher, 'Colonial policy', 534–5; J. McQueen, 'The British colonies; letter to his grace the duke of Wellington, &c., &c.', *BEM* xxiii (June 1828), 891–913, and 'The British colonies: letter third: to his grace the duke of Wellington', ibid. xxvii, pt i (Feb. 1830), 223–53 at pp. 252–3.

[50] Barrow, 'Political importance', 411, which 'reviewed' Anon., *Reflections upon the value of the British West Indian colonies, and of the British North American provinces, 1825*, London 1826. These attempts to quantify the costs and benefits of empire anticipated the interests of economic historians: P. K. O'Brien, 'The costs and benefits of British imperialism, 1846–1914', *P&P* (1988), 163–200; A. Offer, 'The British empire, 1870–1914: a waste of money?', *EcHR* xlvi (1993), 215–38.

The limits of imperium: India and Tory political economy, 1812–29[51]

The intellectual history of Britain's presence in India provides a dramatic demonstration of the distortions risked by imposing 'liberal' teleologies on early nineteenth-century imperial discourse. For, in response to the prescriptions of free traders and Utilitarians, Conservatives and others mounted vigorous defences of the East India Company's monopoly. These justifications of monopoly challenged the appropriateness of both 'free-trade imperialism' and Utilitarianism for British economic development and for her imperium in India. Yet the India question also staked out the limits of Tory imperial political economy. In the Indian case 'constructive conservatism' met 'constructive imperialism' not in the formal fiscal mechanisms of British power nor in colonial settlement. Rather, India was viewed strictly as a dependency whose commerce and governance was controlled by a private chartered company – the East India Company (EIC). Justifications of the EIC's monopoly over the India and China trades dominated Tory attitudes to British imperium in India and mobilised arguments which cannot be dismissed as mere expressions of vested interest. Whereas Britain's colonial empire was justified in explicitly 'underconsumptionist' terms in Tory economic discourse, such economic arguments were explicitly rejected in the Indian case. Instead, Tories defended the fusion of 'sovereign' and 'mercan- tile' functions in the EIC and integrated metropolitan and imperial discourses in rather different ways. If the metropolitan significance of Britain's colonial empire lay in the extension of national self-sufficiency and in the provision of secure markets for the metropolitan economy, the significance of India for the metropolitan state was proscribed by constitutional questions. Fundamentally, the EIC's monopoly was defended in Tory discourse as a mechanism which prevented the constitutional transformation of the British state through direct rule and which was attuned to the limited economic potential of the Indian empire.

Naturally, the most prominent opponents of the EIC's monopoly were those provincial merchants who stood to benefit from the release of London's stranglehold over the eastern trade.[52] Yet the clear pecuniary interests of the merchant petitioners of 1812–13 did not preclude attempts to intellectualise the public debate on the East India Question. In their case for an open eastern trade the petitioners invoked Smithian notions of natural advantage, the international division of labour and trade as a mutually beneficial exchange of equivalents.[53] They maintained that the cessation of the EIC's

---

[51] This periodisation embraces debate from the revocation of the East India Company's (EIC) monopoly over the India trade in 1813 to the start of Lord William Bentinck's governor-generalship in 1828.

[52] See petitions from the merchants and corporation of Liverpool (23 Mar. 1812), *Hansard* xxii. 111–12, 118–19.

[53] For example, *Petitions of the merchants of and manufacturers of Bristol, Liverpool, & c.*

monopoly would maximise the natural advantages enjoyed by both India and Britain and would mobilise an immense demand for the products of British industry. Indeed the Hindu system of castes was lauded as 'the most complete system of division of labour that has ever been, or could be, practised by a whole people'.[54] In parliament, the intellectual attack by the Whigs on the EIC's monopoly also drew on the ideas of Smith. Lord Grenville shared Smith's conviction that this monopoly throttled a vast sea of potential consumption and raised prices of Indian produce in Britain by limiting supply below its natural extent. But he also selected a different Smithian emphasis by insisting on the strict separation of the mercantile and sovereign functions of the East India Company.[55] As Creevy objected, the monopoly 'placed the Company in the situation of both sovereigns and merchants'.[56] What the Whigs objected to was the distortion of civil government in India by the commercial interests of the EIC.

In response to Whig critiques of the conflation of 'commerce' and 'sovereignty' Tories tended to defend the 'commercial sovereignty' of the Company in India. As Warren Hastings maintained in his evidence to a parliamentary committee on the EIC, 'The sovereignty of the Company is certainly beneficial to the country [India]. The union of its commercial with its political interest in it, has never produced ... any detriment to the inhabitants.'[57] Yet the Tory defence of the Company's 'commercial sovereignty' stretched far beyond the assertions of Hastings and mobilised sweeping historicist and constitutionalist arguments. In a number of articles in the *Quarterly* during 1812 and 1813 George Ellis invoked the comparative historicism of David Macpherson.[58] Macpherson's history of the European presence in India traced the progression from Moslem imperium to the Christian rule of the Portuguese and Dutch and finally to the moral fusion of commerce and

---

against the renewal of the Company's charter, &c, London 1812, reviewed by G. Ellis in 'Papers respecting the E. I. Company's charter', *QR* viii (Dec. 1812), 239–86.

54 Ibid. 260–6, 267. Adam Smith assumed the competition in Indian markets could mobilise an 'immense ocean of Indian commerce': *Wealth of nations*, 748.

55 *Substance of the speech of Lord Grenville, on the motion made by the Marquis Wellesley, in the House of Lords, on Friday, the 9th of April, 1813 for the production of certain papers on Indian affairs*, London 1813, 17; Smith, *Wealth of nations*, 637–41, 819.

56 T. Creevy, House of Commons (14 June 1813), *Hansard* xxvi. 631. For a more general survey of Whig and Radical attitudes to the EIC's monopoly see Alborn, *Conceiving companies*, 27–8.

57 Testimony of W. Hastings to a committee of the whole house on the East India Company's affairs: House of Commons (30 Mar. 1813), *Hansard* xxv. 426. See also Alborn, *Conceiving companies*, 30.

58 D. Macpherson, *The history of the European commerce with India; to which is subjoined, a review of the arguments for and against the trade with India, and the management of it by a chartered company; with an appendix of authentic accounts*, London 1812; G. Ellis, 'Macpherson's European commerce with India', *QR* viii (Sept. 1812), 114–44, and 'Papers respecting the E. I. Company's charter'. See also J. Barrow, 'Grant On *maintaining the Indian system*', ibid. ix (Mar. 1813), 218–53.

sovereignty in the dominion of the British East India Company. He interpreted the ultimate collapse of Portuguese power in India as a consequence of their failure to moderate executive power with commercial ethics.[59] Dutch imperium during the seventeenth century was projected, on the contrary, as a fusion of public and private morality in the 'commercial sovereignty' of a private chartered company. Sustained by private capital subscriptions and chartered by a representative legislature Macpherson insisted that the Dutch Company had distilled the moral and political characteristics of the Dutch commonwealth; 'The constitution of this company ... was exactly analagous to that of the commonwealth.'[60] Yet Macpherson located the apotheosis of 'commercial sovereignty' in the monopoly of the British East India Company. Unlike the ventures of the Elizabethan and Stuart periods the privileges conferred in 1708 removed the monopoly from the territory of the crown and located it firmly within the competence of parliament. In this sense, then, the EIC's monopoly was 'exactly analagous' to that of the British commonwealth.[61] This historicist defence of the 'commercial sovereignty' of the EIC therefore drew on a language of parliamentary patriotism which emphasised the pivotal significance of the 'Glorious Revolution'. Far from being 'odious' or 'revolting' the Company's monopoly was presented as an expression of the sovereignty of parliament in the British constitution.[62]

In their defences of the 'commercial sovereignty' of the EIC Tory commentators also introduced a specific historical reading of the origins of British power in India. Historically, Britain's imperium in India was perceived to have originated in the impulse of commerce not sovereignty:

> It is not that the British *nation* has conquered India; rather, unavoidable circumstances have at length almost subdued the *national* aversion to this conquest. Into these, and the influence inseparable from them, were we gradually introduced, in protecting our commercial interests, till we found that to recede would be tantamount to a total abandoning of all future interest in India of any kind whatever.[63]

In this view, the commercial roots of Britain's presence in India legitimated her governance by a chartered company whose administrative structures evolved beside local institutions, customs and social hierarchies. To remove the Company's monopoly, therefore, would be to uproot the evolved consti-

---

[59] Ellis cited from Macpherson's description of the purely 'sovereign' character of Portuguese presence: 'Macpherson's European commerce', 118.
[60] Ibid. 123–4.
[61] Ibid. 125–7. 'Fabius' also endorsed Macpherson's idea of 'commercial sovereignty' in Anon., *A letter to the right honourable the earl of Buckinghamshire, president of the board of commissioners for the affairs of India, on the subject of an open trade to India*, London 1813, 24–5.
[62] Anon., *Considerations on colonial policy, with relation to the renewal of the East India Company's charter, by an impartial observer*, London 1813, 27.
[63] G. R. Gleig, 'Letters on the present state of India', BEM xvii (May 1825), 574–91 at p. 579. See also Ellis, 'Macpherson's European commerce with India', 144.

tution of Indian society.[64] By the same token, the destruction of the EIC's 'commercial sovereignty' was contemplated as a process which would erect an entirely new profile and scope for the British state in India and would drive the British presence beyond the bounds of an essentially temporary imperium.[65] If defenders of the EIC's monopoly invoked particular readings of the origins of British authority in India they also insisted that a direct presence for the British state would exert profound and deleterious influences on the metropolitan constitution. Adam Smith's claim that the territorial acquisitions of the East India Company were the 'undoubted right of the Crown' was refuted as a dangerous violation of the chartered rights of a private company, and indirectly, as a threat to the security of property throughout the empire.[66] Further, the prospect of 'direct rule' in India was presented as a force for the destabilisation of the balanced constitution by the influence which would accrue to the executive through control of the India patronage. As during the 1780s, the confinement of the India patronage to the private sphere was perceived as a safeguard on metropolitan civil liberties.[67] As Samuel Whitbread insisted, 'The Truth was, that the ministerial tools into which the Company would be converted would soon crumble away, and the controul [sic] of India, its patronage and its wealth would quietly fall into the hands of ministers.'[68] The EIC's monopoly was thus defended as an appropriate expression of 'commercial sovereignty' which functioned as a historical corollary of Britain's balanced constitution by preventing the formal expansion of executive power.

The defenders of the Company's monopoly in Tory journals also engaged closely with the economic expectations of their opponents. A common ploy was to represent arguments for open access to the eastern trade as expressions of free-trade theory and to hold up 'experience' of the trade against the sanguine promises of abstract theorising. The Indian infrastructure of ports and credit-houses was presented as inseparable from the Company; without these

---

[64] Barrow, 'Grant On maintaining the Indian system', 218–53; Anon., 'Origin and state of the Indian army', QR xix (May 1818), 385–423 at p. 397; Anon., 'Malcolm – Memoir of central India', ibid. xxix (July 1823), 382–414.

[65] See the citation from a letter of Henry Dundas (president of the India board) to the chairman of the EIC, 2 Apr. 1800, in Anon. ['Cossim'], Considerations on the danger and impolicy of laying open the trade with India and China; including an examination of the objections commonly urged against the East India Company's commercial and financial management, 2nd edn, London 1813, 37.

[66] Smith, Wealth of nations, 945. Ellis challenged Smith's point in 'Macpherson's European commerce with India', 144. On Smith's attitudes to the EIC see Alborn, Conceiving companies, 24–6.

[67] Ellis, 'Macpherson's European commerce with India', 142. For specific appeals to the patronage controversy of 1783–4 see Anon. ['Fabius'], Letter to the earl of Buckinghamshire, 74–5, and Speech of Lord Grenville, 26.

[68] S. Whitbread, House of Commons (11 June 1813), Hansard xxvi. 599; Alborn, Conceiving companies, 28–9.

[69] Anon. ['Cossim'], Considerations on the danger and impolicy, title page and p. 66.

structures an abstract freedom to trade would be meaningless.[69] More commonly, this experiential mode of reasoning was expressed in refutations of the free-trade assumption that competition could liberate 'an immense ocean of Indian commerce'.[70] Thus Tory commentators did not apply underconsumptionist arguments to the justification of monopoly in India but approached the need to proportion supply to demand from the supply side. Here, monopoly was considered to be fundamental in regulating the supply of a limited Indian market for British manufactures. Ellis dismissed Smith's notion that India could become a great mart for British manufactures and also presented a detailed account of the state of European demand for Indian produce as a way of underlining the European limits of a trade which was already restricted by the economic and cultural constraints on the Indian 'means of purchase'.[71] Ellis believed that by opening the India trade parliament would unleash a tide of mercantile speculation which would swamp an essentially limited market with ruinous consequences.[72] Similarly, in their evidence before a parliamentary committee both Sir John Malcolm and Captain Thomas Munro insisted that India could never become a significant mart for British manufacturing industry and identified monopoly as the only sound regulator of this limited market.[73] By appealing to experience, advocates of monopoly attempted to puncture free traders' theoretical expectations of the India trade.[74]

From the metropolitan perspective the Company's monopoly was presented as an instrument which could regulate European demand for Indian produce. It was feared that the intervention of individual mercantile speculators would glut British markets causing extensive commercial failures. Monopolists therefore tended to emphasise the advantages of keeping London the emporium of the Indian import and re-export trades. The EIC could rely on stable sales, the private dealer on sure custom and the revenue on a regular income.[75] In its narrow economic guise the Company's monopoly was presented as a mechanism which apportioned supply to demand and which therefore contributed to the achievement of a lasting balance between supply and demand in the British economy. Yet despite recognising the economic benefits conferred on the nation by the East India Company's monop-

---

[70] Smith, *Wealth of nations*, 748.
[71] Ellis, 'Macpherson's European commerce with India', 133–9
[72] Idem, 'Papers respecting the E.I. Company's charter', 256. See also Anon. ['Fabius'], *A letter*, 19–20, and Anon., *Considerations on the danger and impolicy*, 51–2.
[73] Evidence of Sir J. Malcolm before the committee of the whole House of Commons on the East India Company's affairs (5, 7 Apr. 1813), *Hansard* xxv. 511–12, 632–4; T. Munro (13 Apr. 1813), ibid. 804, 810.
[74] A pamphlet of 1829 drew together all these arguments claiming detailed experience of the Indian commodity trade and pointing to the delusion of India's becoming a mart for British textiles: Anon., *On the territorial government and commerce of the East India Company*, London 1829, 35–46.
[75] A series of progressively increasing statements of sales of goods, 1741–1807, was offered to show that the Company had not artificially kept supply below demand: Anon., *Considerations on the danger and impolicy*, 119–21.

oly, Tory commentators confined their appreciation of the national importance of the East India trade to the efficient remittance of revenue. The state participated in the EIC's territorial revenues and the Company provided structures for the collection of indirect revenues at minimum expense. Moreover the private wealth generated by the East India Trade, it was asserted, constituted 'one fifth of the whole national capital subject to property tax' in 1812.[76] Thus, for many, the EIC's monopoly was merely an efficient device for the remittance of revenue devised by parliament to meet the specific circumstances of India.[77]

Once the East India Company's monopoly over the India trade had been conceded in 1813 the public debate on India shifted to the state of Indian society and administration. The intellectual initiative was appropriated by Utilitarians who attributed the stationary state of the Indian economy to the long-term effect of the EIC's monopoly and to its fusion of commerce with civil administration. In his *History of British India*, James Mill measured the actual state of India against an ideal state based on a conjectural view of historical change where the 'progress' of civilisation was a corollary of economic liberalism. Mill concluded that social and administrative structures had forestalled the emergence of a commercial society in India. For Mill, the stationary condition of India could therefore be transformed by Utilitarian political, administrative and social reforms achieved through a direct rule by the British state.[78] Tory commentators resisted Mill's diagnosis of the state of India and his proposed reforms but did concede that the Company's fiscal reforms had damaged the condition of India and shaken British authority. The particular reforms in question were the introduction of permanent zemindary settlement and the disappropriation of the ryots.[79] In a review of Sir John Malcolm's *Memoir of central India*, the *Quarterly* condemned this reform of the Bengal land tax:

> One of the greatest practical blunders we have yet made in India was the substitution of a plausible theory for ancient usage, in taking the land from the ryots, its rightful owners, and conferring it on the zemindars, the hereditary

---

[76] Ellis, 'Macpherson's European commerce', 130, and 'Papers respecting the E.I. Company's charter', 250, 245.

[77] Melville's policy of 1793 had drawn a clear distinction between colonial trade and a trade of simple remittance. The East India Company's monopoly was described as a parliamentary strategy for efficient remittance of taxes: Anon., *Considerations on the danger and impolicy*, 38.

[78] On Mill's view of the 'progress' of civilisation in India see J. Mill, *History of British India*, London 1817, i. 1–2, 432–80. See also Winch, *Classical political economy and colonies*, 160–2.

[79] Permanent zemindary settlement had been introduced to Bengal in 1793, and to Madras during 1802–4: R. B. Ramsbotham, 'The revenue administration of Bengal, 1765–86', and J. T. Gwynn, 'The Madras district system and land revenue to 1818', in H. H. Dodwell and others (eds), *The Cambridge history of the British Empire*, IV: *British India*, Cambridge 1929, 409–32, 462–82. See also Bayly, *Imperial meridian*, 209–11.

collectors of revenue, under the specious pretext of creating a body of country gentlemen, which would improve the property and secure to the government a permanently fixed rent.[80]

Similarly, G. R. Gleig insisted in *Blackwood's* during 1825-6 that these reforms of the tax system had 'unhinged' and demoralised Indian society; an ancient class of proprietor cultivators had been converted to tenants at will, a new class of zemindars created, native police, courts and magistrates had been swept away, and local religions challenged by Christian missionaries.[81] Thus in response to the Utilitarian prescriptions of James Mill, Tories identified the form and incidence of taxation as the most important influence on the state of the society and economy of India and therefore on the security of British imperium there.[82] In keeping with their defences of the Company's monopoly before 1813, Tory commentators neither indicted the 'commercial sovereignty' of the EIC with the origins of Indian stasis nor endorsed the proposed reforms of Utilitarian and the free-trade case for a direct presence for the British state in India. Instead they pointed to the destructive effects of fiscal reforms on the indigenous structures of Indian society and economy and on the character of Britain's imperial presence.[83]

The intellectual interface between 'constructive conservatism' and 'constructive imperialism' was therefore reinforced by historicist and constitutionalist perspectives on the problem of British imperium in India. The attitudes of Whigs, Radicals and Utilitarians were challenged by an alternative set of approaches which defended the East India Company's monopoly as the fulcrum of Britain's presence in the east. The intellectual defence of monopoly appealed to specific historical constructions of the origins of the British empire in India which legitimised the 'commercial sovereignty' of the Company against the criticisms of free traders and Utilitarians. While Britain's colonial empire in the west was justified in Tory prints as an economic resource which could provide permanent markets and influence the character and durability of the economic advance of metropolitan Britain, the econ-

---

[80] Anon., 'Malcolm – *Memoir of central India*', 409. Tory fiscal critiques also invoked Sir John Malcolm, *A political history of India from 1784 to 1823*, London 1826, Reginald Heber, *Narrative of a journey through the upper provinces of India, from Calcutta to Bombay*, London 1827, and Sir Thomas Munro's arguments for an indigenous ryotwary system in Madras: Gwynn, 'The Madras district system', 470–3.

[81] Gleig, 'Letters on the present state of India: no. I', esp. pp. 581–2, 589–90, and 'Letters on the present state of India', BEM xviii (Oct. 1825), 401–17.

[82] H. Ellis, 'Government of India', QR xxxv (Jan. 1827), 32–66 at pp. 51–2; Anon., *On the territorial government*, 19; Anon., *An inquiry into the causes of the long-continued stationary condition of India and its inhabitants; with a brief examination of the leading principles of two of the most approved revenue systems of British India; by a civil servant of the honourable East India Company*, London 1830, 65–95.

[83] G. R. Gleig, 'Political history of India', BEM xx (Nov. 1826), 689–709 at pp. 701–5; Ellis, 'Government of India', 59; Anon., *On the territorial government*, 31–4; J. G. Lockhart, 'Bishop Heber's *Indian journals*, &c', QR xxxvii (Jan. 1828), 100–47, 119.

omic significance of India as a mart and source of raw materials was considered to be limited. The Company's monopoly was justified as a conduit for the transmission of revenue and as a crucial instrument for the management of structurally limited markets. Yet it was also defended as an imperial device which could prevent the constitutional transformation of the British state which a direct presence in the Indian sub-continent would signify. This historicist and constitutionalist discourse on the India question constitutes one dimension of a 'Conservative imperialism' which consistently challenged the prescriptions of free traders and Utilitarians for Britain's post-Napoleonic empire.

Debating the political economy of emigration, 1817–30

The question of emigration brought the empire to the heart of the public debate about poverty and its causes in early nineteenth-century Britain. Indeed the positions of individual commentators on the desirability of emigration were informed by their perspectives on population growth, the causes of unemployment and the social costs of economic change. To some, for instance R. Wilmot Horton, state-assisted emigration was an instrument which could syphon off the pressure exerted by pauperism on the labour market and on the Old Poor Law.[84] Yet, at a time of acute financial and intellectual pressure on the system of poor relief the solution of 'shovelling out paupers' was consistently challenged in Tory economic discourse.[85] The Tory prints insisted that a pauper emigration could not redress the crises of 'underconsumption' and 'over-capitalisation' which they believed symptomised and caused much domestic poverty. Indeed, Tory commentators protested that the resettlement of the poor within the British Isles, or 'home colonisation', presented a morally and economically superior option for a propertied polity.[86] By resisting the impulse to 'shovel out paupers', however, Tory commentators did not reject the idea that emigration could exert beneficial influences on the metropolitan economy. What amounted to a consensus crystallised around the conviction that public policy should encourage a balanced exportation of both labour and capital to Britain's colonial empire. Not only was such colonial emigration perceived as a response to the oversupply of domestic labour and capital, it was also projected as a strategy which

---

[84] R. Wilmot Horton, *Outline of a plan of emigration in a report of the select committee on the employment of the poor in Ireland*, London 1823; J. R. Poynter, *Society and pauperism: English ideas on poor relief, 1795–1834*, London 1969, esp. pp. 186–329; D. Eastwood, *Governing rural England: tradition and transformation in local government, 1780–1840*, Oxford 1994, 178–9; H. J. M. Johnston, *British emigration policy: 'shovelling out paupers'*, Oxford 1972, 2–56.

[85] See ibid. subtitle.

[86] Anon. 'Extracts from a communication to J. C. Curwen, Esq. chairman of the committee on the poor laws', *BEM* i (June 1817), 241–6 at p. 242.

could address the problems of sustaining British economic advance. Just as the navigation code and imperial preference were presented in Tory economic discourse as mechanisms which maximised demand for the produce of British manufacturing industry, so colonial emigration was identified as an instrument which would ultimately create permanent markets for the metropolitan economy while tightening the bonds of imperial cohesion.

Following the Napoleonic wars Britain's newly formed Colonial Office considered the possibility of giving public assistance to schemes for colonial emigration.[87] Within this context, private strategies like that of Lord Selkirk and public ones such as that supported by N. Vansittart (then Chancellor of the Exchequer) were the subject of some debate in Tory journals.[88] One striking feature of this discourse was that none of the emigration schemes endorsed by the Tory periodicals were purely schemes for 'shovelling out paupers'. Support for Vansittart's policy of state-assisted emigration to the Cape of Good Hope rested on the fact that this scheme was targeted at groups of independent adults not paupers.[89] In *Blackwood's* John Galt presented information on emigration which was aimed explicitly at industrious families who could command £20–£30 of their own capital.[90] As John Barrow observed, the ideal emigrant was no pauper but rather possessed 'a small capital, common prudence, and industrious habits'.[91] Clearly, colonisation schemes were not conceptualised in the Tory periodical press as crude syphons for domestic pauperism. This intellectual characteristic can only be understood by exploring how the emigration question was informed by debates on the social and economic experience of contemporary Britain.

It is at first glance surprising that the political economist Richard Whately chose to publicise his views on emigration in the Tory *Quarterly*. If his views are placed in the context of the Tory discourse on emigration, however, his choice of both genre and organ makes more sense. For it was on the related questions of capital exportation and emigration that Whately diverged from

---

[87] Johnstone, *British emigration policy*, 17–23, 31–4. Emigration was the subject of detailed analysis in parliament by a select committee on the employment of the poor in Ireland (1823), and the select committees on emigration in 1826 and 1826–7: ibid. 89–90, 96–7, 131–4.

[88] On Selkirk's scheme see J. Galt, 'Bandana on emigration: letter first', BEM xv (Apr. 1824), 433–40 at p. 433. See also W. A. Carrothers, *Emigration from the British Isles*, London 1929, 9–11.

[89] On Vansittart's scheme see Anon., 'Emigration to the Cape of Good Hope', BEM v (Aug. 1819), 523–27 at p. 523. See also Anon., 'Emigration to the Cape of Good Hope', ibid. vi (Oct. 1819), 78–83.

[90] J. Galt, 'Howison's Canada', ibid. x (Dec. 1821), 537–45, 540. See also R. Whately, 'Emigration to Canada', QR xxiii (July 1820), 373–400 at pp. 396–7; Anon., 'Van Diemen's Land', ibid. xxvii (Apr. 1822), 99–109 at p. 99. This latter article reproduced the recommendations of George William Evans (surveyor-general of the colony) from *A geographical, historical, and topographical description of Van Diemen's Land, with important hints to emigrants, and useful information respecting the application for grants of land & c. & c.*, London 1822.

[91] J. Barrow, 'Notes on the Cape of Good Hope', QR xxv (July 1821), 453–66 at p. 460.

the 'liberal' orthodoxy. If Richard Whately's economic thought in other areas owed much to Malthus, he explicitly rejected Malthus's belief that emigration would perpetuate poverty by creating a vacuum between population size and the means of subsistence.[92] Whately preferred to analyse emigration in terms of its effect on the fund for wages in the domestic economy and on the state of the labour market and proposed a heavier expenditure on emigration in order to relieve the 'permanent' burden of 'the injurious competition in an overstocked market for labourers'.[93] However, Whately also insisted that far from damaging the domestic economy, the exportation of capital alongside emigrants would be beneficial in providing funds for the employment for emigrants, in creating markets for British trade and industry and in syphoning excess capital away from the domestic economy. In this way Whately presented emigration as an appropriate solution to the over-capitalisation and imbalance between production and consumption which he believed dislocated the metropolitan economy. On this question, then, Whately was at odds with the views of fellow political economists who objected to emigration because it might lead to the exportation of capital.[94] He countered with the argument that the feared capital haemorrhage need not be an abstraction of 'national capital' but a beneficial re-channelling of private funds: 'it is not proposed to lay out the *national* capital in founding a colony at the public expense: but merely to encourage and facilitate the enterprize of those individuals who are willing so to employ their own capital'.[95] If Whately placed more confidence in free-trade political economy than did most other contributors to the Tory periodical press his diagnosis of poverty nevertheless stressed the market's failure to balance the wages and capital funds. Whately's position on the question of emigration can be legitimately located in a broader consensus on the value of a colonial empire in assisting Britain to overcome the social consequences of economic change.

Elsewhere in the Tory periodical press 'emigration' was conceptualised as an appropriate response to the perceived 'over-capitalisation' of the British economy. From this perspective, John Galt presented emigration as a social and economic 'safety-valve' which operated in more complex ways than simply as a syphon for excess paupers.[96] Galt proceeded from the assumption

---

[92] Whately traced changes in Malthus's 'vacuum theory' from the 1798 edition of the *Essay on the principle of population*, to his concession in the 1817 edition that in specific cases emigration was an appropriate response to a short-run surge in population. Whately endorsed emigration as a general solution to domestic poverty in 'Emigration to Canada', 373–400.
[93] Ibid. 387.
[94] For Ricardians, capital haemorrhage was a prominent objection to colonisation. Like Whately, Nassau Senior and Robert Torrens challenged the orthodox Ricardian line on capital exports: Winch, *Classical political economy and colonies*, 65–8.
[95] Whately, 'Emigration to Canada', 389.
[96] John Galt rejected Wilmot Horton's schemes. Horton's *Outline of a plan of emigration* (1823) may have been the focus of Galt's general critique in 'Bandana on emigration: letter first', 433–40.

that, 'as yet no proper "safety-valve" has been introduced into the regular system of the state' which could compensate for the social costs of industrialisation.[97] The 'safety-valve' of emigration, Galt contended, could moderate the unemployment which he attributed to industrialisation and mechanisation:

> In the application of that increased capital, the surplus of which, beyond what is requisite for the business of the country, is even greater than the surplus of population, which is ready to swarm off – in the application, I would say, of that capital, lie the means and materials of constructing a civilised society – EMIGRATION.[98]

Emigrant capital, if concentrated judiciously, would in Galt's view develop imperial powers of production which could then be sustained using the device of imperial preference.[99] More significantly, he believed that the colonial emigration of capital would render metropolitan economic change sustainable and place British social and economic conditions on a steadily progressive trajectory by extending markets for British trade and industry. Following the commercial and financial crises of 1825 Galt sharpened his focus. He declared that social and economic distress was not the product of a Malthusian population mechanism but rather of over-capitalisation. Understood in these terms, the exportation of capital through colonial emigration was an appropriate solution to social and economic dislocation: 'The corrective, I agree with Mr Horton, is emigration. Much of the intelligence, and much of the wealth, at present exclusively directed to improvements in manufactures, would be much more advantageously employed, both for the possessors and for the kingdom, could it be directed to purposes of colonization.'[100] Like Whately, Galt viewed emigration as a way of redressing the domestic maldistribution of resources evidenced in over-capitalisation and unemployment, through the device of empire. Still, few 'emigrationists' advocated a direct role for the state in colonisation; the state could regulate settlement by establishing guidelines for concentration, land clearance and finance and might assist in funding necessary infrastructural projects. But the recruitment, transportation and settlement of emigrants were all firmly located in the province of regulated private agents.[101] As Galt insisted, 'it is not natural that government should be the originator of any scheme of emi-

---

[97] Ibid. 434.
[98] Ibid.
[99] Galt anticipated some of Edward Gibbon Wakefield's views on concentrated colonisation: ibid. 437. Galt argued (p. 439) for the need to reform the Canada Corn preference in order to integrate Canadian with British supply.
[100] J. Galt, 'Bandana on emigration', BEM xx (Sept. 1826), 470–7 at p. 471 (Galt's emphasis).
[101] J. Barrow, 'The Poyais bubble', QR xxviii (Oct. 1822), 157–61, and J. Galt, 'Bandana on colonial undertakings', BEM xx (Aug. 1826), 304–8.

gration, but only the aider of individual adventure. Let it assist, but not plan, protect, but not project'.[102]

The clear boundaries drawn thus around the functions of the early nineteenth-century state did not preclude the presentation of the emigration question as a full-dress critique of free-trade liberalism in Tory economic discourse. In his response to the ideas of Wilmot Horton, David Robinson held up the very existence of a select committee on emigration as evidence that Ricardian economics could not fulfil its promises: 'The Report is a most remarkable production. It in reality, though not in terms, flatly controverts some of the leading tenets of the Ricardo school, and proclaims that Ministers are acting on erroneous and ruinous principles.'[103] Robinson's central point was that Ricardian economic theory possessed no framework for understanding social distress. Neither, in Robinson's view, did Malthus's theory of population. Poverty and pauperism were the results of structural problems in the British economy not the saturation of the labour market by the pressure of population on the means of subsistence. For Robinson, poverty could not be analysed simply in terms of the size of the labour market since he believed a 'political economy of cheapness' had depressed wages and suffocated consumption in the domestic economy. To compound this, foreign produce had been permitted to compete in British markets further diminishing secure demand for British products. Given his reading of the social and economic experience of contemporary Britain, emigration and imperial expansion were remote palliatives for Robinson. Since, in Robinson's understanding, the root of acute poverty in the British Isles was neither 'over-population' nor a lack of capital but rather a structural deficiency of consumption, then emigration could provide no quick fix.[104]

Towards the close of the 1820s Tory critics responded to proposals for pauper emigration with the alternative of resettling the poor in rural areas within the British Isles.[105] Fundamentally, this 'home colonisation' discourse melded responses to two sets of policy debates: those on poverty and on agricultural protection.[106] In parliament Joseph Leycester condemned the emigration schemes of Wilmot Horton as 'a system of statistical suicide' which neglected the possibility of employing the poor at home 'in improving and

---

102 Idem, 'Bandana on emigration: letter first', 435.
103 Robinson responded to *Three reports from the select committee on emigration from the United Kingdom* (1826–7) in 'The surplus population of the United Kingdom', 378.
104 Robinson applied his diagnosis of poverty especially to Ireland: ibid. p. 389, and in his 'Mr McCulloch's Irish evidence', 55–76.
105 But note that domestic resettlement was raised as a preferable alternative to Vansittart's scheme of emigration to the Cape as early as 1819: House of Commons (12 July 1819), *Hansard* xl. 1550–1.
106 There is evidence to suggest that F. J. Robinson (Chancellor of the Exchequer) proposed to use revenue gained by reducing the corn law in 1827–8 to finance pauper emigration: Jones, *Prosperity Robinson*, 127; Johnston, *British emigration policy*, 152–3; Horton (and possibly E. Edwards), 'The corn laws', 269–83.

cultivating waste lands, which would give employment to thousands'.[107] Many advocates of such schemes for 'home colonisation' took for granted the falsity of Ricardian positions on the law of rent and on diminishing returns to capital invested in agriculture.[108] Challenging Ricardo's model in which investment in the cultivation of waste land in the British Isles led inevitably to economic stasis, Edward Edwards made the successful cultivation of such land a corollary of the progress of civilisation.[109] Edwards went on to present empirical evidence derived from experiments in contemporary Holland to demonstrate not only that great productivity advances were possible from less fertile land (and that the British area under cultivation could profitably be extended), but also to present 'home colonisation' as a more effective strategy than the imperial option of emigration.[110] For Robinson, home colonisation was socially and economically preferable to the emigration of paupers to the colonies: home colonies could help forge a stable and mutual demand between the domestic economic sectors and 'would directly and indirectly in all ways provide employment for nearly 200,000 artisans, mechanics, and town-labourers. By providing employment for the first 200,000, Government would provide it for nearly 200,000 more, without being at any more cost or trouble'.[111] Robinson also believed that by borrowing funds to help finance 'home colonisation' the government could combat the effects of a deflationary monetary policy which had swollen the capacity to invest and to produce beyond the British economy's means of consumption.[112] Likewise, in his analysis of the debates of the emigration committees William Johnstone presented the arguments of 'home colonists' as solutions which were better suited to addressing the problems of underconsumption, distribution and deflation than was the imperial option of a pauper emigration.[113]

[107] J. Leycester, House of Commons (4 Mar. 1828), *Hansard* n.s. xviii, 956. See also J. Benett, ibid. and Col. Trench, House of Commons (24 June 1828), ibid. xix. 1511.

[108] See especially J. Weyland, House of Commons (15 Mar. 1832), *Hansard* 3rd ser. xi. 286–90 and above pp. 28–9 n. 15.

[109] Edwards, 'Cultivation of waste lands', 413–14. See also Robinson, 'The surplus population of the United Kingdom', 382.

[110] Edwards's 'Cultivation of waste lands', ostensibly reviewed William Jacob's, *Observations on the cultivation of poor soils, as exemplified in the colonies for the indigent, and for orphans in Holland*, London 1828. Edwards also presented William Cowling's estimates as they appeared in *First, second, and third report of the commissioners appointed to inquire into the nature and extent of the several bogs in Ireland, and the practicability of draining and cultivating them*, London 1814. See also his 'Home colonies', *QR* xli (Nov. 1829), 522–50.

[111] Robinson, 'The surplus population of the United Kingdom', 381. George Croly shared the view that home colonisation was an underconsumptionist strategy for sustaining economic change: 'Mr Wilmot Horton and emigration', *BEM* xxiii (Feb. 1828), 191–4 at pp. 193–4.

[112] Robinson, 'The surplus population of the United Kingdom', 385–6.

[113] Johnstone, 'Emigration', 618–19. See also Edwards, 'Conditions of the English peasantry', 240–84, and Scott, 'On planting waste lands', 558–60.

Yet opposition to 'shovelling out paupers' was not synonymous with anti-colonialism or with a 'Little England' approach to British social and economic problems in Tory economic discourse. Indeed, David Robinson was aware that his preference for 'home colonisation' could be construed as an 'anti-colonial' stance and was therefore anxious to reaffirm his confidence in the political and economic value of the colonies: 'We must not be understood to be saying anything to the disparagement of the Colonies. Of the immense commercial and political worth of the North American ones, we are as sensible as anyone; and we would go perhaps further than the government to benefit them.'[114]

If colonisation was a fractured cause in the Tory periodical press, the consensus against foreign emigration and behind a colonial empire remained solid. Like Robinson, those who advocated domestic solutions to pauperism also tended to regard emigration as a beneficial long-term strategy for Britain's imperial political economy. Fundamentally, the Tory periodicals continually advocated colonial against foreign emigration. Whereas emigration to foreign nations could syphon off paupers and capital as well as could colonial, it could neither be relied upon to forge longterm and reliable demand for the products of Britain's metropolitan economy nor to supplement the primary resources of the British empire. Condemnations of emigration to foreign destinations should therefore be understood as products of a more expansive patriotism which was concerned with the husbanding of Britain's national resources whether human or economic. The *Quarterly*'s review of Birkbeck's *Notes on America* was scathing on the question of British emigration there and subsequent reviews of books about the United States insisted that if colonial emigration was the apotheosis of patriotism then foreign emigration was its antithesis.[115] Thus numerous commentators sought to discourage emigration to foreign countries and to redirect emigrants to Britain's settler colonies.[116] Destinations beyond the empire were recommended only for republicans and subversives.[117]

Yet, discussion of the emigration question was not confined to the spheres of poor relief or economic theory in the Tory periodical press. In the *Quar-*

---

114 Robinson, 'The surplus population of the United Kingdom', 387.
115 J. Barrow, 'Birkbeck's notes on America', *QR* xix (Apr. 1818), 54–78. See also Anon., 'Views, visits and tours in North America', ibid. xxvi (Apr. 1822), 71–99; J. Barrow and W. Gifford, 'Faux – memorable days in America', ibid. xxix (July 1823), 338–70.
116 Anon. ['Barron Field'], 'Van Dieman's Land. – the bush ranger', ibid. xxiii (July 1820), 73–83; J. Barrow, 'Wentworth – Oxley – New South Wales', ibid. xxiv (Oct. 1820), 55–72; Anon., 'Van Dieman's Land', 161–79. Initially the Cape of Good Hope was also presented as an alternative white settler destination: Barrow, 'The Cape of Good Hope', 203–46, and 'Notes on the Cape of Good Hope', 453–66.
117 Whately wrote, 'Those in whom a rooted aversion to our constitution in church and state is one of the principal inducements for emigrating to America, it would neither be easy nor desirable to divert from their purpose. That is the best place for them': 'Emigration to Canada', 399. See also R. Southey, 'Dwight – Travels in New England', *QR* xxx (Oct. 1823), 1–40 esp. at pp. 26–7.

terly, Robert Southey situated his response to the reports of the parliamentary select committees on emigration of 1826-7 in a sweeping analysis of structural and moral crisis affecting contemporary Britain.[118] Southey's moral diagnosis of the state of society was compatible in substance and in genre with the social and economic arguments of commentators like Galt, Robinson and Johnstone. Like them Southey emphasised the preferability of colonisation over emigration. But for Southey colonisation was not only a response to unemployment and economic fluctuation but was also a process which could re-constitute the social, religious and political structures of the metropolitan state in a colonial setting. Southey's review of the select committee reports was in fact a rejection of the Malthusian view that socio-economic crisis originated in 'the system of nature' rather than 'the system of society'.[119] He believed that poverty could not be attributed to population growth, manufacturing, machinery or trade *per se* but rather to the 'profit motive'.[120] Southey nevertheless isolated several economic imbalances in contemporary Britain: the materialistic ethos of competition inevitably resulted in over-production, cheapness, glutted markets and low wages. For him, the rapid growth of manufacturing industry exerted its most damaging effect on society not through the direct impact of industrialisation on material living standards but through its transformation of social and moral relations. One ideological consequence of this transformation was identified by Southey as an increasing tendency to deny to the poor a right to relief from poverty and unemployment. It followed that Southey did not advocate emigration as a material response, whether underconsumptionist or eleemosynary, to domestic poverty.[121] In Southey's postlapsarian perspective human nature and individual selfishness could be controlled and moralised by a constellation of Christian institutions which were the safeguards of an essentially benevolent providence. Therefore Southey advocated emigration as a manifestation of the moral and social duties of government and property to counteract individualism and the profit-motive by reaffirming the right to relief from poverty and reconstructing social and moral bonds.[122]

In his *Colloquies* Southey went on to discuss colonial emigration as a mechanism for re-moralising and re-constituting the fabric of British

---

[118] R. Southey, 'Emigration report', 539-78, in *Essays, moral and political*, ii. 209-75, and *Sir Thomas More: or, colloquies on the progress and prospects of society*, London 1829, ii. 239-334. See also Eastwood, 'Romantic Conservatism', 308-31, and 'Ruinous prosperity, 72-6.
[119] Southey, 'Emigration report', 540.
[120] If Southey did demonstrate a historical association between manufacturing systems and pauperism (here he appealed to Defoe) the cause was the profit motive not modes of production, urbanisation or mechanisation: ibid. 541, 546-9.
[121] However, Southey did recognise that emigration could be targeted at extreme poverty, notably in Ireland: ibid. 562-4.
[122] Southey noted his debt to Blackstone in identifying the right of the poor to relief as an element which reinforced, even constituted, the fabric of society: ibid. 540-1.

society.[123] Just as the moral crisis in metropolitan society was attributed to the dominance of the profit motive so colonisation could become an intrinsically moralising process if it confined individual commercial motives within social and institutional structures.[124] Thus, Southey argued that the 'failure' of the 'home colonisation' of demobilised troops in Scotland, the 'military colonisation' of Upper Canada and numerous schemes for the exportation of paupers had resulted from the absence of hierarchical social structures or religious and administrative civil institutions.[125] In the voice of Sir Thomas More, Southey interpreted the comparative historical endurance of Spanish colonialism as a function of the successful exportation of the fabric of Spanish society. Roman Catholicism aside, Spanish colonialism was held up as an ideal type, a way of controlling and moderating the profit motive which threatened colonial as much as 'metropolitan' social cohesion. Unlike the Portuguese, the Spanish had exported patriarchal social structures beside their political institutions so confining individualism and the profit motive within a constituted social fabric.[126] Thus, in the context of the contemporary public debate on British emigration policy, Southey's historicism served to condemn pauper schemes like those of Horton. For Southey insisted that organised emigration could re-moralise existing commercial societies and colonialism by exporting entire social structures not just the pauper residuum. Appropriately therefore, the *Quarterly*'s review of the *Colloquies* placed considerable emphasis on the functions of empire in Southey's moral economy.[127] If social structures were exported alongside emigration then gold would not be 'bought too dear': trade could be made 'a tributary to the advancement of man in virtue'.[128] Given such appropriate regulation commercially-motivated colonialism could become a 'civilising' force inside and outside the boundaries of empire.[129]

Taking an intellectual approach to the emigration question therefore throws new light on our understanding of Tory economic discourse in early nineteenth-century Britain. Attitudes to emigration were moulded by a cohesive set of interpretations of the origins of poverty, unemployment and economic fluctuations in contemporary Britain. These readings explicitly rejected Ricardian and Malthusian approaches to the problem of poverty and rejected the concept of emigration as a syphon for pauperism. Rather, Tory commentators conceived of emigration to Britain's colonies as a strategy

---

[123] Southey, *Colloquies*, ii. 239–34.
[124] Ibid. 276–7.
[125] Ibid. 272, 274–9.
[126] Ibid. 284–5.
[127] J. J. Blunt, 'Southey's *Colloquies on the progress and prospects of society*', *QR* xli (July 1829), 1–27.
[128] Ibid. 21.
[129] Blunt believed that manufacturing industry could exert a civilising influence on Britain's dependencies when accompanied by religious and social structures: ibid. 22. He exhorted policymakers to apply Southey's ideas to the colonisation of Australia: ibid. 25.

which could, ultimately, reinforce the metropolitan economy by exporting capital and forging secure and permanent markets for British trade and industry. The interventions of William Huskisson (then Colonial Secretary) into the public debate on emigration amplified similar themes. He insisted that if emigration was to address the roots of social and economic crisis then capital should accompany the exportation of paupers.[130] Openly rejecting both the pauper scheme of Wilmot Horton and the general opposition of M. T. Sadler to all emigration, Huskisson stated in June 1829: 'It is only the connection of property with population, that can render emigration useful to this country, or beneficial to the colonists.'[131] Of course, a superficial comparison of Huskisson's attitude to emigration with that of Tory journalists cannot illuminate the motivations behind public policy or the intellectual influences on it. It can be argued, however, that the Tory discourse on emigration voiced criticisms of the free-trade political economy loudly and consistently during the heyday of 'Liberal-Toryism'. The emigration question prompted Tories to analyse the origins of social and economic distress and to debate the importance of Britain's colonial empire in forging the responses of government and of the propertied classes to the problems posed by social and economic modernity.

This survey of Tory imperial discourse has reaffirmed the legitimacy of considering post-Napoleonic imperialism 'in its own right rather than as a plateau to the ascent of liberalism'.[132] Of course the Tory attempt to don the mantle of imperialism was neither exclusive nor uncontested. All the same, the financial scepticism shown by many Whigs and Radicals towards the costs and benefits of the empire and the 'cosmopolitan' assumptions of most free traders were challenged consistently in Tory economic discourse by an alternative imperial political economy. This imperialism elevated the history and experience of the British nation over the theoretical claims of free-trade liberalism and utilitarianism and offered alternative conceptions of both international trade and international relations. In this view the empire was an extension of the Britain which, sustained by political and fiscal structures, could magnify her national presence in the world. The navigation laws, the preferential tariff and emigration were all identifed as imperial instruments which could not only consolidate the British colonies but could also forge permanent markets for the metropolitan economy. In the case of India, the dominant response to free-trade liberalism and utilitarianism was to justify the monopoly and 'commercial sovereignty' of the East India Company. Here, historicist and experiential arguments rejected the free traders' sanguine expectations of a vast eastern mart for British manufactures and amplified the constitutional dangers for the metropolitan state of constructing a

[130] *Speeches of William Huskisson*, iii. 230, 266–8.
[131] Ibid. 473. On emigration as employment for labour and capital see ibid. 471.
[132] See above p. 147.

direct presence in the dependency of India. Yet conceptions of colonialism in Tory economic discourse were moulded by specific readings of the instability, perhaps impermanence, of British economic advance. If the fiscal and economic instruments of colonialism were conceived in Tory economic discourse as devices which could help sustain British economic change and moderate its social costs, they were also understood to be political tools of imperial statecraft. The imperial complexion of post-Napoleonic Conservatism presaged the sweeping critiques of free-trade internationalism which characterised Conservative discourse after 1830.

7

'The Patriotic Principle': The Empire in Conservative Economic Discourse, 1830–1847

The imperial dimensions of Conservative economic argument have not featured prominently in recent approaches to the intellectual history of Britain in the 1830s and 1840s. Indeed, what Disraeli described as 'the great contention between the patriotic and the cosmopolitan principle' has usually been identified as the defining conflict of late Victorian and Edwardian political economy.[1] Owing perhaps to the formalisation of an imperialist response to free-trade internationalism in the tariff reform campaigns of the early twentieth century, the empire has been associated with a 'constructive' Conservative approach to the political, social and economic problems of Edwardian Britain.[2] Undoubtedly, the Edwardian tariff reform movement was conditioned by the specific ideological, electoral, social and economic circumstances of the early twentieth century.[3] Indeed, Joseph Chamberlain's campaign hinged on the perception that Cobdenite free trade had failed to secure economic and social stability or to forestall socialism in Britain.[4] What is less well known is that the promises of Cobden were challenged at their genesis by an alternative imperial political economy. Conservative journals, pamphlets and speeches provided the vehicle through which this intellectual opposition to free-trade cosmopolitanism was chiefly expressed. The imperial political economy of mid nineteenth-century Conservatives was, of course, moulded by the political, constitutional, economic and intellectual circumstances of contemporary Britain. After the 1820s the central problems in imperial policy had shifted from the consolidation of post-Napoleonic acquisitions to questions of colonial governance, settlement and taxation. New intellectual settings for debates on imperial policy were provided by the application of a mentality of retrenchment to the costs of British imperialism during the 1830s and by the cosmopolitan character of Richard Cobden's

---

[1] Disraeli, *Lord George Bentinck*, 583.
[2] See Green, *Crisis of conservatism*, esp. pp. 27–56, 59–77, 159–263.
[3] E. H. H. Green, 'Radical Conservatism: the electoral genesis of tariff reform', *HJ* xxviii (1985), 667–92; P. Cain, 'Political economy in Edwardian England: the tariff reform controversy', in A. O'Day (ed.), *The Edwardian age*, London 1979, 35–59; A. S. Thompson, 'Tariff reform: an imperial strategy, 1903–1913', *HJ* xl (1997), 1033–54.
[4] See C. A. Vince, *Mr Chamberlain's proposals; what they mean and what we shall gain by them, with a preface by the right hon. Joseph Chamberlain M.P.*, London 1903, esp. pp. iii–iv, 19–26, 43–50.

brand of free-trade political economy. In the intellectual contexts furnished by the Great Reform Act and the Poor Law Amendment Act many Conservatives insisted that British commercial policy should remain preferential and protectionist and predicted dire consequences if Britain embarked on a Cobdenite trajectory.

Within these new contexts the established imperial dimensions of Tory economic discourse were reworked after 1830. Conservative writers met financial critiques of British imperialism with empirical demonstrations of the continued value of Britain's colonial empire. Such arguments were subsequently refocused on Richard Cobden's assumption that free trade could furnish solutions to problems posed by both international trade and international relations. By demonstrating the qualitative and quantitative superiority of colonial trade which, crucially, could be sustained by the fiscal structures of protection and preference, Cobden's critics redrew the lineaments of a familiar imperial conception of Britain's economic nationality. These general arguments were frequently framed as responses to specific questions of imperial or commercial policy. The debates surrounding the rescinding of the East India Company's monopoly over the China trade in 1833 furnished opportunities to condemn the assumption that the security of metropolitan manufactures could be grounded on exports of low-value textiles to the east. Such scepticism about the capacity of free trade to forge conditions for sustainable economic advance in Britain was blended with responses to the Whig-Liberal and Utilitarian approaches to the problem of India. Similarly, rebellion in British North America provoked vigorous constitutionalist reactions to Whig-Liberal imperialism in Conservative discourse. But whereas the Whig-Liberal approach to the Canada problem was perceived to emphasise the pivotal importance of colonial self-governance, Conservatives looked to the constitutional conservatism and to the economic instruments of protection, preference and emigration for the bonds of imperial cohesion. It follows, therefore, that the unravelling of colonial preference by the commercial reforms of 1846-7 was frequently interpreted in Conservative economic discourse as a fundamental blow to the cohesion and integrity of the British empire. As Sir W. Heathcote warned in a parliamentary debate about the implications of corn-law repeal for the colonies, 'For the first time, in our history you avow, or at least you act upon, an anticolonial policy.'[5]

Languages of empire: the imperialist response to retrenchment and free trade, 1830-47

From the financial thought of Sir Henry Parnell to the internationalist economics of Richard Cobden, the changing intellectual incarnations of 'anti-

---

5 Sir W. Heathcote, House of Commons (9 Feb. 1846), *Hansard* 3rd ser. lxxxiii. 562.

imperialism' were persistently challenged in Conservative economic discourse. Indeed many Conservative critics located the empire at the heart of their responses to free-trade liberalism whether this flowed from the pens of Parnell, the 'Christian political economists' or Richard Cobden. It is essential, however, to consider the imperial dimensions of Conservative economic argument not on any abstract plane of intellectual engagement but as part of a broader public debate about the imperial costs of retrenchment, the social condition of Britain and the durability of her economic advance.

Sir Henry Parnell's seminal tract of 1830, *On financial reform*, was received as a partisan and anti-imperialist manifesto for free-trade liberalism in the Tory periodicals.[6] This book was interpreted as a doctrinaire addendum to the reports of the select committee on public income and expenditure of 1828 and as the embodiment of a Whig/Radical financial orthodoxy which was the corollary of constitutional reform.[7] Phillip Pusey and David Robinson both viewed Parnell's case for tariff reduction and general retrenchment as a veil for the transformation of the entire system of trade and for the destruction of the fiscal fabric of the British empire. Parnell's emphasis on administrative retrenchment was seen as a mask for abstract principles of free trade which threatened to jerk British commercial policy decisively away from Huskisson's pragmatic, imperialist reformism: 'Sir Henry opposes himself decidedly to that of Mr Huskisson. The latter and his friends always represented that their system was to be one of protection – was at least to give protection equal to the difference between British and foreign taxation.'[8] Parnell's critics targeted his assumption that 'on the whole the public derives no commercial advantage from the colonies, which it might not have without them'.[9] While Pusey devoted considerable energy to exposing inaccuracies in Parnell's rendition of the balance sheet of colonial trade his most basic objection to Parnell was methodological and philosophical.[10] By reducing the empire to an arena for retrenchment, he believed Parnell had ignored politics and reduced political economy to book-balancing, 'Hence we oftner agree in our author's finance than in his political economy; while of politics he appears to us to have altogether lost sight.'[11] Thus Pusey rejected simple pecuniary assessments of colonial worth which ignored the extent of British power relative to rival nations and the strategic importance of imperial possessions. In

---

[6] P. Pusey, 'Sir H. Parnell *On financial reform: the British colonies*', QR xlii (Mar. 1830), 505–36 at p. 505, and Robinson, 'Sir H. Parnell on financial reform', 457. See Newbould, *Whiggery and reform*, 105–7, for a brief assessment of Parnell's influence on Whig policy-makers.
[7] D. Robinson, 'Parties', BEM xxix (Feb. 1831), 346–60 at p. 357; Alison, 'On the financial measures of a reformed parliament: no I: the Whig budget', 971, 975–6.
[8] Robinson, 'Sir H. Parnell on financial reform', 457. See also Pusey, 'Sir H Parnell *On financial reform: the British colonies*', 531–2.
[9] Parnell, *On financial reform*, 231–51 at p. 244; Pusey, 'Sir H. Parnell', 516.
[10] On Parnell's 'imperial accounting', see ibid. 512–14, 517–19.
[11] Ibid. 505.

response to Parnell's emphasis on natural advantage, competition and international trade, Pusey insisted that political imperium and the tariff structure it generated were fundamental to Britain's commercial and manufacturing advance: 'So long as Great Britain is desirous of continuing a manufacturing, commercial, ship-owning country, and a first-rate power, colonies are essential to her.'[12]

Parnell's zeal for retrenchment was challenged by sweeping economic justifications of Britain's colonial empire in the Conservative journals. Both Pusey and Robinson reworked established arguments on the qualitative superiority of a reciprocal and stable colonial trade over the vagaries of foreign competition.[13] For Pusey the maintenance of protection and preference for the North Atlantic empire served a dual purpose: not only did it safeguard natural resources, it also guaranteed a fifth of total employment for British navigation, composed a seventh of the market for British manufactured goods and a substantial proportion of the total demand for West Indian produce.[14] Whereas Parnell maintained that consumption for British manufactures could best be assured by liberating the domestic consumer from the burdens of protection and preference, his Conservative critics insisted on the political and economic importance of these fiscal instruments.[15] For both Robinson and Pusey the essential point was that protection and preference were legislative structures which bound the different classes and interests within the British empire in mutual consumption; only by protecting producers throughout the empire, could the means of consumption be guaranteed and could imperial cohesion be preserved.[16] In parliament J. C. Herries defended imperial preference against Poulett Thompson's proposal to reduce it in 1831: 'It was a principle which was not consistent with what was called political economical doctrines, but it was consistent with a much higher doctrine, that of justice, and of giving to our colonies that protection which they had a right to demand at our hands.'[17] Familiar imperial arguments were thus refocused on the economic pretensions of Parnellite retrenchment. Preferential and protective tariffs were presented as structures which could ensure that British economic change growth was stable and permanent while shoring up the bonds of empire. Conservatives therefore responded to the new 'cosmopolitan' cocktail of retrenchment and free trade with an expansive imperial conception of British political economy.

---

12 Ibid. 528.
13 See above pp. 154–6. See also W. Johnstone, 'Parliamentary sayings and doings: no. III', BEM xxix (Mar. 1831), 526–34 at p. 534, and 'Parliamentary sayings and doings: no. V', ibid. (May 1831), 732–44 at pp. 733–4.
14 Pusey, 'Sir H. Parnell', 529. See also Anon., 'The British North American colonies', FM v (Feb. 1832), 77–84, and Robinson, 'Sir H. Parnell on financial reform', 470–3.
15 Robinson, 'Sir H. Parnell on financial reform', 462; Pusey, 'Sir H. Parnell', 531.
16 Ibid. 469–73.
17 J. C. Herries, House of Commons (11 Mar. 1831), Hansard 3rd ser. iii. 350. See also G. Robinson, ibid. 351–8.

In the early 1830s, Conservative defenders of Britain's colonial empire seldom separated their responses to Parnellite retrenchment and free trade from their analysis of the significance of the Great Reform Act. Indeed, retrenchment, free trade and parliamentary reform were frequently identified as mutually inextricable features of Whig-Liberalism. Beside retrenchment and free trade, the dilution of 'virtual representation' by the 1832 Reform Act was understood as a measure which would weaken the cohesion of the British empire. During the Reform debates in parliament, Sir George Staunton 'was at a loss to conceive any argument that sustained giving Manchester, Birmingham, and Leeds representatives, and denied the same privileges to Canada, Jamaica, and Calcutta'.[18] Like Staunton, Archibald Alison insisted that the numerical strength of small urban property in the reformed constitution would extinguish the virtual representation of imperial interests.[19] Alison maintained that this, in turn, would suffocate the expression of imperial interests in the British tariff by amplifying the political pressures for retrenchment and free trade. Alison even paraphrased David Hume in a bid for intellectual legitimacy for this reading of contemporary fiscal politics: 'Democratic societies never have been able to govern their colonies with justice and liberality, for this simple reason, that their interests interfere with those of their distant subjects; and that they never will cease to sacrifice them to their interests or passions.'[20] Thus, the imperial instruments of navigation laws, preference and protection were presented as instruments of political representation which could counteract the perceived transformation of fiscal politics by parliamentary reform while strengthening the bonds of empire. In the shadow of the Great Reform Act, the politics of protection and preference were explicitly imperial.

The imperial dimensions of Conservative economic discourse must also be located in the intellectual and political context of debates on poor-law reform. Although G. P. Scrope was a Whig MP he found his intellectual home in the Conservative *Quarterly* and it was here that he published his ardent criticisms of anti-colonialism.[21] Indeed, Scrope believed the colonies provided a mechanism by which the science of political economy could be equated with 'social wealth' and governments could influence the distributive characteristics of economic change.[22] Scrope reacted less to Parnell's

---

[18] Sir G. Staunton, House of Commons (16 Aug. 1831), ibid. vi. 130.
[19] Alison, 'The first session of the reformed parliament: Ireland – West Indies – East Indies – domestic and foreign policy of ministers', 776–9, 794–5; 'Progress of social disorganisation: no IV: decay of the wooden walls of England', BEM xxxv (May 1834), 675–90 at pp. 676–7; 'Colonial government and the Jamaica question', ibid. xlvii (July 1839), 75–90 at pp. 82–3.
[20] Idem, 'The East India question', ibid. xxxiii (May 1833), 776–803 at p. 785. For further appeals to Hume see idem, 'Progress of social disorganisation: the prostration of government', 529–31, and 'Colonial government and the Jamaica question', 81.
[21] On Scrope see above p. 66 n. 57.
[22] G. P. Scrope, 'Population and emigration', QR xlv (Apr. 1831), 97–145; 'Amendment

pressure for retrenchment than to the modifications of the thought of Malthus and Ricardo which were tendered by the 'Christian economists', Richard Jones, Richard Whately and Thomas Chalmers during the early 1830s.[23] Scrope's colonialism proceeded from the anti-Ricardian premise that imbalances between production and consumption were inevitable and that 'Say's Law' was erroneous. Scrope insisted that reliance on foreign markets for British manufactures exacerbated economic fluctuations due to fundamental discrepancies between the rate of British and foreign economic advance.[24] Drawing on Richard Jones's criticism of Ricardo's theories of rent and diminishing returns, Scrope also defended investment in colonial agriculture as a beneficial employment for British labour and capital which would retard not accelerate the stationary state.[25] He therefore looked principally to the security of domestic and colonial markets for a stable economic future where all reciprocals were British and where 'excess' capital could be invested in colonial development. It was chiefly in his response to Thomas Chalmers, however, that Scrope applied his colonial political economy to the public debate on poor-law reform.

Fundamentally, Scrope interpreted the writings of Chalmers as paens to 'Population Malthus' which released governments from all responsibility for economic and social conditions. In Scrope's reading, Chalmers placed an ecological straitjacket on social and economic conditions in Britain, where, in the absence of preventative checks, population size would always expand to the limits of available food whether from domestic or colonial sources. Scrope insisted that Chalmers had missed 'the simple and obvious resource – of employing our own surplus labour and capital in raising the required food from the fertile soil of our colonies, – considering them, as we have a right to do, in the light of mere outlying portions of British territory'.[26] Yet Scrope was exercised less by Chalmers's interpretation of the relationship between population and food supply than by the implications of this Malthusianism for social thought and public policy: 'It absolutely frees a government from all

---

of the poor laws', ibid. xlviii (Dec. 1832), 320–45; 'The new poor law', ibid. lii (Aug. 1834), 233–61.
[23] Scrope's reviews responded chiefly to the following works: Nassau Senior, *Two lectures on population, delivered before the University of Oxford in Easter Term, 1828; to which is added, a correspondence between the author and the Rev. T. R. Malthus*, London 1831; J. R. McCulloch, *Principles of political economy with a sketch of the rise and progress of the science*, 2nd edn, London 1830; Jones, *On the distribution of wealth*; Revd R. Whately, *Introductory lectures on political economy*, London 1831; T. Chalmers, *On political economy, in connexion with the moral state and moral prospects of society*, Glasgow 1832.
[24] Scrope explicitly rejected 'Say's Law' in his critique of Mill, *Elements of political economy*, ch. iv, 224ff., in 'The political economists', 23–7.
[25] Scrope, 'Jones on the doctrine of rents', 83–95. Scrope endorsed Richard Jones's anti-Ricardian theory of distribution at pp. 100, 114–17; Jones, *An essay on the distribution of wealth*, i. 253–5.
[26] G. P. Scrope, 'Dr. Chalmers on political economy', *QR* xlviii (Oct. 1832), 39–69 at p. 50. See also his *Political economy for plain people*, 220n.

responsibility for the sufferings of the mass of the community, by throwing the blame entirely on *Nature* and the improvidence of the poor themselves, and declaring the evil to admit of no remedy from any possible exertions of the legislature.'[27] In Scrope's view, therefore, governments could reappropriate some 'responsibility for the sufferings of the mass of the community' by expanding its geographical conception of the British economy and encouraging emigration to the colonies: 'A systematic furtherance of emigration seems to us to be, though long neglected, as essential a branch of the duties of government, as the maintenance of that order and discipline over the poorer classes, which, though necessary for general purposes, prevents their migrating through their own exertions.'[28] Scrope therefore agreed with Richard Whately that political economy could be compatible with 'religion, morality and national happiness' and need not become a demoralised 'study of exchanges, or of wealth, the subject-matter of exchanges'.[29] As a mechanism for the distribution of wealth and for the employment of capital and labour, Britain's colonial empire was, for Scrope, a fundamental component of a remoralised concept of political economy, or, 'The Science of Interests, or Happiness of Nations'.[30] It is striking that such perspectives on the implications of the Malthusianism of Chalmers for British social policy were shared by other Conservative commentators. Though he argued that 'home colonisation', rather than colonial emigration, was to be preferred as a response to domestic poverty, William Maginn was also repulsed by the impact of neo-Malthusianism on British social discourse.[31] Indeed Maginn defended Scrope's arguments, which were condemned by Chalmers as 'the miserable distortions of *The Quarterly*', and insisted that governments had both the duty and capacity to counteract poverty and suffering.[32] Debates on Britain's colonial empire therefore served to amplify the social and economic responsibilities of a propertied polity in Conservative economic discourse.

Within the distinctive intellectual contexts furnished by debates on poor relief, parliamentary reform and retrenchment the Conservative journals represented Britain's colonial policy as a 'patriotic' response to economic and

---

[27] Idem, 'Dr Chalmers on political economy', 69.
[28] Idem, 'The political economists', 50.
[29] Idem, 'The archbishop of Dublin on political economy', *QR* xlvi (Nov. 1831), 46–54 at pp. 47, 50.
[30] Ibid. 50, 53.
[31] W. Maginn, 'The desperate system: poverty, crime and emigration', *FM* i (June 1830), 635–42 at p. 642; 'On national economy (no. I): Chalmers on political economy', ibid. vi (Aug. 1832), 113–21 at pp. 114–18; 'On national economy (no. II): Dr Chalmers on political economy', ibid. (Sept. 1832), 239–48; 'On national economy (no. III): Miss Martineau's *Cousin Marshall*', ibid. (Nov. 1832), 403–13; 'On national economy (no. V): surplus labour and the remedies proposed: I: poor laws for Ireland', ibid. vii (Mar. 1833), 282–91.
[32] Idem, 'On national economy (no. VI): Dr. Chalmers on a right and moral state of the community', ibid. vii (May 1833), 603–14 at p. 603.

social conditions in contemporary Britain. Indeed, this patriotic principle of political economy was increasingly offered as an alternative to the various forms of free-trade internationalism. Not only did Conservative writers reject Cobden's universal and cosmopolitan idea of free trade, they also took issue with more cautious notions of free trade which emphasised bilateral and reciprocal liberality.[33] At the close of the 1830s Archibald Alison stated that Britain faced a stark choice between a colonial system of political economy and an international system based on reciprocal deals with foreign countries: 'Either we trust to our colonies, and consider them as the main stay of our national strength, or we must throw them overboard, and rely on the reciprocity system to maintain an extensive commercial intercourse with foreign and independent nations.'[34] Appealing to history and experience, Alison maintained that reciprocal trade treaties constituted a flimsy foundation on which to construct Britain's economic future since they ignored one fundamental point – the inherent mutual hostility of nations.[35] He insisted that a colonial or national system of trade maximised British maritime power and responded to the realities of international relations.[36] As George Robinson had commented on the 'reciprocity system' in parliament in 1831, 'The fallacious character of that system had been aptly exposed by the former President of the United States, Mr. Munro, and subsequently by Mr. Jefferson, in a work published after his death.'[37] Alison repeatedly pointed out that the colonies took manufactured goods of relatively high value whereas foreign nations accepted a greater proportion of semi-manufactured articles. In this sense, British colonial markets furnished a stable and expanding foundation for British manufacturing advance.[38] In parliament the assumption that colonial markets were both more stable and more valuable than their foreign ones featured large in Henry Goulburn's response to Henry Labouchère's proposal for the reduction of the preference and protection which guarded Britain's colonial trade in 1841.[39] Alison explained the preferability of a colonial political economy in historicist terms. Whereas the interests of different 'old states' necessarily conflicted with each other, the interests of 'old' and 'young' states could be mutually beneficial since 'the old state can always undersell the

---

[33] On the distinction between universal and reciprocal free trade see Howe, *Free trade and Liberal England*, esp. pp. 86–92.
[34] A. Alison, 'The reciprocity and colonial systems', BEM xliv (Sept. 1838), 317–34 at p. 317.
[35] Alison referred to the following 'reciprocity treaties': USA (1816), Prussia, Hanover, Denmark and Oldenburg (1824), Mecklenburg, Bremen, Hamburg, Lubeck, States of Rio de Plata, Colombia (1825), France, Sweden, Norway, Mexico (1826), Brazil (1827) and Austria (1829): ibid. 318.
[36] Idem, 'Progress of social disorganisation: no. IV: decay of the wooden walls of England', 678–9, 682–3, and 'The reciprocity and colonial systems', 320–3.
[37] G. Robinson, House of Commons (18 Mar. 1831), *Hansard* 3rd ser. iii. 569.
[38] Alison, 'The reciprocity and colonial systems', 327.
[39] H. Goulburn, House of Commons (5 Apr. 1841), *Hansard* 3rd ser. lvii. 889.

young one in manufactures, but is everlastingly undersold by them in agriculture'.[40] What Britain's system of protection and preference achieved therefore was to cement a natural commercial conjunction of the 'old' and the 'young' in a colonial political economy.

Thus Conservative commentators responded to the many dimensions of Cobdenite free trade in the 1840s. From Cobden's cost/benefit condemnation of the colonial system to his fervent belief that free trade would inaugurate a new millennium of international peace, the Conservative journals offered a colonial alternative.[41] In *Blackwood's* Alfred Mallalieu engaged directly with Cobden's attempt to demonstrate that the limited gains from colonial trade could not justify the costs of colonial preference and defence.[42] Responding to a speech made by Cobden in June 1843, Mallalieu argued that Cobden had inflated colonial defence costs and ignored the substantial proportion of military expenditure which effectively safeguarded foreign trade.[43] Mallalieu maintained that the higher rates of profit generated by a colonial trade in manufactured goods of relatively high value justified the scale of Britain's expenditure on colonial defence.[44] Yet, Mallalieu's figures did not merely challenge Cobden's financial critique of the empire, they also contributed to a more widely diffused statistical language of imperialism.[45] A number of writers sought to establish the quantitative superiority of colonial and domestic over foreign markets for British manufactures. The comparative abstracts of Richard Burn and James McQueen were appropriated by Conservative writers to bolster the case for the empire as the coping stone of a stable future for industry in metropolitan Britain.[46] Indeed, McQueen not only

---

[40] Alison, 'Free trade and protection', 266. On this point see Macintyre, 'Lord George Bentinck and the protectionists', 156–7.

[41] On Cobden's moral opposition to colonialism as the cause of wars, on his critique of imperial preference and the case for unilateral free trade see Morley, *Life of Richard Cobden*, i. 248, 304–5; ii. 334–7.

[42] Mallalieu, 'Commercial policy – ships, colonies and commerce: no. I', 406–14.

[43] R. Cobden, House of Commons (22 June 1843), *Hansard* 3rd ser. lxx. 205–12, referred to by Morley in *Life of Richard Cobden*, i. 304. Mallalieu's analysis of McQueen's *General statistics of the British empire* [1836], assessed the cost of defending foreign trade at £4,450,000, and colonial at £3,000,000: 'Commercial policy – ships, colonies and commerce: no. II', 640–1.

[44] Ibid. 646–7. On the comparative value of manufactured goods in colonial and foreign trade see ibid. 649.

[45] Preber, *Taxation, revenue, expenditure*, 287–472; G. R. Porter, *The progress of the nation*, London 1838, 92–178, and *The progress of the nation*, London 1843, 311–23.

[46] R. Burn, *Burn's commercial glance by which merchants, manufacturers, spinners, and others, may, at one view, see the quantity of yarn, and all descriptions of manufactured cotton goods, exported from the different ports etc.*, Manchester 1845, esp. nos 1–20. This broadsheet was published annually from 1830. For appropriations of Burn's statistics see Anon., *Our free trade policy examined with respect to its real bearing upon native industry, our colonial system, and the institutions and ultimate destinies of the nation*, London–Liverpool 1846, 17–18, 20–2. On Lord George Bentinck's extensive correspondence with Burn during 1847–8 see Disraeli, *Lord George Bentinck*, 571; McQueen, *Statistics of agriculture, manufactures and commerce*.

offered general comparative abstracts of the value of foreign as against home and colonial trade, he also presented specific comparative figures for exports of cotton manufactures.[47] This imperialist empiricism cannot therefore be read as a reaction against manufacturing modernity itself. For, in Conservative economic discourse, Britain's colonial empire was identified as a political construct which could provide markets for manufacturing industry which were stable and permanent. The appropriateness of Cobden's free-trade cosmopolitanism as a solution to the problem of maintaining Britain's manufacturing economy was consistently challenged in Conservative economic discourse. Indeed the 'patriotic' alternative of a colonial political economy was projected as a system which could better moderate the social condition of industrial Britain. Thus Mallalieu compared the relative vulnerability of industries supplying foreign and colonial trades to gluts and unemployment. He believed that foreign trade was largely concentrated on cheap goods for which demand was low and finite in the domestic market and where a glut in foreign trade could cause severe and general unemployment. On the other hand Mallalieu maintained that the social consequences of gluts in trades dependent on colonial or domestic markets could be moderated by redirecting goods abroad, 'being then pressed upon the foreign market, the superior quality of goods commands a decided preference at once, and that preference ensures comparatively higher rates of price in the midst of the piled up packages of warehouse sweepings and goods made, . . . for sale abroad'.[48]

So the empire figured large in Conservative responses to the changing shape of free-trade political economy after 1830. The retrenching zeal of Whigs and Radicals was challenged by an alternative language of statistics designed to disarm the financial case against the empire. In the context of parliamentary reform, protective and preferential tariffs were presented not only as fiscal structures which could sustain demand for the products of metropolitan capital and labour but also as mechanisms for the legitimate representation of imperial interests. The Conservative journals moved the empire to the centre of the public debate on poor relief by discussing the question of emigration in Anti-Malthusian and Anti-Ricardian terms. In response to the 'cosmopolitan' concepts of 'reciprocity' and 'unilateral' free trade, the Conservative journals offered a 'patriotic' and imperial alternative. Here, the fiscal structures of protection and colonial preference were presented as essential to the fabric of both international relations and international trade. Fundamentally, the empire mattered in Conservative economic discourse as a response to the problem of sustaining British economic change and moderating its social consequences. As a market for British trade and industry and as an employment for her labour and capital, the empire offered an alternative to the Cobdenite trajectory where the stability

[47] Ibid. 17–19.
[48] Mallalieu, 'Commercial policy – ships, colonies and commerce: no. II', 644. See also Anon., *Our free trade policy examined*, 7–8.

of Britain's economy and society was to rest on foreign trade. At their inception, the assumptions of free-trade cosmopolitanism were challenged by a Conservative imperial political economy.

Beyond monopoly: debating British imperium in India and the east, 1830–47

During the 1830s and 1840s the public debate on Britain's imperial presence in the east was focused on two central questions; the East India Company's administration of India and her monopoly over the China trade. The parliamentary select committees of 1830–2 resulted in the removal of the Company's remaining monopoly and in the reform of its political and administrative role in India.[49] Indeed, these reforms have led one historian to conclude that 'The triumph of the anti-monopolist mood and free trade crusade that gathered momentum from the mid-1820s on could not have been more complete.'[50] Yet the 'free trade crusade' was consistently challenged in contemporary imperial discourse. From the polemic of *Fraser's* to the more measured arguments of the *Quarterly* the Conservative journals engaged with the prescriptions of Whigs, Radicals, Utilitarians and free traders for British imperium in the east.[51] The established historicist justifications of the Company's 'commercial sovereignty' were integrated with responses to the Great Reform Act in Conservative economic discourse. With respect to the China trade, Conservative commentators not only condemned free-trade expectations of a vast new market for manufacturing industry, they also predicted that the cessation of the Company's monopoly would undermine the fabric of British relations with China. From the perspectives of Indian governance, the metropolitan economy and international relations, therefore, the 'anti-monopolist mood and free-trade crusade' was challenged in Conservative economic discourse.

The essence of the reformist consensus on Britain's presence in the east was characteristically expressed by T. B. Macaulay when he objected in 1833 to 'The existence of such a body as this gigantic corporation – this political monster of two natures – subject in one hemisphere, sovereign in another.'[52]

---

[49] *Report of the select committee on the affairs of the East India Company (China trade)* (1830); *Report from the Lords on the present state of the affairs of the East India Company, and on the trade between Great Britain, the East Indies and China* (1830); *Report of the select committee on the affairs of the East India Company with appendices* (1831–2).

[50] P. Lawson, *The East India Company: a history*, London 1993, 158. On the free-trade lobby within the EIC see Alborn, *Conceiving companies*, 30–1.

[51] Anon., 'The East India Company – no. II: Messrs. Rickards and Crawfurd', FM i (May 1830), 457–79.

[52] T. B. Macaulay, House of Commons (10 July 1833), *Hansard* 3rd ser. xix. 509. On the distinctions between Macaulay's attitudes and those of Cobden and Bright see Alborn, *Conceiving companies*, 36–9, 40–5.

As early as 1817, of course, James Mill had attempted to slay the two-headed beast with a Utilitarian argument for the direct presence of the British state in India.[53] In the context of the parliamentary select committees of the early 1830s Mill's proposals for Indian reform were revisited by Conservative critics. Typically, Archibald Alison contested the abstract and conjectural view of historical progress which underpinned Mill's assumption that bad governance was the cause of India's 'stationary state'.[54] Indeed, Alison substituted an alternative reading of contemporary history for Mill's historicism. In Alison's account, the decline of the social and economic condition of India and the erosion of British authority there both resulted from the damage caused to the 'commercial sovereignty' of the Company in 1813.[55] If British authority in India rested on the fusion of the 'commercial' with the 'sovereign' functions of the Company then the proposed removal of political discretion from the Company and the transfer of its commercial and territorial assets to the crown in 1833 would further diminish British power in India.[56] Conservative critics continued to insist, then, that the Utilitarians had ignored the fundamental fact that Britain's political authority in India needed to be rooted in property ownership, commerce and indigenous social and political structures.

If the India debates of the 1820s were reworked in the context furnished by the select committees of the early 1830s, they were also refocused as responses to the Great Reform Act by Conservative critics. Crucially, the Indian reforms of 1833 were interpreted as direct consequences of the reform of parliament in 1832. As Alison put it, 'The interests and prejudices of the twelve hundred thousand legislators who now give the law to the British Empire, will soon dissolve the splendid but flimsy fabric.'[57] What Alison, Croly and others objected to was the consequence of a direct presence for the British state in India in the light of parliamentary reform.[58] The constitutional dangers of transferring the vast India patronage from the Company to the state was perceived to be 'incomparably greater' in 1833 than it would have been in 1784.[59] Indeed the beneficiary of the proposed reforms of 1833

---

[53] See above pp. 163–4. On Utilitarian approaches to India see E. T. Stokes, *The English utilitarians and India*, Oxford 1959, 1–80; Winch, *Classical political economy and colonies*, 159–65; E. T. Stokes, 'Bureaucracy and ideology: Britain and India in the nineteenth century', TRHS xxx (1980), 131–56.
[54] Alison, 'The East India question', esp. p. 778.
[55] See above pp. 159–61.
[56] Alison, 'The East India question', 794. See also Anon., 'State and prospects of Asia', QR lxiii (Mar. 1839), 369–402. The latter invoked (p. 329) Adam Smith's *Theory of moral sentiments* [1759] but gave no traceable reference.
[57] Alison, 'The East India question', 788.
[58] Idem, 'The first session of the reformed parliament: Ireland – West Indies – East Indies – domestic and foreign policy of ministers', 776–804.
[59] Croly, 'Edmund Burke: pt III', 674. See also G. Croly's review of Horace Twiss, *The public and private life of Lord Chancellor Eldon*, London 1844, in 'Lord Eldon', BEM lvi (Aug. 1844), 245–64 at p. 256.

was identified as an 'urban democracy' not a Whig aristocracy: 'The little which remains of the balance will infallibly be subverted by such a change; but it will be subverted in a far more dangerous way than in 1784, because, what will kick the beam will not be a firm and stable aristocracy, but a fickle and intemperate populace.'[60] The question of the Company's political independence was not therefore debated merely as an administrative problem in Conservative discourse. For, just as metropolitan constitutional reform was understood to have transformed the pressures on imperial governance, so imperial reforms were seen to impact directly on the balance of the metropolitan constitution.

The connected question of the East India Company's remaining monopoly over the China trade was also debated in broad terms in Conservative economic discourse. The Conservative journals did not merely challenge the appropriateness of free trade for China, they also questioned the general assumption that free trade could best secure markets for Britain's manufacturing economy. The *Quarterly* engaged in detail with the rash of pamphlets published during 1829–30 and proffered a review of G. R. Gleig's *Life of Sir Thomas Munro*.[61] These articles argued that it was naive to attempt to apply abstract principles of free trade to Britain's intercourse with a despotic state. Indeed the case of China seemed to confirm the absolute subordination of 'experience' to 'theory' in free-trade liberalism.[62] On the contrary, Conservative critics identified the East India Company's local knowledge and connections 'as the only legitimate grounds on which to build a sound opinion'.[63] They also insisted that the unregulated participants in an open trade would over-supply limited markets in both China and Britain while antagonising the Chinese.[64] In response to the 'anti-monopolist' claim that by opening her China trade Britain would gain a vast market for her exports of manufactured cotton, writers in the Conservative journals appealed to the commercial history of India since 1813. They insisted that since the India trade had been 'opened' it had been supplied beyond its capacity, markets for British manufactures had collapsed and the long-term ability of India to consume British exports had been fatally undermined by the destruction of the markets of native manufacturers by British imports.[65] Indeed, as Gleig's reviewer warned, the effect of opening the China trade was likely to be more damaging

---

60 Alison, 'The East India question', 792.
61 Anon., 'Trade and intercourse with China', QR xlii (Jan. 1830), 147–70, was explicitly aimed at refuting the arguments of 'writers on free trade and colonisation' (p. 152). See also Anon., 'Life and correspondence of Sir Thomas Munro', ibid. xliii (May 1830), 81–111 at p. 81.
62 J. Barrow, 'Free trade to China', ibid. l (Jan. 1834), 430–67 at p. 460. See especially Alison's engagement with J. R. McCulloch in 'The East India question', 799–802.
63 Anon., 'Trade and intercourse with China', 147.
64 J. Barrow, 'The Chinese', QR lvi (July 1836), 489–521 at pp. 518–21, and 'Chinese affairs', ibid. lxv (Mar. 1840), 537–81 at p. 538.
65 Anon., 'Trade and intercourse with China', 152.

than it had been in the case of India because Britain could not rely on political influence to sustain her commercial position:

> It *is our political power*, acquired by the Company's arms, which has made the *trade* to India what it is. . . . but until we are prepared to follow the advice of those liberal and enlightened persons who have already proposed carrying *free trade* at the point of the bayonet, let us not hear of India and China talked of in the same breath.[66]

Thus the case for the continuance of the EIC's monopoly over the China trade went far beyond the defence of vested interest. In Conservative economic discourse the China question was presented as an issue which exposed the inadequacies of free-trade templates for both the metropolitan economy and for British imperial practice.

Critics of the reforms of 1833 also questioned the fundamental assumption that free-trade policies could pacify international relations. Numerous Conservative commentators insisted that the eastern wars of the thirties and forties were attributable to the transformation of Britain's imperial presence in the east by free trade. In particular, the war in China during 1839–41 was condemned as a direct and *predicted* consequence of the withdrawal of the Company's monopoly over the China trade in 1833. Claiming a precise identity of opinion with the duke of Wellington, Thomas De Quincey maintained that the sole cause of the Opium War was free trade with China: 'Hitherto the enterprising parties (the final controllers) have been cautious and intelligent capitalists – now they will be desperate adventurers.'[67] John Barrow also suggested that he had predicted that free trade would precipitate war with China: 'We foresaw and stated, some years ago in this Journal (see Quar. Rev. No. C), what would be the probable issue of depriving the East India Company of their exclusive privilege of trading to China, of substituting the *free trade* system, and encouraging an indiscriminate intercourse with that country.'[68] Similarly, Britain's Afghan war was not explained merely in terms of diplomatic failure or Russian aggression. This also was presented as the result of retrenchment and centralisation in Indian administration combined with the consequences of glutting Indian markets with cheap British manufactures after the removal of the Company's monopoly in 1813.[69] George Croly even maintained that the termination of the EIC's 'commercial sover-

---

[66] Anon., 'Life and correspondence of Sir Thomas Munro', 100 (Anon.'s emphasis).
[67] T. De Quincey, 'The opium and the China question', BEM xlvii (June 1840), 717–38 at pp. 731–2. De Quincey went on to assert that this article (which he claimed went to press on 11 May) anticipated the arguments of the duke of Wellington in the House of Lords (12 May 1840), Hansard 3rd ser. liv. 34–43 esp. at pp. 40–1, in T. De Quincey, 'Postscript on the China and opium question', BEM xlvii (June 1840), 847–53 at p. 847.
[68] Barrow, 'Chinese affairs', 538. The article referred to was Barrow's own, 'Free trade to China' (Barrow's emphasis). See also Sir J. Graham, House of Commons (7 Apr. 1840), Hansard 3rd ser. liii. 675.
[69] A. Alison, 'The Affghanistan expedition', BEM xlvii (Feb. 1840), 241–52 at p. 248.

eignty' in India had transformed the commercial spirit of British imperium into a military ethos which shattered the established basis and boundaries of British power. In 1842 Croly detected a new 'principle of perpetual conquest' which was fundamentally at odds with what he identified as the 'original' principle of 'connexion' with India: 'We went there as merchants and settlers, and as such we should have continued; and on this principle alone. . . . India can be rendered either a safe government, or an advantageous dependence.'[70] Of course, contrary to Croly's assumption, the military and commercial aspects of British imperium were not mutually exclusive.[71] Nevertheless, Conservative commentators looked to Lord Ellenborough's administration of India for a commercial rather than a military approach to the consolidation of British power in the east.[72] By attributing eastern wars to a combination of administrative, political and free-trade reforms, Conservative commentators attempted to discredit Whig-Liberal imperialism.

The 'triumph of the anti-monopolist mood and free trade crusade' was therefore far from complete in the public debate on British imperium in India. Conservative commentators challenged the assumptions of anti-monopolists on the prospects of an open Chinese trade, and on the capacity of free trade to secure a stable foundation for Britain's manufacturing economy. They also engaged in detail with the intellectual foundations of Utilitarian reformism and its application to India. Conservative commentators continued to locate Britain's authority in India in the institutional fusion of sovereignty, commerce and property ownership by the EIC. In the aftermath of the Great Reform Act the prospect of a direct presence for the British state in India was mediated as an issue which could transform the balance of the British constitution. If the eastern empire was seldom justified in underconsumptionist terms, Conservative commentators continued to insist that the system of monopoly forged the substructure of an essentially commercial presence for Britain in the east. Indeed, Conservative critics maintained that by replacing the commercial fabric of empire with free trade and administrative reforms Whig imperial policy became unavoidably dependent on military power and launched the British empire in the east on a wholly new trajectory.

---

[70] G. Croly, 'Cabul and Affghanistan', ibid. li (May 1842), 676–90 at p. 679. See also Anon., *Letter to his grace the duke of Wellington &c. &c. &c. on the present state of affairs in India*, London 1842.
[71] On the military despotism of the EIC see Lawson, *The East India Company*, 145–49, and Bayly, *Imperial meridian*, 119–20.
[72] F. Holme, 'Affghanistan and India', BEM lii (July 1842), 100–12 at pp. 111–12. Rueing his dismissal in 1844, Lockhart described Ellenborough as the 'regenerator of India': 'Capt. Neill's *Narrative – General Nott in Affghanistan*', QR lxxviii (Sept. 1846), 463–510.

Corn, colonisation and the constitution: the Canada question, 1830–47

In 1837 Britain's western empire was once again shaken to its foundations by rebellion in Lower Canada. It is striking, however, that this imperial crisis has figured small in most histories of Britain during this period.[73] Where Canada has penetrated 'metropolitan' historiography it has usually been cast as an issue which merely exposed existing tensions within the Whig and Conservative parties.[74] Historians have, of course, recognised the long-term significance of the Whigs' solution to the Canada crisis – the Durham Report. This blueprint for colonial constitutional reform established a distinctive Whig-Liberal approach to the problem of imperial governance in the nineteenth century.[75] It is only by inhabiting contemporary intellectual debate, however, that the broader ideological significance of the Canada crisis can be fully appreciated. The Whig-Liberal solution was challenged in a Conservative imperial discourse which emphasised constitutional conservation but also looked to the economic instruments of protection, preference and colonisation for a coherent response to imperial crisis. This imperial political economy needs to be recognised as a defining characteristic of Conservative fiscal discourse during the thirties and forties and as an integral feature of the ideological schism of 1846.

In contemporary debate the 1837 rebellion in Lower Canada was constructed chiefly as a constitutional question. Indeed, Conservatives brought a distinctive constitutionalist historicism to their explanations of the origins of the crisis in Canada. From the vantage point of 1838–9 Conservatives interpreted the Canadian rebellion of 1837 as a necessary confluence of Whig constitutional reform and revolutionary nationalism.[76] By ceding control over Canadian finances to the House of Assembly in 1831, the Whigs were understood to have subordinated the executive and the royal prerogative to representative elements within the colonial constitution.[77] This fundamental tendency of Whig-Liberal constitutionalism was, in this reading, consolidated in the Great Reform Act and further expressed in the Whig commission of inquiry into the state of Canada and Lord John Russell's reso-

---

[73] See, for instance, Brent, *Liberal Anglican politics*; Mandler, *Aristocratic government*; Parry, *The rise and fall of Liberal government*.
[74] Newbould, *Whiggery and reform*, 216–23; Gash, *Sir Robert Peel*, 203–5, 231, 245–46.
[75] G. Martin, *Britain and the origins of Canadian confederation, 1837–67*, London 1995, 27–202; *The Gladstone diaries*, iii, pp. xxxivff.; x, pp. cxxix–cxxx.
[76] J. W. Croker, 'Canada', *QR* lxi (Jan. 1838), 249–72 at p. 253; G. Croly, 'A sketch of the Canadas', *BEM* xliii (Feb. 1838), 214–27 at 225–7; A. Mallalieu, 'Ministerial policy in the Canadas', ibid. 228–47 at pp. 232–42.
[77] On the reform of 1831 see Croker, 'Canada', 253, and Mallalieu, 'Ministerial policy in the Canadas', 236–7; C. E. Fryer, 'British North America under representative Government: (A) Lower Canada (1815–1837)', in J. H. Rose and others (eds), *The Cambridge history of the British empire*, vi, Cambridge 1930, 234–50.

lutions of 1837.[78] In this setting it seemed inevitable to Conservatives that Papineau, the Canadian republican and nationalist, should become the colonial *alter ego* of Daniel O'Connell.[79] Lord Durham's intervention in the politics of Lower Canada was therefore received in Conservative discourse as a more extreme expression of the established characteristics of Whig constitutionalism.[80] Of course, Durham's handling of the Canada problem was the subject of intense censure across the political spectrum.[81] Yet it remains that Durham's proposals for Canadian governance provoked a distinctive Conservative response. Whereas the Conservative party's leaders were reluctant to oppose Whig policy in Canada in 1839, the *Quarterly* insisted that colonial misgovernment demanded the abandonment of the parliamentary strategy of 'constructive opposition'.[82] Durham's proposal for the legislative union of the Canadian provinces under a single congress was condemned as a policy which would undermine the subsidiarity of the provincial legislatures to Westminster and would ultimately result in the secession of Canada from the British empire.[83] Conservatives therefore offered several constitutional alternatives to Durham's model for the legislative union of the Canadas. Wilmot Horton revived Bathurst's proposal for an alternative 'executive' union where the governor of the united provinces would have remained closely accountable to Westminster and would have retained control over the civil list.[84] A *Narrative* by Sir F. B. Head was elevated in the public debate as the constitutional antithesis of the Durham Report. Head's 1839 text rejected the entire

---

[78] Croker, 'Sir Robert Peel's address', 266; Sir C. Grey, *Remarks on the proceedings as to Canada, in the present session of parliament: by one of the commissioners, 10 April 1837*, London 1837, esp. pp. 9, 11, 14–15 (endorsed by Croker in 'Canada'). On Whig reformism before the Durham Report see Anon., *The Canadian controversy: its origin, nature and merits*, London 1838, described by Croker as 'ministerial' in 'Canada', at p. 260.

[79] On the parallel between Papineau and O'Connell see Croly, 'A sketch of the Canadas', 227, and Anon., *Hints on the case of Canada, for the consideration of members of parliament*, London 1838, 10, 19–20, (reviewed by Croker in 'Canada').

[80] Anon., 'Colonial misgovernment', BEM xliv (Nov. 1838), 624–37; J. W. Croker, 'Colonial government – Head's *Narrative* – Lord Durham's *Report*', QR lxiii (Mar. 1839), 457–525 at p. 524, and 'Political affairs, ibid. lxiii (Jan. 1839), 223–77 at pp. 234–7, 248–9, 261–5; T. C. Haliburton, *A reply to the report of the earl of Durham; by a colonist*, London 1839, 5–6 (letter i).

[81] Henry Brougham was the chief critic of Durham in parliament: H. Brougham, House of Lords (30 July, 7 Aug. 1838), *Hansard* 3rd ser. xliv. 755–6, 1019–22. See also House of Commons (8 Feb. 1839), ibid. 192–6.

[82] Croker, 'Colonial government – Head's *Narrative* – Lord Durham's *Report*', 524; Sir F. B. Head, 'British policy', QR lxiv (Oct. 1839), 462–512 at p. 509.

[83] Haliburton, *A reply to the report of the earl of Durham*, 50–62, 53 (letter v); 12–21 (letter ii) (authorship was attributed to Haliburton by Croker who had recognised him as the author of a series of letters to *The Times* on Whig policy in Canada: 'Colonial government', 522).

[84] R. Wilmot Horton, *Exposition and defence of the Earl Bathurst's administration of the affairs of Canada, when colonial secretary, during the years 1822 to 1827, inclusive*, London 1838, 5–6, 41–51. See also Mallalieu, 'Ministerial policy in the Canadas', 243.

notion of unifying the Canadian provinces and looked instead to an active executive for the rejuvenation of colonial governance in the Canadas.[85] What both Conservative approaches shared was an unshakeable faith in the *status quo* of 1830 and in the predominance of executive authority over representative structures in colonial constitutions.

Yet constitutional conservatism was blended with distinctive attitudes to the socio-economic instruments of British imperial statecraft in Conservative discourse. Indeed, Horton insisted that Henry Bathurst's Tory colonial policy had belonged to the 'science of political economy' not colonial administration.[86] Accordingly, Horton combined his revival of Bathurst's constitutional proposal for British North America with his own schemes for the exportation of labour and capital to the Canadas: Here, the ties of imperial cohesion would be strengthened by the mutual bonds of commerce.[87] Similarly, Croker endorsed Head's territorial and economic perspective on the consolidation of British North America. If Montreal was transferred to Upper Canada then the loyal province would be 'at full liberty to push the long and vigorous arms of *commerce* to the Atlantic, and of *colonization* into the boundless West'.[88] Of course, constitutional and economic perspectives were also blended together in Whig-Liberal attitudes to the Canada question. Lord Durham embraced the ideas of Edward Gibbon Wakefield and the National Colonisation Society as the socio-economic corollary of his constitutional blueprint.[89] In common with many Conservative writers Wakefield diagnosed the basic problem of the British economy as the difficulty of balancing production with consumption. He believed that colonial expansion would provide markets for British trade and industry and would raise profits by multiplying opportunities to invest and by syphoning off excess capital. On the face of it, then, Wakefield's imperial political economy shared some of the fundamental assumptions of Conservative imperial discourse.[90] It is instructive therefore to examine how Conservatives distinguished their positions on colonisation from that of Wakefield and the National Colonisation Society.

There were two specific features of Wakefield's colonial political economy which Conservative critics tended to reject – 'land finance' and 'concentrated

---

[85] *A narrative by Sir Francis Head, Bart*, 2nd edn, London 1839, was lauded as a Conservative model for British North America by the following: Croker, 'Colonial government', 457–99; duke of Wellington, House of Lords (15 Feb. 1839), *Hansard* 3rd ser. xlv. 436; J. G. Lockhart, 'Hochelga and the emigrant', *QR* lxxviii (Sept. 1846), 510–35 at p. 511.
[86] Horton, *Earl Bathurst's administration*, 39.
[87] Ibid. 29–31.
[88] Croker, 'Colonial government', 505. See also Mallalieu, 'Ministerial policy in the Canadas', 245–7, and Alison, 'The reciprocity and colonial systems', 326–7.
[89] On Wakefield and his influence see Winch, *Classical political economy and colonies*, 73–121, and Morrell, *British colonial policy*, 5–15. Croker condemned Wakefield's appointment as an adviser to Lord Durham: 'Political affairs', 232.
[90] For instance J. Barrow, 'Emigration – letters from Canada', *QR* liv (Sept. 1835), 413–29 at p. 418. See above pp. 154–6, 166–9.

settlement'.[91] Wakefield's proposal to finance colonisation through the sale of land was received critically in Conservative journals. Lord Elgin objected that the stipulation of a minimum price would discourage capitalists and might lead to an unbalanced exportation of labour and capital.[92] G. P. Scrope, however, feared the intrusion of the profit motive into the colonisation process which he viewed as a distributive mechanism of 'social economy'.[93] Wakefield's concept of 'concentrated settlement' was an essential feature of his proposals for 'land finance' and also met with criticism in the Conservative press. Invoking Tocqueville, Talleyrand and Burke, J. G. Phillimore insisted that the essence of colonisation consisted in the dispersal not the concentration of emigrants.[94] Moreover, he maintained that the institutional and legal structures which accompanied colonisation needed to grow historically from social and economic conditions and could not be imposed by a Benthamite strategy of organised and concentrated colonisation.[95]

Beyond their specific objections to the imperial political economy of Wakefield, Conservatives offered a broader perspective on the political instruments of British imperialism. Some Conservative critics of Wakefield objected that government-assisted schemes of colonisation ought to predominate over those of private companies or individuals if the object was a truly 'national' colonisation.[96] Others objected fiercely to the connection of Wakefieldian colonialism to Whig constitutionalism and religious liberalism. Thus H. H. Milman, T. C. Haliburton and others insisted that the established Protestant Church with its episcopal and parochial structures was crucial to the consolidation of Britain's imperial authority in North America.[97] As one reviewer commented on the role of the established Church: 'If we regard it

---

[91] On Wakefield's land schemes see Winch, *Classical political economy and colonies*, 90–4, 99–103. On 'concentrated settlement' see ibid. 100–3.

[92] Elgin engaged directly with the ideas of Robert Gouger and Edward Gibbon Wakefield in a review of *A statement of the objects of a society for effecting systematic colonization*, London 1830, in 'Causes and remedies of pauperism in the United Kingdom', 243–4, 255–7, 270–1.

[93] Scrope, 'Ammendment of the poor laws', 320–45, and 'The new poor law', 245–53. See also Scrope's criticism of the National Colonisation Society's 'land finance' as detailed in C. Tennant, *Letters on systematic colonization and the bill now before parliament*, London 1831, in 'Population and emigration', 139–43.

[94] J. G. Phillimore, 'Merivale on colonies and colonization', BEM lii (Aug. 1842), 206–23 at p. 212. See ibid. pp. 219–20 for citations from C. M. de Talleyrand-Périgord, *Essai sur les avantages à retirer des colonies nouvelles*, repr. Paris 1840, and A. de Tocqueville, *De la democratie en Amérique*, Paris 1836. Of the latter Phillimore wrote (p. 219): 'It seems as if it had been written for the express purpose of contradicting Mr. Wakefield.'

[95] Ibid. 211; J. G. Phillimore, 'Lewis on the government of dependencies', BEM li (Feb. 1842), 213–23 re. Sir G. C. Lewis, *Essay on the government of dependencies* London 1841. See also Winch, *Classical political economy and colonies*, 116.

[96] J. G. Lockhart, 'Pringle and Moodie on South Africa', QR lv (Dec. 1835), 74–96; J. Barrow, 'Travels and adventures in Eastern Africa; the manners, customs, &c., of the Zoolus', ibid. lviii (Feb. 1837), 1–29, and 'The Australian colonies', ibid. lxviii (June 1841), 88–145.

[97] H. H. Milman, 'Guizot's edition of Gibbon', ibid. l (Jan. 1834), 273–307 at pp. 275, 282–3, 293–7; Haliburton, *A reply to the report of the earl of Durham*, 63–74 (letter vi), 84–7

merely on the grounds of civil and commercial policy, we must remember that the leaven of loyalty has uniformly been conveyed to the people through the medium of the Church.'[98] Many Conservatives conceptualised colonisation as a process of nationalisation not merely as a transfer of capital and population from the metropole to the colonies. In this sense colonisation was viewed as a device which could dampen the flames of French nationalism in North America through sheer force of numbers. Even before the rebellion of 1837 Thomas De Quincey observed that, beside British laws and an established Church, the foundation of 'a civic and patriotic spirit' in the Canadas was the emigration of Britons: 'It is probable, also, that the tide of emigration being in so large an overbalance British, may have the effect of diffusing and sustaining a British state of political feeling.'[99] For S. T. Coleridge also, English nationality was crucial to the construction of colonial society in North America.[100] As Alfred Mallalieu ventured, 'Thus might 50,000 annually ... be poured into the province and advantageously located, until the balance of origin was established in favour of British blood.'[101] George Croly explained Britain's relative success in colonisation in terms of the influence of English language and culture in unifying colonial settlement and edifying the baser commercial motives behind imperial expansion.[102] Of course, it would be absurd to suggest that Conservative imperial commentators held a monopoly over political and cultural notions of colonisation. Nevertheless, the idea of emigration as 'exported nationality' was used to delineate a distinctive position against Whig-Liberal emphases on constitutional reform, Wakefieldian colonisation and religious liberalism within the public debate of the 1830s.

Yet the distinctiveness of Conservative imperial discourse rested principally in the prominence afforded to maintaining the fiscal fabric of the British empire. While Wakefield was prepared to interfere with the market's allocations of land and labour in order to construct a colonial empire, he never seriously challenged free-trade liberalism. In parliament and in print, however, Conservatives presented protection and preference as essential instruments of British imperial statecraft. Indeed, it was axiomatic in many Conservative commentaries on the colonisation of North America that the transfer of capital and labour to the colonies needed to be supported by the fiscal structures of protection and preference.[103] Not only was the imperial

---

(letter vii); Anon., 'Ecclesiatical state of the colonies', *QR* lxxv (Dec. 1844), 201–22 at p. 219.
[98] Ibid. 221.
[99] T. De Quincey, 'McGregor's British America', *BEM* xxxi (June 1832), 907–27 at p. 907.
[100] S. T. Coleridge, 4 May 1833, in *Specimens of the table-talk of the late S. T. Coleridge*, ed. H. N. Coleridge, London 1835, i. 166–7, cited in Lockhart, 'Coleridge's *Table-Talk*', 100.
[101] Mallalieu, 'Ministerial policy in the Canadas', 245. See also Sir R. Peel, House of Commons (2 June 1840), *Hansard* 3rd ser. iv, 892.
[102] G. Croly, 'Africa', *BEM* xlix (Jan. 1841), 109–13 at p. 113.
[103] Anon. (poss. J. Galt), 'The British North American provinces', *FM* v (Feb. 1832),

tariff understood to safeguard Canadian raw producers from the competition of the United States, it was also viewed as a mechanism which maintained the muscle of Britain's mercantile marine and which addressed the structural problem of 'a superfluity of manufactures and a paucity of consumers' in the metropolitan economy.[104] In parliament the Canadian timber preference was repeatedly defended during the thirties and forties as a device which sustained markets for British manufactures and which cemented the bonds of empire.[105] Moreover, Sir Howard Douglas presented his argument for the retention of the timber preference in 1842 as a general defence of the colonial system against the promises held out by free-trade internationalists: 'what our manufacturers want, and what all our interests require is not increased production but increased consumption. This we can command in the colonies'.[106] By defending the traditional fiscal implements of British imperium thus, many Conservatives located the empire at the heart of their intellectual challenge to free-trade liberalism.

It is essential, therefore, to reclaim the empire as a fundamental feature of Conservative fiscal discourse during the 1840s. For, as early twentieth-century historians of the period noted, the imperial significance of protection and preference figured large in the public debate on free trade in general and on corn-law repeal in particular.[107] Strikingly, Peel's reformist protectionism of 1842–3 was both presented and received as imperial statecraft, not as an instalment of cosmopolitan free trade. Indeed, in a parliamentary debate on Peel's 1842 budget, Gladstone and Stanley justified their adjustment of the tariff of Britain's North American colonies and their imposition of duties on imports from the USA in imperial terms. As Gladstone stated, 'These were what he called intercolonial principles; he meant principles of equality and impartiality in the commercial relations established by Parliament between colony and colony.'[108] Naturally, the Conservative journals celebrated the imperialist credentials of Peel's great reforming budget: 'The powerful protec-

---

77–84 at pp. 78–9; De Quincey, 'McGregor's British America', 907–27 esp. pp. 908–9, 919–20.

[104] J. Wilson, 'Upper Canada: by a backwoodsman', BEM xxii (Aug. 1832), 238–62 at p. 246. Wilson was influenced by a *Report of Mr Richards to the colonial secretary, respecting the waste lands in Canada, and emigration,* repr. in *The Canadas, compiled from documents furnished by John Galt, Esq. with the fullest information for emigrants,* ed. Andrew Picken, London 1832.

[105] Alderman Thompson resisted C. P. Villiers's motion for the equalisation of foreign and colonial timber duties in House of Commons (9 July 1839), Hansard 3rd ser. xlix. 102. See also H. Goulburn, House of Commons (1 June 1840), ibid. liv. 802–3.

[106] Sir H. Douglas opposed Roebuck's bill for the equalisation of timber duties, House of Commons (6 June 1842), ibid. lxiii. 1289.

[107] See Holland, *The fall of protection,* 118–26, and Morrell, *British colonial policy,* 171–80, 191–5. Macintyre also touched on the imperial dimensions of protectionist argument in 'Lord George Bentinck and the protectionists', esp. p. 157 n. 49.

[108] W. E. Gladstone, House of Commons (15 Apr. 1842), Hansard 3rd ser. lxii. 550; E. Stanley, ibid. 559. Both defended Peel's policy against the free-trade opposition of H. Labouchère, ibid. 541.

tion afforded by the new tariff to our colonial produce is one of its most interesting and satisfactory features.'[109] The Canada corn law of 1843 was similarly interpreted as a fiscal instrument of Britain's imperial political economy. In parliament Stanley defended the reduction of the duty on corn imported into the United Kingdom as a measure of imperial statecraft:

> I do not bring that measure forward as a measure of free-trade; I do not submit it to you as a bill for the admission of foreign corn; but I do bring the measure forward as a great boon to one of our most important colonies. I submit it to the house as a colonial and not as a fiscal question.[110]

Of course, a large minority of British protectionists did not accept Stanley's imperialist reasoning.[111] Yet there were many who accepted the Canada corn law as an expression of Britain's imperial political economy and as the antithesis of Cobdenite cosmopolitanism.[112] As H. T. Liddell claimed in 1846: 'He regarded the Canada Corn Bill as a far-seeing act of policy. Why did he so regard it? Because, so far from its being an abandonment of the protective system, it was a means of extending it to the remotest parts of our distant colonies.'[113]

The repeal of the corn laws and the abandonment of the Canadian corn preference in 1846 was therefore received in Conservative economic discourse as a fundamental shift outside the established imperial paradigm of British commercial policy. Peel was considered by many to have abandoned the fiscal tools of imperial statecraft and to have adopted Cobden's cosmopolitan political economy. As *Fraser's* countered, 'if you want corn, Canada alone will supply you, and . . . Canada, if you deal fairly by her, will take more of your manufactured goods than all the continent of Europe put together'.[114] By relinquishing colonial preference, then, Peel was widely thought to have

---

[109] Warren, 'Great Britain at the commencement of the year 1843', 12. See also the retrospective claim in Anon., *Protection and free trade; or, the interests of an empire and not of a party; considered in a letter to Lord Viscount Sandon*, London 1846, esp. p. 19.

[110] E. Stanley, House of Commons (19 May 1843), Hansard 3rd ser. lxix. 579.

[111] On the opposition of 'metropolitan' protectionists to the Canada Corn Bill see G. Heathcote and P. Miles, ibid. 619–22, 622–4. See also Holland, *The fall of protection*, 129.

[112] Note the care taken by a member of the Essex Agricultural Society to retain imperialist credentials in Anon., *Notes on Canada, with reference to the Act 6–7 Vict. 1843, c. 29 for reducing the duties on Canadian wheat and wheat flour imported into the United Kingdom*, London 1845, esp. pp. 3–21, 41–3. Note also the vehement opposition of the free traders Gibson, Bowring and Villiers in the House of Commons (29 May 1843), Hansard 3rd ser. lxix. 988–92.

[113] H. T. Liddell, House of Commons (27 Jan. 1846), ibid. lxxxiii. 295. See also Sir H. Douglas, House of Commons (13 Feb. 1846), ibid. 848, and Anon., *Our free trade policy examined with respect to its real bearing upon native industry, our colonial system, and the institutions and ultimate destinies of the nation*, London–Liverpool 1846, 28. This pamphlet appealed to various authorities including Sir Howard Douglas, ibid. 9–10, Richard Burn, ibid. 17–18, 28–9, and Lord George Bentinck, ibid. 30–1.

[114] Anon., 'What is the policy of Sir Robert Peel and his cabinet?', FM xxxiii (Apr. 1846),

undermined the foundations of stable economic advance in metropolitan Britain: 'The British manufacturer, in consequence, has found in their markets a second *Home Market*. Commercially speaking, as well as politically, they have been a portion of Great Britain itself.'[115] In the context of Britain's boundary dispute with the USA therefore, J. W. Croker read the removal of Canada's corn preference as a naive endorsement of free-trade theories on trade and international relations:

> If it succeeds, even to any considerable degree, we may *clothe* them, and they may *feed* us, but only so long as they please, and that will be until they have nursed up their own manufactures to the point of doing without us. . . . And it may be remembered that the stoppage of the *food* must necessarily be accompanied by a rejection of the *clothing*; so that the misery will be double – destitution at once of work and food.[116]

In this reading the cosmopolitan reform of 1846 ignored the realities of international relations and ransomed the stability of the British economy to the maintenance of a palpably precarious peace.

Not only was the transformation of 1846 considered to have destroyed the socio-economic security of colonialism, it was also received as a potentially shattering blow to the cohesion and integrity of the British empire. As Alison opined, 'Protection to domestic industry, at home or colonial, is the unseen but strongly felt bond which unites together the far distant provinces of the British empire by the firm bond of mutual interest.'[117] The politics of preference also preponderated in the parliamentary reaction against the cosmopolitan departure of 1846. Thus Phillip Miles urged an alternative imperial conception of British political economy on Peel:

> Treat them in all respects as integral parts of the Empire. Extend to them the principle of your Canada Corn Bill – permit them to import their grain, meal, and maize and all other produce, and I will vote with you. Give them the some greater benefit than you now propose, and you will draw the bonds of union closer, and knit them more firmly to the mother country.[118]

369–78 at p. 371. On Canadian corn as an imperial resource see the following: F. Scott, House of Commons (13 Feb. 1846), *Hansard* 3rd ser. lxxxiii. 866–7; Anon., *Our free trade policy examined*, 5, and *Speech of Mr. Disraeli*, 32–3.

[115] Anon., *Our free trade policy examined*, 15. This reasoning was applied to Ireland as well as to Canada in Anon., *Protection and free trade*, 20–5, 39, and by Col. Connolly and Viscount Ingestre, House of Commons (24 Feb. 1846), *Hansard* 3rd ser. lxxx. 23, 34.

[116] J. W. Croker, 'The Oregon question: postscript', *QR* lxxvii (Mar. 1846), 603–10 at p. 605. This argument was continued in Croker's, 'Close of Sir Robert Peel's administration', 535–80 at p. 545. For a rendition of this view in parliament see G. Finch, House of Commons (3 Mar. 1846), *Hansard* 3rd ser. lxxxv. 538. For a brief summary of the Oregon boundary dispute see J. W. Croker, 'The Oregon question', *QR* lxxvii (Mar. 1846), 563–602.

[117] Alison, 'The Roman Campagna', 355. See also his 'The fall of Rome: its causes at work in the British empire', 692–718.

[118] P. Miles, House of Commons (9 Feb. 1846), *Hansard* 3rd ser. lxxxiii. 558. See also Sir W. Heathcote, ibid. 562.

'THE PATRIOTIC PRINCIPLE'

Sir Howard Douglas also contemplated Peel's repeal of the corn laws as the symbol of a free-trade policy which amounted to 'a virtual dissolution of our colonial system'.[119] In place of Cobdenite cosmopolitanism or the *ad hoc* pragmatism of 'reciprocal' free trade, Douglas offered the alternative of a British imperial *zollverein*:

> it might really be possible to treat Colonies like counties of the country, not only in direct trade with the United Kingdom, but in commercial intercourse with each other, by free trade among ourselves, under a reasonable moderate degree of protection from without, and so resolve the United Kingdom, and all her colonies and possessions, into a commercial union such as might defy all rivalry, and defeat all combinations.[120]

Thus, when Lord George Bentinck asserted during the corn-law debates of 1846 that the abandonment of Canada's corn and timber preferences would damage the integrity of Britain's North American empire, he articulated a widely held view that Britain had abandoned the certainties of an imperial political economy for the chimerical expectations of cosmopolitanism.[121] The empire played a pivotal role, therefore, in the protectionist case against free trade in 1846 and loomed large in Conservatives' explanations of their break with Peel. Indeed, Peel's critics appealed to the concept of empire in order to 'get rid of the absurd notion that there is *only one* course safely open to us'.[122] As one anonymous pamphleteer warned: 'Go on in your present course; throw off your colonies, destroy our native industry; ruin you commercial marine; and the *progress of this country towards extinction as a great state is fixed and inevitable.*'[123]

---

[119] Sir H. Douglas, House of Commons (13 Feb. 1846), ibid. 850.
[120] Ibid. 850.
[121] Lord G. Bentinck, House of Commons (14, 18 May 1846), ibid. lxxxvi. 553–68, 828–30; Disraeli, *Lord George Bentinck*, esp. pp. 180, 224–5, 458, 579, 583.
[122] Anon., *Our free trade policy examined*, 4 (Anon.'s emphasis).
[123] Ibid. 41 (Anon.'s emphasis).

PART IV

AFTER REPEAL

8

'Dead and Buried?': The Protectionist Challenge, 1847–1852

'Freedom for what? Freedom to employ the lightly taxed foreigner instead of our own heavily burdened countrymen. Freedom to sever every holy tie that should bind colonies to their mother country, Briton to Briton, rich to poor – freedom to reduce the working classes from their bread, bacon, beef and beer, to the tea-pot washings and slave labour cake of 1849': Anon. ['Britannicus'], *Political principles: an answer to the letter from Sir Robert Peel Bart., to his constituents*, 2nd edn, London 1847, 20.

'[T]his long story is over, and the moral of it is, that Protection is dead and buried': G. W. Dasent, 'The story of free trade', FM xliii (June 1851), 716–22 at p. 722.

Most histories of economic ideas and policy in nineteenth-century Britain have tended to treat 1846 either as a pivotal moment or as a chronological terminus. It has generally been assumed that the hegemony of free trade over policy, elections and the public debate was complete if not by 1846 then certainly by 1852.[1] Almost automatically, historians have tended to assume that protection died and was buried with a haste which was more appropriate than it was unseemly. Of course, at the level of policy and elections the free-trade *telos* tells an accurate tale: Corn law repeal was swiftly followed by the abandonment of the colonial sugar preference, by the repeal of the navigation laws in 1849 and by the recognition of protection as an electoral incubus by the leaders of the Conservative party.[2] Yet, in reality, this apparently seamless consolidation of a free-trade consensus was vigorously challenged. Far from dying obligingly, protectionist discourse flourished in pamphlets and journals, in parliament and, in its new institutional incarnation, the National Association for the Protection of Industry and Capital throughout the British Empire from 1849. Protectionists sustained their broad economic and social response to free-trade liberalism and insisted on the continuing political and constitutional significance of protection in mid nineteenth-century Conservatism.

By rejecting the assumption that free trade was a great electoral fact after

---

[1] See, for instance, Hirst, *Free trade and other fundamental doctrines*, 117–238, and more recently, Harling, *The waning of 'Old Corruption'*, 228–54, and Howe, *Free trade and Liberal England*, 111.
[2] But note the argument that Britain remained more protectionist than France between 1846 and 1860 in Nye, 'Myth of free-trade Britain', 23–46.

1846 protectionists were forced to address the problem of shifting public opinion back to protection. From the middle of 1849 protectionists attempted an organised onslaught on the public mind. G. F. Young and the National Association urged protectionists to engage in active opinion-forming, 'to use their best endeavours, through the daily and periodical press – by the circulation of pamphlets and tracts – and by such other means as might be at their disposal, to awaken those to whom the appeal was made to a full sense of the importance of the crisis'.[3] The National Association itself sent regular circulars to affiliated provincial associations frequently enclosing copies of the reports of its own committees and other protectionist tracts. Such texts were often accompanied by requests that provincial associations attempt to persuade their local newspapers to reprint all or part of the National Association's enclosures.[4] Young's own series of letters to the *Morning Herald*, designed as a 'manual of facts and arguments' for every 'true protectionist', was distributed in this manner.[5] Indeed, as the chairman of the acting committee of the National Association, as a witness to parliamentary committees and as pamphleteer and contributor to the *Quarterly*, Young personified the numerous facets of protectionist opinion-forming. Like the *Quarterly*, *Blackwood's* was instrumental in propagating the arguments of the National Association and could even sport David Low, W. E. Aytoun and John Blackwood among the delegates of both the Scottish Protective Association and the National Association.[6] The contributions of both major Conservative periodicals were recognised unequivocally by the National Association in 1850: 'To the *Quarterly Review* and to *Blackwood's Magazine*, the cause of Protection owes a debt of obligation scarcely to be expressed; the masterly and unanswerable reasonings by which the important facts, adduced in those publications, are supported, having defied the assaults of the whole Free Trade press.'[7] Responses in the daily, weekly, provincial and metropolitan press to a particular *Blackwood's* article of January 1850 would seem to justify this fulsome gratitude. For the reviews of Aytoun's article on 'British agriculture and foreign competition' reveal not only that his arguments were accurately and widely understood but also that the local press connected

---

[3] NAPIC, citation from the circular of 24 July 1850 in *Report of the acting committee to the special meeting of the general committee of the National Association for the Protection of Industry and Capital throughout the British Empire*, London 1850, 6. See also G. F. Young, 'Free trade', *QR* lxxxvi (Dec. 1849), 148–83 at p. 182.

[4] NAPIC's circular of 3 June 1850 enclosed the *Report of the subcommittee on currency*, London 1850. A circular of Nov. 1850 enclosed J. H. Merridew's tract on freehold land societies while that of March 1851 distributed the *Report of the conference of provincial delegates with the acting committee* (3 Mar. 1851) and pressed local associations to reprint it.

[5] G. F. Young, *Free-trade fallacies refuted; in a series of letters to the editor of the Morning Herald*, repr. London 1852, 4.

[6] W. E. Aytoun, 'The great protection meeting in London', *BEM* lxvii (June 1850), 738–82 at pp. 746, 748, 776.

[7] [NAPIC], *Report of the acting committee to the special meeting*, 10.

general protectionist discourse to specific local instances of protest and association.[8] Clearly, the protectionist effort to re-form public opinion relied heavily on the perceived power of 'Print'.

Interests, nation and empire: protectionist economics, 1847–52

While the National Association provided a new institutional framework for the co-ordination of a protectionist campaign in print, the texts themselves must be located in a long tradition of protectionist argument. After 1846 the advocates of protection continued to project it as a national economic philosophy which could not be reduced to the special pleading of agriculture. Contemplating the general election of 1847, Croker urged Conservatives to pledge themselves to 'the great principles of *protection to every class of national industry*'.[9] And, as Aytoun insisted in 1851, 'To argue the Agricultural case alone, however important that may be, is to weaken the general cause, which is the cause of labour . . . the cause is that of the whole industrious population of Britain, not of a section or class.'[10] In practice therefore protectionists appealed to a range of urban, commercial and manufacturing interests in their campaign for the restoration of protection.[11] In parliament Lord Stanley underlined the catholicity of interests behind protection when he presented a petition from Lancastrian landowners, occupiers, manufacturers, tradesmen and artisans to the House of Lords in 1850.[12] Echoing Stanley's insistence that protection should not be constructed solely as an agriculturists' question, Aytoun chose to cite the address and protectionist resolutions of the Metropolitan Trades Delegates to the National Association's conference of May 1850.[13] Protection, then, was projected as an inclusive and national economic philosophy which would unite the different sectors and social classes. As Young insisted, 'It was by *dividing* interests that Free-trade overthrew Pro-

---

[8] W. E. Aytoun, 'British agriculture and foreign competition', *BEM* lxvii (Jan. 1850), 94–136; 'Appendix to Blackwood's Magazine, no. cccciii, Feb. 1850: opinions of the press', ibid. lxvii (Feb. 1850), 1–122. For explicit connections of protectionist ideas to local contexts see the *Nottingham Guardian* on meetings at Ripon and Driffield, the *West of England Conservative's* reference to an association at Callington and the *Morning Herald's* use of the meeting of protectionists at Shrewsbury as a setting for its review of *BEM* ibid. 14, 48, 53.
[9] J. W. Croker, 'Peel policy', *QR* lxxxi (June 1847), 274–316 at p. 309 (Croker's emphasis).
[10] W. E. Aytoun, 'Autumn politics', *BEM* lxx (Nov. 1851), 607–28 at pp. 614–15.
[11] See Young's appeal to shipping and imperial interests in *Free-trade fallacies refuted*, 17–23 (letter iv).
[12] Stanley, House of Lords (19 July 1850), *Hansard* 3rd ser. cxiii. 1.
[13] Aytoun, 'The great protection meeting', 749–52. See also Aytoun's citation from an 'Address of the metropolitan trades delegates to the working classes of Great Britain and Ireland', in 'Latter days of the free-trade ministry', *BEM* lxix (Apr. 1851), 491–512 at p. 510. [Isaac Wilson and Augustus Delaforce], *Proclamation of the working classes against free trade and for protection, produced by the metropolitan trades delegates* (19 Nov. 1852).

tection. It is by *uniting* interests that Protection must triumph over Free-trade.'[14]

The plausibility of this strategy was acutely dependent on the effectiveness of protectionists' attempts to present free trade as a narrow and sectional alternative. Such responses combined political and constitutional explanations of the ascendancy of free trade with particular protectionist readings of Britain's contemporary economic experience. Thus Alison continued to attribute the dominance of the sectional 'philosophy' of free trade to the Great Reform Act. Building on arguments first formulated during 1832–3, Alison insisted that free trade was an inevitable legislative consequence of the electoral position of urban interests after 1832.[15] In this view parliamentary reform had established the numerical dominance of urban consumers and retrenchers and had annihilated the unreformed constitution's virtual representation of a range of urban, imperial and agricultural interests:

> *all* interests were attended to; and that worst of tyrannies, the tyranny of one class over another class, was effectually prevented. . . . Had any one class or interest been predominant . . . to the subversion or injury of other classes in the state, such a storm of discontent must have arisen as would speedily have proved fatal to the unanimity, and with it to the growth and prosperity of the empire.[16]

Thus it appeared to Alison that through his commercial legislation Peel had 'made himself not the representative of the nation, but of a section of the nation; not of the British empire in every part of the world, but of Manchester and Glasgow'.[17]

Protectionists insisted that the essential sectionalism of free trade was being expressed in contemporary economic experience. Far from distributing prosperity across all manufacturing and commercial interests, the reforms of the 1840s benefited manufacturing exporters almost exclusively: 'Free-trade, in so far as it lessens the cost of production, is clearly in the interest of the master manufacturer who exports for the foreign market; but, we repeat, it is the interest of no one else in the community.'[18] Aytoun argued that Britain's four main exporting industries – cotton, iron, wool and linen – were gaining at the expense of domestic non-exporting trades whose markets were being

---

[14] G. F. Young, *Address of the general committee of the National Association for the Protection of Industry and Capital throughout the British Empire to the friends of protection to all British interests, 12 Dec. 1850*, London 1850, 3.

[15] A. Alison, 'Thirty years of Liberal legislation', *BEM* lxiii (Jan. 1848), 1–28 at p. 4.

[16] Idem, 'The crowning of the column and the crushing of the pedestal', ibid. lvi (July 1849), 108–32 at p. 111.

[17] Idem, 'The dinner to Lord Stanley', ibid. lxix (May 1851), 635–40 at p. 636. For an example of the diffusion of this type of constitutional reading see *Leicester Journal* (18 Jan. 1850) cited in 'Appendix to Blackwood's Magazine', 88.

[18] W. E. Aytoun, 'A review of the last session', *BEM* lxiv (Sept. 1848), 261–90 at p. 268.

assailed by imports of foreign goods.[19] Britain's relative advancement in industrialisation meant that her staple export trades had little to fear from competition with the foreigner in the home market and much to gain from wider and deeper access to foreign markets. Thus Aytoun went on to maintain that Britain's comparative advantage in cotton, wool and iron was crushing the share of the smaller trades in foreign as well as domestic markets: 'The truth is, that the whole scheme of free trade was erected and framed, not for the purpose of benefiting the manufacturers at the expense of the landed interest, but rather to get a monopoly of export for one or two of the leading manufacturers of the empire.'[20] Charles Newdegate injected an identical point into parliamentary debates on the free-trade 'experiment'. He characterised Richard Cobden as the representative of 'only a section of the manufacturers, the section of a class who were determined to sacrifice their neighbours for their own advantage'.[21] Thus it seemed to protectionists that British commercial legislation was in danger of reducing the British economy to a 'circle of smoking factories'.[22] For Aytoun, here was a political economy which ignored the bulk of the UK beyond the 'smoking circle' and which rested Britain's economic future on exporting low-value textiles to 'semi-barbarous countries'.[23] For G. F. Young free trade did not forge secure foundations for the continued advance of the British economy but rather acted as a dangerous fillip to speculative exports rendering domestic economic fluctuations inevitable.[24] Clearly the insistence of protectionists on the confined and sectional benefits of free trade was not merely a strategy for splitting the urban free-trade consensus.

The primary purpose of contesting the economic gains from free trade was, of course, to present protection as the only route to secure and permanent prosperity. In keeping with established arguments, protectionists continued to maintain that secure growth could only be guaranteed if the sectors were balanced and if the home market was strong. Thus in 1847 Alison turned on its head the free-trade claim that Britain was shielded from the immediate benefits of economic liberalism by the Irish famine. By substituting foreign for domestic agricultural produce, by diminishing the capacity of British producers to consume manufactured goods, and by failing to establish a reciprocal trade with European nations, Alison claimed that famine in Ireland showed how free trade would eventually work for the United Kingdom as a whole.[25] In line with Alison's predictions, the faltering performance of manufactures during 1849 and 1850 was attributed to the devastating impact of

---

[19] Ibid. 269–72.
[20] Idem, 'The opening of the session', ibid. lxv (Mar. 1849), 357–82 at pp. 378–9.
[21] C. N. Newdegate, House of Commons (14 May 1850), *Hansard* 3rd ser. cxi. 96.
[22] Aytoun, 'British agriculture and foreign competition', 136.
[23] Ibid. 119, 133.
[24] Young, *Free trade fallacies refuted*, 25–6 (letter v).
[25] A. Alison, 'Lessons from the famine', *BEM* lxi (May 1847), 515–24 at pp. 520–1.

free trade on domestic and colonial markets. Using evidence from trade circulars and from *Burn's commercial glance*, J. B. Johnson attempted to demonstrate serious decline in the home market after 1846.[26] Similarly, Disraeli claimed in parliament in 1849 that free trade measures had directly caused the destruction of around a quarter of the home market for manufactures.[27] As Aytoun put it 'The home trade is a thing altogether kept out of the account in the . . . splendid vision of the calico millenium.'[28] Protection, by contrast, was presented as an economic strategy which guaranteed mutual consumption in domestic markets and which encouraged the balanced development of economic sectors. Thus the decline of domestic agriculture in the face of cheaper foreign imports was presented as permanently damaging to the stability and growth of the entire British economy.[29]

This emphasis on the fundamental importance of protection in maintaining domestic markets was, of course, nothing new in British economic discourse. Yet these established arguments were creatively reworked in a number of new intellectual contexts. The first of these was furnished by the insistence of free traders that corn law repeal had not destroyed the home market and that British agriculturists could secure their own profits and ability to consume by adopting modern 'high farming' techniques. As Disraeli recognised, *Blackwood's* was at the vanguard of the attack on the manifesto of 'high farming', James Caird's, *High farming under Liberal covenants*.[30] Reasoning from specific case studies, Aytoun showed that even given the most modern farming methods and moderate rents British agriculture could not withstand the scale of foreign competition. To protectionists, of course, foreign imports not only destroyed agricultural profits, they also annihilated the mainstay of the domestic market for manufactures. The presiding importance of the idea of the home market in British protectionist argument was reworked in a second new intellectual context, the interplay between Henry Carey (the American critic of English 'orthodox' political economy) and British protectionists. In an article of 1851 Aytoun cited extensively from Carey's *Harmony of interests* which he read (to Carey's evident satisfaction) as a 'remarkable' treatise on 'the causes of the progress and decline of industrial communi-

---

[26] J. B. Johnson, 'Tenor of the trade circulars', ibid. lxvii (May 1850), 589–604, and 'Our commercial and manufacturing prosperity', ibid. lxix (June 1851), 700–16
[27] Disraeli, House of Commons (2 July 1849), *Hansard* 3rd ser. civ. 1157–8.
[28] W. E. Aytoun, 'The industry of the people', BEM lxviii (July 1850), 106–22 at p. 114.
[29] Young, *Free trade fallacies refuted*, 14–15 (letter iii); W. B. Ferrand, *The speech of W. Busfeild Ferrand Esq., at Aylsham in Norfolk, March 4th 1851*, London 1851, 27; [NAPIC], *Tracts on protection: no. 2: the occupations of the people*, 5, 7, 11, 13. This estimate of the national economic importance of agriculture appealed to Aytoun's 'British agriculture and foreign competition', 105–19.
[30] Ibid. esp. pp. 104–30. On 1 Jan. 1850 Disraeli admitted to having 'read the last article in the new "Blackwood". I think it has knocked up Scotch high farming, the last imposition': *Lord Beaconsfield's correspondence with his sister*, 238; J. Caird, *High farming under liberal covenants the best substitute for protection*, Edinburgh 1849.

ties'.³¹ Aytoun was impressed by Carey's argument that the social and economic stability of a state needed to be rooted in production which in turn laid the foundations of the home market. For Carey's principal criticism of what he called 'the English school of political economists' was their elevation of '*conversion* and *exchange*' over production in 'the advance towards perfect prosperity'.³² Carey maintained that whereas 'exchangers' simply 'converted' wealth, producers added permanently to 'the amount of things to be exchanged' creating a permanent capacity to consume the products of other productive classes: 'Consumption and production go hand in hand, and when there is a glut of anything it is the result of error in the system that requires to be corrected.'³³ In the British context Carey was convinced that agriculture ought to constitute the bulk of the home market; a mechanism for securing both the 'harmony of interests' and balanced economic development. Axiomatic in Carey's protectionism was a rejection of the agrarian theories of Malthus and Ricardo.³⁴ Indeed, Carey had engaged at length with both theorists in a prior work which had elevated historical experience of cultivation, settlement, and population growth over theory.³⁵ It is surely suggestive that Carey chose in this 'lesson of the past to the present' to single out the *Blackwood's* contributor Thomas De Quincey as an important critic of Ricardian theory.³⁶

If British protectionists insisted on the primacy of the home market they also argued that the destruction of domestic consumption had not been vindicated by a commensurate increase in foreign trade. Consistently, protectionists emphasised two points: the decline of British manufactured exports to corn-producing nations, and the absence of reciprocal tariff liberalisations by foreign nations. In 1847 Croker reiterated the *Quarterly*'s established interpretation of the official trade figures: 'for a series of years, our commerce with the four great corn-growing countries of the Continent had exhibited so extraordinary a phenomenon, as that, the more of their produce we imported, the less of our manufactures they took in return'.³⁷ Similarly, *Blackwood's* insisted that there was no positive correlation between corn imports and

---

31 W. E. Aytoun, 'British labour and foreign reciprocity', BEM lxix (Jan. 1851), 112–30 at p. 117; H. C. Carey, *The harmony of interests, agricultural, manufacturing and commercial*, 2nd edn, Philadelphia 1851. Carey cited Aytoun's fulsome praise on the title page of this edition.
32 Carey, *Harmony of interests*, 46; Aytoun, 'British labour and foreign reciprocity', 121–2.
33 Carey, *Harmony of interests*, 48; W. E. Aytoun, 'To the shopkeepers of Great Britain', BEM lxx (Dec. 1851), 629–48 at p. 640.
34 Carey, *Harmony of interests*, 63–4.
35 Idem, *The past, the present, and the future*, London 1848, 17–76, 77–93.
36 Ibid. 20–1. Carey referred to T. De Quincey, *The logic of political economy*, London 1844.
37 J. W. Croker, 'Parliamentary prospects', QR lxxxi (Sept. 1847), 541–78 at p. 558. This comment referred back to his article of 1846, 'Close of Sir Robert Peel's administration', 541. For identical points see Anon., *The case of the farmer and labourer stated, in a letter to Benjamin D'Israeli, Esq., MP.*, London 1851, 33, and Young, *Free-trade fallacies refuted*, 22 (letter iv).

exports of manufactured goods. In the context of 1847–52 this argument responded to the claim that it was the revolutions of 1848 and not free trade which caused the disruption of foreign markets: 'The evil of which we complain is chronic, and has not been caused by any sudden or violent convulsions.'[38] Aytoun went on to demonstrate this structural change in a heavily empirical analysis of the regional distribution of Britain's foreign trade which showed that British exports of cotton manufactures to grain-exporting nations had fallen or remained stationary.[39] The second central theme, that Britain's unilateral initiative had not generated an international 'reciprocity' was perhaps best exemplified by Disraeli in parliament. In a speech of March 1848 Disraeli insisted that the commercial policy of 1846 had violated Pitt's and Huskisson's shared legacy of 'regulated competition and reciprocal intercourse'. In this view unilateralism misunderstood the reality of international relations and dispensed with the fabric of international commerce – bilateral trade agreements.[40] Protectionist texts echoed Disraeli's despair at the absence of 'reciprocity' and pointed to American protectionism as overwhelming evidence of the visionary character of Cobdenism.[41] The difficulty here lay perhaps in distinguishing the protectionist position on 'reciprocity' from the similar arguments of Cobden's free-trade critics.[42]

Protectionists carved out a more distinctive intellectual niche by exploring the impact of the commercial reforms on Britain's balance of trade. Following Lord George Bentinck, the MP Charles Newdigate Newdegate maintained that Britain's official trade figures were dominated by a language of statistics which misrepresented the real economic impact of free trade.[43] In

---

[38] W. E. Aytoun, 'Conservative union', *BEM* lxiv (Nov. 1848), 632–40 at p. 634. See also his 'The opening of the session', 374–6, and Alison, 'Thirty years of Liberal legislation', 10, and 'The currency extension act of nature', *BEM* lxix (Jan. 1851), 1–19 at p. 16.

[39] W. R. Callender and W. E. Aytoun, 'Free trade and our cotton manufactures', ibid. lxviii (Aug. 1850), 123–40 at pp. 126–9.

[40] Disraeli, House of Commons (6 Mar. 1848), *Hansard* 3rd ser. xcvii. 417, 420–2. This speech responded to a free-trade pamphlet: Anon., *The commercial policy of Pitt and Peel, 1783–1846*, London 1847. Croker offered a fiercely critical review of the latter in 'Peel policy', 276–82. Reciprocity remained a central theme for Disraeli: House of Commons (8 Mar. 1849), *Hansard* 3rd ser. ciii. 425; (2 July 1848), ibid. 1155.

[41] Aytoun cited Disraeli's speech on reciprocity in 'The opening of the session', 377. See also J. L. Elliot, *A letter to the electors of Westminster from a Conservative*, London 1847, 23. On American protectionism see Aytoun, 'British agriculture and foreign competition', 248, and 'Free trade and our cotton manufactures', 131. See also [NAPIC], *Tracts on protection: no. 10: home trade – colonial trade – foreign trade: the respective advantages of each examined: part II*, London 1850, 15–6.

[42] See, for instance, W. Ward, *Remarks on the commercial legislation of 1846; addressed to the Lord Mayor and the livery of London*, London 1847, 54–5. On Cobden's free-trade critics see Howe, *Free trade and Liberal England*, 17–18, 70–92.

[43] Lord George Bentinck, House of Commons (23 May 1848), *Hansard* 3rd ser. xcviii. 1265–80, esp. p. 1266; C. N. Newdegate, House of Commons (22 Aug. 1848), ibid. ci. 398–400. Newdegate acknowledged his debt to Bentinck in his *Letter to the right hon. H. Labouchere, M. P. & c. & c; on the balance of trade, ascertained from the value of all articles imported during the last four years*, London 1849, 1.

a series of influential published letters to Presidents of the Board of Trade, Newdegate isolated a number of key features of 'free-trade statistics'.[44] The central problem in Newdegate's view was that official scales for assessing the value of imports and exports were antiquated. Many valuable imported items were absent from official tables, there was no way of checking the declared value of exports and there was insufficient information on the 'real' or 'market' value of imports.[45] Yet, 'the most remarkable omission from our official documents' was, for Newdegate, 'the absence of any account of the precious metals imported or exported'.[46] The combined tendency of these omissions, he maintained, was to over-estimate exports, to under-estimate imports and to obscure the reality of successively large deficits in Britain's balance of trade: 'The Returns may be accurate according to the scale by which they are made up, but they are eminently calculated to deceive the public and most members of the Legislature.'[47] Consequently Newdegate presented the public with an alternative language of statistics in 'returns' which he painstakingly compiled and revised.[48]

Fundamentally, Newdegate's protectionist empiricism was designed to expose the combined effects of British commercial and monetary legislation on the British economy: 'The result has been, that we have sacrificed what Adam Smith calls the Balance of Produce and Consumption.'[49] Of course, in pursuing his didactic purpose Newdegate was highly selective in his use of Adam Smith. Indeed Newdegate noted that Smith had rejected the 'mercantilist' concept of the balance of trade. Newdegate maintained that precisely because he dismissed the concept of the balance of trade Smith had missed the crucial connections between commercial and monetary policy; based on Smithian assumptions, British official figures replicated this omission.[50] It was therefore to another contemporary economic thinker that Newdegate appealed in order to legitimate his own views on the balance of trade. The writer he turned to was G. F. List, 'the founder of the Zollverein, the guide and teacher of a large and by no means the least intelligent section of Europe'.[51] What Newdegate found in List's work was a mirror to his own understanding of how monetary and commercial legislation combined to in-

---

[44] On the influence of Newdegate's letters see Young, 'Free trade', 162; Alison, 'The crowning of the column', 123–4; Croker, 'Parliamentary prospects', 550–1.
[45] Newdegate, *Letter*, 9–10.
[46] Ibid. 9.
[47] Ibid. 8.
[48] Idem, *A second letter to the right hon. H. Labouchere*, 2nd edn, London 1849; *A third letter to the right hon. H. Labouchere*, London 1851; *A fourth letter to the right hon. H. Labouchere*, London 1851; *A letter to the right hon. J. W. Henley, M P. & c. & c., on the balance of trade, ascertained from the market value of all articles imported, as compared with the market value of all articles exported, during the year 1851*, London 1852.
[49] Idem, *A letter*, 14.
[50] Ibid. 4.
[51] Ibid. 15. On List's influence in America and in the German states see W. O. Henderson,

fluence a nation's balance of trade.[52] This was less an appeal to an external intellectual authority than an attempt to integrate the political economy of List into an established tradition of British protectionist thought.

List's political economy rejected 'cosmopolitical' economics and was dominated by an idea of the nation. Viewed in this context, what was striking about the British response to Cobden's cosmopolitanism was its imperial character. Just as protectionists challenged Cobden's expectations of unilateral free trade with countless examples of the absence of 'reciprocity', so they engaged with Cobden at the abstract level. The larger question at stake was, as Disraeli recognised, 'the great contention between the patriotic and the cosmopolitan principle which has hardly begun'.[53] Offering a critique of 'chimerical *cosmopolitanism*, which does not comprehend nationality, and which has no regard for national interests' List provided a fitting point of reference.[54] In the British context, of course, 'comprehending nationality' meant integrating the empire into the idea and practice of political economy.[55] Thus both Croker and Disraeli challenged the 'cosmopolitanism' of the free-trade pamphlet *The commercial policy of Pitt and Peel* in imperial terms.[56] Both responses undermined Cobdenite teleology with an alternative protectionist historicism. Here, Peel had severed the continuous history of British commercial policy when he abandoned imperial preference and 'reciprocity'.[57] Thus Croker and Disraeli located the empire at the heart of a protectionist idea of Britain's economic nationality. This imperial concept was more concretely expressed in arguments for the superiority of colonial over foreign markets. In a series of tracts on the value of colonial trade the National Association maintained that free trade was permanently damaging colonial markets for British manufactures.[58] Of course protectionists could not and did not argue that on aggregate colonial trade was more valuable than foreign trade. However, they did demonstrate that items for colonial

---

Friedrich List: economist and visionary, 1789–1846, London 1983, esp. pp. 68–89, 90–123, 143–202, and K. Tribe, *Strategies of economic order: German economic discourse*, Cambridge 1995, 32–65.

[52] The work referred to in Newdegate's, *A letter*, 15–16, and *A second letter*, p. iv, was possibly G. F. List, *Das nationale system der politischen oekonomie*, 2nd edn, Stuttgart 1844. Using counterfactual analysis D. McCloskey concluded that 'free trade caused the British terms of trade to deteriorate, reducing national income': 'Magnanimous Albion', 318.

[53] Disraeli, *Lord George Bentinck*, 583.

[54] G. F. List, *National system of political economy*, ed. S. Colwell, trans. G. A. Matile, Philadelphia 1856, 262.

[55] See, for instance, Newdegate's insistence on the imperial scope of the British economy in his *A third letter*, esp. pp. xvii–xx.

[56] Anon., *The commercial policy of Pitt and Peel*, reviewed by Croker in 'Peel policy', 274–316, and criticised by Disraeli in the House of Commons (Mar. 6 1848), *Hansard* 3rd ser. xcvii. 416–21.

[57] Ibid. 416, and Croker, 'Peel policy', esp. pp. 277–82.

[58] [NAPIC], *Tracts on protection: nos 9–11: home trade – colonial trade – foreign trade*, parts I–III, London 1850.

export were of higher value than the crude manufactures which comprised the bulk of foreign trade. And Adam Smith's point, that in colonial trade all reciprocals were British, was again thrown back at free traders.[59] Beyond these customary arguments, the National Association attempted to show that the consumption of British manufactures in the colonies (when analysed per head of population and in terms of the proportion made up by enumerated articles in total colonial exports) was worth more than foreign trade.[60] What this new empiricism underlined was the traditional importance of Britain's colonial empire in the protectionist search for stable economic advance based on the balance of production and consumption. It was in this intellectual context that Bentinck and John Byles advocated the abolition of all duties on the importation of colonial produce into metropolitan Britain and recommended the construction of 'one Great British Zollverein'.[61] Thus, during 1847–52 protectionists once again turned to the empire to provide the permanent markets which 'cosmopolitan' free trade had seemingly failed to secure: empire was a fundamental element in the protectionist approach to preserving Britain's economic nationality.

The abstract term 'empire' represented a complex mesh of political relationships which protectionists considered fundamental to the political economy of Britain. By the same token, the commercial instruments of navigation legislation and imperial preference were presented as pillars which supported the political edifice of the empire. Many protectionists interpreted the repeal of the navigation laws in 1849 not only as a fatal blow to British shipping interests but also as the destruction of the fabric of Britain's maritime and commercial supremacy.[62] Whereas free traders hailed the repeal of the navigation laws as the 'crowning of the column of free trade' Alison claimed that it represented 'the *crushing of the pedestal*' of the British empire.[63] Similarly, Croker condemned this repeal as the abandonment of that 'grand system of mutual insurance' which had bound the colonies to the mother country and underwrote Britain's 'national independence'.[64] Strikingly, pro-

---

[59] Ibid. *no. 10*, 5–8, 3; *no. 11*, 7. J. Byles invoked Smith on the reciprocals of colonial trade in *Sophisms of free trade, and political economy examined*, 2nd edn, London 1850, 10–15.
[60] [NAPIC], *Tracts on protection: no. 10*, 2; *no. 11*, 6.
[61] Byles used this term in *Sophisms*, 84. See also Disraeli's account of Bentinck's belief that 'our colonial empire ought to be reconstructed by a total abolition of all duties on Her Majesty's dominions abroad': *Lord George Bentinck*, 579.
[62] For surveys of the decline of British tonnage under the reciprocity system see T. Ogilvy, *Statistical evidence affecting the question of the navigation laws*, Edinburgh–London 1849; Young, *Free trade fallacies refuted*, 31–2; H. T. Liddell, House of Commons (9 Feb. 1847), *Hansard* 3rd ser. lxxxix, 1021–30.
[63] Alison, 'The crowning of the column', 108. See also his 'The navigation laws', BEM lxiv (July 1848), 114–18.
[64] J. W. Croker, 'Political prospects of Britain and France', QR lxxxiii (June 1848), 250–304 at p. 294. Croker praised Young's arguments in the press and Bentinck's in parliament; Bentinck, House of Commons (2 July 1847), *Hansard* 3rd ser. xciii. 1136–39, and (15 May 1848), ibid. xcviii. 1031–40.

tectionists also presented the diminution of imperial preference as the undermining of the political fabric of the empire. This general point frequently appeared in protectionist condemnations of specific instances of free-trade policy. Corn law repeal continued to be represented as a fatal rupture of the imperial bond between Britain and the Canadian provinces.[65] Similarly the abandonment of the sugar preference resounded as the death knell of the West Indian empire in protectionist discourse.[66]

Yet the identification of the tariff as an essentially political instrument also featured large in more general critiques of free-trade political economy. Alison argued that 'the abandonment of the principle of protection to native industry' of both the mother country and the colonies was tantamount to the erosion of 'the cement which alone has hitherto held together the vast and multifarious parts of the British empire'.[67] For Alison, imperial preference and protection constituted the 'sole bond' binding the colonies to the metropole following what he understood to be the annihilation of the virtual representation of colonial interests by the borough disfranchisement schedules of the Great Reform Act of 1832: 'Schedules A and B at one blow disfranchised the whole colonial empire of Great Britain, because it closed the avenue by which colonial wealth had hitherto found an entrance to the House of Commons.'[68] Clearly Alison viewed the tariff as a representative mechanism which could be substituted for virtual or direct representation and which could express electorally unrepresented interests in commercial policy. By the same token Croker viewed the abandonment of imperial preference as the relinquishment of a political instrument of imperial integrity: 'as to the Colonies, ... the two new principles adopted – the giving them governments responsible to local legislatures, and the releasing them from all reciprocation of commercial favour with the mother country – are neither more nor less than *discolonization*'.[69] Thus protectionists continued to respond to Cobden's 'cosmopolitanism' with an imperial political economy. Whereas Cobden looked to the pacifying influence of mutual trade between nations his critics held fast to an imperial and 'patriotic' idea of international relations: protection and preference constituted 'a great principle, the only principle on which a large and expansive system of commerce can be founded'.[70]

---

[65] Croker, 'Parliamentary prospects', 571; A. Williams, *Curious lights on strange anomalies; a letter to Lord George Bentinck*, London 1847; Anon., *Remarks on the consequences of the entire change of our colonial policy in British North America*, Edinburgh–London 1847; Young, 'Free trade', 179, and *Fallacies of free trade*, 33.
[66] Ibid. 32–3; Anon., 'Cheap sugar and the slave trade', QR lxxxviii (Dec. 1850), 129–36 at p. 130–1; M. J. Higgins, *Is cheap sugar the triumph of free trade?: a letter to Lord John Russell*, London 1847, 3–4.
[67] Alison, 'The dinner to Lord Stanley', 636.
[68] Idem, 'How to disarm the Chartists', BEM lxiii (June 1848), 653–73 at p. 672, and 'The crowning of the column', 113, 111–12. On the disfranchisement schedules see Brock, *The Great Reform Act*, 137–8, 148, 161, 183–4, 262, 264–5.
[69] Croker, 'Parliamentary prospects', 571.
[70] Disraeli cited by Aytoun in 'The opening of the session', 377.

Thus 1846 was no terminus for protectionist economics in Britain. The experience of financial and commercial crisis in 1847, agricultural depression in 1849–52 and the sluggish performance of manufactures in 1848 provided new contexts within which established arguments could be reworked. Free trade was represented as a sectional strategy which benefited manufacturing exporters at the expense of agriculturists, small exporters and non-exporting manufacturers. Thus in the immediate aftermath of corn-law repeal, free trade stood indicted of political injustice and economic myopia. Reciprocal international free trade had failed to materialise and the importance of a colonial empire in sustaining secure economic advance was restated in a nationalist and imperial protectionist alternative. Protectionist empiricism showed that in place of Cobden's promises British commercial and monetary policy was generating successively large deficits in the balance of trade. Protection was, on the contrary, presented as a philosophy which not only secured the 'harmony of interests' but laid foundations for the stable, diverse and balanced advance of an imperial economy:

> Reciprocity, like charity, begins at home. Unless the agricultural and the manufacturing bodies reciprocate – cordially, kindly, and without jealousy – it is impossible for either body to thrive. Free Trade at present stands entirely in the way of such reciprocity.[71]

The boundaries of political economy: protectionist social argument, 1847–52

'There can scarcely be a higher science than Political Economy; it is one for philosophers to investigate and for statesmen to learn. But the mere science of wealth is the science of brokers and usurers. It is Political Economy narrowed to the dimensions of one of its really inferior subjects: a great, miserable, mistake': [NAPIC], *Tracts on protection: introductory tract*, London 1850, 7.

The National Association's condemnation of orthodox political economy as a 'mere science of wealth' should be located in an extensive protectionist discourse on the distribution of wealth, the social condition of Britain and the social responsibilities of the state. These themes had, of course, defined the protectionist response to freer trade throughout the first half of the nineteenth century in Britain. During 1847–52, however, the 'social question' was refocused as a central element in the campaign to present protection as a national not a sectional strategy. The Anti-Corn-Law League's powerful cry of 'cheap bread' had masked a deeper assumption that free trade was in general beneficial to the labouring classes. After 1846 protectionists sharp-

---

[71] W. R. Callender and W. E. Aytoun, 'Free trade and our cotton manufactures', *BEM* lxviii (Aug. 1850), 123–40 at pp. 137–8.

ened their challenge to this assumption at a number of levels. Protectionist texts presented social deterioration as an empirically demonstrable consequence of free trade and moved the issues of employment and British relative living standards to the centre of the public debate. By explaining social suffering and political protest as direct consequences of commercial and monetary policy protectionists attempted to shift the intellectual boundaries of political economy and public policy onto the territory of distribution and social cohesion. As Aytoun put it, 'Our firm belief is, that what are termed social grievances are simply the consequence of a faulty or erroneous commercial and national system.'[72]

Protectionists challenged the presumption that free trade and social progress automatically went hand in hand. In parliament, periodicals and tracts, social statistics were presented as evidence of the deterioration of Britain's social condition under free trade. During 1848, 1849 and 1852 Bentinck, Disraeli and Newdegate attributed the rise in pauperism in both manufacturing and agricultural districts directly to free trade.[73] In similar fashion Young and Alison identified poverty and poor relief as central features of the response to free trade in the Conservative periodicals.[74] Other social indices such as rates of crime and emigration and the volume of deposits in savings banks were offered as further evidence of social deterioration under free trade.[75] In a striking anti-Malthusian interpretation of the census of 1851 Alison read the structural decline in the rate of population growth (beside increases in rates of crime, poverty and emigration) as evidence of national decline. What for Alison were statistics of social decay were directly attributable to commercial and monetary policy: 'They have accomplished what no British statesman since the days of Alfred has been able to effect. They have *stopped the growth of our population, and for the first time during five centuries rendered it retrograde.*'[76] Of course protectionists did not and could not prove their argument that social deterioration was directly attributable to free trade. Rather social indices forged a protectionist language of statistics which can only be understood as part of a broader discourse on how free trade was thought to influence social conditions in mid nineteenth-century Britain.

In 1850 the National Association insisted that 'the struggle we are maintaining is chiefly and essentially for the rights and interests of labour: – that Protection is the poor man's question . . . that Free-Trade is a gigantic fraud,

---

[72] Aytoun, 'British labour and foreign reciprocity', 113.
[73] Bentinck, House of Commons (6 Mar. 1848), *Hansard* 3rd ser. xcvii. 299–300; Disraeli, House of Commons (2 July 1849), ibid. civ. 1144–6; Newdegate, House of Commons (15 Mar. 1852), ibid. cxix. 1119–20. D. T. Coulton praised Newdegate's presentation of protectionists as the guardians of the poor in 'California versus free trade', *QR* xc (Mar. 1852), 492–502 at p. 502.
[74] Young, 'Free trade', 156–7; A. Alison, 'Free trade at its zenith', *BEM* lxvi (Dec. 1849), 756–78 at p. 772.
[75] Ibid.; Croker, 'Parliamentary prospects,' 544–5.
[76] A. Alison, 'The census and free trade', *BEM* lxx (Aug. 1851), 123–41 at p. 141.

of which *they* are destined ultimately to be the victims'.[77] In attempting to cast protection as a 'poor man's question' the National Association faced the formidable obstacle of the 'cheap loaf'. The presentation of cheapness as a scourge not a blessing relied on three central themes: the impact of free trade on employment, on the relative living standards of British labourers and on the 'value of labour'. In his open letter to the labouring classes of 1850 Lord Stanhope stated the protectionist position starkly: 'Protection is that policy which secures the employment of British labourers instead of foreigners, and encourages British industry in preference to that of other countries.'[78] Similarly, the National Association's declaration of December 1851 stated that free trade had 'a direct and inevitable tendency to diminish the demand for British labour'.[79] Yet protectionists also understood that the 'scourge of cheapness' affected the labour market in more complex ways than by simply diminishing the aggregate demand for labour. As the address of the Metropolitan Trades Delegates to the National Association's general meeting of May 1850 had maintained, 'The labour of the working man thus becomes a superfluous commodity in the market, so that he must either be an outcast altogether from society, or else find some way of doing more work for less materials of consumption.'[80] Thus it was argued that foreign competition was driving employers to exact more labour for less wages or to employ the cheaper labour of women, children and machines.[81] The diminution of the exchangeable value of British labour was perceived, then, to be a necessary consequence of the 'competitive system' and a counterbalance to the assumed benefits of the 'cheap loaf'.[82]

To protectionists the ultimate logic of the 'system of cheapness' was to drive British living standards down to those of foreign competing nations. Thus protectionism became not only a defence of British living standards *per se* but also a means of preserving what was perceived to be Britain's superior social 'scale of civilisation'. Implicit in this well-established protectionist stance was the assumption that the social and economic condition of individual nations was distinctively defined by history and social custom. As Alison observed, 'The Protectionists reasoned after an entirely different manner. The doctrines of free-trade, they observed, perfectly just in their application to different provinces of the same empire, are entirely misplaced if extended

---

77 [G. F. Young], *Address of the general committee*, 2.
78 Lord Stanhope, *Letter to the labouring classes of Great Britain and Ireland, October 7th, 1850*, London 1850, 3.
79 [NAPIC], *Declaration read, approved and unanimously adopted at a meeting of the members and friends of the National Association for the Protection of Industry and Capital throughout the British Empire, 12th Dec. 1851*, London 1851. This declaration was sent out to local protection societies for signatures.
80 Address of the Metropolitan Trades Delegate, cited in Aytoun, 'The great protection meeting', 750.
81 [NAPIC], *Tracts on protection: no. 5: the blessings of cheapness*, London 1850, 7–15.
82 Ibid. 4.

to different *countries* of the world.'[83] During 1847–52 these customary arguments were refocused. Thus Alison went on to maintain that the contemporary competitiveness of foreign nations such as Poland and Russia was the result of precise social conditions: 'It is the comparative poverty, the *scarcity of money* . . . which is the cause of the difference. . . . We shall be able to raise grain as cheap as the serfs of Poland, or the peasants of the Ukraine, when we are as poor as they are, but *not till then.*'[84] In the same vein the National Association presented comparative lists of wage rates in a number of European countries and concluded that 'a free competition with all the nations of Europe must include a lowering of wages to the standard of those nations'.[85] The condition of Ireland was frequently held up as evidence that free trade hastened social decline. As John Byles noted, 'Without temporary protection, Irish industry is undersold, smothered, rendered impossible. Universal, hereditary, and national idleness, poverty and discontent, are the necessary consequences.'[86] The assumption that free trade would ultimately annihilate the distinctive and superior social condition of the rest of the UK was widely shared. J. S. Barty presented protection as a legislative shield which had preserved the condition of civilised labour: 'It defended them against competition with the serf labour of Continental countries; and it kept them from the physical, intellectual and moral degradation in which the toil-worn sons of labour in many other lands are so deeply sunk.'[87] In parliament protectionists mounted critiques of free trade which assumed that Britain's 'scale of civilisation' was superior and could be guarded by protection. Indeed Grantley Berkeley defied 'any man to justify a system which places serf and slave labour on the same footing as English labour'.[88] In this way Protectionists met the free-trade cry of 'cheap bread' with an overtly nationalistic discourse on relative standards of living.

It followed that protectionists interpreted working-class political protest as a direct consequence of a political economy which reduced the exchangeable value of labour. As the National Association commented on the revolutions of 1848, 'The danger of Europe has a social source altogether; and lies,

---

[83] Alison, 'Lessons from the famine', 515.

[84] Idem, 'The crowning of the column', 120. See also his 'Free trade finance', *BEM* lxvii (May 1850), 513–25 at p. 520.

[85] Figures for wages in Dantzig, Holstein, Freisland, Istria, Lombardy and Tuscany were drawn from Porter's official tables: [NAPIC], *Tracts on protection: no. 8: is free trade fair trade?: part II*, London 1850, 7.

[86] Byles, *Sophisms of free trade*, no. xvii, 'Free trade is good for Ireland', 160–70 at p. 170. See also Carey, *Harmony of interests*, 60, cited in Aytoun, 'British labour and foreign reciprocity', 125–6.

[87] J. S. Barty, 'The experiment', *BEM* lxx (Oct. 1851), 488–504 at p. 498. This essay responded to the 'social protectionism' of E. Bulwer Lytton: *Letters to John Bull, Esq., on affairs connected with his landed property, and the persons who live thereon*, London 1851. See also Aytoun, 'Autumn politics', 628, and Anon. [W. W. N.], 'Justice to John Bull', 17.

[88] G. Berkeley, House of Commons (14 May 1850), *Hansard* 3rd ser. cxi. 31. See also Disraeli (2 July 1849), ibid. 1156.

not in the dearness of provisions, but in the unprofitableness of labour. Our Poor-Law has probably saved us hitherto. But the sources of mischief are not removed.'[89] Thus protectionist tracts disputed Peel's claim that the budget of 1842 had begun a process of elevating working-class living standards. Instead they read the fiscal settlement of 1842 as the inauguration of a pernicious political economy of cheapness, 'And the epoch of their poverty is, by an almost universal consent, the year 1842, – the year of Sir Robert Peel's reformation of the tariff.'[90] In this view Chartism was a creature of the distributive realities of free trade: 'Free trade has been the great incentive to Chartism.'[91] For Aytoun the prominence of labourers from the struggling small exporting and domestic trades in the ranks of the Chartists demonstrated that political protest was the direct consequence of a commercial policy which benefited the large exporting trades at their expense.[92] Alison's determinist reading of the origins of Chartism also focused on the distributive consequences of free trade. The universality of depression in 1847–8 was attributable in Alison's view to unemployment caused by foreign competition.[93] This foreign competition was the predictable and direct consequence of legislation passed by a parliament where the voice of retrenchers, consumers and 'the moneyed classes' had dominated since 1832.[94] For Alison social distress was the logical consequence of 'class legislation' which ignored domestic producers and assumed that the market could solve the social problem of distribution. In this view the specifically political response of the Chartists – 'that the legislature and the government are alike indifferent to their representations'[95] – merely acknowledged the problem of 'class legislation' and misgovernment. For it was only through protectionist commercial legislation and monetary reform that employment and the exchangeable value of labour could be restored, that 'democracy' could be defused and the propertied constitution legitimated:

> What is required is not to augment the political power of the working classes, but to remove their grievances; – not to give them the government of the state, which they can exercise only to their own and the nation's ruin, but to place them in such a condition that they may no longer desire to govern it. This can only be done by abandoning the system of class government . . . and returning to the old system of general protective and national administration.[96]

---

[89] [NAPIC], *Tracts on protection: no. 6: the blessings of cheapness no. 2*, London 1850, 8.
[90] [NAPIC], *Tracts on protection: no. 5: the blessings of cheapness no. 1*, London 1850, 16.
[91] Aytoun, 'A review of the last session', 272.
[92] Ibid. 269–71, and 'The opening of the session', 378–80.
[93] Alison, 'How to disarm the Chartists', 655–8.
[94] Ibid. esp. pp. 660, 663–4.
[95] Ibid. 658.
[96] Ibid. 665–6.

Protectionist interpretations of the social consequences of free trade therefore shifted the state to the centre of a debate on the social crisis of distribution. This intellectual response to *laissez-faire* attempted to push out the boundaries of British political economy beyond the limitations of a mere 'science of wealth'. Protectionists attacked two central assumptions: that the problem of distribution lay beyond the province of the mid nineteenth-century state, and that free trade was a natural and inherently Christian system. Responding to the removal of the sugar preference, *Blackwood's* challenged the general claim of free traders to the moral high ground:

> When we find people, in a tone of profound piety putting forth the purely commercial principle of buying in the cheapest and selling in the dearest market, as an inviolable law of the Great Parent of the Universe . . . then, I say, that this servile liberality, this Evangelical cupidity, this Christianity of the 'Change, is beyond all expression detestable, and more worthy of the shafts of Voltaire's satire than the Christianity of the Inquisition.[97]

Having exposed the specious religiosity of free trade, the writer proceeded to identify appropriate territory for a genuinely Christian state. He urged the British state to embrace definite distributive functions for legislation which 'will require an interference with the market of labour, and with the lordly privileges of capital'.[98] Similarly, in his influential *Sophisms of political economy*, John Byles threw down the gauntlet of distribution as a fundamental criticism of orthodox political economy:

> The need of a political economy, very different from the inert and barren system now in fashion, is but too apparent to any one. . . . Modern society presents to the serious observer, as the consequences of past and present systems of political economy, practical results by no means flattering. The immense progress of physical science has multiplied a thousand-fold the means of producing wealth. . . . Yet some mysterious and invisible, but impassable barrier, for the present impedes its distribution, and shuts out the masses from the promised land.[99]

Byles's position, of course, contributed to a long-established protectionist consensus on the contracted boundaries of Ricardian political economy. Interestingly, both *Blackwood's* and *Fraser's* welcomed the social and moral breadth of J. S. Mill's *Principles of political economy*. Neither journal endorsed his specific policy prescriptions but both welcomed Mill's recognition of the

---

[97] Anon., 'Reflections suggested by the career of the late premier', BEM lxi (Jan. 1847), 93–128 at pp. 111–12.
[98] Ibid. 128.
[99] Byles, *Sophisms*, 5. The first edition of this work was 'reviewed' by Young in 'Free trade', 148–83. The eighth edition was printed (without attribution to Byles) by the Manchester Reciprocity Association c. 1870. The ninth edition was reprinted in 1904 with notes by the Edwardian tariff reformers W. S. Lilly and C. S. Devas.

problem of distribution: 'The functions of government become the subject of economical science through the influence which they exercise upon the production, distribution, and interchange of the wealth of a community.'[100] Mill's extension of the boundaries of orthodox political economy perhaps impeded the ability of protectionists to appropriate the moral high ground on distribution and on the social responsibilities of government.

Notwithstanding the problem of Mill, protection was consistently presented as a distributive strategy which could secure social cohesion and political stability beside stable prosperity. By guarding the markets of domestic producers protection preserved employment dependencies and placed the emphasis of legislation on achieving a high exchangeable value for British labour. As Disraeli noted in 1849, 'In every way the application of the principle of reciprocity would produce its intended effect, the enhancement of the value and efficiency of British labour.'[101] For Byles greater distributive justice made economic sense since 'Every increase in the rate of wages enormously increases the power of the BULK OF THE NATION to consume, and *pay for what they consume*. It creates a new and enormous demand. It creates a new and immense home market.'[102] A similar assumption motivated Aytoun's injection of Henry Carey's *Harmony of interests* into British protectionist discourse. For Carey's treatise fused social harmony with secure economic advance in direct response to the socially destructive tendencies of 'the whole English politico-economical system':[103] 'The object of protection is to produce dear labour, that is, high-priced and valuable labour, and its effect is to cause it to increase in value from day to day, and to increase the equivalents to be exchanged, to the great increase of commerce.'[104]

Yet protection remained one among a number of possible legislative responses to the problem of distribution. As the National Association claimed, 'THE GREAT OBJECT OF MODERN LEGISLATION SHOULD BE TO MAKE LABOUR DEAR, NOT TO MAKE PRODUCTIONS CHEAP.'[105] Thus, in his essay on Chartism, Alison couched his proposal to return to protection beside a number of distributive options for a responsive state. These included schemes for work creation by government, grants for railway construction and state-assisted emigration to the colonies, 'to provide on a great scale, and by government machinery, for the relief of the *labour market*'.[106] Others proposed extensive state involvement in the social and

---

[100] Anon., 'Mill's political economy', FM xxxviii (Sept. 1848), 245–60 at p. 259. See also W. H. Smith, 'Political economy by J. S. Mill', BEM lxiv (Oct. 1848), 407–28 at pp. 410–14; J. S. Mill, *Principles of political economy, with some of their applications to social philosophy*, London 1848, ed. W. J. Ashley, London 1909.
[101] Disraeli, House of Commons (6 July 1849), Hansard 3rd ser. ciii. 1496.
[102] Byles, *Sophisms*, 224.
[103] Aytoun, 'British labour and foreign reciprocity', 130; Carey, *Harmony of interests*, 64.
[104] Ibid. 72. See also [NAPIC], *Tracts on protection: no. 6: the blessings of cheapness no. 2*, 7.
[105] Ibid. 7 (NAPIC's emphasis).
[106] Alison, 'How to disarm the Chartists', 668, 667–70.

economic regeneration of Ireland which would also consolidate the Union. Through focused investment and the resettlement of depopulated areas it was argued that Irish separatism could be appeased while relieving pressure on the English labour market and extending the home market for manufactures.[107] Furthermore, in keeping with their response to Peelite banking legislation, protectionists continued to pose monetary reform as a problem of distribution.

The mask of gold: protection, Conservatism and monetary reform, 1847–52

Notwithstanding the unshakeable parliamentary consensus behind the Bank Charter Act of 1844, criticism of Britain's monetary and banking legislation persisted after 1847. The dimensions of the monetary criticism in protectionist texts and Conservative journals were broadly unchanged. A monetary policy which was inherently deflationary and which exposed the means of trade to periodic contraction was indicted as damaging to the productive classes. This fundamental assumption – that monetary legislation was not neutral – led critics of Peel's system to emphasise the political and constitutional objections to legislation which was, in effect, redistributive and confiscatory. This constitutional language of monetary criticism gained new resonances in the light of both commercial crisis and corn-law repeal. Naturally, the commercial and financial crisis of 1847–8 enabled protectionists to confirm the accuracy of their central prediction, that the combination of 'free trade and a fettered currency' would be catastrophic. Yet protectionists and Conservatives faced two new problems when attempting to establish a distinctive position on monetary reform in contemporary economic discourse. First, the effect of the commercial and monetary crisis of 1847–8 was to strengthen criticism of Peel's monetary system by free traders. Not only did free-trade critics adopt many similar positions on the social and economic consequences of deflation and monetary contraction, some also focused on the political consequences of redistributive legislation in Radical constitutional languages. Second, the inflationary effect of the discovery of gold in California, combined with the recovery of commerce, posed fundamental problems of credibility for the protectionist campaign against 'free trade and a fettered currency'.

The inseparability of monetary reform from protection was explicitly recognised by the National Association's sub-committee on currency in 1850: 'their enquiry has resulted in the strong conviction that any plan of protec-

---

[107] Disraeli, *Lord George Bentinck*, 139; Anon., 'The great and comprehensive measure', *FM* xxxv (Mar. 1847), 370–8 esp. pp. 375–7; Aytoun, 'A review of the last session', 282; W. R. Greg, 'Highland destitution and Irish emigration', *QR* xc (Dec. 1851), 163–205 at pp. 199–201; Alison, 'The crowning of the column', 130–1.

tion which is formed without a due consideration of this important element of the question must prove incomplete'.[108] Thus the slogan 'free trade and a fettered currency' retained its totemic status and it was to its author, Archibald Alison, that the sub-committee referred for intellectual authority.[109] After 1847 Alison reiterated what had become protectionist monetary orthodoxy; not only were bullionism and free trade mutually incompatible, together they institutionalised commercial and financial crises.[110] Free trade in corn made Britain dependent on importations of food from foreign countries which frequently took only gold in exchange. Each time bullion was exchanged for food the strict convertibility conditions of the Bank Charter Act dictated that the domestic currency and credit system was contracted in order to counteract the bullion drain by reversing the state of the exchanges. Thus Alison could present the dramatic effect of the Irish famine on international bullion flows and Britain's balance of trade not as an exceptional circumstance but as an example of the normal behaviour of a system of 'free trade and a fettered currency'.[111] In this view famine merely amplified the combined catastrophic tendencies of monetary and commercial legislation: 'what Free-traders and Sir Robert Peel are chargeable with, is having established a system of currency so fettered and restricted by absurd regulations, that the exportation of sovereigns *led necessarily and inevitably to a contraction of the paper accommodation, and a shock to credit all over the whole country*'.[112]

This protectionist orthodoxy was reinforced by several new perspectives on 'free trade and a fettered currency'. In parliament and in print Newdegate dressed Alison's arguments with rigorous empirical analysis of Britain's balance of trade.[113] Newdegate's alternative 'returns' included bullion as an enumerated item which accounted for a large proportion of Britain's adverse balance of trade during 1848–51.[114] Interpretatively, Newdegate's tables were designed to show that 'the amount of bullion in the Bank is the mere creature of the Balance of Trade' which, given the extent of imports under the new commercial system, was destined to be adverse.[115] Newdegate's empiricism therefore complemented the protectionist monetary orthodoxy established by Alison.[116] Similarly the National Association's sub-committee on cur-

---

[108] [NAPIC], *Report of the sub-committee on currency, to the acting committee of the National Association for the Protection of Industry and Capital throughout the British Empire*, London 1850, 1.
[109] Ibid. 17. The report directed readers (p. 13) to Alison's, *Free trade and a fettered currency*, and his *England in 1815 and 1845*.
[110] Idem, 'Thirty years of Liberal legislation', 26.
[111] Idem, 'Lessons from the famine', 518–22.
[112] Idem, 'Free trade at its zenith', 762. See also J. L. Elliot, *A letter to the electors of Westminster from a protectionist*, 2nd edn, London 1848, 22.
[113] C. N. Newdegate, House of Commons (10 May 1847), *Hansard* 3rd ser. xcii. 609–17; (22 Aug. 1848), ibid. ci. 398–400.
[114] Idem, *Letter to the right hon. H. Labouchere*, appendix.
[115] Ibid. 4.
[116] Newdegate cited Alison's *England in 1815 and 1845* in his *A third letter*, p. v.

rency voiced the orthodox protectionist line on the inevitability of crises of credit under Peel's policy of 'regulating the foreign exchanges'. Yet their report also introduced a new suggestion that the monetary settlement of 1819 had neutered the protective system long before 1846; '*On the one hand they promised protection up to a given sum per quarter for wheat, on the other hand, by an unperceived action on the monetary system, rendered that protection periodically inoperative.*'[117] The sub-committee's purpose in projecting 'free trade and a fettered currency' back onto the period before 1846 was to sharpen the significance of monetary reform in the new context created by repeal: 'In truth, a fall in the value of money would be tantamount to an equivalent Protection; while a rise in the value of money is an aggravation of the effects of "Free Trade", in proportion to its degree.'[118] Like protection, monetary reform was at one level merely a distributive instrument within a broader political economy.

As the National Association's report on the currency question suggested, monetary reform retained its prominence in contemporary debates about distribution. The distributive consequences – economic, social and political – of bullionist monetary policy remained central features of protectionist and Conservative monetary criticism. John Byles exemplified the protectionist position when he argued that monetary deflation – or as he put it 'cheapness' caused by the 'scarcity and inaccessibility of the precious metals' – signified 'a transfer from the industrious to the idle classes'.[119] A highly valued currency and a contracted means of payment were, in Byles's opinion, wholly inappropriate to a nation labouring under a large public debt and heavy taxes.[120] Moreover, the financial and commercial fluctuations caused by the contractions of the domestic circulation (legally required under the Bank Charter Act as a response to external gold drains) amounted to the 'torture of industry'.[121] This torture undermined the capacity of capital to provide secure employment for labour in town or country: 'What the masses want, is, *the means of purchase*. If the means of purchase be wholly absent, it is a matter of supreme indifference to them, whether things be dear or cheap.'[122] Of course protectionists did maintain that tight credit had particularly harmed farmers

---

117 [NAPIC], *Report of the sub-committee on currency*, 8 (NAPIC's emphasis). On this point the sub-committee referred readers to the 'speeches, evidences, and writings of Mr Matthias Attwood, Lord Ashburton, Mr John Taylor, and Mr James Taylor, of *"The Scotch Banker"* and the *"Circular to Bankers"* '.
118 Ibid. 10.
119 Byles, *Sophisms*, 113–14.
120 Ibid. 115. See also Anon. ['Agricola'], *An oppressed poor in an insolvent nation: a letter to the members of the new parliament*, London 1847, 4–9.
121 Byles, *Sophisms*, 150–1. Byles invoked David Hume's argument that periods of inflation tended to envigorate industry (p. 114).
122 Ibid. 113. See also J. Harvey, *Remunerative price the desideratum, not cheapness*, London 1851, esp. p. 9. Aytoun claimed Harvey as a convert to protectionism in 'To the shopkeepers of Great Britain', 644.

suffering the simultaneous impact of foreign competition.[123] Yet the monetary question provided opportunities to underline the mutual advantages to be derived for the industrious classes of all sectors from reversing Peel's policy of 'free trade and fettered currency'.[124] A more relaxed monetary standard, attuned to the size of population and to the needs of the domestic market, would release the productive classes from the yoke of deflation and would lay the monetary foundations for the restoration of protection to domestic producers.[125]

It was the direct agency of legislation in the 'transfer from the productive to the idle classes' which made monetary reform a political and constitutional question. Hence Croker focused on the confiscatory profile of the state in his account of the impact of Peel's banking and monetary laws in 1847: 'It is impossible to estimate the change operated in the value of property of every description by thus spending the medium of all internal circulation to meet the foreign balance against us.'[126] The redistributive effects of Britain's monetary laws were, the National Association claimed, creating a political crisis of confidence in the propertied constitution: 'The inquietude and dissatisfaction thus engendered, have exposed the middle and labouring classes to the fallacious doctrines of demagogues.'[127] Thus, in his attempt to explain how the state had adopted this dangerous profile Alison turned, once again, to his interpretation of the Great Reform Act. The makers of the 1832 act had 'shown themselves entirely ignorant of the effect of the great monetary change of 1819' which had 'crippled the means and weakened the influence of the landowners as much as it added to the powers of the moneyed interest'.[128] The redistributive effects of resuming cash payments therefore underpinned the 'over-representation' of creditor interests in the reformed parliament. Alison believed that 'the moneyed interest' was over-represented in the reformed parliament. This preponderance of 'the moneyed or consumer interest' had fatally distorted the balance of interests in the state after 1832 causing 'fiscal iniquity and spoilation'.[129] For Alison therefore, inflationary monetary reform was a way of re-legitimating the propertied constitution by readjusting the balance of interests in the state.

Though this precise reasoning was peculiar to Alison, Disraeli's response to the queen's speech of February 1851 also assumed that the commercial and banking legislation of the 1840s had fundamentally transformed the balance

---

[123] Disraeli, House of Commons (11 Feb. 1851), *Hansard* 3rd ser. cxiv. 406; [NAPIC], *Report of the sub-committee on currency*, 2–3.
[124] Alison, 'The crowning of the column', 122–3.
[125] [NAPIC], *Report of the sub-committee on currency*, 13; Alison, 'How to disarm the Chartists', 666–7.
[126] Croker, 'Parliamentary prospects', 558.
[127] [NAPIC], *Report of the sub-committee on currency*, 15.
[128] Alison, 'The crowning of the column', 114. Alison estimated the scale of deflation (therefore the magnitude of redistribution) at 40%.
[129] Ibid. 115.

of interests in the state: 'in 1844, you passed a law in this House, the whole object of which was to restrict the employment of capital – the whole object of which was to restrict the distribution of capital in those channels which communicate with the cultivators of the soil'.[130] In the light of corn law repeal this inequity appeared even greater: 'In my opinion, you ought to have prepared for this great change – the repeal of the corn laws – by placing the cultivator of the soil ... in a juster relation, not only with your financial, but with your banking and industrial laws.'[131] Thus Disraeli incorporated banking reform in his broad schema for the equitable readjustment of Britain's entire commercial and fiscal system in response to the inequities of the free-trade system. Conservatives therefore continued to debate monetary reform in political languages which questioned the direct involvement of the state in the redistribution of property.

Despite their wide currency, protectionist and Conservative critiques of Peelite monetary orthodoxy faced the problem of maintaining a distinctive position in contemporary economic discourse. Of course Conservatives and protectionists had never exercised a monopoly over critiques of bullionist monetary policy and banking legislation. But what was new during 1847–52 was the organised opposition of the National Anti-Gold-Law League to the Peelite consensus. Jonathan Duncan's speech to the League's meeting of August 1847 shared a number of arguments with Peel's protectionist critics.[132] Duncan argued that the size of the circulation should be regulated by the principles of supply and demand, that a deflationary monetary system redistributed wealth from the productive to the idle classes, and that the domestic means of trade should be insulated from the fluctuations of the foreign exchanges. Yet he firmly distanced the League's monetary argument from that of protectionists insisting 'on the same free trade in the commodity of gold, as I could wish to enforce in respect to every other commodity'.[133] Similarly, in parliament the Conservative David Urquhart questioned the constitutionality of Peel's redistributive monetary legislation.[134] In print Urquhart extended his critique of Peel's banking reforms into a debate about the location of monetary sovereignty in mid nineteenth-century Britain.[135] It could be surmised that the existence of monetary 'co-thinkers' like Duncan who were neither Conservatives nor protectionists ought to have strengthened the purchase of the latter's arguments. As one pamphleteer asked, 'Can

---

[130] Disraeli, House of Commons (11 Feb. 1851), *Hansard* 3rd ser. cxiv. 406.
[131] Ibid. 406–7.
[132] J. Duncan [The National Anti-Gold-Law League], *The principles of the League explained, versus Sir R. Peel's currency measures, and the partial remedy advocated by the Scotch Banks in a speech delivered at the City Hall, Glasgow, 7th August, 1847*, London 1847, esp. pp. 2–3, 5–9, 13–16.
[133] Ibid. 7.
[134] D. Urquhart, House of Commons (2 Dec. 1847), *Hansard* 3rd ser. xcv. 533–4.
[135] Ibid. 532; idem, *The parliamentary usurpations of 1819 and 1844, in respect to money, considered: in a letter to the burgesses and electors of Stafford*, London 1847, 6–10.

it then for a moment be credited by intelligent Englishmen . . . that such astute politicians as Blackwood, Alison, Attwood, Spooner, Muntz and . . . the late Mr. Cobbett, together with thousands of well-educated men . . . of all parties, are so far at sea on the subject?'[136] Yet the failure of an 'anti-Peelite' monetary consensus to emerge can be explained only with reference to wider contexts. From the protectionist perspective, monetary argument was only one element in an integrated political economy which embraced social, political, economic and imperial dimensions. Thus, mere similarity between the monetary ideas of, say, Alison and Muntz masked profound dissension on the central questions of political economy.

Perhaps the greatest impediment to protectionist monetary argument during 1847–52 was geological not intellectual: the discovery of gold in California. Protectionists viewed this addition to the world's stock of gold as an event which diminished the purchase of their arguments whilst shielding Britain from the full effects of free trade. They argued that the flow of gold from California 'had the effect of keeping up the exchanges, which our large purchases of corn would otherwise have turned against us'.[137] Consequently G. F. Young could maintain that 'Free-trade is thus, for the moment, relieved from the exposure of its rottenness, and the people are yet a little longer continued in a delusive belief in its blessings.'[138] Writing in the *Quarterly* D. T. Coulton welcomed monetary inflation and attributed the prosperity of 1852 not to free trade but to Californian gold.[139] He went on to predict that 'the superior abundance of gold will very materially lessen the chance of those commercial panics, which, since the currency settlement of 1819, have been the plague of the industry of this country'.[140] While Alison shared this reading of the immediate inflationary impact of the Californian gold discoveries, or 'the currency extension act of nature', he insisted that they did not remove the incubus of 'free trade and a fettered currency': 'while it tends by its beneficent influence to conceal for a time the pernicious effects of other measures, it is by no means a remedy for them . . . it has no tendency to diminish the dreadful evils of Free Trade and a currency mainly dependent on the retention of the precious metals at all times in the country'.[141] Though Alison refused to relinquish protectionist monetary orthodoxy its purchase in contemporary debate was eroded by the inflationary consequences of events in California.

---

[136] T. Linkwater, *How to right the nation by an equitable adjustment of capital as a compromise under free trade and cash payments*, London 1848, 14–15.
[137] Anon., *The case of the farmer and labourer stated*, 37.
[138] Young, *Free trade fallacies*, 43.
[139] D. T. Coulton, 'California versus free trade', *QR* xc (Mar. 1852), 492–502 esp. pp. 494–7.
[140] Idem, 'Gold discoveries', ibid. xci (Sept. 1852), 504–40 at p. 538.
[141] A. Alison, 'The currency extension act of nature', *BEM* lxix (Jan. 1851), 1–19 at p. 17.

This survey has shown that far from being 'dead and buried' protectionism persisted as a vigorous intellectual current in British economic discourse during 1847–52. The economic justifications of protection continued to focus on protecting producers in order that secure and balanced economic growth could rest on stable domestic and colonial markets. In both political and economic terms, empire remained an integral feature of the protectionist response to Cobdenite free trade. The customary presentation of protection as a national economic philosophy and not a sectional strategy persisted. Protectionists continued to emphasise the constitutional importance of representing the full range of productive interests in commercial legislation. In their social discourse protectionists reworked their established condemnation of orthodox liberal economics as a contracted science which ignored the problem of distribution and which diverted the state from its social duties. Similarly protectionist monetary argument continued to combine criticism of the economic impact of both monetary deflation and contracted credit with critiques of redistributive legislation which were essentially political and constitutional.

It should come as no surprise therefore that protectionists rejected the liberal idea of modernity which was celebrated in the Great Exhibition, or 'Exhibition of the World's Industry', of 1851.[142] To protectionists the Great Exhibition was at best a diversion and at worst the pernicious embodiment of a flawed political economy. As Newdegate warned, 'that novelty will die out. It may, for a time divert public attention from the consideration of the general position of the country in its commercial and social aspect'.[143] To Aytoun the Great Exhibition was a monstrous and misguided celebration of 'progress' which betrayed widespread ignorance of the social condition of Britain. The exhibition's metropolitan location and prohibitive ticket prices symbolised the socially divisive tendencies of free trade.[144] From the economic perspective Newdegate insisted that the exhibition symbolised no permanent apotheosis of British prosperity: 'Trade has always had its cycles of prosperity, and I think we have reached the meridian of one.'[145] Indeed Aytoun warned that the exhibition would expose the unfounded complacency of the Manchester School by revealing the extent of scientific and manufacturing advance in the exhibits of foreign nations.[146] Fundamentally, Aytoun objected that the international ideal of the Great Exhibition was a product of Cobden's chimerical notion of the 'fraternity of nations': 'He still talks of reciprocity, as enthusiasts talk of the Millenium, forgetful of or blind to the fact that no Government whatever has stepped forward frankly to

---

[142] Cobden was a member of the organising executive: Ceadel, *The origins of war prevention*, 459.
[143] Newdegate, *A third letter*, p. xxix.
[144] W. E. Aytoun, 'The proposed exhibition of 1851', *BEM* lxviii (Sept. 1850), 278–90 at pp. 279–82.
[145] Newdegate, *A third letter*, p. xxix.
[146] Aytoun, 'The proposed exhibition of 1851', 284.

ratify the bargain, and to contribute to the emancipation of trade.'[147] In rejecting the Great Exhibition protectionists therefore reiterated many of those arguments which had forged a cohesive and continuous critique of free trade throughout the first half of the nineteenth century.

---

[147] Ibid. 283.

9

Epilogue

Why, therefore, did protectionists fail in their attempt to persuade public opinion back to protection by 1852? One answer to this question – that the Conservative party simply ditched what had become an electoral liability – still dominates the historiography.[1] Of course, it cannot be disputed that by 1852 the leaders of the Conservative party had abandoned protection as a policy which lay beyond the bounds of 'practical politics'.[2] However, by adopting an intellectual perspective this epilogue suggests a more complex reading. As the 1852 election clearly demonstrated and as that of 1906 was to underline, the fate of protectionist economics in Victorian and Edwardian Britain was uniquely dependent on the political will of the Conservative party. It is impossible, however, fully to understand the party's mid Victorian surrender of protection without a deeper examination of two intellectual contexts. It is firstly necessary to examine the formidable 'external' obstacles faced by protectionists in their battle for public opinion. Secondly, and perhaps most importantly, it is essential to examine how protection was forced to compete with alternative fiscal strategies in a vigorous Conservative debate on taxation.

Although historians differ as to the precise timing of the surrender of protection by Disraeli and Stanley, there is broad agreement on two central points: the Conservative leadership condemned protection as an electoral incubus before 1852 and embraced the settlement of 1846 thereafter.[3] In this way the years 1847–52 are woven into a history of the nineteenth century which is dominated by the concept of a 'mid-Victorian liberal consensus' where free trade was a defining element.[4] At the level of elections and policy the broad contours of the historiographical consensus are, of course, unquestionable. Yet, the assumption that the Peelite compact – free trade, direct

---

[1] On the 1852 election and its aftermath see McDowell, *British Conservatism*, 55; Stewart, *The politics of protection*, 77–188; J. B. Conacher, *The Peelites and the party system, 1846–52*, Newton Abbott 1972, 111–70; R. Blake, *The Conservative party from Peel to Thatcher*, London 1985, esp. pp. 74–95.
[2] Stewart, *The politics of protection*, 186.
[3] McDowell maintained that Disraeli had 'lost all hope of restoring protection' before the end of 1848: *British Conservatism*, 52. Ghosh endorses this view in 'Disraelian Conservatism: a financial approach', *EHR* xcix (1984), 268–96, esp. p. 269. Stewart dates Disraeli's relinquishment of protection from May 1849, and that of Lord Stanley (created earl of Derby, 1851) from June 1851: *The politics of protection*, 140–1, 186.
[4] See, for instance, Parry, *The rise and fall of Liberal government*, 167–94.

taxation, retrenchment, and bullionist monetary orthodoxy – would inevitably dominate the late nineteenth-century state has imposed a one-sided perspective on Victorian economic discourse. With the striking exception of Ewen Green, historians have generally endorsed the idea that Conservatives had buried protection in an intellectual as well as a political sense by 1852.[5]

A close reading of Conservative fiscal discourse during 1847–52 shows that protection was not straightforwardly ditched in the interests of electoral expediency. Of course electoral realism featured prominently in Conservative argument but the 'relegation' of protection in the hierarchy of Conservative issues cannot be fully understood within such determinist terms of reference. Fundamentally, protection had always been presented as a political and constitutional instrument in Conservative economic discourse. Beside its social and economic functions, protection was perceived as an interface between the state and the interests which comprised the nineteenth-century political nation. Thus the 'relegation' of protection was a function of its political and constitutional character and was not simply a consequence of the lower status of economic and social questions in mid nineteenth-century Conservatism. Just as the Great Reform Act had refocused Conservative debate on the importance of protection in the politics of taxation, so the repeal of the corn laws generated a distinctively Conservative discourse on the politics of Peel's fiscal settlement. During 1847–52 Conservatives debated the relative merits of restoring protection and reconstructing the entire fiscal system. Both strategies were essentially means to the same political end: an equitable balance of taxation which could confirm the state as even-handed and accountable without sacrificing the finances necessary to the maintenance of establishments. Exploring the tension between protection and financial reconstruction and the common ground on which both issues stood is essential to a more sophisticated reading of the fate of protection. For, increasingly, corn-law repeal was seen by many protectionists and Conservatives as the thin end of an ever-thickening 'democratic' wedge. Of course, this presentation of free trade as a destructive political strategy was to a large extent the product of powerful protectionist political languages. Yet faced with renewed Radical campaigns for retrenchment and new proposals for parliamentary reform protection could no longer be viewed as a sufficient strategy of constitutional conservation. Thus protection took its place within a hierarchy of 'Conservative principles' which together constructed a broad bulwark of constitutional defence.[6]

---

[5] Green, 'Radical Conservatism: the electoral genesis of tariff reform', 667–92, and *Crisis of Conservatism*, esp. pp. 159–83, 311–19.
[6] See, for example, E. W. Cox, *Conservative principles and Conservative policy, a letter to the electors of Tewkesbury*, London 1852.

The electoral incubus: Conservatives, protection and public opinion

Self-evidently protection was never the exclusive preserve of Conservatives in nineteenth-century Britain. All the same it is impossible to deny that protection chiefly depended for its political expression on Conservative prints and politicians. Indeed it was no foregone conclusion that Peel's opponents would relinquish the object of rallying the electoral fortunes of the Conservatism around the standard of protection after 1846. The National Association attempted to forge a protectionist and Conservative parliament through electoral and constituency organisation. From July 1850 the National Association instructed local protectionist organisations in electoral registration.[7] The National Association targeted the problems of non-residence and absenteeism in a campaign by its metropolitan committee to co-ordinate and finance the transportation of voters back to their rural constituencies.[8] The conference of provincial delegates with the acting committee in March 1851 was concerned with the selection of protectionist candidates and with dividing up constituencies into divisions for canvassing. This conference also highlighted the need to secure the active support of local notables and to establish local election committees which would regularly report to the National Association.[9] Particular efforts were directed at securing the urban protectionist vote particularly in the counties and the maritime boroughs.[10] Indeed, by April 1851 Aytoun observed protectionist by-election victories and boasted that 'Almost every vacancy which has occurred was filled up by a protectionist member.'[11]

However, as the general election of 1852 approached it was generally recognised that the issue of protection was imposing intractable electoral limits on the fortunes of the Conservative party. As early as July 1850 Aytoun had recognised that it was unrealistic to expect Stanley and Disraeli to achieve a reversal of free trade in the current House of Commons.[12] Thus in his response to Disraeli's amendment of the queen's speech of February 1851 Aytoun conceded that 'We have no wish to precipitate matters, or to effect by a *coup de main* that alteration which never can be permanent unless based on the conviction of the majority of the constituencies of the Empire.'[13] Con-

---

[7] [NAPIC], *Report of the acting committee to the special meeting of the general committee*, 8 (distributed with the circular of 1 July 1850).
[8] [NAPIC], *Circular, 15th July, 1850*.
[9] [NAPIC], *Report of the conference of provincial delegates*, 2–4.
[10] Ibid. 2; [NAPIC], *Circular, 12th May, 1851*.
[11] W. E. Aytoun, 'Latter days of the free-trade ministry', BEM lxix (Apr. 1851), 491–512, 495. On the protectionist victories in Cirencester, Kidderminster, Reading, South Staffordshire, North Hampshire and Cork see Stewart, *The politics of protection*, 143–4.
[12] W. E. Aytoun, 'The industry of the people', BEM lxviii (July 1850), 106–22 at pp. 110–11. See also his rendition of Stanley's response to a delegation of the *National Association*, in 'The great protection meeting in London', 778–9.
[13] Idem, 'The ministry and the agricultural interest', BEM lxix (Mar. 1851), 368–84 at p. 369; Disraeli, House of Commons (11 Feb. 1851), *Hansard* 3rd ser. cxiv. 387.

templating the general election of 1852 even G. F. Young brought himself to endorse the limited pledge of Stanley (now Derby) to 'carry out the Protective principle to the extent to which the constituencies may give him power. ... He can do no more'.[14] Although protectionists interpreted the electoral hegemony of free trade as a damaging force which distanced parliament from a large minority of the people,[15] the election of 1852 forced them to admit the electoral limits of protection.

This recognition of the electoral limitations of protectionism resulted from the attitudes of Conservatives to a number of intellectual and economic factors. On key issues it became increasingly difficult for protectionists to establish a distinctive position in contemporary economic discourse. The Anti-Gold-Law League adopted monetary and constitutional critiques of Peel's banking and currency policies which replicated protectionist and Conservative positions. As A. C. Howe has shown, 'moderate' free traders also urged the necessity of returning to commercial treaties in order to guarantee reciprocal free trade.[16] The moral and social dimensions of J. S. Mill's economic thought seemed to respond to the criticism that orthodox Ricardian political economy had contracted the discipline to a mere science of wealth creation. Moreover, in their attempts to present protection as a national economic philosophy and to distance the cause from the special pleading of sectional interests, protectionists faced formidable problems. As a federal organisation which attempted to co-ordinate the campaigns of regional and industry-based protectionist associations, the National Association could readily be represented as an agglomeration of sectional interests. This problem was compounded by the fact that in parliament protectionist argument was usually located in specific debates on the relief of agricultural distress.[17] Neither could the National Association match the efficiency of the Anti-Corn-Law League in exerting extra-parliamentary pressure on parliament. Thus protectionists bemoaned the lassitude of colonial and shipping interests in the campaign for the restoration of protection and observed the relative difficulty of mobilising a dispersed and rural population.[18]

Beside these impediments protectionist opinion-forming faced two further formidable problems: prosperity and the 'bread tax'. The return of prosperity in 1851 opened up a gaping credibility gap between protectionist argument and contemporary economic experience. Thus, when he resigned from the chairmanship of the acting committee of the Association, Young deplored,

---

14 Young, *Free-trade fallacies refuted*, 46.
15 Aytoun, 'The industry of the people', 111–12, and 'The experiences of free trade', BEM lxix (June 1851), 748–66, 750.
16 Howe, *Free trade and Liberal England*, esp. pp. 17–18, 70–92.
17 See, for instance, Disraeli's resolutions and speech on agricultural distress: House of Commons (1 Mar. 1849), *Hansard* 3rd ser. ciii. 424–53, and subsequent debates (14 Mar. 1849), ibid. 731–46, and (15 Mar. 1849), ibid. 767–72, 781–90.
18 [NAPIC], *Circular* (12 May 1851); Aytoun, 'Latter days of the free-trade ministry', 508.

'the incautious facility with which many of our party have admitted the assumed connexion between the policy they have opposed and the prosperity vaunted as its result'.[19] Protectionists were forced to admit the vulnerability of their general arguments for a protected economy to the potent cry of 'cheap bread'.[20] As *Fraser's* noted, 'For good or evil free trade is an accomplished fact. It is a measure, moreover, not likely to be reversed, unless the agricultural interest can convince the public that a return to protection will benefit the classes more numerous than their own.'[21] Like their Edwardian counterparts the protectionists of 1847–52 were impeded by the electoral incubus of the 'bread tax'. And, like Chamberlainite tariff reform, mid nineteenth-century protectionism was forced to compete with a range of other issues for intellectual prominence in Conservatism.[22]

The fiscal fix: Conservative debates on taxation, 1847–52

The bare bones of electoral politics can tell us little about why Conservatives perceived protection as dispensable by 1852. Fundamentally, protection was forced to compete with financial reform within a complex and fractured Conservative fiscal discourse. The dominant voice in this debate about taxes and tariffs was, of course, Disraeli's. It is well known that Disraeli responded to the electoral ascendancy of free trade with a coherent and distinctive campaign for the equitable adjustment of taxation.[23] What is less commonly understood is that Disraeli aimed to relocate the constitutional and political functions of protection – the equitable representation of interests by an impartial state – in new fiscal instruments.

It was axiomatic that Disraeli's various strategies for financial reform were predicated on the abandonment of protection by Peel in 1846. Presenting his financial resolutions on the 'impolitic and unjust' incidence of local and excise taxes in March 1849, Disraeli explained the logic of financial reform as a question of political justice: 'more than one third of the whole revenue derived from the Excise, is levied upon agricultural produce, exposed, by the

---

[19] G. F. Young, *Letter from G. F. Young to the duke of Richmond, Dec., 18th, 1852*, London 1853, 1 (distributed with the National Association's circular of 17 Jan. 1853).
[20] J. W. Croker, 'Parliamentary prospects', *QR* xci (Sept. 1852), 541–67 at p. 547; Coulton, 'California versus free trade', 497.
[21] Anon., 'Foreign competition and British agriculture', *FM* xliii (Feb. 1851), 236–48 at p. 237.
[22] A. Sykes, *Tariff reform in British politics, 1903–1913*, Oxford 1979, 58–9, 272–3; J. Ramsden, *The age of Balfour and Baldwin, 1902–1940*, London 1978, 7–10, 13–14, 30–44, 65–86; Green, 'Radical conservatism: the electoral genesis of tariff reform', 667–9, 684–6.
[23] Ghosh, 'Disraelian Conservatism: a financial approach', 268–96, disputed the notion that Disraeli's financial thought was derivative and opportunist; cf. H. C. G. Matthew, 'Disraeli, Gladstone, and the politics of mid-Victorian budgets', *HJ* xxii (1979), 615–43 at pp. 620–2.

recent changes in the Law, to direct competition with the untaxed produce of Foreign countries'.[24] Similarly, Disraeli predicated his argument for the reform of poor-law rating on the legislature's destabilisation of the general balance of taxation by its repeal of the corn laws.[25] In this view, the effect of corn-law repeal was to retain the heavy burden of taxation on the land while removing protection from agriculture and relieving other interests from the payment of import duties. As Disraeli explained, 'The principle of the present proposition was that, that the whole property of the country should not enjoy great advantages supplied by taxes on one particular portion of property.'[26] In his response to the queen's speech of 1851, Disraeli made his position even more explicit: while British agriculture suffered from competition with relatively lightly taxed foreigners the principal fiscal problem was both political and domestic.[27] The entire structure of British taxation, local and national, had been predicated on the assumption that the profits and 'taxability' of agriculture were protected by legislation. Repeal had rendered insupportable 'a financial system, which is the creature of protection, and which protection alone could have upheld'.[28]

Thus Disraeli's proposals for the reform of local taxation, for the repeal of the malt tax, for the reweighting of the assessed taxes, and ultimately for the permanent reconstruction of the income tax, were all based on one assumption.[29] The abandonment of protection had toppled the balance of taxation and had exposed the state to charges of inequitability, redistribution and confiscation: 'In fact, if you maintain that the essence of direct taxation is, that it should be limited to class, that it should be founded upon large exemptions, your impost is not so much a direct tax as a forced contribution.'[30] Disraeli's proposals for a permanent and extended income tax were therefore designed not only to preserve the financial muscle of the state from the inroads of retrenchers, but also to retrieve the impartiality of the fiscal state.[31] Indeed Disraeli's valedictory on the failure of a financial amendment of April 1851 might equally be read as a statement of the Conservative fiscal politics which underpinned his thinking on the income tax: 'You might have commenced a course of legislation the tendency of which would have been to put an end to that war of classes and that fatal controversy raging between the rival indus-

---

[24] Disraeli, House of Commons (1 Mar. 1849), *Hansard* ciii. 11.
[25] Disraeli, House of Commons (19 Feb. 1850), ibid. cviii. 1029–30.
[26] Disraeli, House of Commons (21 Feb. 1850), ibid. 1265.
[27] Disraeli, House of Commons (11 Feb. 1851), ibid. 388.
[28] Ibid. 403. See also cols 397, 400.
[29] On assessed taxes and poor rates see Disraeli, House of Commons (11 Apr. 1851), ibid. cxvi. 26–48. On Malt tax see Disraeli, House of Commons (8 May 1851), ibid. 711–15.
[30] Disraeli, House of Commons (30 June 1851), ibid. cxvii. 1420.
[31] Disraeli's financial proposals must be distinguished from those of parliamentary radicals and the radical associations for financial reform: Disraeli, House of Commons (6 Mar. 1848), ibid. xcvii. 436. See also Ghosh, 'Disraelian Conservatism: a financial approach', 268–71.

tries of the country. You might have commenced a vast system of remedial legislation.'[32]

In spite of his abandonment of protection, Disraeli's political language was widely echoed in Conservative fiscal discourse. Most notably, Archibald Alison reached beyond protection for a new fiscal expression of Conservatism. Though he had vehemently opposed direct taxation prior to the repeal of the corn laws, in an article of February 1847 Archibald Alison advocated the refocusing of some of the constitutional functions of protection in different fiscal instruments: the equalisation and deepening of direct taxation, and the establishment of a sinking fund to begin paying off the public debt.[33] For Alison, the fiscal consequences of repeal held two principal constitutional ramifications. Firstly, repeal represented a retreat from indirect taxation which, in the absence of other sources of public income, potentially undermined the financial capacity of the British state. Secondly, by conceding the indirect tariff, Alison believed Peel had relinquished a crucial device for balancing the interests of different forms of property and that he had exposed financial policy to the whims of a numerous, vocal and concentrated urban interest.[34] Alison's fusion of fiscal and constitutional argument in his proposals for financial reconstruction are similarly suggestive. His case for equalising direct taxation was as much a constitutional response to repeal as it was a pecuniary *quid pro quo* for the loss of agricultural protection. From a survey of the incidence of local and national direct taxes Alison concluded that the needs of public finance and the imbalance of interests occasioned by repeal demanded more equitable and comprehensive approaches to direct taxation.[35] By facilitating a sinking fund Alison believed fiscal reconstruction could protect the state from further imperial and military emasculations.[36] Moreover, by lowering the threshold of the property tax and by extending it to Ireland, he hoped simultaneously to harness a new swathe of propertied taxpayers behind constitutional conservation. Deepening the incidence of direct taxation was for Alison a strategy which could confine the confiscatory potential of direct taxation: 'What is wanted is not their money, but their breath; not their contribution, but their clamour. In a serious conflict their voice would be decisive in favour of any side espoused. Exempted from direct taxation, they will promote its increase until it has swallowed up the state.'[37]

---

[32] Disraeli, House of Commons (11 Apr. 1851), *Hansard* cxvi. 39.
[33] A. Alison, 'Direct taxation', *BEM* lxi (Feb. 1847), 243–60. See also the hints on equalisation of the burdens of direct tax in C. Neaves, 'The crisis', ibid. lix (Jan. 1846), 124–8 at p. 125, and Aytoun, 'Ministerial measures', 381.
[34] Alison, 'Direct taxation', esp. pp. 243–6.
[35] Ibid. 247–54.
[36] See above pp. 60–2.
[37] Alison, 'Direct taxation', 258.

Thus, for Alison, direct taxation was designed to serve the same political and constitutional ends as had protection.

Within a fractured fiscal discourse, therefore, many protectionists and Conservatives shared Disraeli's political language without abandoning protection. Just as protectionists avidly supported Disraeli's proposals for agricultural relief in parliament, so in print did protectionists endorse Disraeli's campaign for the equitable adjustment of the tax burden.[38] Yet many others viewed equitable adjustment as a stark alternative to protection and wished, therefore, to see 'partial protection, through fiscality, deprecated'.[39] As Young argued in 1850, *'no remission of taxation can enable the British producer to maintain successfully an unrestricted competition with foreigners. . . . As an equivalent for the deprivation of Protection, therefore, we regard the expedient of the reduction of public burdens as a delusion and a snare'*.[40] This view – that the readjustment of taxation could not compensate for the removal of protection – was widely echoed.[41] Thus Disraeli's campaign for the equitable adjustment of taxation was seen by many protectionists at worst as a betrayal and at best as 'too clever by half'.[42] Aytoun surmised that Disraeli might have been attempting to secure a return to protection by forcing retrenchments in taxation and the consequent re-adoption of import duties for revenue purposes. Yet he warned that 'The farmers will not stand finessing. They neither comprehend circuitous *coups d'état*, nor will they follow those who attempt them.'[43] While many protectionists shared Disraeli's Conservative fiscal language, they could not embrace any financial strategy which was not 'distinctly and unequivocally subordinate to the grand cause'.[44]

This conflict between equitable adjustment and protection masked a more sophisticated Conservative debate about the politics of Peel's financial settlement, or, the 'fiscal fix'. This debate was conducted on the common intellectual ground which Disraeli shared with protectionists and other Conservative critics of Peelite finance. As early as July 1847 Bentinck had mounted a coherent financial critique of Peel's income tax and the commercial reforms this had facilitated. Bentinck argued that Peel's experiment had operated on much less than one-third of Britain's ordinary revenue and demonstrated that

---

[38] Among Disraeli's supporters on 15 Mar. 1849 were Miles, Newdegate, Cayley and the marquess of Granby: House of Commons (15 Mar. 1849), *Hansard* ciii. 781–90, 802–5, 809–16, 816–24; Anon. [W. W. N], *Justice to John Bull*, 42.
[39] Harvey, *Remunerative price the desideratum, not cheapness*, 41.
[40] Young, *Address of the general committee*, 2 (Young's emphasis). See also Aytoun, 'The great protection meeting in London', 763, and J. W. Croker, 'The budget', *QR* xcii (Dec. 1852), 236–74 at p. 236.
[41] Anon., *The case of the farmer and labourer stated*, 6–9; Anon. ['W. Bull'], *Letter to Sir E. Bulwer Lytton, Bart., commenting upon the policy advocated in his letters to John Bull, Esq.*, London 1851, 6.
[42] Disraeli noted protectionist accusations of betrayal in the House of Commons (11 Feb. 1851), *Hansard* cviii. 413–14; (30 June 1851), ibid. cxvii. 1428–9.
[43] W. E. Aytoun, 'Autumn politics', *BEM* lxx (Nov. 1851), 607–28 at p. 615.
[44] Ibid. 616.

'the revenue which was not touched by Sir Robert Peel's legislation . . . rose from £37,388,251 on the 5th of January 1842 to £41,538,573 on the 5th January, 1847'.[45] Bentinck's revivification of the tariff as a financial instrument was echoed in another response to Peel's self-justificatory *Letter to the electors of Tamworth*.[46] Here, Croker maintained that Peel's reputation for financial wizardry was entirely based on the temporary income tax and on the growth in revenue from items which Peel had not touched.[47] During 1848 this financial critique was modified in the light of Peel's claim, in his famous letter to the electors of Elbing, that he had explicitly presented the income tax in 1842 as the financial foundation of a complete transformation of Britain's commercial policy.[48] This statement provoked an extensive protectionist response which hinged on the political and constitutional implications of Peel's retrospective interpretation of the 1842 budget.[49] Beyond merely reacting to what they viewed as a political subterfuge, Peel's critics objected to the explicitly redistributive stance which Peel had foisted on the British state. Thus Aytoun repeatedly condemned the financial politics of free trade as a system of confiscation and redistribution. What the state was taking in one hand from the land (in the form of an apparently permanent income tax) it was giving in the other to those commercial and manufacturing interests which benefited from the repeal of import duties. For Aytoun this amounted to a form of 'monetary conscription' which brought the very constitutionality of taxation into question:

> It is contrary to the constitution of a free country, that any class should be selected as the subjects of isolated taxation, and doubly so when the selection is made for the almost avowed purpose of relieving some other class from the impost. Equal laws and equal rights can only be maintained when there is a proper equality of burdens.[50]

Self-evidently Aytoun's constitutional language shared much with Disraeli's proposals for the equitable adjustment of taxation. Yet a Conservative fiscal consensus failed to cohere not only because Disraeli relinquished protection but also because he too looked forward to a permanent, albeit reconstructed, income tax.

---

[45] Bentinck, House of Commons (20 July 1847), *Hansard* xciv. 617–26 at p. 620.
[46] Ibid. 617. Croker 'reviewed' both *A letter from Sir Robert Peel to the electors of Tamworth*, London 1847, and *Speech of Lord George Bentinck in the House of Commons, on Sir Robert Peel's letter to the electors of Tamworth, July 20, 1847*, London 1847, in his 'Parliamentary prospects'.
[47] Ibid. esp. pp. 548–51.
[48] On the 'Elbing letter' see Howe, *Free trade and Liberal England*, 11.
[49] For Bentinck's response to the 'Elbing letter' see House of Commons (6 Mar. 1848), *Hansard* 3rd ser. xcvii. 297.
[50] W. E. Aytoun, 'The budget', *BEM* lxiii (Mar. 1848), 383–92 at pp. 386, 388. See also his 'The opening of the session', 359, and 'To the shopkeepers of Great Britain', 645.

EPILOGUE

Without protection a putative Disraelian income tax was almost as objectionable as the Peelite reality to many protectionists and Conservatives. For protection was repeatedly presented as the *sine qua non* of the heavy burdens of local and national taxes in Britain. As Albert Williams noted in 1847, 'the burden of fixed money payment is first laid on him [the farmer] for State purposes and ecclesiastical, territorial and local requirements; and protective measures given to him as some kind of equivalent'.[51] This idea – that protection and direct taxation were mutually contingent and not mutually exclusive – was widely shared by Conservative writers. As a mechanism through which the state guaranteed that British producers could afford to pay taxes (whether direct or indirect, national or local) protection made financial sense.[52] Because Disraeli relinquished protection and proposed a permanent but reformed income tax, he was perceived to be perpetuating the Peelite settlement by many of those Conservatives who accepted the principle of taxing property directly.[53] Clearly Conservative financial discourse cohered around the idea that Peelite finance constituted a 'fiscal fix' which was objectionable in financial, economic and political senses. Yet means mattered as much as ends in Conservative argument. Regardless of the electoral prospects of protection the complexity of the Conservative financial discourse of 1847–52 meant that the electoral regeneration of Conservatism could not be rooted in fiscal territory.

Confronted with the general election of 1852, Conservatives situated protection in a re-ordered hierarchy of constitutional issues. The persistence of party disunity, the perceived threats to the Church and to other establishments, and the revivification of the issue of parliamentary reform in 1851 presented traditional constitutional issues on which the Conservatives could fight the 1852 election.[54] It would be simplistic, however, to assume that protection was simply 'relegated' because it was a fiscal and commercial question of a lower order than constitutional and religious matters. For protection had traditionally appealed to Conservatives as a constitutional question. Indeed during 1847–52 the constitutionalist language of protectionists was refocused in response to Radical reformism in three respects. Firstly, protection was presented as an instrument which could galvanise all the great national interests behind the Conservative party, itself an organ of constitutional defence. Alison even maintained that protection had laid the foundation of 'a great

---

51 Williams, *Curious lights on strange anomalies*, 14.
52 Alison, 'Free trade at its zenith', 770; Aytoun, 'British agriculture and foreign competition', 241; A. Alison, 'Free trade finance', BEM lxvii (May 1850), 513–25 esp. p. 524; Anon. [Justus], *An address to the electors of England, Scotland, and Ireland, for the year 1847 with an introductory letter to his grace the duke of Newcastle*, Leamington–London 1847, 14.
53 For a standard preference for indirect over direct taxation see Aytoun, 'The renewal of the income tax', 622–5.
54 On Radical pressure for parliamentary reform see Parry, *The rise and fall of Liberal government*, 171–5.

NATIONAL PARTY', since 'PROTECTION TO NATIVE INDUSTRY in all its branches – agricultural manufacturing, and colonial – was the principle which had banded the majority together'.[55] Similarly, for Aytoun protection represented a mechanism which could give political direction to 'INTEREST, which in all political questions is the principle motive power'.[56] Secondly, agricultural protection was justified as a mechanism for the defence of the territorial constitution. As Croker opined,

> All government . . . must be based on property, and especially on the most solid and substantial species of property – *the land*. Nothing else can afford any fair prospect or even any chance of stability to national institutions. . . . This territorial influence is in the political world what the terrestrial influence of gravity is in the physical world.[57]

Similarly, in his reading of the constitutional consequences of the loss of agricultural protection and subsequent justifications of equitable adjustment, Disraeli emphasised the political importance of maintaining a sizeable agricultural middle class.[58] Thirdly, and most importantly, free trade itself was interpreted in constitutional terms as the thin end of the wedge of democratic reform.

In the context of renewed Radical campaigns for retrenchment, and new pressure for parliamentary reform, it was not difficult to present free trade as the mere stalking horse of a broad-bottomed campaign for political democracy.[59] As Croker argued, 'It will not be pretended that the English Chartists and Socialists have been conciliated and converted by the repeal of the Corn-Laws; it is avowed that they look upon it as a mere instalment – a step – towards their own revolutionary objects.'[60] The idea that economic liberalism and political democracy were opposite sides of the same coin dominated Conservative justifications of protection.[61] Thus the National Association publicised the view that the Anti-Corn-Law agitation was merely the start of a sustained 'war of the classes' directed at the destruction of the aristocracy, the empire and Britain's military might: 'we must not overlook the political objects of which Free Trade is made the stalking horse . . . the schemes of the Free Trade party involve the downfall of the English constitution'.[62] The

---

[55] Alison, 'The dinner to Lord Stanley', 635.
[56] Aytoun, 'The experiences of free trade', 753.
[57] Croker, 'Peel policy', 307.
[58] Disraeli, House of Commons (11 Feb. 1851), *Hansard* cviii. 385–6.
[59] Of course the 'Manchester School' itself insisted that free trade was only one feature of its doctrines: Hirst, *Free trade*, 239–379. On Lord John Russell's 'conversion' to parliamentary reform by 1851 see Parry, *The rise and fall of Liberal Government*, 175.
[60] J. W. Croker, 'M. Guizot on democracy', *QR* lxxxviii (June 1849), 260–312 at p. 293.
[61] Alison, 'Thirty years of Liberal legislation', 42–5, and 'The crowning of the column', 110–11; Aytoun, 'British agriculture and foreign competition', 134.
[62] [NAPIC], *Tracts on protection: no. 4: the war of the classes*, London 1850, 1.

Radical campaigns for financial retrenchment conducted by Financial Reform Associations seemed to vindicate this Conservative constitutionalist critique.[63] As *Fraser's* warned, 'the old machinery of the Anti-Corn-Law League will be brought to work again for the furtherance of an extensive democratic movement'.[64] In this light, Lord John Russell's proposed extension of the franchise appeared to be 'a new Reform Bill, cut and carved so as to adjust the franchise to a particular party question; so as to create a constitution for the purpose of enforcing an experiment in political economy'.[65]

Ironically, it was in part as a result of this presentation of free trade as the 'thin end of the wedge' that Conservatives came to view protection as an important but insufficient instrument of constitutional defence. In several responses to Derby's identification of the Constitution and the Church as the territory on which the Conservatives would fight the 1852 election, the *Quarterly* identified protection as one instrument among a number of strategies for constitutional defence. Reviewing E. W. Cox's pamphlet, *Conservative principles and Conservative policy*, D. T. Coulton argued against the tendency of some to view protection as 'the whole sum and substance of their political creed. We think there are other and even greater objects to be contended for – that *Protection* is urgently wanted for still higher interests than those in question'.[66] Those higher interests were the defence of the constitution in Church and State. Thus in his reading of Derby's attempt to form a government in March 1852 Croker argued that the direct defence of the constitution in Church and State was 'the *immediate and imperious*' object.[67] Protection was an important but subordinate issue given that '*the first and most pressing duty of the country is to try to preserve itself from a revolutionary Government*. This is the great danger that in our view swallows up all others. The antagonism of Free Trade and Protection is but a corollary of that greater question'.[68]

---

63 Ibid. 4. See also [NAPIC], *Tracts on protection: no. 13: reply to the Edinburgh Review: part 1*, London 1850, 9.
64 Anon., 'Current history: chronicle and comment', FM xxxix (May 1849), 237–44, 239.
65 Lytton, *Letters to John Bull Esq.*, 12–13.
66 Coulton, 'California versus free trade', 493.
67 J. W. Croker, 'The old and new ministries', QR xc (Mar. 1852), 567–92 at p. 582.
68 Ibid. 592.

Biographical Appendix

Note on Sources

These biographical details are limited to the period 1815–52, and are derived from: *The dictionary of national biography on CD-rom*; *The complete peerage*; *The new Palgrave dictionary of economics*; M. Blaug (ed.), *Who's who in economics: a biographical dictionary of major economists, 1700–1986*, 2nd edn, London 1986; R. G. Thorne (ed.), *The history of parliament: the House of Commons, 1790–1820*, London 1986; M. Stenton (ed.), *Who's who of British members of parliament*, I: *1832–1885*, Hassocks 1976; *The Wellesley index to Victorian periodicals, 1824–1900*, Toronto 1972; F. W. Fetter, 'The economic articles in Blackwood's Edinburgh Magazine and their authors', *SJPE* vii (June 1960), 85–107, 213–31, and 'The economic articles in the *Quarterly Review*: articles, authors and sources', *JPE* lxvi (1958), 150–70.

Alison, Sir *Archibald* (1792–1867), historian and lawyer; author of *History of Europe* (1833–42), *Lives of Lord Castlereagh and Sir Charles Stewart* (1861).

Arnold, *Thomas* (1795–1842), Fellow of Oriel College, Oxford (1815–19); headmaster of Rugby School (1828–42).

Ashburton, *Lord*, see Baring, Alexander.

Attwood, *Matthias* (1779–1851), Conservative MP for Fowey (1819), Callington (1820–30), Boroughbridge (1830–2), Whitehaven (1832–47); banker; brother of Thomas Attwood; patronised by the Tory Viscount Lowther.

Attwood, *Thomas* (1783–1856), MP for Birmingham (1832–40); banker and Radical; key member of 'Birmingham School' and Birmingham Political Union (1830); author of *Observations on currency, poverty and pauperism* (1818), and *The Scotch banker* (1828).

Aytoun, *William Edmonstoune* (1813–65), poet; barrister; Professor of Rhetoric and Belles Lettres, University of Edinburgh (1845–64); Sheriff of Orkney (1852); acquaintance of Disraeli; DCL Oxon. (1853).

Baker-Holroyd, *John* (1735–1821), 1st Baron Sheffield (1802), Tory peer; promoter of the union with Ireland; member of the Board of Trade (1809–21).

Bankes, *Henry* (1757–1834), Tory MP for Corfe Castle (1780–1826), Dorset (1826–31).

Baring, *Alexander* (1774–1848), Baron Ashburton (1835), MP for Taunton (1806–26), Callington (1826–31), Thetford (1831–32), Essex North (1832–5); President of the Board of Trade (1834–5); banker and merchant; politics drifted from Whig to Conservative.

Baring, Hon. *Francis* (1800–68), Conservative MP for Thetford (1832–41, 1848–57).

Baring, Sir Francis Thornhill (1796–1866), Whig MP for Portsmouth (1826–65); Chancellor of the Exchequer (1839–41).

Barrow, Sir John (1764–1848), Second Secretary of the Admiralty (1807–45); intimate of Sir George Staunton; explorer and cartographer.

Barton, John (1789–1852), political economist critical of Ricardo and Malthus; wrote on poverty.

Bathurst, Henry, 3rd Earl Bathurst (1762–1834), Tory peer; Secretary for War and the Colonies (1812–27).

Benett, John (b. 1773), Conservative MP for Wiltshire South (1819–52); voted for agricultural protection and for income tax in the 1840s.

Bennett, Hon. Henry Grey (1777–1836), Whig MP for Shrewsbury (1806–24); advocate of retrenchment and parliamentary reform.

Bentinck, Lord William George Frederick (1802–48), Conservative MP for Lyme Regis (1828–48); leader of protectionist party in the House of Commons (1846–8).

Berkeley, Hon. George Charles Grantley Fitz-Hardinge (1800–81), MP for Gloucestershire West (1832–47); severed connection with the Whig Earl FitzHardinge (1847); brought motion for agricultural protection (1850).

Blunt, John James (1794–1855), divine; Fellow of St John's College, Cambridge; Lady Margaret Professor of Divinity, University of Cambridge (1839–55).

Brougham, Henry (1778–1868), Whig-Radical MP for Winchelsea (1815–30), Knaresborough (1830); Lord Chancellor (1830–4); extensive contributor to the *Edinburgh Review*.

Browne, Robert Dillon (d. 1850), MP for Mayo (1836–50).

Buckland, William (1784–1856), Fellow of Corpus Christi College, Oxford (1808–25); Professor of Mineralogy, University of Oxford (1813); Reader in Geology, University of Oxford; FRS (1818); canon of Christ Church (1824); dean of Westminster (1845).

Buller, Charles (1806–48), Radical MP for Liskeard (1832–48); chief secretary to Lord Durham in Canada (1838–9); contributor to *Edinburgh* and *Westminster Reviews*.

Byles, Sir John Barnard (1801–84), judge and commercial lawyer; wrote on usury laws, bills of exchange and protection.

Caird, Sir James (1816–92), agriculturist, author and adviser to parliament on agricultural questions.

Canning, George (1770–1827), Pittite MP for Liverpool (1812–22), Harwich (1823–6), Newport (1826–7), Seaford (1827); Secretary of State for Foreign Affairs (1822–7); Prime Minister (1827).

Carey, Henry Charles (1793–1879), American political economist and critic of Ricardo and Malthus; author of *Essay on the rate of wages* (1835); *Principles of political economy* (1837–40); *The slave trade* (1853); *Principles of social science* (1858–60).

Cayley, Edward Stillingfleet (1802–62), MP for North Riding (1832–62); described himself as 'not a Whig but a reformer'.

Chalmers, Thomas (1780–1847), evangelical divine; Professor of Moral Philosophy and Political Economy, University of St Andrews (1823–8); Professor of Theology, University of Edinburgh (1828–43); author of

Commercial discourses (1820–1), and *On political economy* (1832); DCL Oxon. (1835).

Clay, Henry (1777–1852), American statesman; secured protective tariffs (1824, 1840); presidential candidate (1824, 1832, 1844); Secretary of State (1824–8).

Clay, Sir William (1791–1869), Liberal MP for Tower Hamlets (1832–57).

Cobbett, William (1762–1835), Radical MP for Oldham (1832–5); founder of the *Political Register* (1802–35); author of *Rural rides* (1830).

Cobden, Richard (1804–65), Radical MP for Stockport (1841–7), West Riding (1847–57); cotton printer; director of Manchester chamber of commerce; leading member of Anti-Corn-Law League; writer on free trade and pacifism.

Colebrooke, Henry Thomas (1765–1837), Sanskrit scholar in service of East India Company (1782–1814).

Colquhoun, John Campbell (1802–70), Conservative MP for Dumbartonshire (1832–3), Kilmarnock Burghs (1837–41), Newcastle-under-Lyme (1841–7).

Colquhoun, Patrick (1745–1820), city magistrate, London (1792–1818); social reformer and statistical writer.

Conolly, Col. Edward Michael (1786–1849), Conservative MP for Donegal (1831–49); voted for protection in 1846.

Copleston, Edward (1776–1849), Tutor, Dean and Provost of Oriel College, Oxford; bishop of Llandaff (1827–49); writer on theology and political economy.

Coulton, David Trevena (1810–57), journalist; founded Conservative newspaper *Britannia* (1839).

Cox, Edward William (1809–79), barrister; contested Tewkesbury as a Conservative (1852, 1857); writer on legal questions.

Creevy, Thomas (1768–1838), Whig MP for Thetford (1807–18), Appleby (1820–6), Downton (1831–2).

Croker, John Wilson (1780–1857), politician and essayist; Tory MP for numerous seats (1812–18, 1819–32); 'Political editor', *Quarterly Review* (1832–54).

Croly, Revd George (1780–1860), divine and author; contributed to the *New Times*, *Britannia* and the *Literary Gazette*.

Crombie, Alexander (1762–1840) schoolmaster and writer on philology, agriculture, monetary policy and theology; often used pseudonymn 'Titus'.

Curteis, Edward J., MP for Sussex (1820–30).

Curwen, John Christian (1756–1828), MP for Carlisle (1816–20), Cumberland (1820–8); Whig but self-confessedly never 'what is called a good party man'; protectionist and retrencher.

Dalbiac, Sir James Charles (1776–1847), Conservative MP for Ripon (1835–7); lieutenant-general (1838).

Dallas, Eneas Sweetland (1828–79), journalist and author; staff writer for *The Times* and regular contributor to weeklies as well as to *Blackwood's*.

Dasent, George Webb (1817–96), scholar and linguist; contributor to *Blackwood's*; assistant editor of *The Times* (1845).

De Quincey, Thomas (1785–1859), Lakeland poet friend of S. T. Coleridge and John Wilson; contributed to *Tait's Magazine*; author of *Confessions of an opium eater* (1821).

Disraeli, Benjamin (1805–81), Conservative MP for Maidstone (1837–41),

Shrewsbury (1841–7), Buckinghamshire (1847–76); Chancellor of the Exchequer (1852).

Douglas, Sir Howard (1776–1861), Conservative MP for Liverpool (1842–7); voted for protection in 1846.

Drummond, Henry (1786–1860), MP for West Surrey (1847–60); founder of the Drummond Chair of Political Economy, University of Oxford.

Duncan, Jonathan (1799–1865), founder member of National Anti-Gold-Law League and critic of the 'currency school'.

Eden, Sir Frederick Morton (1766–1809), wrote on population (1800), friendly societies (1801), the peace (1802), national self-sufficiency (1808).

Edwards, Revd Edward (?1789–1832), Anglican clergyman; literary adviser to John Murray.

Elgin, Thomas Bruce, 7th earl of Elgin (1766–1841), Tory peer and diplomat.

Ellice, Edward (1781–1863), Whig MP for Coventry (1818–26, 1830–63).

Elliot, Sir Francis Perceval (?1756–1818), commissioner of audit, Somerset House (1806–18); volunteer and financial writer; contributor to the weekly, *Aegis*.

Elliot, William (1766–1818), Whig MP for Peterborough (1766–1818); supported 1815 corn law and 1816 property tax; increasingly distanced from Whigs by his opposition to parliamentary reform.

Ellis, Charles Rose (1771–1845), Pittite MP for Seaford (1812–26); Canningite with West India interests.

Ellis, George (1753–1815), Pittite MP for Seaford (1796–1802); co-founded *Anti-Jacobin* with Canning.

Ellman, John (1753–1832), agriculturist; founder of Sussex Agricultural Association; commissioner of taxes.

Ferrand, William Busfeild (1809–89), Conservative MP for Knaresborough (1841–7); voted for protection in 1846.

Finch, George (d. 1870), Conservative MP for Rutlandshire (1846–7); protectionist.

Flood, Sir Frederick (1741–1824), 'Independent' MP for Co. Wexford (1812–18); agricultural protectionist.

Fullarton, John (?1780–1849), banker; 'banking school' theorist and traveller; a founder of the Carlton Club.

Galt, John (1779–1839), novelist and poet known to Lord Byron and Sir Walter Scott; secretary to Canada Company; member of a government commission to investigate the colonisation of Upper Canada.

Gladstone, John (1764–1851), Conservative MP for Lancaster (1818–20), New Woodstock (1820–26), Berwick-upon-Tweed (1826–7); Liverpool merchant with West India interests; father of W. E. Gladstone.

Gladstone, William Ewart (1809–98), Conservative MP for Newark (1832–45), University of Oxford (1847–65); Vice-President of the Board of Trade (1841–3); Secretary of State for the Colonies (1845–6).

Gleig, Revd George Robert (1796–1888), chaplain-general of the forces; military historian; biographer.

Gooch, Thomas Sherlock (1767–1851), Tory MP for Suffolk (1802–56).

Goulburn, Henry (1784–1856), Conservative MP for numerous boroughs (1810–26), Cambridge University (1831–56); Under-Secretary of State for the Colonies (1812–21); Secretary of State for Ireland (1821–8); Chancellor of the Exchequer (1828–30, 1841–6).

BIOGRAPHICAL APPENDIX

Graham, Sir James Robert George (1792–1861), MP for Hull (1818–20), Carlisle (1826–9), Cumberland East (1830–7), Pembroke (1838–41), Dorchester (1841–7), Ripon (1847–52); Secretary of State for the Home Department (1841–6).

Granby, Marquess of (John Henry Manners, 5th duke of Rutland) (1778–1857), Recorder of Cambridge (1800–35); Tory peer.

Greenfield, William (d. 1827), cleric; Professor of Rhetoric at the University of Edinburgh.

Gregory, William (1803–58), chemist; Professor of Medicine and Chemistry, King's College, Aberdeen; Professor of Chemistry, Edinburgh University; pupil of Justus Liebig.

Grenville, William Windham, 1st Baron Grenville (1759–1834), First Lord of the Treasury (1806–7).

Gurney, Hudson (1775–1864), 'Independent' MP for Newtown, Isle of Wight (1816–32).

Haliburton, Thomas Chandler (1796–1865), Chief Justice of Court of Common Pleas, Nova Scotia (1829); Judge of Supreme Court of Nova Scotia (1840).

Hawes, Sir Benjamin (1797–1862), Liberal MP for Lambeth (1832–47), Kinsale (1848–52); Under-Secretary of State for the Colonies (1846–51); advocate of corn-law repeal and critic of Bank Charter Act.

Head, Sir Francis Bond (1793–1875), naval lieutenant; manager of the Rio Plata Mining Association (1825–6); Assistant Poor Law Commissioner (1834); Lieutenant-Governor of Upper Canada (1835–37).

Heathcote, Sir William (1801–1), Conservative MP for Hampshire (1826–32), North Hampshire (1837–49); Fellow of All Souls, Oxford; DCL (1830).

Herries, John Charles (1778–1855), Conservative MP for Harwich (1823–41), Stamford (1847–53); Secretary to the Treasury (1823–7); Chancellor of the Exchequer (1827–8); President of the Board of Trade (1830); Secretary at War (1834–5).

Heygate, William (1782–1844), 'Independent' MP for Sudbury (1818–26); banker and anti-bullionist.

Higgins, Godfrey (1773–1833), archaeologist; Justice of the Peace; writer on social and economic reform.

Higgins, Matthew James ['Jacob Omnium'] (1810–68), writer on the West Indies; newspaper correspondent; contested Westbury (1847) as a Peelite.

Holland, George Calvert (1801–65); physician; prominent in Sheffield Literary and Philosophical Society; bank director; protectionist.

Horner, Francis (1778–1817), Whig MP for Wendover (1807–12), St Mawes (1813–17); student of Dugald Stewart; chairman of the bullion committee; contributor to the *Edinburgh Review*.

Horton, Robert John Wilmot (1784–1841), MP for Newcastle-under-Lyme; Under-Secretary of State for War and Colonies (1821–8); Governor of Ceylon (1831–7).

Hume, Joseph (1777–1855), Radical MP for Montrose (1818–30, 1842–55), Middlesex (1830–7), Kilkenny (1837–41).

Huskisson, William (1789–1830), Tory MP for Chichester (1812–23), Liverpool (1823–30); Commissioner of Woods, Forests and Land Revenues (1814–23); President of the Board of Trade (1823–27); Secretary of State for the Colonies (1827–8).

Ingestre, Viscount (Henry John Chetwynde Talbot) (1803–68), Conservative MP for Hertford (1830, 1832), Armagh (1831), Staffordshire South (1837–49); voted for protection in 1846.

Jacob, William (1762?–1851), Tory MP for Rye (1808–12); merchant trading to South America; FRS (1807); comptroller of the corn returns for the Board of Trade (1822–42); contributor to the 7th edn of *Encyclopaedia Britannica*.

Johnston, James Finlay Weir (1796–1855), Reader in Chemistry at the University of Durham (1833–55); Chemist to the Agricultural Society of Scotland (1843).

Johnstone, William, Irish journalist; briefly personal secretary to William Lowther (2nd earl of Lonsdale and First Commissioner of Woods and Forests [1828]).

Jones, Richard, Revd (1790–1855), Professor of Political Economy, King's College, University of London (1833–5); headmaster of Haileybury College (1835–55).

Labouchère, Henry (1798–1859), Liberal MP for St Michael's (1826–30), Taunton (1830–59); Vice-President of the Board of Trade (1835–9); President of the Board of Trade (1839–41, 1847–52); Chief Secretary for Ireland (1846–7).

Lauderdale, Lord (James Maitland, 8th earl) (1759–1839), Whig Protectionist peer; author of *Inquiry into the nature and causes of Public Wealth* (1804).

Lethbridge, Thomas Buckler (1778–1849), 'Independent' MP for Somerset (1820–30); protectionist; anti-Radical.

Leycester, Joseph (b. 1784), Conservative MP for numerous Irish boroughs incl. Cork City (1835); agent of the Bank of Ireland.

Liddell, Hon. Henry Thomas (1797–1878), Conservative MP for Northumberland (1826–30), Durham North (1837–47); protectionist.

List, G. Friedrich (1789–1846), Political economist and economic journalist; proponent of Prussian *zollverein* and concept of 'National Economy'.

Liverpool, Lord (Henry Bankes Jenkinson, 2nd earl) (1770–1828), Tory premier (1812–27).

Lockhart, John Gibson (1794–1854), author and biographer; editor of the *Quarterly Review* (1826–53).

Lockhart, John Ingram (1765–1835), MP for Oxford (1807–18, 1820–30); supporter of protection and the property tax.

Low, David (1786–1859), editor of the *Quarterly Journal of Agriculture* (from 1826); Professor of Agriculture at the University of Edinburgh (1831).

Loyd, Samuel Jones (1796–1883), banker and currency-school theorist; witness to 1832 Committee on the Bank Charter; Peel's adviser on the Bank Charter Act (1844).

Lytton, Sir Edward George Earle Lytton Bulwer- (1st Baron Lytton) (1803–73), MP for St Ives (1831), Lincoln (1832–41), Conservative MP for Hertfordshire (1852–66); novelist, poet and friend of Disraeli.

Macaulay, Thomas Babington (1800–59), Whig MP for Calne (1830–2), Leeds (1832–4), Edinburgh (1840–7); member of and legal adviser to Supreme Council in India; Secretary at War (1839–41); historian and essayist.

McCulloch, John Ramsay (1789–1864), Ricardian political economist and economic journalist; author of formal treatises and contributions to the *Edinburgh Review* and *Encyclopaedia Britannica*.

BIOGRAPHICAL APPENDIX

Macdonnell, Alexander (1798–1835), West India merchant; secretary to the West India Committee of Merchants (1830).
Macpherson, David (1746–1816), historian of Scotland, of commerce and of navigation.
McQueen (or Macqueen), James (1778–1870), manager of a sugar plantation; geographer; journalist; editor and part-owner of the *Glasgow Courier* (1821).
Maginn, William (1793–1842), poet, journalist; joint-editor of the *Standard*; editor of *Fraser's Magazine*.
Malcolm, Sir John (1769–1833), soldier and administrator in service of East India Company; writer on Indian administration.
Mallalieu, Alfred, journalist; employee of the foreign office.
Malthus, Thomas Robert (1766–1834), political economist; clergyman (1797–1834); Professor of Political Economy, East India College, Haileybury (1805–34).
Marryat, Joseph (1757–1824), 'Independent' MP for Sandwich (1812–24); West India merchant; chairman and parliamentary spokesman for Lloyds; banker.
Marshall, John (1783–1841), statistical author; member of the boundary commission (1831); factory inspector.
Mathews, Henry (1789–1828), judge; advocate-fiscal of Ceylon.
Miles, Philip William Skinner (d. 1881), Conservative MP for Bristol 1837–52; protectionist.
Mill, James (1773–1836), Benthamite and 'Philosophic Radical'; economic journalist and historian of India; contributed extensively to the *Edinburgh Review*.
Mill, John Stewart (1806–73), moral philosopher and political economist; contributor to *London and Westminster Review* during 1830s.
Miller, John, barrister of Lincoln's Inn.
Milman, Henry Hart (1791–1868), Professor of Poetry, University of Oxford (1821–31).
Mirabeau, Victor Riquetti, Marquis de (1715–89), physiocrat influenced by Quesnay; wrote on population, agriculture, commerce and taxation.
Munro, Sir Thomas (1761–1827), major-general; governor of Madras (1819–27).
Muntz, George Frederick (1794–1857), Radical MP for Birmingham (1840–57); Birmingham School currency theorist; co-founder of Birmingham Political Union.
Napier, Sir William Francis Patrick (1785–1860), general; historian of peninsular war; political radical.
Neaves, Charles (1800–76), Scottish judge; Solicitor-General for Scotland (1852–3).
Newdegate, Charles Newdigate (1816–87), Conservative MP for Warwickshire (1843–85); DCL (Christ Church, Oxford).
Newport, Sir Simon John (1756–1843), Tory MP for Waterford (1803–32).
Palgrave, Sir Francis (1788–1861), historian; Municipal Corporations Commissioner; Deputy-keeper of Her Majesty's Records.
Parnell, Sir Henry Brook (1776–1842), MP for Queen's County (1805–32), Dundee (1833–41); Chairman of the Finance Committee (1828).
Peel, Sir Robert (1788–1850), 2nd baronet (1830), MP for Oxford University (1818–28), Westbury (1828–30), Tamworth (1830–50); Home Secretary (1822–7, 1828–30); Prime Minister and Chancellor of the Exchequer (1834–5); Prime Minister (1841–6).

Phillimore, John George (1808–65), clerk in the Board of Control for India (1827–32); QC; Reader in Constitutional Law and Legal History to Inns of Court (1852).

Preston, Richard (1768–1850), MP for Ashburton (1812–18); Professor of Law, King's College, London.

Pusey, Philip (1799–1855), Conservative MP for Chippenham (1830–1), Cashel (1832), Berkshire (1835–52).

Quesnay, François (1694–1774), French philosopher and physiocrat; author of *Tableau économique* (1758).

Redesdale, Lord (John Freeman-Mitford, 1st Baron) (1748–1830), Tory peer.

Ricardo, David (1772–1823), MP for Portarlington (1772–1823); political economist; stockbroker; founder of the Political Economy Club.

Robinson, David (d. 1849), London-based political journalist.

Robinson, Hon. Frederick John (1782–1859), Viscount Goderich (1827), earl of Ripon (1833), Tory MP for Ripon (1807–27); President of the Board of Trade (1818–23, 1841–3); Chancellor of the Exchequer (1823–7); Secretary of State for War and Colonies (1827, 1830–3); First Lord of Treasury (1827–8); President of the Board of Control (1843–6).

Robinson, George Richard (d. 1850), Conservative MP for Worcester (1826–37); merchant and shipowner; Chairman of Lloyds; East India proprietor

Rose, George (1744–1818), Pittite MP for Christchurch (1790–1818); Vice-President of the Board of Trade (1807–12).

Salomons, Sir David (1797–1873), Liberal MP for Greenwich (1851); Lord Mayor of London; co-founder of London and Westminster Bank.

Sandon, Viscount (Hon. Granville Dudley Ryder) (1799–1879), Conservative MP for Hertfordshire (1841–7); voted for protection in 1846.

Say, Jean-Baptiste (1767–1832); political economist, econonomic journalist and professor of political economy.

Scott, Hon. Francis (1806–84), Conservative MP for Roxburghshire (1841–7), Berwickshire (1847–59); barrister; parliamentary agent for Port Phillip, New South Wales.

Scott, Sir Walter (1771–1832), novelist; partner in the publishing company Constable and Cadell which was ruined by the financial crisis of 1825–6.

Scrope, George Julius Poulett (1797–1876), Liberal MP for Stroud (1833–67); geologist; political economist.

Seeley, Robert Benton (1798–1886), publisher; writer on religion and history for *The Times*, the *Morning Herald* and *Fraser's*.

Selkirk, Lord (Thomas Douglas, 5th earl) (1771–1820), Whig peer.

Senior, Nassau William (1790–1864), Drummond Professor of Political Economy, University of Oxford (1825–30, 1847–52).

Sheffield, Lord, see Baker-Holroyd, John.

Sibthorpe, Col. Charles Delaet Waldo (d. 1855), Conservative MP for Lincoln (1826–32, 1835–55); voted for protection in 1846.

Sidmouth, Lord (Henry Addington, 1st Viscount) (1757–1844), Tory peer; Home Secretary (1812–22).

Sinclair, Sir John (1754–1835), MP (1780–1811); President of Board of Agriculture (1793–8, 1806–14); Cashier of Excise (1811–30); author of *Statistical account of Scotland* (1791–9).

Sismondi, Jean Charles Leonard Simonde de (1773–1842), Swiss historian and political economist; abandoned theoretical economics of *De la richesse commerciale* (1803); his 'anti-Ricardian' *Nouveaux principes* (1819, 1827) was attacked in the *Edinburgh Review*.

Smith, Adam (1723–90), moral philospher and political economist.

Southey, Robert (1774–1843), poet, historian and biographer.

Spence, William (1783–1860), entomologist and political economist.

Stanhope, Philip Henry (1781–1855), Viscount Mahon (1816), MP for Midhurst (1812–16); Tory peer.

Stanley, Edward (1799–1869), 14th earl of Derby (1851), Whig MP from 1822; held numerous cabinet posts; joined Tory party (1835); Colonial Secretary (1841–5); opposed repeal of the corn laws; leader of the Protectionist/Conservative party (1846–52); Prime Minister (1852).

Staunton, Sir George Thomas (1781–1859), Conservative MP for Mitchell (1818–26), Heytesbury (1830–2), Hampshire South (1832–4), Portsmouth (1838–52); adviser to East India Company and to successive governments on the China trade.

Stevenson, William (1772–1829), Keeper of the Records at the Treasury; editor of the *Scots Magazine*; compiler of the *Annual Register*; author of surveys of agriculture, commerce and navigation.

Tatham, Revd Edward (1749–1834), logician; author of pamphlets on the income tax and the national debt; sub-Rector of Lincoln College, Oxford.

Taylor, George (1772–1851), writer on social and economic questions; secretary to the Commission of Inquiry into the Poor Laws (1832).

Thompson, William ['Alderman'] (1793–1854), Conservative MP for Callington (1820–6), London (1826–30), Sunderland (1833–41), Westmoreland (1841–54); Lord Mayor of London (1828–9); shipowner; ironmaster; voted for protection in 1846 and 1852.

Thomson, Charles Poulett (d. 1841), Lord Sydenham (1840), Whig MP for Dover (1826–39), and Manchester (1839–40); Vice-President of the Board of Trade (1830–4); President of the Board of Trade (1834); Governor-General of Canada (1839).

Thornton, Henry (1760–1815), MP for Southwark (1782–1815); banker; helped to write the report of the Bullion Committee (1811).

Tooke, Thomas (1774–1858), free trader and banking school theorist; author (with W. Newmarch) of *A history of prices and the state of circulation from 1792 to 1856* (1838–57).

Torrens, Robert (1780–1864), Whig MP for Ashburton (1831), Bolton (1832–5); writer on economic subjects; proprietor of *The Globe* newspaper.

Trelawny, Sir John Salusbury (1816–85), Liberal MP for Tavistock (1843–52).

Trench, Frederick William (?1777–1859), Conservative MP for Cambridge (1819–32), Scarborough (1835–47).

Turgot, Anne Robert Jacques, Baron de L'Aulne (1727–81), French philosopher, economist and administrator.

Urquhart, David (1805–77), Conservative MP for Stafford (1847–52); secretary of the British embassy at Constantinople (1837); founded the *Free Press* (1855) and *Diplomatic Review* (1866).

Vansittart, Nicholas (1766–1851), Baron Bexley (1823), Conservative MP for Harwich (1812–23); Chancellor of the Exchequer (1812–23).

Vyvyan, Sir Richard Rawlinson (1800–79), Conservative MP for Bristol, (1825–30, 1832–7), Helstone (1841–57).

Wakefield, Edward Gibbon (1796–1862), advocate of 'systematic colonisation'; author of appendix to Lord Durham's *Report on the affairs of North America* (1839).

Wallace, Robert (d. 1855), MP for Greenock (1832–45); West India proprietor and protectionist.

Walsh, Sir John (1798–1881), Conservative MP for Sudbury (1830–4, 1839–40), Radnorshire (1840–68).

Ward, William (1787–1849), Tory MP for City of London (1826–31); financier; Director of the Bank of England; Chairman of the East India Committee (1832).

Warren, Samuel (1807–77), lawyer; poet and author; FRS (1835); DCL Oxon. (1853).

Wellesley, Richard Colley, Marquis Wellesley (1760–1842), Governor-General of India (1797); Lord Lieutenant of Ireland (1821).

West, Edward (1782–1828), Fellow of University College, Oxford.

Western, Charles Callis (1767–1844), Whig MP for Maldon (1807–12), Essex (1812–32).

Weyland, John (1774–1854), MP for Hindon (1830–2); writer on population and poor laws.

Whately, Richard (1787–1863), Drummond Professor of Political Economy University of Oxford (1829–31); archbishop of Dublin (1831–63).

Whitbread, Samuel (1764–1815), Whig MP for Bedford (1790–1815); campaigner for poor law, parliamentary and economical reform.

Whitmore, William Wolryche (1787–1858), Whig MP for Bridgenorth (1826–32), Wolverhampton (1832–5).

Willoughby, Sir Henry (1796–1865), Reform MP for Yarmouth (1831), Conservative MP for Newcastle-under-Lyme (1832–5), Evesham (1847–65).

Wilson, John (1785–1854), the author 'Christopher North'; Professor of Moral Philosophy, University of Edinburgh; friend of Sir Walter Scott and S. T. Coleridge.

Wood, Col. Thomas (d. 1872), Conservative MP for Brecknockshire (1806–47); declared for protection but voted for repeal in 1846.

Young, George Frederick (d. 1870), MP for Tynemouth (1831–8), Scarborough (1851–2); shipowner and shipbuilder; chairman, National Association for the Protection of Industry and Capital.

Young, Thomas (1773–1829), physician and physicist.

Select Bibliography

Bibliographical note

This book draws on an exhaustive reading of the *Quarterly Review* (1809–52), *Blackwood's Edinburgh Magazine* (1817–52) and *Fraser's Magazine* (1830–52). Owing to shortage of space the bibliography does not list individual journal articles. The reader is referred to the first footnote to each article for full bibliographical information. This omission is not intended to imply that periodicals are less important historical sources than those listed below.

Published primary sources

Official documents and publications
Hansard's parliamentary debates, 1st, new and 3rd series, 1809–52

Periodicals
Blackwood's Edinburgh Magazine
Fraser's Magazine
The Edinburgh Review
The Quarterly Review

Contemporary books and pamphlets

Alison, Archibald, *The principles of population and their connection with human happiness*, London 1840
―――― *England in 1815 and 1845 or a sufficient and a contracted currency*, 1st, 2nd edns, London 1845
―――― *Free trade and a fettered currency*, London 1847
Almack, John, *Character, motives and proceedings of the Anti-Corn Law Leaguers, with a few general remarks on the consequences that would result from a free trade in corn; dedicated to W. R. Greg*, London 1843
―――― *Cheap bread and low wages* (printed for the Agricultural Protection Society), London 1844
Andrews, A., *The history of British journalism, from the foundation of the newspaper press in England, to the repeal of the Stamp Act in 1855*, London 1859
Anon., *Petitions of the merchants of and manufacturers of Bristol, Liverpool, & c. against the renewal of the Company's Charter, & c*, London 1812
Anon., *Considerations on colonial policy, with relation to the renewal of the East India Company's Charter, by an impartial observer*, London 1813
Anon. ['Cossim'], *Considerations on the danger and impolicy of laying open the trade with India and China; including an examination of the objections commonly urged*

against the East India Company's commercial and financial management, 2nd edn, London 1813

Anon. ['Fabius'], *A letter to the right honourable the earl of Buckinghamshire, president of the board of commissioners for the affairs of India, on the subject of an open trade to India*, London 1813

Anon., *A letter to the earl of Liverpool, on the probable effect of a great reduction of corn prices, by importation; upon the relative condition of the state and its creditors, and of debtors and creditors in general*, London 1814

Anon., *An address to the nation on the relative importance of agriculture and manufactures, and the means of advancing them both to the highest degree of improvement of which they are capable; together with remarks on the doctrines lately advanced by Mr. Malthus on the nature of rent, and the relation it has to the amount of national income; and a prefaratory letter to C. M. Talleyrand Perigord, prince of Benevento, on the late exposé of the financial state of the French nation*, London 1815

Anon., *An address to the two houses of parliament on the importance of the corn laws to the national revenue*, London 1815

Anon., *Considerations upon the corn bill; suggested by a recent declaration from a high authority, that it was calculated 'to throw the burden from those upon whom it ought to rest, to those upon whom it ought not'*, London 1815

Anon., *England may be extricated from her difficulties consistently with the strictest principles of policy, honour and justice, by a country gentleman*, London 1816

Anon., *Remedies proposed as certain, speedy and effectual, for the relief of our present embarrassments, by an independent gentleman*, London 1816

Anon., *Three letters of Paul Silent to his country cousins*, 2nd edn, London 1816

Anon., *A view of the causes of our late prosperity, and of means which have been proposed for our relief*, Exeter 1816

Anon., *On the relation of corn and currency*, London 1819

Anon., *Brief thoughts on the agricultural report by a musing bee within the hive*, London 1821

Anon., *An inquiry into the capacity of government to administer relief (and into the best mode of administering relief) to agricultural distress; with an examination into the actual operation of Mr Peel's bill upon the existing prices*, London 1822

Anon., *A letter to the earl of Liverpool on agricultural distress; its extent, cause and remedy by an old Tory*, London 1822

Anon., *A letter to the right hon. the earl of Eldon on the present state of the agricultural lessees, and their right to relief from the payment of rent*, London 1822

Anon., *A statement of the claims of the West India colonies to a protecting duty against East India sugar, dedicated to William Manning, Esq., M.P.*, London 1823

Anon., *Emancipation of the negro slaves in the West India colonies, with reference to its impolicy and injustice; in answer to Mr. Wilberforce's appeal: by the author of 'A statement of the claims of the West India colonies to a protecting duty against East India sugar'*, London 1824

Anon., *The periodical press of Great Britain and Ireland: or an inquiry into the state of the public journals, chiefly as regards their moral and political influence*, London 1824

Anon., *The corn laws considered, in their effect on the labourer, tenant, landlord &c., &c.*, London 1826

Anon., *Reflections upon the value of the British West Indian colonies, and of the British North American provinces, 1825*, London 1826

SELECT BIBLIOGRAPHY

Anon., *The high price of bread shown to be the result of commercial prosperity, not the cause of national distress; and the dangers of a free trade in corn pointed out; by a warning voice*, London 1827

Anon. ['Atticus'], *Observations on the corn laws*, London 1827

Anon., *Observations on the corn laws, addressed to W. W. Whitmore, Esq. M.P. in consequence of his letter to the electors of Bridgenorth*, London 1827

Anon., *Remarks on certain modern theories respecting rents and prices*, Edinburgh 1827

Anon., *Thoughts on the policy of the proposed alteration of the corn laws*, London 1827

Anon., *On the territorial government and commerce of the East India Company*, London 1829

Anon., *An inquiry into the causes of the long-continued stationary condition of India and its inhabitants; with a brief examination of the leading principles of two of the most approved revenue systems of British India; by a civil servant of the honourable East India Company*, London 1830

Anon., *Public economy concentrated; or a connected view of currency, agriculture, and manufactures*, Carlisle 1833

Anon., *Cheap corn, but no bread: or the results of free corn trade*, London 1835

Anon., *Domestic prospects of the country under a new parliament*, London 1837

Anon., *Canada*, London 1838

Anon., *The Canadian controversy; its origin, nature and merits*, London 1838

Anon., *Hints on the case of Canada, for the consideration of members of parliament*, London 1838

Anon., *Corn and currency; or, how shall we get through the winter?*, London 1839

Anon., *Letter to the duke of Buckingham, on the corn laws; by a practical farmer: 'live and let live'*, London 1839

Anon., *Cheap bread and its consequences; a plain statement*, 9th edn, London 1841

Anon., *A counterplea for the poor, shewing that the cause of their distress is not attributable to the corn laws; by the poor man's friend: in a reply to a pamphlet by the Hon. and Rev. Baptist Noel*, 3rd edn, London 1841

Anon., *The farmers of England; foreign corn, the cost price of producing wheat in some foreign countries*, London 1841

Anon., *The farmers of England: foreign corn: the cost price of producing wheat in some foreign countries, and matters therewith connected: by a merchant, formerly a farmer of sixty thousand acres on the continent*, 2nd edn, London 1841

Anon. ['Veritas'], *A plea from the poor, versus many canting pleas for the poor; showing the ignorant and absurd notions of anti-protection and free-trade mania being advantageous to the commercial polity of the British nation; but, on the contrary, particularly injurious to the working classes; in reply to pamphlets written by J. R. McCulloch, Esq., W. W. Whitmore, Esq., and Rev. B. Noel, M. A.*, London 1841

Anon., *Guilty or not guilty?: being an inquest on the Conservative parliament and ministry*, London–Plymouth 1842

Anon., *Letter to his grace the duke of Wellington &c. &c. &c. on the present state of affairs in India*, London 1842

Anon. ['Britannicus'], *Corn laws defended; or, agriculture our first interest, and the mainstay of trade and commerce*, Leeds 1844

Anon. ['T. B.'], *A few words of friendly caution to the Tories in the houses of parliament*, London 1844

Anon., *The Gemini letters* London 1844

Anon, *How much would the four-pound loaf be lowered by the repeal of the corn laws?*, London 1844

Anon. ['Anglia'], *Is the strong heart of England broken that she does not rise?: being a few words upon the want of high principle and some remarks upon the tergiversation of the periodical press*, London 1844

Anon., *Notes on Canada, with reference to the Act 6–7 Vict.1843, c.29 for reducing the duties on Canadian wheat and wheat flour imported into the United Kingdom*, London 1845

Anon., *An address on the corn laws; by a protectionist*, London 1846

Anon., *Brief considerations with reference to the corn laws, and on the theory of protection generally*, London 1846

Anon., *British industry or foreign labour; a few words addressed to the working classes*, London 1846

Anon., *Corn and consistency; a few remarks in reply to a pamphlet entitled 'Sir Robert Peel and the corn law crisis'*, London 1846

Anon., *A few words on the repeal of the corn laws*, London 1846

Anon., *Our free trade policy examined with respect to its real bearing upon native industry, our colonial system, and the institutions and ultimate destinies of the nation: by a Liverpool merchant*, London–Liverpool 1846

Anon., *Popkins' protest addressed to the House of Lords*, London 1846

Anon. ['F. C.'], *Present condition and future prospects of the country, in reference to free trade and its recent application*, London 1846

Anon., *Protection and free trade; or, the interests of an empire and not of a party; considered in a letter to Lord Viscount Sandon*, London 1846

Anon. ['Cincinnatus'], *Remarks on the Anti-Corn-Law mania, in a letter to his grace the duke of Buckingham*, London 1846

Anon, *Upon the probable influence of a repeal of the corn laws upon the trade in corn*, London 1846

Anon. ['Justus'], *An address to the electors of England, Scotland, and Ireland, for the year 1847 with an introductory letter to his grace the duke of Newcastle*, Leamington–London 1847

Anon., *The commercial policy of Pitt and Peel, 1783–1846*, London 1847

Anon. ['Agricola'], *An oppressed poor in an insolvent nation; a letter to the members of the new parliament*, London 1847

Anon. ['Britannicus'], *Political principles: an answer to the letter from Sir Robert Peel Bart., to his constituents*, 2nd edn, London 1847

Anon., *Remarks on the consequences of the entire change of our colonial policy in British North America*, Edinburgh–London 1847

Anon., *The case of the farmer and labourer stated, in a letter to Benjamin D'Israeli, Esq., M. P.*, London 1851

Anon. ['W. Bull'], *Letter to Sir E. Bulwer Lytton, Bart., commenting upon the policy advocated in his letters to John Bull, Esq.*, London 1851

Anon. [W. W. N.], *'Justice to John Bull'; or, the fallacies of the existing policy called 'free trade': addressed to the 'pupils' of the 'Manchester School', and to the working portion generally of 'John Bull's family', by one of the latter class*, London 1852

[Aristotle], *The politics of Aristotle*, trans. B. Jowett, Oxford 1885

SELECT BIBLIOGRAPHY

—— *Aristotle: the politics*, ed. T. J. Saunders, London 1981

Ashburton, Lord, *The financial and commercial crisis considered*, 3rd edn, London 1847

Bain, Donald, *The egregious and dangerous fallacies of the Anti-Corn-Law league; or, the protection of agriculture not a question with landlords but for the whole kingdom*, Edinburgh 1843

Baines E., *History of the cotton manufacture in Great Britain*, London 1835

Banfield, T. C., *Six letters to the right hon. Sir Robert Peel, Bart., being an attempt to expose the dangerous tendency of the theory of rent advocated by Mr. Ricardo, and by the writers of his school; by a political economist*, London 1843

Barton, John, *Observations on the circumstances which influence the condition of the labouring classes of society*, London 1817

—— *An inquiry into the causes of the progressive depreciation of agricultural labour in modern times*, London 1820

—— *In defence of the corn laws being an inquiry into the expediency of the existing restrictions on the importation of foreign corn with observations on the present social and political prospects of Great Britain*, London 1833, repr. in *John Barton: economic writings*, ed. G. Sotiroff, Regina, Sask. 1962, ii. 5–136

—— *The influence of the price of corn on the rate of mortality*, London 1844, repr. in *John Barton: economic writings*, ii. 139–46

Bell, J., *A vindication of the rights of British landowners, farmers and labourers against the claims of the cotton capitalists to a free trade in corn*, London 1839

[Bentinck, Lord George], *Speech of Lord George Bentinck in the House of Commons, on Sir Robert Peel's letter to the electors of Tamworth, July 20, 1847*, London 1847

Booth, George, *Observations on lowering the rent of land, and on the corn laws*, Liverpool 1814

Boucherett, Auscoghe, *A few observations on corn, currency, and c. with a plan for promoting the interests of agriculture and manufactures*, London 1841

Boyes, John, *Observations addressed to the right hon. Lord Stourton, occasioned by his two letters to the earl of Liverpool*, York 1821

Brougham, Henry, *An inquiry into the colonial policy of the European powers*, Edinburgh 1803

—— *Political philosophy*, London 1843

Burke, Edmund, *Thoughts and details on scarcity originally presented to the right hon. William Pitt in the month of November, 1795*, London 1800

Burn, Richard, *Burn's commercial glance by which merchants, manufacturers, spinners, and others, may, at one view, see the quantity of yarn, and all descriptions of manufactured cotton goods, exported from the different ports etc.*, Manchester 1845

Byles, John, *Sophisms of free trade, and political economy examined*, 2nd edn, London 1850

Caird, J. E., *English agriculture in 1850–1*, London 1852

—— *High farming under liberal covenants the best substitute for protection*, Edinburgh 1849

[Canning, George], *Speech of the right. hon. George Canning in the House of Commons, on the 16th day of March, 1824, on laying before the house the 'Papers in explanation of the measures adopted by His Majesty's government, for the amelioration of the condition of the slave population in the West Indies'*, London 1824

Carey, Henry Charles, *The past, the present, and the future*, London 1848

―――― *The harmony of interests, agricultural, manufacturing and commercial*, 2nd edn, Philadelphia 1851

Cayley, Edward, S., *Corn trade, wages, and rent*, London 1826

―――― *Reasons for the formation of the Agricultural Protection Society, addressed to the industrious classes of the United Kingdom*; published by the Society, London 1844

―――― *Letters to the right honourable Lord John Russell, MP., on the corn laws*, London 1846

Chalmers, T., *On political economy, in connexion with the moral state and moral prospects of society*, Glasgow 1832.

Chapman, William, *Observations on the effects that would be produced by the proposed corn laws on the agriculture, commerce, & population of the United Kingdom*, London 1815

Clarigny, M. Cucheval, *Histoire de la presse en Angleterre et aux États-Unis*, Paris 1857

Colebrook, H. T., *On import of colonial corn*, London 1818

Coleridge, H. N. (ed.), *Specimens of the table-talk of the late S. T. Coleridge*, London 1835

Colquhoun, John Campbell, *The effects of Sir R. Peel's administration on the political state and prospects of England*, 2nd edn, London 1847

Colquhoun, Patrick, *Treatise on the wealth, power and resources of the British empire*, London 1815

Comber, W. T., *An inquiry into the state of national subsistence, as connected with the progress of wealth and population*, London 1808

Copleston, Revd Edward, *A letter to the right hon. Robert Peel, M.P. for the University of Oxford, on the pernicious effects of a variable standard of value, especially as it regards the condition of the lower orders and the poor laws*, Oxford 1819

―――― *A second letter to the right hon. Robert Peel, M.P. for the University of Oxford, on the causes of the increase of pauperism and on the poor laws*, Oxford 1819

Cox, Edward William, *Conservative principles and Conservative policy, a letter to the electors of Tewkesbury*, London 1852

Croker, John Wilson, *Two letters on Scottish affairs from Edward Brawardine Waverley, Esq. to Malachi Malgrowther Esq.*, London–Edinburgh 1826

―――― *The Croker papers, 1808–1857*, ed. B. Pool, London 1967

Crombie, Revd Alexander, *Letters on the present state of the agricultural interest, addressed to Charles Forbes., Esq. M.P*, London 1816

―――― *A letter to Lieut. Col. Torrens M. P. in answer to his address to the farmers of the United Kingdom*, London 1832

Dalbiac, Sir James Charles, *A few words on the corn laws, wherein are brought under consideration certain of the statements which are to be found in the third edition of Mr. McCulloch's pamphlet on the same subject*, London 1841

Davenant, Charles, *Discourses on the public revenues and on the trade of England*, London 1698

Davies, Richard, *A defence of the agricultural interest, comprising, also, a refutation of the statements of the Anti-Corn-Law-League: addressed to the landed proprietors, &c., &c.; to which is added a letter to Lord John Russell*, London 1846

Davy, Sir Humphry, *Elements of agricultural chemistry, in a course of lectures for the Board of Agriculture*, 2nd edn, London 1814

SELECT BIBLIOGRAPHY

Day, George Game, *The farmers and the League: the speech of Mr George Game Day, of St Ives, at Huntingdon, January 27, 1844, on the occasion of forming an Anti-League Association for the county of Huntingon*, 5th edn, London 1844

De Quincey, Thomas, *The logic of political economy* [1844], in *Thomas De Quincey's works*, Edinburgh 1863, repr. 1884, xiii. 234–452

[Disraeli, Benjamin], *The speech of Mr Disraeli, in the House of Commons, on Friday, 15th May, 1846*, London 1846

—— *Lord George Bentinck: a political biography*, 3rd edn, London 1852

—— *Lord Beaconsfield's correspondence with his sister, 1832–52*, London 1886

Drummond, Henry, *Cheap corn best for farmers proved in a letter to George Holme Sumner, Esq. M. P. for the county of Surrey, by one of his constituents*, London 1826

Duncan, Jonathan [The National Anti-Gold-Law League], *The principles of the League explained, versus Sir R. Peel's currency measures, and the partial remedy advocated by the Scotch Banks in a speech delivered at the City Hall, Glasgow, 7th August, 1847*, London 1847

Eden, Sir F. M., *The state of the poor*, 1st publ. 1797, ed. A. G. L. Rogers, London 1926, repr. London 1966

Edye, John, *A letter to William Wilberforce, Esq., M. P., on the consequences of the unrestrained importation of foreign corn*, London 1815

Eliot, Sir Francis Perceval ['Falkland'], *Letters on the political and financial situation of the country in the year 1814, addressed to the earl of Liverpool*, London 1814

—— *Three letters on the financial and political situation of the country, in the year 1815; being a continuation to those of the preceding year*, London 1815

Elliot, John Lettsom, *A letter to the electors of Westminster from a Conservative*, London 1847

—— *A letter to the electors of Westminster from a protectionist*, 2nd edn, London 1848

Ellman, John, *Considerations on the propriety of granting protection to the agriculture of the United Kingdom; with remarks on the report of the select committee of the House of Commons thereon*, London 1821

Evans, George William, *A geographical, historical, and topographical description of Van Diemen's Land, with important hints to emigrants, and useful information respecting the application for grants of land & c. & c.*, London 1822

Ferrand, William Busfeild., *The speech of W. Busfeild Ferrand Esq., at Aylsham in Norfolk, March 4th 1851*, London 1851

Francis, Sir Philip, *Reflections on the abundance of paper in circulation, and the scarcity of specie*, London 1810

Franklin, Benjamin, 'Papers on subjects of general politics', in *The works of Benjamin Franklin*, London 1806

Fullarton, John, *On the regulation of currencies; being an examination of the principles on which it is proposed to restrict within certain limits the future issues in credit of the Bank of England and of other banking establishments throughout the country*, London 1844, 2nd edn, London 1845

Gladstone, John, *The repeal of the corn laws; with its probable consequences briefly examined and considered*, London 1839

—— *Plain facts intimately connected with the intended repeal of the corn laws, its probable effects on the public revenue, and the prosperity of the country*, London 1846

Graham, Sir James, *Corn and currency, in an address to the landowners*, London 1826

[Grenville, Lord], *Substance of the speech of Lord Grenville, on the motion made by the Marquis Wellesley, in the House of Lords, on Friday, the 9th of April, 1813 for the production of certain papers on Indian affairs*, London 1813

Grey, Sir Charles, *Remarks on the proceedings as to Canada, in the present session of parliament: by one of the commissioners, 10 April 1837*, London 1837

Haliburton, T. C., *A reply to the report of the earl of Durham; by a colonist*, London 1839

Hall, George Webb, *Letters on the importance of encouraging the growth of corn and wool, in the United Kingdom of Great Britain and Ireland*, London 1815

────── *The connexion between landlord and tenant, and tenant and labourer, in the cultivation of the British soil; their rights, their duties, and their interests*, London 1841

Harvey, James, *Remunerative price the desideratum, not cheapness*, London 1851

Hawes, Benjamin, *Speech of Benjamin Hawes, Jun., Esq., in opposition to the second reading of the bank charter*, London 1844

Head, Sir Francis Bond, *A narrative by Sir Francis Head, Bart*, 2nd edn, London 1839

Heathfield, Richard, *Elements of a plan for the liquidation of the national debt &c*, London 1819

Heber, Reginald, *Narrative of a journey through the upper provinces of India, from Calcutta to Bombay*, London 1827

Higgins, Godfrey, *An address to the Houses of Lords and Commons, in defence of the corn laws*, London 1826

Higgins, Matthew James, *Is cheap sugar the triumph of free trade?: a letter to Lord John Russell*, London 1847

Hill, John, *An inquiry into the causes of the present high price of bullion*, London 1811

Hoare, Peter Richard, *Thoughts on the alleged depression of agriculture*, London 1816

Holland, George Calvert, *An analysis of the address of F. H. Fawkes, Esq., to the landowners of England*, 2nd edn, London 1841

────── *Letter to J. R. McCulloch, Esq., in answer to his statements on the corn laws*, London 1841

────── *The millocrat: letters to J. G. Marshall in answer to his letter to Lord Fitzwilliam, on the the manufacturing classes*, London 1841

────── *Suggestions towards improving on the present system of the corn-laws; inscribed by permission, to the right hon. Sir Robert Peel, Bart.*, London 1841

Hopkins, Thomas, *Economical enquiries relative to the laws which regulate rent, profit, wages and the value of money*, London 1822

[Horner, Francis], *The Horner papers: selections from the letters and miscellaneous writings of Francis Horner M. P., 1795–1817*, ed. K. Bourne and W. B. Taylor, Edinburgh 1994

Horton, Robert Wilmot, *Outline of a plan of emigration in a report of the Select Committee on the Employment of the Poor in Ireland*, London 1823

────── *Exposition and defence of the Earl Bathurst's administration of the affairs of Canada, when colonial secretary, during the years 1822 to 1827, inclusive*, London 1838

Humboldt, Friedrich Heinrich Alexander von, *Personal narrative of travels to the*

SELECT BIBLIOGRAPHY

equinoctial regions of the new continent during the years 1799–1804, London 1814–29

―――― *The travels and researches of Alexander von Humboldt, being a condensed narrative of his journeys in the equinoctial regions of America and Asiatic Russia*, ed. W. Macgillvray, London 1832

Hume, David, 'Of public credit' [1752], 'Of commerce' [1752], and 'Of money' [1752], in *Hume*, ed. K. Haakonssen, Cambridge 1994

Huskisson, William, *The question concerning the depreciation of our currency, stated and examined*, London–Edinburgh–Dublin 1810

―――― *Speech of the right hon. W. Huskisson in the House of Commons, Tuesday, the 11th of June, 1822 on Mr Western's motion concerning the resumption of cash payments*, London 1823

―――― *The speeches of the right honourable William Huskisson, with a biographical memoir, supplied to the editor from authentic sources*, London 1831

Jackson, Samuel, *Commercial distress temporary; arising from natural and periodical causes, and not from the effects of the corn laws: letter I: addressed to the right hon. Earl Fitzwilliam*, London 1839

Jacob, William, *Considerations on the protection required by British agriculture, and on the influence of the price of corn on exportable productions*, London 1814

―――― *A letter to Samuel Whitbread, Esq. M.P, being a sequel to 'Considerations on the protection required by British agriculture', to which are added remarks on the publications of a fellow of University College Oxford: of Mr. Ricardo, and Mr Torrens*, London 1815

―――― *Report on the trade in foreign corn, and on the agriculture of the north of Europe: to which is added, an appendix of official documents, averages of prices, shipments, stock on hand in the various exporting countries, &c., &c. &c.*, London 1826

―――― *Observations on the cultivation of poor soils, as exemplified in the colonies for the indigent, and for orphans in Holland*, London 1828

―――― *Report presented to the Lords of the committee of His Majesty's Privy Council for Trade respecting the agriculture and the trade in corn, in some of the continental states of Europe*, London 1828

―――― *An historical inquiry into the production and consumption of precious metals*, London 1831

Johnston, J. F. W., *What can be done for British agriculture?*, London 1842

Jones, Revd Richard, *An essay on the distribution of wealth and on the sources of taxation*, London 1831

Liebig, Justus, *Organic chemistry, in its applications to agriculture and physiology*, London 1842

Linkwater, Timothy, *How to right the nation by an equitable adjustment of capital as a compromise under free trade and cash payments*, London 1848

List, G. Friedrich, *Das nationale system der politischen oekonomie*, 2nd edn, Stuttgart 1844

―――― *National system of political economy*, trans. G. A. Matile, ed. S. Colwell, Philadelphia 1856

[Liverpool, Lord], *The speech of the earl of Liverpool, delivered in the House of Lords, on Tuesday, the 26th day of Feb., 1822, on the subject of the agricultural distress of the country, and financial measures proposed for its relief*, London 1822

Lloyd, Samuel Jones, *Thoughts on the separation of the departments of the Bank of England*, London 1844

Locke, John, *Short observations on a printed paper, entitled, 'For encouraging the coining of silver in England, and after for keeping it here'*, 1st publ. London 1691, in *The works of John Locke Esq.*, fol. edn, London 1714, ii

────── *Some considerations of the consequences of the lowering of interest and raising of the value of money: in a letter sent to a member of parliament*, London 1692

────── *Further considerations concerning raising the value of money; wherein Mr Lowndes's arguments for it in his late report concerning 'An essay for the ammendment of the silver coins', are particularly examined*, 1st publ. London 1695, fol. edn, London 1714

Lockhart, J. G., *Narrative of the life of Sir Walter Scott*, London 1906, repr. London 1931

Logan, W. H., *The Scottish banker; or a popular exposition of the practice of banking in Scotland*, London 1838, 2nd edn, London 1844

[Londonderry, Lord], *Substance of the speech of the marquis of Londonderry, delivered in the House of Commons, on Friday, the 15th day of Feb., 1822, on the subject of the agricultural distress of the country, and the financial measures proposed for its relief*, London 1822

Low, David, *Elements of practical agriculture; comprehending the cultivation of plants, the husbandry of the domestic animals, and the economy of the farm*, Edinburgh 1834

Lowe, Joseph, *The present state of England in regard to agriculture, trade and finance; with a comparison of the prospects of England and France*, London 1822

Loyd, Samuel Jones, *Thoughts on the separation of the departments of the Bank of England*, London 1844

Lushington, W. J., *Six letters addressed to the agriculturists of the county of Kent, on the doctrines of the Anti-Corn-Law League, and the subject of free trade*, London 1843

Lytton, E. Bulwer, *Letters to John Bull, Esq., on affairs connected with his landed property, and the persons who live thereon*, London 1851

McCulloch, John Ramsay, *Principles of political economy, with a sketch of the rise and progress of the science*, 2nd edn, London 1830

────── *Statements illustrative of the policy and probable consequences of the proposed repeal of the corn laws, and the imposition in their stead of a moderate and fixed duty on foreign corn when entered for consumption*, London 1841

Macdonnell, Alexander, *Considerations on negro slavery with authentic reports illustrative of the actual condition of the negroes in Demerara*, London 1824

────── *Free trade; or an inquiry into the expediency of the present corn laws; the relations of our foreign and colonial trade; the advantages of our navigation system; the propriety of preventing combinations among workmen; and the circumstances which occasion a derangement of the currency; comprising a general investigation of the alterations lately adopted, and still further meditated in the commercial policy of the country*, London 1826

────── *Colonial commerce; comprising an inquiry into the principles upon which discriminating duties should be levied on sugar, the growth respectively of the West India possessions, of the East Indies, and of foreign countries*, London 1828

────── *An address to the members of both houses of parliament on the West India question*, London 1830

SELECT BIBLIOGRAPHY

Macpherson, D., *The history of the European commerce with India; to which is subjoined, a review of the arguments for and against the trade with India, and the management of it by a chartered company, with an appendix of authentic accounts*, London 1812

McQueen, James, *The West India colonies; the misrepresentations circulated against them by the Edinburgh Review, Mr Clarkson, Mr Cropper, &c. &c. examined and refuted*, London 1824

——— *General statistics of the British empire*, London 1836

——— *Statistics of agriculture, manufactures and commerce drawn up from official and authentic documents*, Edinburgh–London 1850

Malcolm, Sir John, *A political history of India from 1784 to 1823*, London 1826

Malthus, Thomas Robert, *An essay on the principle of population*, 1st edn, London 1798, ed. 'Royal Economic Society', London 1926, repr. London 1966

——— *An essay on the principle of population or a view of its past and present effects on human happiness; with an inquiry into our prospects respecting the future removal or mitigation of the evils which it occasions*, 2nd edn, London 1803, ed. D. Winch, Cambridge 1992

——— *Observations on the effects of the corn laws and of a rise or fall in the price of corn on the agriculture and general wealth of the country*, London 1814

——— *The grounds of an opinion on the policy of restricting the importation of foreign corn*, London 1815

——— *Principles of political economy considered with a view to their practical application*, 1st publ. 1820, ed. J. Pullen, Cambridge 1989

Marryat, John, *A reply to the arguments in various publications recommending an equalization of the duties on East and West Indian sugar*, London 1823

Marshall, George, *A view of the silver coin and coinage of Great Britain from 1662 to 1837*, London 1837

Marshall, John, *A digest of all the accounts relating to the population, productions, revenues, financial operations, manufactures, shipping, colonies, commerce, &c. &c, of the United Kingdom of Great Britain and Ireland*, London 1834

[Maydwell], *Maydwell's analysis of Cobden's addresses, with remarks on Mr Greg's speech at the great League meeting at Manchester*, London 1843

Miers, John, *Travels in Chile and La Plata*, London 1826

Mill, James, *Commerce defended*, London 1808

——— *History of British India*, London 1817

——— *Elements of political economy*, London 1821

Mill, John Stuart, *Principles of political economy, with some of their applications to social philosophy*, 1st publ. London 1848, ed. W. J. Ashley, London 1909

Miller, Samuel, *Suggestions for the equalisation of the land tax; with a view to provide the means of reducing the malt duties: and a statement of the legal rights and remedies unequally assessed to land tax in particular districts or places*, London 1843

[Mirabeau, Marquis de], *On the corn laws; being a digest from the oeconomical table: an attempt towards ascertaining and exhibiting the source, progress, and employment of riches, with explanations, by the friend of mankind, the celebrated marquis de Mirabeau: digested from the English translation as printed for W. Owen*, trans. 1766, repr. London 1815

Moreau, César, *State of the trade of Great Britain with all parts of the world, 1697–1822*, London 1822

Moreton, A. H., *Thoughts on the corn laws, addressed to the working classes of the county of Gloucester*, London 1839

[NAPIC], *Circulars*, 1850–1

────── *Report of the acting committee to the special meeting of the general committee of the National Association for the Protection of Industry and Capital throughout the British Empire*, London 1850

────── *Report of the sub-committee on currency, to the acting committee of the National Association for the Protection of Industry and Capital throughout the British Empire*, London 1850

────── *Tracts on protection*, London 1850

────── *Declaration read, approved and unanimously adopted at a meeting of the members and friends of the National Association for the Protection of Industry and Capital throughout the British Empire, 12th Dec. 1851*, London 1851

────── *Report of the conference of provincial delegates with the acting committee*, 3 March 1851

Napier, W. F. P., *Observations on the corn law, addressed to Lord Ashley*, 2nd edn, London 1841

Nevile, Revd Christopher, *The new tariff*, London 1842

────── *The sliding scale, or a fixed duty*, London 1842

────── *Corn and currency, in a letter to A. Alison, Esq.*, London 1846

Newdegate, Charles Newdigate, *Letter to the right hon. H. Labouchere, M. P. & c. & c; on the balance of trade, ascertained from the value of all articles imported during the last four years*, London 1849

────── *A second letter to the right hon. H. Labouchere*, 2nd edn, London 1849

────── *A third letter to the right. hon. H. Labouchere*, London 1851

────── *A fourth letter to the right hon., H. Labouchere*, London 1851

────── *A letter to the right hon. J. W. Henley, M. P. & c. & c., on the balance of trade, ascertained from the market value of all articles imported, as compared with the market value of all articles exported, during the year 1851*, London 1852

Ogilvy, T., *Statistical evidence affecting the question of the navigation laws*, Edinburgh–London 1849

Ogle, Nathaniel, *Direct or indirect taxation?: or, should the laws, customs and excise duties be abolished, how is the revenue now obtained from them to be replaced?*, London 1843

Parker, C. S. (ed.), *Sir Robert Peel from his private papers*, London 1891–9

────── (ed.), *Life and letters of Sir James Graham, 1792–1861*, London 1907

Parnell, Sir Henry, *On financial reform*, 3rd edn, London 1830

Parry, Charles Henry, *The question of the necessity of the corn laws, considered, in their relation to the agricultural labourer, the tenantry, the landholder, and the country*, London 1816

[Peel, Sir Robert], *The speech of the right honourable Sir Robert Peel, Bart. in the House of Commons, on Mr Villiers' motion on the corn laws*, 2nd edn, London 1839

────── *A letter from Sir Robert Peel to the electors of Tamworth*, London 1847

────── *Memoirs by the right honourable Sir Robert Peel*, ed. Lord Mahon and E. Cardwell, London 1857

Porter, G. R., *The progress of the nation, in its various social and economical relations from the beginning of the nineteenth century*, London 1836–43

Preber, A. L. R. P. de V. M., *Taxation, revenue, expenditure, power, statistics, and*

SELECT BIBLIOGRAPHY

debt of the whole British empire; their origin, progress, and present state; with an estimate of the capital resources of the empire, and a practical plan for applying them to the liquidation of the national debt, London 1833

Preston, Richard, An address to the fundholder, the manufacturer, the mechanic and the poor; on the subject of the corn laws, London 1815

—— Further observations on the state of the nation, London 1816

Putt, Charles, Observations on the corn laws, or bread for thirty millions of inhabitants; without the importation of a single grain of corn: without loss to the farmer, the landlord, or the fundholder, London 1840

[Redesdale, Lord], Observations upon the importation of foreign corn: with the resolutions moved by Lord Redesdale in the House of Lords, March 29, 1827; and his speech thereupon, May 15, 1827, London 1828

Renny, J. H., Reflections upon the corn laws, and upon the their effects on the trade, manufactures, and agriculture of the country, and on the condition of the working classes, London 1841

Report from the committee of the Cirencester and Fairford Farmers' Club, to a meeting of the agriculturists of Gloucestershire and the adjoining counties, held at the King's Head in Cirencester, on Monday the 22nd April, 1844, London 1844

Report from the select committee on the high price of bullion, London 1819 in E. Cannan (ed.), The paper pound, 1797–1821, London 1819

Report of the proceedings at a meeting of the landowners, farmers, and others resident in the county of York, interested in the welfare of British agriculture, for the establishment of the Yorkshire Protective Society, London 1844

Ricardo, David, The high price of bullion, a proof of the depreciation of bank notes, London 1810

—— An essay on the influence of a low price of corn on the profits of stock; shewing the inexpediency of restrictions on importation; with remarks on Mr Malthus's two last publications 'An inquiry into the nature and progress of rent'; and 'Grounds of an opinion on the policy of restricting the importation of foreign corn', 2nd edn, London 1815

—— On the principles of political economy and taxation, London 1817, in The works and correspondence of David Ricardo, ed. P. Sraffa, Cambridge 1951, i

—— On protection to agriculture, 4th edn, London 1822, in Works and correspondence of David Ricardo, iv. 201–26

—— Essay on political economy: supplement to the Encyclopedia Britannica, vi, pt i, Edinburgh 1823.

[Richards], Report of Mr Richards to the Colonial Secretary, respecting the waste lands in Canada, and emigration, repr. in The Canadas, compiled from documents furnished by John Galt, Esq. with the fullest information for emigrants, ed. Andrew Picken, London 1832

Richards, James, A letter to the earl of Liverpool, on the agricultural distress of the country; its cause demonstrated in the unequal system of taxation; and a just system suggested, 2nd edn, London 1822

Salomons, David, The corn laws; their effects on the trade of the country considered, with suggestions for a compromise, London 1841

[Saunders, Otley & Co.], Hints for the formation of reading and book societies in every part of the United Kingdom with an improved plan for rendering them more extensively available and efficient, London 1841

Say, Jean-Baptiste, *A treatise on political economy; or the production, distribution, and consumption of wealth*, trans. C. R. Princep, London 1821

Scott, Sir Walter, *A letter to the editor of the Edinburgh Weekly Journal, from Malachi Malagrowther Esq. on the proposed change of currency and other late alterations, as they affect or are intended to affect the kingdom of Scotland*, 3rd edn, Edinburgh 1826

——— *A second letter to the editor of the Edinburgh Weekly Journal, from Malachi Malagrowther, Esq. on the proposed change of currency and other late alterations, as they affect or are intended to affect the kingdom of Scotland*, 3rd edn, Edinburgh 1826.

——— *A third letter to the editor of the Edinburgh Weekly Journal from Malachi Malagrowther, Esq., on the proposed change of currency and other late alterations, as they affect, or are intended to affect, the kingdom of Scotland*, London–Edinburgh 1826

——— *Thoughts on the proposed change of currency and other late alterations, as they affect, or are intended to affect, the kingdom of Scotland*, Edinburgh 1826

Scrope, George Julius Poulett, *On credit currency, and its superiority to coin, in support of a petition to the establishment of a cheap, safe, and sufficient circulating medium*, London 1830

——— *The currency question freed from mystery*, London 1830

——— *An examination of the bank charter question, with an inquiry into the nature of a just standard of value, and suggestions for the improvement of our monetary system*, London 1833

——— *Political economy for plain people applied to the past and present state of Britain*, 1st publ. London 1833, 3rd edn, London 1873

Senior, Nassau, *Two lectures on population, delivered to the University of Oxford in Easter Term, 1828; to which is added, a correspondence between the author and the Rev. T. R. Malthus*, London 1829

Sheffield, Lord, *A letter on the corn laws and on the means of obviating the mischiefs and distress, which are rapidly increasing*, 2nd edn, London 1815

Sinclair, Sir John, *Observations on the report of the bullion committee*, London 1810

——— *Address to the owners and occupiers of land, in Great Britain and Ireland*, Edinburgh 1822

Sismondi, J.-C.-L. Simonde de, *Nouveaux principes d'économie politique, ou de la richesse dans ses rapports avec la population*, 2nd edn, Paris 1827

——— *Études sur les sciences sociales*, Paris 1837

Smith, Adam, *Theory of moral sentiments*, London 1759

——— *An inquiry into the nature and causes of the wealth of nations*, ed. R. H. Campbell, A. S. Skinner and W. B. Todd, Oxford 1976

Smith, J. B., *Report of the directors to a special general meeting of the chamber of commerce and manufactures at Manchester, on the effects of the administration of the Bank of England upon the commercial and manufacturing interests of the country*, London 1840

Smith, T. S., *On the economy of nations*, London 1842

Southey, Robert, *Sir Thomas More: or, colloquies on the progress and prospects of society*, London 1829

Spence, William, *Britain independent of commerce; or proofs, deduced from an investigation into the true causes of the wealth of nations, that our riches, prosperity, and*

power are derived from resources inherent in ourselves and would not be affected, even though our commerce were annihilated, 2nd edn, London 1807
—— *Agriculture the source of the wealth of Britain; a reply to the objections urged by Mr. Mill, the Edinburgh Reviewers, and others, against the doctrines of a pamphlet entitled 'Britain independent of commerce', with remarks on the criticism of the monthly reviewers on that work*, London 1808
—— *The objections against the corn bill refuted; and the necessity of this measure to the vital interests of every class of the community, demonstrated*, 4th edn, London 1815
—— *Tracts on political economy*, London 1822
Stanhope, Lord, *Letter to the labouring classes of Great Britain and Ireland, October 7th 1850*, London 1850
Stanley, A. P. (ed.), *The life and correspondence of Thomas Arnold*, London 1844
Talleyrand-Périgord, C. M. de, *Essai sur les avantages à retirer des colonies nouvelles*, repr. Paris 1840
Tatham, Revd Edward, *On the scarcity of money and its effects upon the public; with the expedients by which they alone can be remedied and the nation saved from ruin*, 5th edn, Oxford 1819
Taylor, G, *An enquiry into the principles which ought to regulate the imposition of duties on foreign corn, in answer to 'Statements illustrative of the policy and probable consequences of the proposed repeal of the existing corn laws', by J. R. McCulloch, Esq.*, London 1842
Taylor, John, *A catechism of the currency*, 3rd edn, London 1836
Taylor, John (ed.), *Selections from the works of the Baron de Humboldt*, London 1824
Tennant, C., *Letters on systematic colonization and the bill now before parliament*, London 1831
Thompson, Henry, *Free corn ruinous to England*, 4th edn, London 1839
Thompson, Perronet, *Catechism of the corn laws*, London 1828
Thornton, Henry, *An enquiry into the nature and effects of the paper credit of Great Britain*, 1st publ. London 1802, ed. F. A. Hayek, London 1939
Tocqueville, Alexis de, *De la democratie en Amérique*, Paris 1836
Tooke, Thomas, *Thoughts and details on the high and low prices of the last thirty years*, London 1823
—— *An inquiry into the currency principle; the connexion of currency with prices*, 2nd edn, London 1844
Torrens, Robert, *Essay on the external corn trade*, London 1815
—— *A letter to the right honourable, the earl of Liverpool, on the state of the agriculture of the United Kingdom, and on the means of relieving the present distress of the farmer, and of securing him against the recurrence of similar embarassment*, London 1816
—— *Address to the farmers of the United Kingdom, on low rates of profit in agriculture and in trade*, London 1831
—— *A letter to the right honourable Sir Robert Peel, Bart. M. P., on the condition of England and on the means of removing causes of distress*, London 1843
—— *An inquiry into the practical working of the proposed arrangements for the renewal of the charter of the Bank of England*, London 1844
Turner, Samuel, *Considerations upon the agriculture, commerce, and manufactures of the British empire; with observations on the practical effect of the bill of the right.*

hon. Robert Peel, for the resumption of cash payments by the Bank of England; and also upon the pamphlet lately published by David Ricardo, Esq., entitled, 'Protection to agriculture', London 1822

Ure, Andrew, *The philosophy of manufactures: or, an exposition of the scientific, moral, and commercial economy of the factory system of Great Britain*, London 1835

Urquhart, David, *The parliamentary usurpations of 1819 and 1844, in respect to money, considered: in a letter to the burgesses and electors of Stafford*, London 1847

Vince, C. A., *Mr. Chamberlain's proposals; what they mean and what we shall gain by them, with a preface by the right. hon. Joseph Chamberlain M.P.*, London 1903

Vyvyan, Sir Richard, *A letter from Sir Richard Vyvyan Bart., M.P., to his constituents upon the commercial and financial policy of Sir Robert Peel's administration*, London 1842

Ward, Sir Henry George, *Mexico in 1827*, London 1828

Ward, William, *Remarks on the commercial legislation of 1846: addressed to the Lord Mayor and the livery of London*, London 1847

West, Edward, *Essay on the application of capital to land*, London 1815

Weyland, John, *The principles of population and production, as they are affected by the progress of society; with a view to moral and political consequences*, London 1816

Whately, Revd Richard, *Introductory lectures on political economy*, London 1831

Whitmore, William Woolryche, *A letter to the electors of Bridgenorth, upon the corn laws*, London 1826

Williams, Albert, *The law or the league: which?: a letter to Robert Palmer, Esq., M.P.*, London 1843

—— *Curious lights on strange anomalies; a letter to Lord George Bentinck*, London 1847

[Wilson, Isaac and Augustus Delaforce], *Proclamation of the working classes against free trade and for protection, produced by the metropolitan trades delegates*, London 1852

Wilson, John, *Some illustrations of Mr McCulloch's political economy*, Edinburgh–London 1826

Wilson, Robert, *An enquiry into the causes of the high prices of corn and labour, the depression of our foreign exchanges and high prices of bullion, during the late war; and consideration of the measures to be adopted for relieving our farming interest*, Edinburgh 1815

Wright, John, *Remarks on the erroneous opinions which led to the new corn law; and also on those of the bullionists, on a circulating medium; and pointing out the only protection to agriculture*, London 1823

Wyatt, Harvey, *An address to the owners and occupiers of land on the importance of an adequate protection to agriculture*, London 1827

Young, George Frederick, *Address of the general committee of the National Association for the Protection of Industry and Capital throughout the British Empire to the friends of protection to all British interests, 12 Dec. 1850*, London 1850

—— *Free-trade fallacies refuted; in a series of letters to the editor of the Morning Herald*, repr. London 1852

—— *Letter from G. F. Young to the duke of Richmond, Dec. 18th, 1852*, London 1853

SELECT BIBLIOGRAPHY

Secondary sources

Acworth, A. W., *Financial reconstruction in England, 1815–22*, London 1925

Alborn, T., *Conceiving companies: joint-stock politics in Victorian England*, London 1998

Aspinall, A., *Politics and the press, c. 1780–1850*, London 1949

Barber, W. J., *A history of economic thought*, London 1967

Barnes, D. G., *A history of the English corn laws*, London 1930

Barnes, J. J., *Authors, publishers and politicians: the quest for an Anglo-American copyright agreement, 1815–1854*, London 1974

Baumol, W. J., 'Say's (at least) eight laws, or what Say and James Mill may really have meant', *Economica* xliv (1977), 145–62

Bayly, C. A., *Imperial meridian: the British empire and the world, 1780–1830*, London 1989

Beer, M., *An inquiry into physiocracy*, London 1939

Bennet, S., 'Revolutions in thought: serial publication and the mass market for reading', in Shattock and Wolff, *Victorian periodical press*, 225–57

Berg, M., *The machinery question and the making of political economy, 1815–1848*, Cambridge 1980

Biagini, E., *Liberty, retrenchment and reform: popular Liberalism in the age of Gladstone, 1860–1880*, Cambridge 1992

Black, R. D. Collinson, *A catalogue of pamphlets on economic subjects published between 1750 and 1900 and now housed in Irish libraries*, Belfast 1969

Blake, R., *The Conservative party from Peel to Thatcher*, London 1985

Blaug, M., *Economic theory in retrospect*, Cambridge 1962

Bowen, I., 'Country banking, the note issues and banking controversies in 1825', *Economic Journal History Supplement* iii (1938), 68–88

Bradfield, B. T., 'Sir Richard Vyvyan and the country gentlemen, 1830–1834', *EHR* lxxxiii (1968), 729–43

Brady, A., *William Huskisson and Liberal reform: an essay on the changes in the economic policy in the twenties of the nineteenth century*, Oxford 1928

Brent, R., *Liberal Anglican politics: Whiggery, religion, and reform, 1830–1841*, Oxford 1987

Briggs, A., 'Thomas Attwood and the economic background of the Birmingham Political Union', *CHJ* ix (1948), 190–216

Brock, M., *The Great Reform Act*, London 1973

Brock, W., *Lord Liverpool and Liberal Toryism, 1820–1827*, 2nd edn, London 1967

Brown, L., 'The Board of Trade and the tariff problem', *EHR* lxviii (1953), 394–421

—— *The Board of Trade and the free trade movement, 1830–1842*, Oxford 1958

Brown, L., *Victorian news and newspapers*, Oxford 1985

Burrow, J. W., *Whigs and Liberals: continuity and change in English political thought*, Oxford 1988

Cain, P. J., 'J. A. Hobson, Cobdenism and the radical theory of economic imperialism, 1898–1914', *EcHR* xxxi (1978), 565–84

—— 'Political economy in Edwardian England: the tariff reform controversy', in A. O'Day (ed.), *The Edwardian age*, London 1979, 35–59

—— 'Gentlemanly capitalism and British expansion overseas, II: new imperialism, 1850–1945', *EcHR* xl (1987), 3–11

────── *British imperialism: innovation and expansion, 1688–1914*, London 1993
────── and A. G. Hopkins, 'The political economy of British expansion overseas, 1750–1914', *EcHR* xxxiii (1980), 463–90
Carrothers, W. A., *Emigration from the British Isles*, London 1929
Ceadel, M., *The origins of war prevention: the British peace movement and international relations, 1730–1854*, Oxford 1996
Checkland, S. G., 'The Birmingham economists, 1815–50', *EcHR* 2nd ser. i (1948), 1–19
────── 'The propagation of Ricardian economics in England', *Economica* xvi (1949), 40–52
────── 'The prescriptions of the classical economists', *Economica* xx (1953), 43–70
────── *Scottish banking: a history, 1695–1973*, London 1975
Claeys, G. and P. Kerr, 'Mechanical political economy', *CJE* v (1981), 251–72
Clapham, Sir J., *The Bank of England: a history*, Cambridge 1944
Clive, J., *Scotch reviewers: the Edinburgh Review, 1802–1815*, London 1957
Coats, A. W. (ed.), *The classical economists and economic policy*, London 1971
Coleman, B., *Conservatism and the Conservative Party in nineteenth-century Britain*, London 1988
Coleman, D. C. (ed.), *Revisions in mercantilism*, London 1969
Collins, M., *Money and banking in the UK: a history*, London 1988
Conacher, J. B., *The Peelites and the party system, 1846–52*, Newton Abbot 1972
Cookson, J. E., *Lord Liverpool's administration, 1815–1822: the crucial years*, Edinburgh 1975
Corry, B. A., 'The theory of the economic effects of government expenditure in English classical political economy', *Economica* xxv (1958), 34–48
Crosby, T. L., *Sir Robert Peel's administration, 1841–46*, London 1976
────── *English farmers and the politics of protection, 1815–1852*, Hassocks 1977
Crowley, J. E., 'Neo-mercantilism and "The wealth of nations": British commercial policy', *HJ* xxxiii (1990), 339–60
Daunton, M. J., 'Payment and participation: welfare and state-formation in Britain, 1900–1951', *P&P* cl (Feb. 1996), 169–216
Davis, L. E. and R. A. Huttenback, *Mammon and the pursuit of empire: the economics of British imperialism*, Cambridge 1988
Deane, P., *The evolution of economic ideas*, Cambridge 1978
Eastwood, D., 'Robert Southey and the intellectual origins of romantic Conservatism', *EHR* civ (1989), 308–31
────── *Governing rural England: tradition and transformation in local government, 1780–1840*, Oxford 1994
────── 'Ruinous prosperity: Robert Southey's critique of the commercial system', *The Wordsworth Circle* xxv (Spring 1994), 72–6
Edsall, N. C., *Richard Cobden: independent Radical*, Cambridge, Mass. 1986
Ellegård, A., 'The readership of the periodical press in mid Victorian Britain', *Göteborgs Universitets Årsskrift* lxiii (1957), 1–28
Erickson, A. B., *The public career of Sir James Graham, 1792–1861*, Oxford 1952
Fairlie, S., 'The nineteenth-century corn law reconsidered', *EcHR* 2nd ser. xviii (1965), 562–75
────── 'The corn laws and British wheat production, 1829–76', *EcHR* 2nd ser. xxii (1969), 88–116

Farrant, S., 'John Ellman of Glynde in Sussex', *AgHR* xxvi (1978), 77–88

Fay, C. R., *Great Britain from Adam Smith to the present day: an economic and social survey*, London 1929

―――― *The corn laws and social England*, Cambridge 1932

Feaveryear, A., *The pound sterling: a history of English money*, 2nd edn, Oxford 1963

Fetter, F. W., 'The economic articles in the *Quarterly Review* and their authors, 1809–52', *JPE* lxvi (1958), 45–64

―――― 'The economic articles in the *Quarterly Review*: articles, authors and sources', *JPE* lxvi (1958), 150–70

―――― 'The politics of the bullion report', *Economica* xxvi (1959), 99–120

―――― 'The economic articles in *Blackwood's Edinburgh Magazine*, and their authors, 1817–1853, pts i, ii', *SJPE* vii (June 1960), 85–107, 213–31

―――― 'Economic controversy in the British reviews, 1802–1850', *Economica* xxxii (1965), 424–37

―――― *The development of British monetary orthodoxy, 1797–1875*, Cambridge, Mass. 1965

―――― 'The rise and decline of Ricardian economics', *HPE* i (1969), 767–841

―――― *The economist in parliament, 1780–1868*, Durham, NC 1980

Fisher, D. R., 'Peel and the Conservative party: the sugar crisis of 1844 reconsidered', *HJ* xviii (1975), 279–302

Fontana, B., *Rethinking the politics of commercial society: the Edinburgh Review, 1802–1832*, Cambridge 1985

Fryer, C. E., 'British North America under representative government: (A) Lower Canada (1815–1837)', in J. H. Rose and others (eds), *The Cambridge history of the British empire*, vi, Cambridge 1830, 234–50

Gambles, A., 'Rethinking the politics of protection: Conservatism and the corn laws, 1830–1852', *EHR* cxiii (1998), 928–52

―――― 'Free trade and state formation: the political economy of fisheries policy in Britain and the UK, c. 1780–c. 1850', *JBS* forthcoming

Gash, N., *Reaction and reconstruction in English politics, 1832–1852*, Oxford 1965

―――― 'After Waterloo: British society and the legacy of the Napoleonic wars', *TRHS* 5th ser. xxviii (1978), 145–57

―――― *Lord Liverpool: the life and political career of Robert Bankes Jenkinson, second earl of Liverpool*, Cambridge, Mass. 1984

―――― *Mr Secretary Peel: the life of Sir Robert Peel to 1830*, 2nd edn, London 1985

―――― *Pillars of government and other essays on state and society, c. 1770–c. 1880*, London 1986

―――― *Sir Robert Peel: the life of Sir Robert Peel after 1830*, 2nd edn, London 1986

Ghosh, P. R., 'Disraelian Conservatism: a financial approach', *EHR* xcix (1984), 268–96

Gordon, B., 'Say's law, effective demand, and the contemporary British periodicals, 1820–1850', *Economica* xxxii (1965), 438–46

―――― 'Criticism of Ricardian views on value and distribution in the British periodicals, 1820–1850', *HPE* i (1969), 370–87

―――― *Political economy in parliament, 1819–1823*, London 1976

―――― *Economic doctrine and Tory-Liberalism, 1824–1830*, London 1979

Graham, Walter, *Tory criticism in the Quarterly Review, 1809–1853*, New York 1918

Grampp, W. D., 'How Britain turned to free trade', *Business History Review* lxi (Spring 1987), 86–112
Green, E. H. H., 'Radical Conservatism: the electoral genesis of tariff reform', *HJ* xxviii (1985), 667–92
────── 'Rentiers versus producers?: the political economy of the bimetallic controversy', *EHR* ciii (1988), 588–612
────── 'The bimetallic controversy: empiricism belimed or the case for the issues', *EHR* cv (1990), 673–83
────── *The crisis of Conservatism: the politics, economics and ideology of the British Conservative party, 1880–1914*, London 1995
Gregory, T. E. (ed.), *British banking statutes and reports, 1832–1928*, Oxford 1929
Gwynn, J. T., 'The Madras district system and land revenue to 1818', in H. H. Dodwell and others (eds), *The Cambridge history of the British empire*, IV: *British India*, Cambridge 1929
Harling, P., 'Rethinking "Old Corruption"', *P&P* cxlvii (1995), 127–58
────── *The waning of 'Old Corruption': the politics of economical reform in Britain, 1779–1846*, Oxford 1996
────── and P. Mandler, 'From "fiscal-military" state to laissez-faire state', *JBS* xxxii (1993), 44–70
Harlow, V. T., *The founding of the second British empire*, London 1952–64
Hawkins, A., 'Lord Derby and Victorian Conservatism: a reappraisal', *ParlHist* vi (1987), 280–301
Heckscher, E. F., *Mercantilism*, 1st publ. 1935, repr. London 1994
Henderson, W. O., *Friedrich List: economist and visionary, 1789–1846*, London 1983
Higgs, H., *The physiocrats: six lectures on the French Économistes of the 18th century*, London 1897
Hill, R. L., *Toryism and the people, 1832–1846*, London 1929
Hilton, A. J. B., *Corn, cash, commerce: the economic policies of the Tory governments, 1815–1830*, Oxford 1977
────── 'Peel: a reappraisal', *HJ* xxii (1979), 585–614
────── *The age of atonement: the influence of evangelicalism on social and economic thought, 1785–1865*, Oxford 1988
Hirst, F. W., *Free trade and other fundamental doctrines of the Manchester School*, New York 1968
Holland, B., *The fall of protection, 1840–1850*, London 1913, repr. Philadelphia 1980
Hollander, S., 'Malthus and the post-Napoleonic depression', *HPE* i (1969), 306–35
────── 'Ricardo and the corn laws: a revision', *HPE* ix (1977), 1–47
────── *Classical economics*, Oxford 1987
────── 'More on Malthus and protection', *HPE* xxvii (1995), 531–7
Hont, I. and M. Ignatieff (eds), *Wealth and virtue: the shaping of political economy in the Scottish enlightenment*, Cambridge 1983
Horsefield, J. K., 'The bankers and the bullionists in 1819', *Journal of Political Economy* lvii (1949), 442–8
────── 'The origins of the Bank Charter Act, 1844', in T. S. Ashton and R. Sayers (eds), *Papers in English monetary history*, Oxford 1953, 109–25

Howe, A. C., 'Bimetallism, c. 1880–1898: a controversy re-opened?', *EHR* cv (1990), 377–91
────── 'Free trade and the City of London, c. 1820–1870', *History* lxxvii (1992), 391–410
────── *Free trade and Liberal England, 1846–1946*, Oxford 1997
Imlah, A. H., *Economic elements in the pax Britannica*, Cambridge, Mass. 1958
Jenkins, B., *Henry Goulburn, 1784–1856: a political biography*, Liverpool 1996
Johnston, H. J. M., *British emigration policy, 1815–1830: 'shovelling out paupers'*, Oxford 1972
Jones, A., *Powers of the press: newspapers, power and the public in nineteenth-century England*, Aldershot 1996
Jones, W. D., *Prosperity Robinson: the life of Viscount Goderich, 1782–1859*, London 1967
Kemp, B., 'The general election of 1841', *History* xxxvii (1952), 146–57
────── 'Reflections on the repeal of the corn laws', *VS* v (1962), 189–205
Kennedy, P., 'The costs and benefits of British imperialism', *P&P* cxxv (1989), 186–92
Kitson-Clark, G., *Peel and the Conservative Party: a study in party politics, 1832–41*, 2nd edn, London 1964
Koss, S., *The rise and fall of the political press in Britain*, I: *The nineteenth century*, London 1981
Lawrence, J. *Speaking for the people: party, language and popular politics in England, 1867–1914*, Cambridge 1998
Lawson, P., *The East India Company: a history*, London 1993
Lubenow, W. C., *The politics of government growth: early Victorian attitudes toward state intervention, 1833–1848*, Newton Abbot 1971
McCloskey, D. N., 'Magnanimous Albion: free trade and British national income, 1841–1881', *Explorations in Economic History* xvii (1980), 303–20
────── 'Reply to Peter Cain', *Explorations in Economic History* ix (1982), 208–10
McCord, N., *The Anti-Corn-Law League, 1838–46*, London 1958
Macdonagh, O. O. M., *Early Victorian government, 1830–1870*, London 1977
McDowell, R. B., *British Conservatism, 1832–1914*, London 1955
Macintyre, A., 'Lord George Bentinck and the protectionists: a lost cause?', *TRHS* 5th ser. xxxix (1989), 141–65
McKeown, T., 'The politics of corn law repeal and theories of commercial policy', *British Journal of Political Science* xix (1989), 353–80
Magnusson, L., *Mercantilism: the shaping of an economic language*, London 1994
Mandler, P., *Aristocratic government in the age of reform: Whigs and Liberals, 1830–1852*, Oxford 1990
────── 'Tories and paupers: Christian political economy and the making of the new poor law', *HJ* xxxiii (1990), 81–103
Marrison, A., *British business and protection, 1903–1932*, Oxford 1996
────── (ed.), *Free trade and its reception, 1815–1960*, London 1998
Martin, G., *Britain and the origins of Canadian confederation, 1837–67*, London 1995
Matthew, H. C. G. (ed.), *The Gladstone diaries*, VI: *1861–1868*, Oxford 1978
────── 'Disraeli, Gladstone, and the politics of mid-Victorian budgets', *HJ* xxii (1979), 615–43
────── *Gladstone, 1809–1874*, Oxford 1986

────── *The Gladstone diaries*, X: *1881–83*, Oxford 1990
Meek, R. L., *The economics of physiocracy: essays and translations*, London 1962
Michie, M., *An enlightenment Tory in Victorian Scotland: the career of Sir Archibald Alison*, McGill 1997
Milgate, M. and S. C. Stimson, *Ricardian politics*, Princeton 1991
Milne, M., 'The "veiled editor" unveiled: William Blackwood and his magazine', *Publishing History* xvi (1984), 87–103
────── 'The management of a nineteenth-century magazine: William Blackwood and Sons, 1827–47', *Journal of Newspaper and Periodical History* i (1985), 24–33
Moore, D. C., 'The other face of reform', *VS* v (1961–2), 7–34
────── 'The corn laws and high farming', *EcHR* xviii (1965), 544–61
Morgan, E. V., *The theory and practice of central banking, 1797–1813*, Cambridge 1943
Morley, J., *The life of Richard Cobden*, London 1908
Morley, T., ' " The arcana of that great machine": politicians and *The Times* in the late 1840's', *History* lxxiii (1988), 38–54
Morrell, W. P., *British colonial policy in the age of Peel and Russell*, 2nd edn, London 1960
Neeson, J., *Commoners: common right, enclosure and social change in England, 1700–1820*, Cambridge 1993
Newbould, I., 'Sir Robert Peel and the Conservative party, 1832–1841: a study in failure?', *EHR* lxcviii (1983), 529–57
────── *Whiggery and reform, 1830–41: the politics of government*, London 1990
Northcote, Sir S. H., *Twenty years of financial policy: a summary of the chief financial measures passed between 1842 and 1861, with a table of budgets*, London 1862
Nye, J. V., 'The myth of free-trade Britain and fortress France: tariffs and trade in the nineteenth century', *JEcH* li (1991), 23–46
O'Brien, D. P., *The classical economists*, Oxford 1974
────── *Thomas Joplin and classical macroeconomics: a re-appraisal of classical monetary thought*, London 1993
O'Brien, P. K, 'The costs and benefits of British imperialism, 1846–1914', *P&P* cxx (1988), 163–200
────── 'The costs and benefits of British imperialism, 1846–1914: reply', *P&P* cxxv (1989), 186–99
Offer, A., 'The British empire, 1870–1914: a waste of money?', *EcHR* xlvi (1993), 215–38
Oliphant, M., *Annals of a publishing house: William Blackwood and his sons: their magazine and friends*, Edinburgh 1897
Paglin, M., *Malthus and Lauderdale: the anti-Ricardian tradition*, New York 1961
Palmer, R. R., *J.-B. Say: an economist in troubled times*, Princeton 1997
Palmer, S., *Politics, shipping and the repeal of the navigation laws*, Manchester 1990
Parry, J. P., *Democracy and religion: Gladstone and the Liberal Party, 1867–1875*, Cambridge 1986
────── *The rise and fall of Liberal government in Victorian Britain*, London 1993
Peake, C. F., 'Henry Thornton and the development of Ricardo's economic thought', *HPE* x (1978), 193–212

Peers, D. M., 'Between Mars and Mammon: the East India Company and efforts to reform its army, 1796–1832', *HJ* xxxiii (1990), 385–401
Perkin, H., *Origins of modern English society*, London 1969
Pocock, J. G. A., *Virtue, commerce and history: essays on political thought and history, chiefly in the eighteenth century*, Cambridge 1985
Potter, J., 'The British timber duties, 1815–60', *Economica* xxii (1955), 122–36
Poynter, J. R., *Society and pauperism: English ideas on poor relief, 1795–1834*, London 1969
Prentice, A., *History of the Anti-Corn-Law League*, 1st publ. 1853, ed. W. H. Challoner, London 1968
Pressnell, L. S., *Country banking in the industrial revolution*, Oxford 1956
Prest, J., *Politics in the age of Cobden*, London 1977
——— 'A large amount or a small?: revenue and the nineteenth-century corn laws', *HJ* xxxix (1996), 467–78
Pullen, J., 'Malthus on agricultural protection: an alternative view', *HPE* xxvii (1995), 517–29
Ramsay, A. A. W., *Sir Robert Peel*, London 1928
Ramsbotham, R. B., 'The revenue administration of Bengal, 1765–86', in H. H. Dodwell and others (eds), *The Cambridge history of the British empire*, IV: *British India*, Cambridge 1929
Ramsden, J., *The age of Balfour and Baldwin, 1902–1940*, London 1978
Rashid, S., 'David Robinson and the Tory macroeconomics of *Blackwood's Edinburgh Magazine*', *HPE* x (1978), 258–70
Read, D., *Peel and the Victorians*, Oxford 1987
Roberts, D., *Victorian origins of the British welfare state*, New Haven 1960
Robinson, R. and J. Gallagher, 'The imperialism of free trade, 1814–1915', *EcHR* 2nd ser. vi (1953), 1–15
Rothschild, E., 'Adam Smith and conservative economics', *EcHR* xlv (1992), 74–96
Sabine, B. E. V., *A history of the income tax*, London 1966
Sack, J. J., 'The memory of Pitt and the memory of Burke: English Conservatism confronts its past, 1806–1829', *HJ* xxx (1987), 623–40
——— *From Jacobite to Conservative: reaction and orthodoxy in Britain, c. 1760–1832*, Cambridge 1993
Schonhardt-Bailey, C., 'Linking constituency interests to legislative voting behaviour: the role of district economic composition in the repeal of the corn laws', in J. A. Phillips (ed.), *Computing parliamentary history: George III to Victoria*, Edinburgh 1994, 86–118
——— *The rise of free trade*, London 1997
——— 'Interests, ideology and politics: agricultural trade policy in nineteenth-century Britain and Germany', in A. Marrison (ed.), *Free trade and its reception, 1815–1960*, London 1998, i. 63–81
——— (ed.), *Free trade: the repeal of the corn laws*, Bristol 1996
Schumpeter, J. A., *History of economic analysis*, New York 1954
Semmel, B., 'Malthus: "physiocracy" and the commercial system', *EcHR* xvii (1965), 522–35
——— *The rise of free trade imperialism: classical political economy and the empire of free trade imperialism, 1750–1850*, Cambridge 1970

────── *The Liberal ideal and the demons of empire: theories of imperialism from Adam Smith to Lenin*, London 1993

Shattock, J., *Politics and reviewers: the Edinburgh and the Quarterly in the early Victorian age*, Leicester 1989

────── and M. Wolf (eds), *The Victorian periodical press: samplings and soundings*, Leicester 1982

Shehab, F., *Progressive taxation: a study of the development of the progressive principle in the British income tax*, Oxford 1953

Shine, H. C., *The Quarterly Review under Gifford: identification of contributors, 1809–1824*, Chapel Hill 1949

Skinner, A. S. and T. Wilson (eds), *Essays on Adam Smith*, Oxford 1976

Smith, R. B., *The Gothic bequest: medieval institutions in British thought, 1688–1863*, Cambridge 1987

Spring, D., 'Earl Fitzwilliam and the corn laws', *American Historical Review* lix (1954), 287–304

────── and T. L. Crosby, 'George Webb Hall and the Agricultural Association', *JBS* ii (1986), 115–31

Stedman-Jones, G., 'Rethinking Chartism', in his *Languages of class: studies in English working-class history, 1832–1982*, Cambridge 1983, 90–178

Stewart, R. M., 'The ten hours and sugar crises of 1844', *HJ* xxii (1969), 35–57

Stewart, R. W., *The politics of protection: Lord Derby and the protectionist party, 1841–1852*, Cambridge 1971

────── *The foundation of the Conservative party, 1830–1867*, London 1978

Stokes, E. T., *The English Utilitarians and India*, Oxford 1959

────── 'Bureaucracy and ideology: Britain and India in the nineteenth century', *TRHS* 5th ser. xxx (1980), 131–56

Strout, A. L., *A bibliography of articles in Blackwood's Magazine, 1817–1825*, Lubbock, Texas 1959

────── (ed.), 'Some unpublished letters of John Gibson Lockhart to John Wilson Croker', *Notes & Queries* clxxxv (9 Oct. 1943), 222; clxxxvi (4 Nov. 1944), 207; clxxxix (22 Sept. 1945), 124

Sykes, A., *Tariff reform in British politics, 1903–1913*, Oxford 1979

Thompson, A. S., 'Tariff reform: an imperial strategy, 1903–1913', *HJ* xl (1997), 1033–54.

Thompson, N., *The people's science: the popular political economy of exploitation and crisis, 1816–1834*, Cambridge 1984

Trentmann, F., 'The transformation of fiscal reform: reciprocity, modernisation, and the fiscal debate within the business community in early-twentieth-century Britain', *HJ* xxxix (1996), 1005–48

Tribe, K., *Land, labour and economic discourse*, London 1978

────── *Strategies of economic order: German economic discourse*, Cambridge 1995

Turner, M. J., 'Before the Manchester School: economic theory in early nineteenth-century Manchester', *History* lxxix (1994), 216–41

Vann, J. D. and R. T. Van Arsdel, *Victorian periodicals: a guide to research*, New York 1978

────── and R. T. Van Arsdel (eds), *Victorian periodicals and Victorian society*, Aldershot 1994

Wahrman, D., *Imagining the middle class: the political representation of class in Britain, c. 1780–1840*, Cambridge 1995

Walker-Smith, D., *The protectionist case in the 1840s*, Oxford 1933, repr. New York 1970
Ward, J. T., *Sir James Graham*, London 1967
Waterman, A. M. C., *Revolution, economics and religion: Christian political economy, 1798–1833*, Cambridge 1991
The Wellesley index to Victorian periodicals, 1824–1900, Toronto 1972
White, L. H., *Free banking in Britain: theory, experience and debate, 1800–1845*, Cambridge 1984
Winch, D., *Classical political economy and colonies*, London 1965
—— 'Adam Smith: Scottish moral philosopher as political economist', HJ xxxv (1992), 91–113
—— *Riches and poverty: an intellectual history of political economy in Britain, 1750–1834*, Cambridge 1996
Wood, J. C., *British economists and empire*, Beckenham 1983
Wrigley, E. A., 'The classical economists, the stationary state, and the industrial revolution', in G. D. Snooks (ed.), *Was the industrial revolution necessary?*, London 1994, 27–42

Unpublished theses

Hardy, W. E., 'Conceptions of manufacturing advance in British politics, c. 1800–1847, with special reference to parliament, governments and their advisers', unpubl. DPhil. diss. Oxford 1994
Milne, M., 'The politics of *Blackwood's*, 1817–1846: a study of the political, economic and social articles in *Blackwood's Edinburgh Magazine*, and of selected contributors', unpubl. PhD diss. Newcastle 1984

Index

agriculture: as domestic market for manufactures, 34, 49, 52, 71, 72, 207–9; and employment, 81, 221; improvement of, 28–9, 66–7, 208; size of sector, 71. *See also* protectionism
Alborn, Timothy, 91–2
Alison, Sir Archibald, 243; on 1832 Reform Act and Bank of England, 128; on 1832 Reform Act and deflation, 123; on 1832 Reform Act and rise of free trade, 206; on 1832 Reform Act and governance of India, 187–8; on 1832 Reform Act and representation of interests, 59, 60, 180, 214, 219; on agriculture's economic importance, 71, 72, 81; on Bank Charter Act (1844), 137–8, 139; on Chartism, 219, 221–2; on colonial system, 183–4; on commercial crisis (1837), 137, 94n; on commercial crisis (1847), 141; on corn imports and manufactured exports, 68; on direct taxation, 236; on economic consequences of corn law repeal, 207; on education, 84–5; on foreign and colonial trade, 71–2; *Free trade and a fettered currency*, 134, 223; California gold discoveries, 227; on governance of India, 187, 189; on indirect taxation, 75; on Irish famine, 207–8; on living standards, 218; on repeal of navigation laws, 213; on philanthropy, 85; on definition of political economy, 78; on population, 67, 139; on Whig budgets, 61
allotments, 52
Almack, John: on Anti-Corn-Law League, 80
Anti-Corn-Law League: *Anti-bread tax circular*, 79; as 'Anti-national faction', 81; and 'bread tax', 83; and class, 79, 83–4; and distribution of wealth, 79–80; and Ricardianism, 66; and social discourse, 79–84
Anti-Malthusianism, 168, 169, 172, 181–2, 216
Aristotle, 95
Arnold, Thomas, 135, 243

Ashburton, *see* Baring, Alexander
Attwood, Matthias, 243; on deflation, 102, 105; on monetary policy and economic depression, 120
Attwood, Thomas, 243; on currency, 117
Aytoun, William Edmonstoune, 243; on A. Alison, 142; 'British agriculture and foreign competition' (1850), 204; on Chartism, 219; on corn law repeal and Bank Charter Act, 141; and Disraeli, 16; on domestic markets, 74–5; on electoral limits of protection, 232; on foreign trade, 210; on free trade as a sectional strategy, 206; on Great Exhibition (1851), 228; on Henry Carey, 208–9, 221; on 'high farming', 208; and NAPIC, 204; on Peel's financial politics, 238; on periodical press, 10; on protection as the 'cause of labour', 205

balance of trade: impact of free trade and monetary policy on, 210–11
Bank Charter Act (1833), 126–7; committee of secrecy on, 127–8
Bank Charter Act (1844), 117–18, 127, 135; and contraction of the money supply, 137–42, 224–5; constitutionalist critiques of, 137, 225–6; and currency school, 135–6; as deflationary, 137, 138, 224–7; and distribution of wealth, 134, 138, 224–7; and economic instability, 134, 140, 141, 223; and financial crisis (1847), 136, 141, 142, 223; fixed fiduciary issue, 136, 139; and fixed value of gold standard, 136; and home market, 139, 140; impact of combined with free trade, 140–1, 222–4; and living standards, 139; and unitary issue, 132
Bank of England: Bank Charter Act (1833), 126–7, (1844), 117–18, 127; branch banking of, 111, 115, 127; and centralisation of note issue, 127, 130; committee of secrecy on (1832), 127–8; monopoly of joint-stock status,

127–8; publication of accounts of, 127, 128; suspension of cash payments (1797), 92. *See also* Bank Charter Act, resumption of cash payments, monetary sovereignty
banking, *see* Bank of England, Bank Charter Act (1833), Bank Charter Act (1844), banking school, country banks, currency school, joint stock banks, monetary sovereignty
Banking Act (Scottish and Irish) 8 & 9 Vict.c.38, 127, 132, 133
Banking Copartnership Act (1826), 109, 122, 123. *See also* joint stock banks
banking school, 117, 135, 136
Baring, Alexander, 243; criticism of bullionism, 94; on deflation, 103; on financial crisis (1847), 137; on advantages of a paper currency, 97
Baring, Francis, 243; on provincial banks, 133
Barrow, John, 244; on emigration, 166; on financial anti-colonialism, 157, 48n.; on Opium War, 189
Barton, John, 244; on relationship between corn prices and mortality, 81–2; on manufacturing industry, 72; on national self-sufficiency in food, 48, 135n.; debate with Ricardo on mechanisation, 78; on the definition of wealth, 77–8
Barty, J. S.: on relative living standards, 218
Bayly, C. A., 147, 150
Bell, John: on deflationary consequences of corn law repeal, 76
Bennet, Scott, 12
Bentinck, Lord William George Frederick, 76, 244; on balance of trade, 210; on Bank Charter Act (1844), 134, 78n.; on imperial preference, 199, 213, n.61; on social consequences of free trade, 216
Berg, Maxine, 3
Berkeley, George Grantley, 243; on relative living standards, 218
bimetallism, 102, 104 n.82, 131
Birmingham School, 136–7
Blackwood, John: and NAPIC, 204
Blackwood, William, 13, 15
Blackwood's Edinburgh Magazine: circulation of, 11–13; Conservatism of, 13–14: content of, 16–17; editorial character of, 13–14; protectionism of, 204–5
Booth, George: on politics of warehousing, 30; on free trade and unemployment, 32–3
Boucherett, Auscoghe, 140
Brady, Alexander, 149
Brent, Richard, 5
British North America, *see* Canada
budget of 1842, 61–2, 62–3, 66, 74, 196–7, 219, 237–8
bullionism, 90; and Bank Charter Act (1844), 117, 135; and banking panic (1825), 108–9; and resumption of cash payments, 93; and currency school, 127; and free trade in corn, 113; and neutrality of money, 92, 96; and relative property values, 97–8; *Report from the select committee on the high price of bullion* (1810–11), 92; theory of convertibility, 92–3, 127; theory of depreciation, 93, 97–8; theory of foreign exchange, 93; theory of intrinsic value, 93; theory of overissue, 93, 108
bullionism, criticisms of: constitutionalist, 98–9, 105–6, 121, 137, 142, 225–6; for contraction of money supply, 112–13, 122–3, 137–41, 223–4; by advocates of convertibility, 93; on exchangeable value of gold, 120–1; on relationship with free trade in corn, 113, 114, 118, 140–1, 223–4; on social and economic influence of monetary policy, 92, 95, 96, 97, 100, 104, 105, 118, 124, 127, 129, 130, 131, 133, 137, 138, 224–5; on theory of depreciation, 101–2; on theory of exchanges, 94; on theory of intrinsic value, 94–5; on theory of overissue, 94
Burke, Edmund: biography of, 58; *Thoughts and details on scarcity*, 30
Burn, Richard: *Burn's commercial glance*, 208; commercial statistics of, 184 n.46
Burrow, J., 5
Byles, John, 244; on the 'Great British zollverein', 213; *Sophisms of political economy*, 220; on deflation and redistribution, 224; on wages and consumption, 221

Caird, John, 244; *High farming and liberal covenants*, 108

INDEX

California gold discoveries: inflationary impact of, 227
Canada: corn law (1843), 196–7; debates on colonisation of, 193–4; constitutionalist case against Durham's report, 192–3; corn preference, 196–7; and demand for British manufactures, 179, 198; Durham's report (1838), 191, 192, 193; the Oregon dispute, 198; rebellion (1837), 177, 191, 195; impact of repeal of corn laws on, 197–8, 214; timber preference, 155, 156, 157, 196–7
Canning, George, 244; and Conservative press, 15; on powers of the executive, 98; on mercantilism, 95; on neutrality of money, 96
Carey, Henry, 244; on agriculture and the home market, 209; criticisms of Malthus and Ricardo, 209; *Harmony of interests*, 208–9; on T. de Quincey, 209; on relationship between social harmony and economic change, 221
Cayley, Edward Stillingfleet, 244; on agriculture as market for manufactures, 72; on economic diversification, 74; on free trade and bullionism, 140–1; on free trade and manufacturing exports, 68; on living standards, 82–3; on the relationship between the price of corn and wages, 51; on the profit motive, 77
census of 1851, 216
Chalmers, Thomas, 181–2, 244–5
Chamberlain, Joseph: and 'bread tax', 234; critique of Cobden, 176
Chartism: and 'class legislation', 219; as a consequence of free trade, 219; responses to, 221
chrematistics, 78
Christian political economy, 5–7. *See also* evangelical economics
Clay, Henry, 245; protectionism of, 69
Cobbett, William, 245; on small notes, 109
Cobden, Richard, 245; opposition to 1842 budget, 61, 63; on contraction of foreign markets by corn laws, 68; cosmopolitan free trade, 176–7, 212; on cost of empire, 184; on free trade and international relations, 69–70, 148, 177, 214, 228; on imperialism, 148, 184 n.41
Coleridge, Samuel Taylor: on colonisation of Canada, 195

colonial trade: security of, 35, 154, 155, 165, 179, 181, 183, 198, 213; and economic stability, 70, 153–4, 155, 185, 193, 198; comparative value of, 155, 156, 183, 184, 212. *See also* empire: political economy of
colonies, *see* Canada, colonial trade, colonisation, emigration
colonisation: 'concentrated' colonisation, 168 n.99, 194; importance of social and religious institutions to, 173, 194; as nationalisation, 195; patriotism of, 171, 182–3; Spanish, 173
Colquhoun, John Campbell, 245; on corn law repeal and unemployment, 81
commerce, 31. *See also* colonial trade, domestic markets, foreign trade
'Condition of England Question', 45, 53, 55, 77, 82, 134
conservative, 6 n.26
conservatism: constitutional language of, 1–2, 8–9, 19–22, 57–64, 97–9, 105–8, 114–15, 122–4, 127–30, 132–4, 137–8, 159–61, 187–8, 191–3, 213–14, 225–6, 230–1, 234–8, 239–41; 'constructive conservatism', 150, 158, 164, 176; and critiques of economic liberalism, 1; and historicism, 19, 42, 150, 151, 152; and imperialism, 150, 158, 185–6, 191, 196; and social and economic thought, 7–9
Conservative party: as an organ of constitutional defence, 59, 62, 239; split of (1846), 56, 199, 239
consumption, *see* demand
convertibility: as distinct from bullionism, 93–4, 131, 135; concept of, 92–3; flexible gold standard, 124. *See also* bimetallism, bullionism, gold standard
Copleston, Edward, 245; critique of bullionist theory of depreciation, 101–2; on deflation after 1819, 101; on redistribution by depreciation of currency, 98; on recomposition of national debt, 106; on property tax, 107
corn law (1804), 27
corn law (1814): select committee (1813), 29; terms of, 27
corn law (1815), 27; and agricultural productivity, 28–9; and deflation, 31–2; and food policy, 27–30; and international relations, 27; and Ireland, 29; and population growth, 27–8; and relationship between price

281

of corn and wages, 32–3; and profits in manufacturing, 33–4; and national self-sufficiency, 28–9; and warehousing, 29, 37

corn law (1822), 37, 113 n.136

corn law (1828), 45–6, 47–8; and national self-sufficiency, 45–6

corn law (1842), 65; as food policy, 65–6; sliding scale as opposed to fixed duty, 65, 66

corn law (1843), 196–7

corn law, repeal of (1846): and Bank Charter Act (1844), 140–2, 222–5; as a constitutional concession, 58, 64; and deflation, 76; and democratic reform, 231, 240–1; financial consequences of, 75; and foreign trade, 209–10; and destruction of home market for manufactures, 72, 74, 207–8; imperial consequences of, 177, 197–8, 199, 214; and Ireland, 66, 207

Coulton, David Trevena, 245; on 1852 general election, 241; on California gold discoveries, 227

country banks: criticisms of 1825, 108, 112; social and economic benefits of, 110–12, 115

Cox, Edward William, 245; *Conservative principles and conservative policy*, 241

Creevy, Thomas, 245; on EIC monopoly, 159

Croker, John Wilson, 245; on Anti-Corn-Law League, 79; on 1842 budget, 63; on Whig reforms in Canada, 192; on constitutional defence, 241; on relationship between corn law and manufactured exports, 69, 209; on corn law repeal and democracy, 240; on corn law repeal and the empire, 198, 212; on distribution, 80; on imperial preference, 214; his intimacy with ministers, 15; on repeal of the navigation laws, 213; on the representation of interests, 62; on Scottish small notes, 114–15; as 'Edward Brawardine Waverley', 114 139n.

Croly, George, 245; on colonisation of Canada, 195; on deflation and debts, 105; on deflation and demand, 103; on governance of India, 187, 189–90; on the territorial constitution, 58

Crosby, T. L., 9

currency: contraction of money supply, 112–13, 113–14, 117, 122, 124, 138, 139, 141, 142; effect of depreciation of value of, 97–8, 225; expansion of money supply, 118, 124–6, 138–9; insulation of from foreign exchange fluctuations, 130–1, 133. *See also* bullionism, bullionism criticisms of, deflation, gold standard, monetary sovereignty

currency school, 117, 127, 135

Curwen, John Christian, 245; on property tax, 39–40

Dallas, Eneas Sweetland, 245; on the influence of the press, 14–15, 17

Davenant, C., 126 40n.

Day, George Game: on Anti-Corn-Law League, 80

De Quincey, Thomas, 245; on agricultural improvement, 66; on Anti-Corn-Law League, 79; on colonisation of Canada, 195; and Henry Carey, 209; on Ricardo's view of the corn laws, 73; on Ricardo's theory of diminishing returns, 65; on the Opium War, 189

deflation: and capital market, 122; and corn law repeal, 76; and contraction of supply of money and credit, 100, 103; and burden of debt, 31, 100, 102, 103, 105, 106–7, 121, 138; and destruction of demand, 103–4; and economic depression, 37–8, 125; and home colonisation, 170; and legitimacy of government, 123; magnitude of, 100–1, 120; and national debt management, 122; and protectionism, 31–2, 224; and sectoral balance, 103; and abolition of small notes, 109; and social conditions, 138; and burden of taxes, 32, 100, 102, 138

demand: and country banks, 111–12; impact of deflation on, 103–4; and avoidance of depressions, 50–1, 73, 83, 168, 207–9; impact of free trade on, 75; impact of national debt on, 108; deficiency of and poverty, 169; Malthus on, 154; protection as a device for the boosting of, 44–5, 54–5, 68, 140, 170, 208–9; and small notes, 109–11. *See also* distribution, underconsumption

depression, 1816, 1821–2: and monetary policy, 38, 100, 102, 106; protectionist response to, 37–9, 40

INDEX

depression, 1825: bullionist interpretations of, 108, 112; and country banks, 108; and the empire, 154 n.36; and excess capital, 168; monetary policy as cause of, 109, 112–13, 117

depression, 1829, 48, 122

depression, 1836–7, 1839, 72; culpability of Bank of England for, 127, 129; monetary policy as cause of, 119–20, 121–2; and underconsumption, 83

depression, 1847, 137; and Bank Charter Act, 136, 141, 142, 223; and foreign competition, 219

Dickenson, John: on domestic currency and the foreign exchanges, 130, 131; on joint-stock banks, 130

direct taxation: assessed taxes, 235; and distribution of wealth, 55, 84 n.171; economic benefits of, 40; equalisation of burdens of, 75–6, 235–7; local, 234; poor rates, 235; as a corollary of protection, 55, 234. *See also* property tax

Disraeli, Benjamin, 245; on banking reform, 225–6; and *Blackwood's*, 208 n.30; and Conservative press, 15–16; on the empire, 176; on Huskisson, 210; on imperial preference, 212; on the Irish railways loan (1847), 142; on nature of manufacturing industry, 72; on the Queen's speech (Feb. 1851), 232, 235; on reciprocity, 210, 212, 221; on social consequences of free trade, 216

distribution of wealth: of capital, 53; effect of colonisation on, 180, 182; strategies for greater equitability of, 55, 77, 82, 138–9, 170, 221; effect of free trade on, 80; effect of expansion of money supply on, 118, 124–6; and political stability, 57, 124–6, 219; debate on the role of the state in, 220–2. *See also* living standards, underconsumption

domestic markets: and corn law repeal, 72, 74, 207–9; and balanced economic change, 54–5, 103, 134–5, 139–40, 154, 170, 181, 207–9, 228; and stable manufacturing advance, 35–6, 70, 71, 72, 215; and political stability, 54–5, 221–3. *See also* demand, colonial trade, foreign trade

Douglas, Howard, 246; on the colonial system, 197; on corn law repeal and unemployment, 81; on imperial preference, 196

Duncan, Jonathan, 246; on monetary policy, 226

East India Company (EIC), criticisms of monopoly over India trade: by merchants, 158–9; by Adam Smith, 159; by Whig constitutionalists, 159

East India Company (EIC), defences of monopoly over India trade: concept of 'commercial sovereignty', 159–60, 186–7; constitutional, 160, 161; economic, 162; experiential, 161–2; financial, 163; historical, 160

East India Company (EIC), removal of monopoly over China trade, 186, 189; constitutionalist case against, 187–8; constitutionalist case for, 186–7; historicist case against, 187; and wars, 189

East Indies: Dutch empire in, 160; value of exports to, 155; patronage in, 161; Portugese empire in, 160; trade, 161–2

Eastwood, David, 7 n.29

Eden, Sir Frederick Morton, 246; on working-class consumption, 33

Edinburgh Review: on imperialism, 151, 157; political economy of, 3

education, 84–5

Edwards, Edward, 246; on deflation and agricultural depression, 121; on deflation and redistribution, 122–3; on home colonisation, 170; on inflation 124; on joint-stock banks, 131; on rural poverty, 52–3

Elgin, Thomas Bruce, 246; on colonisation, 194; on rural poverty, 52–3; on relationship between taxation and distribution, 55

Elliot, William, 246; on Ireland as a granary, 29

Ellis, George, 95–6, 246; on British empire in India, 159–60; on Malthus's principle of population, 28

Ellman, John, 246; on agricultural report (1821), 37

emigration, colonial, 149; and exportation of capital, 165, 166, 167, 168, 181, 194; and economic stability, 165, 167, 168, 172, 181, 185, 193; and cohesion of the empire, 166, 193; and exportation of labour, 165, 166, 167, 181; and markets for British manufactures, 165, 168, 181,

283

183, 193, 198; patriotism of, 171; and poverty, 165–6; state assisted, 166, 168, 182, 194. See also colonisation, home colonisation
emigration, foreign, 171
empire: and conservatism, 150; decline of French, 151; and historicism, 150–2; and international relations, 149; and national power, 149; 'Second British Empire', 147. See also colonial markets, colonisation, emigration, imperialism
empire, political economy of: autarchy, 156; and employment of capital, 187; and character of economic change, 149, 154, 155, 179, 198; and markets for manufactures, 154, 179, 181, 183, 185, 193, 198; and profits, 153, 193; and stationary state, 153–4, 181. See also colonial trade, colonisation, emigration, imperialism
evangelical economics, 6–7; and Liberal Toryism, 6–7

Fay, C. R., 149
Fetter, F. W., 4
financial crisis, see depression
financial reform association, 241
Fletcher, M.: on colonial trade, 153; on free trade and domestic markets, 44; on navigation laws, 151; on theoretical reasoning, 151
Fontana, B., 3
foreign exchanges: bullionist theory of, 93–4; insulation of domestic money supply from fluctuations of, 130–1, 133–4
foreign trade: and corn law repeal, 209–10; compared with home and colonial, 35, 70, 71, 155, 181, 183–5, 212–13; idea of, 70; insecurity of, 35–6, 69, 185, 207; effect of value of sterling on, 70. See also colonial trade, domestic markets
Fraser's Magazine: circulation of, 12; content of, 16
free trade: and bullionism, 134, 138, 140; cosmopolitan, 69–70, 148, 176–7; and democratic reform, 240–1; and financial policy, 75; and imperialism, 147–8; and international relations, 152–3, 189–90; and manufacturing profits, 67; and reciprocity, 183. See also Cobden, Ricardo

free trade, criticisms of: and Christianity, 220; and domestic demand, 50; and British economic growth, 9–10; as food policy, 65; philosophical, 57, 78–9, 151, 161–2, 215–16; as a sectional strategy, 206, 207; social, 57, 77–85, 169, 216–19. See also protectionism
Fullarton, John, 246; and 'banking school', 135

Gallagher, J., 147
Galt, John, 246; on depression of 1821–2, 40; on economic benefits of direct taxation, 40; on emigration, 166, 167–8; on imperial preference, 157; on national debt redemption, 38–9, 107
Gash, N., 7
Gemini letters, 136
general election: 1847, 205; 1852, 230, 232, 233, 239, 241
gentlemanly capitalism, 148
Gladstone, William Ewart, 246; on imperial preference, 196
Gleig, George Robert, 246; on Indian tax reforms, 164
gold standard: constitutionalist case for, 97–8; and 'Old Corruption', 91; return to (1819), 93, 100–8; suspension of (1797), 92; and mid Victorian orthodoxy, 89–90. See also bullionism, resumption of cash payments
gold standard, criticisms of: constitutionalist, 97–9; advantages of paper currency, 96, 97, 124; mutable value of gold, 94–5, 99, 121, 124. See also bullionism, criticisms of, deflation
Gooch, Thomas Sherlock, 246; on property tax, 39
Gordon, B., 4
Goulburn, Henry, 246; on imperial preference, 183
Graham, Sir James, 247; *Corn and currency* (1826), 136; on domestic market for manufactures, 72
Granby, Marquess of (John Henry Manners, 5th duke of Rutland), 247; on national self-sufficiency in food, 67
Great Exhibition, 1851: protectionist criticism of, 228–9
Green, E. H. H.: 231
Greenfield, William, 247; on convertibility, 93–4
Grenville, Lord, 247; on East India Company's monopoly, 159

INDEX

Harling, P., 2, 5, 58
Harlow, V. T., 147
Hawes, Benjamin, 247; and 'banking school', 135
Head, Sir Francis Bond, 247; on the constitution of the Canadas, 193
Heathfield, Richard: on capital levy, 107
Herries, John Charles, 247; on imperial preference, 179
high farming: protectionist attitude to, 208
Hilton, A. J. B.: 5, 6, 7, 45 n.119, 46 n.120, 118, 149–50
Holland, George Calvert, 247; and 1842 corn law, 63; on corn law repeal and unemployment, 81; on domestic markets and economic stability, 70
home colonisation: impact on the economy of, 170; as an alternative to emigration, 149; as a response to poverty, 52–3, 165, 169, 182; as a corollary of protection, 53, 169
Hopkins, T.: critique of Ricardo, 42–3
Horton, Robert John Wilmot, 247; on union of the Canadas, 192–3; and state-assisted emigration, 165, 169, 174
Howe, A. C.: 2, 5, 233
Hume, David: *Of money*, 104
Hume, David, appeals to: on constitutional reform and colonial governance, 180; on money supply and distribution, 126 n.40; on economic diversification, 74; on money supply, 104
Hume, James Deacon, 65
Hume, Joseph, 247; anti-imperialism of, 157 n.48; opposition to 1842 income tax, 61
Huskisson, William, 247; and Conservative press, 15; on emigration, 174; and imperial preference, 149, 152, 178; on Ireland as a market for British manufactures, 29; appeals to legacy of, 69, 178, 210; and mercantilism, 95; and Ricardo, 36 n.64

imperialism: 'free trade imperialism', 147–8, 158; and national power, 149, 153, 178. *See also* Canada, empire, India, West Indies
imperial preference, 148, 152; and balance of British economy, 155–6, 179, 183, 196; and international relations, 152; and political cohesion of the empire, 156, 157, 177, 179, 196–7, 198, 213, 214; as an instrument of political representation, 180, 214; and shipping, 179, 196; and timber, 155, 196–7. *See also* corn law (1843), corn law, repeal of (1846), imperial consequences of
income tax, *see* direct taxation, property tax
India: Afghan war, 189; debate on British direct rule in, 163, 187; character of British imperium in, 161, 164, 190; as a market for British manufactures, 159, 162, 177; patronage in, 160–1, 187; tax reforms in, 163–4; zemindary settlement, 163–4. *See also* East India Company (EIC), East Indies
indirect taxation, 75, 238: excise, 234; malt tax, 235. *See also* direct taxation
inflation: economic benefits of, 104, 118–19, 124, 126, 225–6, 227; social consequences of, 109–10, 124–5, 138–9. *See also*, currency, deflation
interests: balancing of, 30, 54–5, 57, 58, 62–3, 64, 105–6, 225, 236; concept of, 8–9, 231, 240; creditor, 99, 105–6, 108, 225; landed, 39, 58–9, 79, 234, 240; representation of, 62, 63; urban, 59, 61, 63, 79, 123, 205, 206–7, 236
Ireland: and banking legislation, 132; and corn law debates 1814–15, 29, 38; and famine in, 207, 223; impact of free trade on, 218; as a market for British manufactures, 29; as a pretext for corn law repeal, 66

Jackson, Samuel: on the Anti-Corn-Law League, 83
Jacob, William, 248; criticism of 1828 corn law, 46–7; on European grain supplies, 46–7; on Huskisson's commercial reforms, 152; on international relations, 27; on precious metals, 120 n.12; on the relationship between the price of corn and wages, 33–4, 46; on profit rate in manufacturing, 33–4; *Report on the trade in foreign corn, and on the agriculture of the north of Europe* (1826), 46–7; on Ricardo, Torrens and West, 34; on self-sufficiency in food, 28; on warehousing of corn, 29–30
Johnson, J. B.: on corn law repeal and the home market, 208

Johnston, James Finlay Weir, 248; on agricultural improvement, 66
Johnstone, William, 248; on the unequal distribution of wealth, 45; on small notes and distribution, 109–10
joint-stock banks, 117; and crisis of 1839, 130; monopoly of Bank of England in London, 127–8; social and economic benefits of, 131, 132–3
Jones, Richard, 181, 248

labour, see living standards, protectionism and condition of labouring classes
laissez faire, 77, 89. See also free trade, free trade criticisms of
Lauderdale, Lord (James Maitland, 8th earl), 248; on agriculture as a market for manufactures, 35; on mutable value of gold, 94
legal tender, 97–8
Leycester, Joseph, 248; on emigration, 169
Liberal Toryism: and bullionist monetary policy, 91, 95, 116, 118; definition of, 6, 7; and evangelical political economy, 6, 91; influence of, 26, 174; and tariff reform, 149–50
Liddell, Henry Thomas, 248; on imperial preference, 197
Liebig, Justus: on agricultural chemistry, 66
List, G. Friedrich, 248; critique of cosmopolitan economics, 212
Liverpool, Lord (Henry Bankes Jenkinson, 2nd earl), 248; on depression of 1822, 100–1; on Ireland as a granary, 38
living standards: British relative to European, 82–3, 139, 217–18, 221–2. See also protectionism and condition of labouring classes
Locke, John: appeals to, 94, 98, 99, 137 n.93; on constitutional significance of the monetary standard, 98; on redistributive effect of changing the value of money, 99
Lockhart, John Gibson, 248; on colonial trade, 153; as editor of the *Quarterly Review*, 13; on Sir Walter Scott, 114
Low, David, 248; and NAPIC, 204
Loyd, Samuel Jones, 135, 248
Londonderry, marquis of: on depression of 1822, 100–1
Lower Canada, see Canada

Macaulay, Thomas Babington, 248; on East India Company's monopoly, 186
McCloskey, D., 9–10
McCulloch, John Ramsay, 248; responses to his views on landlord absenteeism, 55 n.173; anti-imperialism of, 151, 157 n.48; and *Edinburgh Review*, 151; on low fixed duty on corn (1841), 65; on Jacob's report (1826), 46; and diffusion of Ricardianism, 47; response of D. Robinson to, 47
Macdonnell, Alexander, 249; on colonial trade, 153–4; on foreign trade, 154; on British living standards, 49; on relationship between profits and wages, 49; on Say's law, 50; on importance of high wages, 52
Macintyre, Angus, 10
Macpherson, David, 249; on history of Europeans in India, 159–60
McQueen, James, 249; on emancipation of French slaves, 151; on theoretical reasoning, 151–2; on comparative value of domestic, colonial and foreign trade, 72, 184
Maginn, William, 249; on Conservatism, 60; on Malthusianism and social policy, 182; on the relationship between poverty and deflation, 121
Malcolm, Sir John: on India as a market for British manufactures, 162
Mallalieu, Alfred, 249; on Anti-Corn-Law League, 79; on bimetallism, 131; on colonisation of Canada, 195; on centralisation of note issue, 130; on colonial trade, 184–5; on protection for infant industry, 74; on competitiveness of manufacturing, 73; on monetary sovereignty, 129; on profit motive, 83; on foreign and domestic trade, 71, 185; on urban interests, 62; on relationship between wages, corn prices and profits, 67
Malthus, Thomas Robert, 249; on demand, 154; on sectoral balance in economic change, 34–5; on emigration and population growth, 167; *Essay on the principle of population*, 28; on international relations, 27; on population growth, 27–8, 139; on relationship between the price of corn and wages, 33; on prices, 43–5; *Principles of political economy*, 154; on rate of profit in manufacturing, 44–5;

INDEX

on agricultural protection, 28, 32; influence of on social thought, 181–2
Mandler, Peter, 5
manufactures: importance of domestic agriculture to, 34–5, 50–1, 54–5, 71, 72, 74; colonial markets for, 154, 155, 166, 179, 183, 184, 185, 193, 213; and competition, 73; competitiveness of, 80; tendency of to decay, 72–3; durability of advance of, 50–1, 68, 72, 73; foreign markets for, 69, 141; free trade as beneficial for exporters of, 206–7; and mechanisation, 78, 83, 168; moralisation of, 84–5, 172–3; overcapitalisation of, 165, 167; overproduction of, 68, 73, 83, 101, 125, 129 n.56
Marryat, Joseph, 249; on timber preference, 155, 156
Marshall, John, 249; on employment dependencies, 71; on degeneration of working classes, 83
mercantilism, 26, 95, 148
Miles, Philip, 249; on imperial preference, 198
Mill, James, 249; *History of British India*, 163; on governance of India, 187; on physiocracy, 31
Mill, John Stuart, 249; *Principles of political economy*, 220–1, 233
Mirabeau, Victor Riquetti marquis de: *Oeconomical table*, 31, 249
monetary sovereignty, 127, 129, 130, 131, 133, 137, 142, 226
Munro, Thomas, 249; on India as a market for British manufactures, 162

Napier, Sir William Francis Patrick, 249; corn law repeal and unemployment, 81
National Anti-Gold-Law League, 226, 233
National Association for the Protection of Industry and Capital throughout the British Empire (NAPIC), 203, 233; conference of (May 1850), 205; on colonial trade, 212, 213; on corn law repeal and democratic reform, 240–1; on currency question, 222–3, 224; delegates of, 204; electoral organisation of, 232; on concept of political economy, 215; on protection and the labouring classes, 216–17, 221–2; and public opinion, 204–5; on revolutions of 1848, 218–19
national debt, 38–9; deflation and, 106; economic benefits of, 108; recomposition of, 106–7; redemption of, 107–8
navigation laws, 148, 151, 152, 153; repeal of, 213–14
Nevile, Christopher: on repeal of corn laws, 63
Newdegate, Charles Newdigate, 249; on balance of trade, 210–11, 223; on Bank Charter Act (1844), 137, 138, 139; on corn and currency, 138; on sectionalism of free trade, 207; on social consequences of free trade, 216; on Great Exhibition (1851), 228; on protection as a duty of government, 76; on value of sterling, 140; on Adam Smith, 211
Newport, Sir John, 249; on Ireland as a market for manufactures, 29
newspapers: local, 204–5; and protectionism, 204. *See also* periodicals
Nilan, H. A.: on currency and social cohesion, 126; on exchangeable value of gold, 121

Old Corruption, 91–2

Paglin, M., 4
Palgrave, Sir Francis, 249; on scope of political economy, 78; on rural poverty, 52
paper currency: arguments for, 96, 97, 124, 136. *See also* currency
parliamentary reform, proposals for: Conservative 59–60; Radical, 231, 239; Lord John Russell (1851), 240–1. *See also* Reform Act, 1832
Parnell, Sir Henry, 249; on free trade and consumption, 75, 179; *On financial reform*, 178; and imperialism, 178–9
Parry, J., 5
Peel, Sir Robert (2nd baronet), 249; and Bank Charter Act (1844), 118, 135, 142; and 1842 budget, 61–2, 62–3, 66, 74, 196–7, 219, 237–8; on commercial treaties, 69; on competitiveness of manufacturing, 73; on depression of 1842, 74; on *Gemini Letters*, 136; historiography of, 56; and imperial preference, 196–7, 198–9, 212; income tax, 61, 237–8; Irish Railways Loan (1847), 142; letter to the electors of Elbing, 238; perception of as a protectionist, 57, 62–3; on protection

(1847), 80; and repeal of corn laws, 58, 64; and resumption of cash payments (1819), 93, 97–8; Tamworth manifesto, 62

periodicals: anonymous authorship of, 17–18; authors of, 16–17; binding and indexing of, 13; circulation of, 12–13; and Conservative party, 13–14; content of, 16–17, 18; cultural significance of, 10–11; as 'fourth estate', 14–15; as distinct from newspapers, 12; and politicians, 15–16; and public opinion, 10–11, 13–14; readers of, 13–14

Perkin, H., 4

philanthropy, 84–5

Phillimore, John George, 250; on colonisation, 194

philosophic radicalism, 148

physiocracy, 26, 30–1, 148

plug riots (1842), 80

political economy, concept of: 2–3, 77–9, 124–5, 178, 180–1, 182, 215, 220, 233

poor law: old, 52–3, 165; new, 219

population growth: Alison on, 67; anti-Malthusianism, 28, 67, 168, 169, 172, 181–2, 216; capacity of agriculture to keep pace with, 37–8; Malthus on, 27–8

Porter, G. R., 71–2

poverty, 52–3, 82, 165; causes of, 165, 169, 172; impact of deflation on, 121; and emigration, 165–70, 172–3; and free trade, 216, 217–18

Preber, Antonio, Pablo, 71

press, see newspapers, periodicals

prices: and size of money supply, 90; and value of money, 90

profit motive, 77

property tax: and deflation, 107–8; proposals for equitable adjustment of, 75–6, 235–7; 1842 income tax, 61, 237–8; and political legitimacy, 55; protectionist defences of (1820s), 39–40, 55, 239; proposals for reform of (1820s), 39–40, 107. *See also* direct taxation

protectionism: and importance of agriculture to manufacturing industry, 34–5, 50–1, 72, 74, 207–8; on balance of production and consumption, 34–5, 50–1, 68, 72, 73, 74, 78, 83, 208–9; and 'bread tax', 233–4; and critiques of bullionism, 140–1; on distribution of capital, 53; and Conservative constitutionalism, 8–9, 54–5, 57–64, 206, 214, 231, 235–9; and deflation, 5; and domestic demand, 44–5, 54–5, 68, 82, 140; as an electoral incubus, 203, 230, 232; of European nations, 69; on foreign markets and economic depressions, 36–8, 50; and infant industry, 14; and international relations, 27, 69, 183, 210; and condition of labouring classes, 32–3, 48–50, 51–5, 77–85, 217; on durability of manufacturing advance, 50, 54–5, 68, 72; pejorative view of, 9, 25, 56; and political stability, 54–5; on relationship between corn imports and manufactured exports, 33–4, 68, 209–10; on impact of corn laws on manufacturing profits, 33–4, 43–5, 45–6, 49, 68; on representation of interests, 62, 231, 241; on Ricardo's theory of diminishing returns, 43, 49, 65; on Ricardo's theoretical method, 42, 47; on Ricardo's theory of rent, 42–3, 48–9; and sectoral balance in economic change, 34–5, 50–1, 72, 74, 207–8; and self-sufficiency in food, 28–30, 45–8, 67; and stability of the economy, 44–5, 50–1, 70–1, 72, 207; and territorial constitution, 240; in United States, 69, 210; and value of labour, 221–2; on relationship between wages and profits, 49–50, 53–4, 67–8

Pusey, Philip, 250; on imperial preference, 179; criticism of Sir H. Parnell, 178

Quarterly Review: and Conservative party, 14; content of, 16–17; editorial character of, 13–14; protectionism of, 204; readers of, 13

reciprocity: and commercial treaties, 69–70, 183; and free trade, 183

Reciprocity of Duties Act (1823), 152

Redesdale, Lord (John Freeman-Mitford, 1st Baron), 250; on corn and currency, 114

Reform Act, 1832, Conservative readings of: and banking policy, 128; and colonial representation, 180, 215; and repeal of the corn laws, 63–4; and role of the executive, 61; fiscal politics of, 58, 60–1, 77, 79; and rise of free trade, 206, 219; and governance of India,

INDEX

187; and interaction with monetary policy, 123, 126, 225; and representation, 59, 61; and territorial constitution, 58–9; and urban electorate, 59

reports: *Report of the select committee on the high price of gold bullion* (1810), 92, 115; *Report of the select committee to whom the several petitions complaining of the depressed state of the agriculture of the United Kingdom were referred* (1821), 36–7, 40–1; *Report of the select committee appointed to inquire into …the distressed state of the agriculture of the United Kingdom* (1822), 36; *Reports from the select committee on emigration from the United Kingdom* (1826–7), 169; *Report of the select committee on public income and expenditure* (1828), 178; *Report of the select committee on import duties* (1840), 57

resumption of cash payments (1819): bullionist case for, 93; as deflationary, 95, 99, 100, 102–3, 105, 106–7, 119, 120–2, 224; timing of, 101. *See also* bullionism, deflation, gold standard

retrenchment, 36–7, 38, 39–40, 60, 170, 178, 179, 231, 240

revolutions of 1848, 210, 218–19

Ricardo, David, 250; on deflation after 1819, 101; on agricultural depression (1821), 37; on diminishing returns, 41–2; *Essay on the influence of a low price of corn on the profits of stock*, 33; influence of, 3, 4, 5, 40–1; on the relationship between the price of corn and wages, 41–3; on the rate of profit in manufacturing, 41, 67; *On protection to agriculture*, 40–1, 42–3; on rent, 41; on the stationary state, 41–2

Ricardo, David, criticisms of: on diminishing returns, 43, 49, 65; methodology of, 42, 47; on relationship between price of corn and wages, 33, 43–4, 46, 49–50, 51, 67, 80–1; on effect of corn laws on manufacturing profits, 43–5, 45–6, 49; on rent, 42–3, 48–9, 170; on relationship between wages and profits, 49–50, 53–4, 67–8

Ricardianism: and Anti-Corn-Law League, 66; definition of, 35

Robinson, David, 250; on Bank of England branch banks, 115; on distribution of capital, 54; on colonial trade, 155, 179; on country banks, 111–12; on deflation, 120, 123; on demand, 50; on emigration, 169; on financial panic (1825), 112–13; on impact of free trade on demand, 75; imperial preference, 179; on Jacob's 1826 report, 46; on J. R. McCulloch, 47; on national debt management, 122; on paper currency, 124; criticism of Sir H. Parnell, 178; on causes of poverty, 169; on relationship between price of corn and wages, 49–50; on property tax, 55; on Say's Law, 50; on sliding scale 1828, 47–8; on small notes, 110–11; on relationship between wages and profits, 53–4

Robinson, George, 250; on reciprocity system, 183

Robinson, R., 147

Rose, George, 250; on mutable value of gold, 94

Russell, Lord John: on franchise reform, 241

Sack, J. J., 7–8
Sadler, Michael Thomas, 174
Say, J. P., 250
Say's law: criticism of, 50, 181; definition of, 44
Scott, Sir Walter, 250; appeals to, 131, 132; on home colonisation, 52 n.160, as Malachi Malagrowther, 114 n.139; on Scottish banks, 110, 111; on Scottish small notes, 110, 114–15
Scottish banks: issue policies of, 110; lending policies of, 131; morality of, 132; self-regulation of, 111; socio-economic benefits of, 131–2, 133
Scrope, George Poulett, 66 n.57, 250; on Bank of England, 129; on colonial emigration, 180–2; on contraction of the money supply, 122; on deflation, 123; on distribution, 124–5; on flexible gold standard, 124; on government bank, 129; on Malthusianism and social policy, 181–2; on monetary sovereignty, 129; on expansion of the money supply, 125–6; on overproduction of manufactures, 73; on political economy, 77, 124–5; on the exchangeable value of gold
Seeley, Robert Benton, 250; on the Conservative party, 62

Selkirk, Lord (Thomas Douglas, 5th earl), 250; on emigration, 166
Semmel, Bernard, 148
Shattock, Joanne, 12
Sheffield, Lord (John Baker Holroyd), 243; on warehousing, 29–30
shipping, 156, 179, 213
Sinclair, Sir John, 250; on agricultural improvement, 28; on currency, 89; on Ricardo's theory of diminishing returns, 43; on the socio-economic influence of monetary policy, 96
Sismondi, Jean Charles Leonard Simonde de, 250; on chrematistics, 78
slavery: emancipation of French slaves, 151
sliding scale, see corn law (1828), corn law (1842)
small notes, abolition of: and central/local relations, 114–15; as deflationary, 109; impact on distribution, 109–10, 111, 115; Scottish, 110, 114; social consequences of, 109, 110–11; and union of Scotland and England, 115
Smith, Adam, 251; on colonial trade, 153, 213; on East India Company, 159, 161; on mercantilism, 96; on monopoly, 158; on navigation laws, 152; on profits, 73; on stationary state, 153–4; on value, 33
Southey, Robert, 251; *Colloquies*, 172; on colonisation, 172–3; on deflation and poverty, 121; on emigration, 172; moral economics of, 172–3; on poverty, 52, 172; on the profit motive, 172–3
Sowler, Robert: on employer philanthropy, 84
speculation, 113
Spence, William, 251; on agriculture and manufactures, 31, 35; on commerce, 31; on periodicals, 18; on physiocracy, 30–1
Stanhope, Lord (Philip Henry), 251; on protection and employment, 217
Stanley, Lord (Edward, 14th earl of Derby), 251; on electoral limits of protection, 233; on imperial preference, 196–7; on protection as a national strategy, 205
Staunton, Sir George, 251; on imperial representation, 180
Stedman Jones, G., 8 n.37
Stevenson, William, 251; on history and economic reasoning, 42

Stewart, R. W., 9
sugar preference, 155, 157, 214

tariff reform, 149, 176; as a financial instrument, 238. See also corn law, imperial preference
Tatham, Edward, 251; on bullionist theory of value, 94, 99; on deflation and relative property values, 106; on monetary liquidity, 103
Ten Hours campaign, 84
territorial constitution, 42, 58, 240
Thompson, Perronett, 65, 77
Thomson, Poulett, 65, 179, 251
Thornton, Henry, 251; on theory of depreciation, 93–4
timber preference, 155, 156, 157, 196–7
Tooke, Thomas, 251; on currency and prices, 135
Torrens, Robert, 251; on the relationship between the corn laws and wages, 80; on currency, 135; on manufacturing profits, 73
Tory, 6 n.26
trade, see domestic markets, colonial trade, foreign trade
Turner, Michael, 5
Turner, Samuel: on depression of 1822, 106; on Ricardo's *On protection to agriculture*, 42–3

underconsumption: protection as a solution to, 43, 52, 68, 82; as a cause of depression, 50–1, 73, 83, 104; colonial empire as a solution to, 167–8, 179, 181, 183–5, 193, 196, 212–13; home colonisation as a solution to, 170; and imperialism, 148; high exchangeable value of labour as a solution to, 221–3; as a cause of poverty, 165. See also demand
unemployment: competition and, 219; corn law repeal and, 81; emigration as a response to, 168, 172; foreign trade and, 185
Upper Canada, see Canada
Urquhart, David, 251; on the constitutionality of the Bank Charter Act (1844), 226
utilitarianism: and government of India, 163, 187

Vansittart, Nicholas, 251; and state-assisted emigration, 166; on

constitutionality of suspending the gold standard, 97–8; on the mutable value of gold, 99
virtual representation: and banking reform, 93; of imperial interests, 180, 214; and 1832 Reform Act, 61, 182; and unreformed constitution, 59. *See also* Reform Act

Wakefield, Edward Gibbon, 252; on concentrated colonisation, 168 n.99, 194; criticisms of, 194–5; on finance of colonisation, 193–4; on political economy of colonisation, 193–4
Walker-Smith, Derek, 10
Walsh, Sir John, 252; on consequences of free trade, 65
Warren, Samuel, 252; on Anti-Corn-Law League, 79; on 1842 budget, 74; on conservative fiscal policy, 63
Wellesley, Richard Colley, 252; on loss of American colonies, 151
West Indies: and consumption of manufactures, 155; and sugar preference, 155, 157, 214; and trade with the Canadas, 179
Western, Charles Callis, 252; on the benefits of inflation, 104
Weyland, John: on population, 29

Whately, Richard: on emigration and capital export, 166–7; on the scope of political economy, 182
Whiggism, Conservative readings of, 60, 61, 63, 128, 180, 190
Whigs: and free trade, 5, 57; and East India Company's monopoly, 159; and imperial reform, 177, 190, 191, 195; and low fixed duty on corn, 64; and monetary policy, 120; and 'Old Corruption', 91–2; and protection, 26, 56–7; and retrenchment, 60, 75, 178
Whitbread, Samuel, 252; on East India patronage, 161
Williams, Albert: on direct taxation, 239
Willoughby, Sir Henry, 122, 252
Winch, Donald, 3, 148
working classes, *see* 'Condition of England Question', distribution, living standards, protectionism and condition of labouring classes
Wyatt, Harvey: on free trade and foreign economies, 47

Young, George Frederick, 252; on electoral limits of protection, 233; on California gold discoveries, 227; on insecurity of foreign trade, 207; and protectionist opinion forming, 204; on sectionalism of free trade, 205